Practical
Environmental Law

EDITORIAL ADVISORS

Deborah E. Bouchoux, Esq.
Georgetown University

Therese A. Cannon
Executive Associate Director
Western Association of Schools and Colleges

Katherine A. Currier
Chair, Department of Paralegal and Legal Studies
Elms College

Cathy Kennedy
Paralegal Program Director
Legal Studies Department
Globe University/Minnesota School of Business

Susan M. Sullivan
Director, Graduate Career Programs
University of San Diego

Laurel A. Vietzen
Professor and Instructional Coordinator
Elgin Community College

William I. Weston
Dean, College of Legal Studies
Kaplan University

ASPEN PUBLISHERS

Practical Environmental Law

◆ ◆ ◆

Laurel A. Vietzen

Elgin Community College

Wolters Kluwer
Law & Business

AUSTIN   BOSTON   CHICAGO   NEW YORK   THE NETHERLANDS

Aspen Publishers
Attn: Permissions Department
76 Ninth Avenue, 7th Floor
New York, NY 10011-5201

To contact Customer Care, e-mail customer.care@aspenpublishers.com, call 1-800-234-1660, fax 1-800-901-9075, or mail correspondence to:

Aspen Publishers
Attn: Order Department
PO Box 990
Frederick, MD 21705

Printed in the United States of America.

1 2 3 4 5 6 7 8 9 0

ISBN 978-0-7355-7242-3

Library of Congress Cataloging-in-Publication Data

Vietzen, Laurel A.
   Practical environmental law / Laurel A. Vietzen.
       p. cm.
   Includes index.
   ISBN 978-0-7355-7242-3 (pbk. : alk. paper) 1. Environmental law—United States. I. Title.

KF3775.V54 2008
344.7304'6—dc22

2008014103

About Wolters Kluwer Law & Business

Wolters Kluwer Law & Business is a leading provider of research information and workflow solutions in key specialty areas. The strengths of the individual brands of Aspen Publishers, CCH, Kluwer Law International and Loislaw are aligned within Wolters Kluwer Law & Business to provide comprehensive, in-depth solutions and expert-authored content for the legal, professional and education markets.

CCH was founded in 1913 and has served more than four generations of business professionals and their clients. The CCH products in the Wolters Kluwer Law & Business group are highly regarded electronic and print resources for legal, securities, antitrust and trade regulation, government contracting, banking, pension, payroll, employment and labor, and healthcare reimbursement and compliance professionals.

Aspen Publishers is a leading information provider for attorneys, business professionals and law students. Written by preeminent authorities, Aspen products offer analytical and practical information in a range of specialty practice areas from securities law and intellectual property to mergers and acquisitions and pension/benefits. Aspen's trusted legal education resources provide professors and students with high-quality, up-to-date and effective resources for successful instruction and study in all areas of the law.

Kluwer Law International supplies the global business community with comprehensive English-language international legal information. Legal practitioners, corporate counsel and business executives around the world rely on the Kluwer Law International journals, loose-leafs, books and electronic products for authoritative information in many areas of international legal practice.

Loislaw is a premier provider of digitized legal content to small law firm practitioners of various specializations. Loislaw provides attorneys with the ability to quickly and efficiently find the necessary legal information they need, when and where they need it, by facilitating access to primary law as well as state-specific law, records, forms and treatises.

Wolters Kluwer Law & Business, a unit of Wolters Kluwer, is headquartered in New York and Riverwoods, Illinois. Wolters Kluwer is a leading multinational publisher and information services company.

To my husband, Bob Warski, who supports me in everything I undertake,
Lora Lucero, who has helped me learn this area of law, and the many students and graduates
who contributed to this book and to my understanding of many things.

Summary of Contents

Part I
Implementation of Environmental Law

Part II
The Statutes

Contents

PART I

♦ ♦ ♦

Implementation of Environmental Law

1

♦ ♦ ♦

Introduction to the Study of Law

2

◆ ◆ ◆

Administrative Agencies in Environmental Law

3

◆ ◆ ◆

The Courts in Environmental Law

4

◆ ◆ ◆

The Constitution and the Executive in Environmental Law

5
◆ ◆ ◆

Protection of the Environment at the Local and International Levels

6
◆ ◆ ◆

Due Diligence in Transactional Law

PART II

◆ ◆ ◆

The Statutes

7

◆ ◆ ◆

National Environmental Policy Act (NEPA)

8

◆ ◆ ◆

The Air We Breathe

9

◆ ◆ ◆

Water

10
◆ ◆ ◆

CERCLA, SARA, EPCRA, and TSCA

11

◆ ◆ ◆

Solid Waste, Hazardous Waste

12

◆ ◆ ◆

Wild Things, Wild Places: ESA, Federal Land, and FIFRA

Preface

Environmental law is vast and complicated. While there are many resources for learning about risks and damage to the environment and how we could better protect the environment, there are few resources to help non-lawyers understand and work with the law in this field. This book is intended to be accessible to those who want to work in the field without going to law school and to those who learn best from hands-on projects.

Laurel A. Vietzen

April 2008

Acknowledgments

I would like to thank the following for helping me with this text.

American Planning Association, Lora Lucero, Editor of Planning and Environmental Law, Colorado Bar Association

Illinois Legislative Reference Bureau

Office of Revisor of Statutes, State of Minnesota

The Wonderful, Patient, and Creative Folks at the Iowa Department of Natural Resources, especially Sean Fitzsimmons

Student Assistants:
Samira Qureshi
Sue Ann Najdzin

Professional Profiles:
Connie S. Kubajak, Paralegal
Dan Pava, Los Alamos National Laboratory
Tracie Rose, Principal with ENVIRON Corp.

Practical
Environmental Law

◆ ◆ ◆

PART I

◆ ◆ ◆

IMPLEMENTATION OF ENVIRONMENTAL LAW

◆ ◆ ◆

1

◆ ◆ ◆

Introduction to the Study of Law

◆ ◆ ◆

This text requires that the student do a substantial amount of independent research to find recent developments and the law applicable in the student's jurisdiction. This chapter provides an overview or refresher course on the concepts necessary to find and analyze law: sources of primary law, use of secondary sources, formulating a search query, reading and analyzing legal authority, and the consequences of bad research.

A. Sources and Types of Legal Authority
   1. Five Sources of Authority
   2. Enforcement
B. Steps in Preparing to Research a Legal Issue
C. Formulating a Query
D. Primary Authority
   1. Statutes
   2. Judicial Decisions
      a. Trial Courts versus Appellate Courts
      b. Reading Cases
      c. Briefing Cases
E. In the Field
   1. Employment Opportunities
   2. Ethical Issue: Confidentiality

A.   Sources of Legal Authority

Some students will have taken an introduction to law or a legal research class before using this book. For them, the special features of this book will provide an unusual and very valuable opportunity to practice their research skills. By reading this chapter, students who have not taken a previous introductory class can learn enough about the basics of research to do well in this class and to conduct basic environmental law research on the job.

Let's start with some basics. Success in law is not about enjoying a good argument; it is about having legal authority to support your arguments.

1.   Five Sources of Authority

There are five types of sources of legal authority. Environmental law comes from all of these sources and this book is organized accordingly. These sources exist within the bodies of federal law, state law, tribal law, and most exist in even local (**municipal**) law. Environmental law can be federal, state, tribal, or local law.

a.   **Constitution** (even municipalities have a charter or other governing document), describes the structure of government and the basic rights of the governed;

b.   **Legislation**, enacted by an elected body such as Congress, a state legislature, a county board, or city council (also called **code** or **statute**), is intended to govern future conduct and applies to large groups (example: city enacts ordinance prohibiting all open burning after a certain date);

c.   **Judicial decisions**, also called **common law, case law, or precedent**, generally determines consequences of past conduct and deals with individual situations (example: a resident of the city is prosecuted or sued for having burned leaves in his yard);

d.   **Administrative agency regulations and rulings**, such as the "rules and regs" of the Environmental Protection Agency (EPA), the Department of Agriculture, your state environmental protection department, or a local zoning board. An administrative agency is established to administer a particular law or program (e.g., the National Labor Relations Board was created to administer the National Labor Relations Act); and

e.   **Executive action**, executive orders signed by the President or governor (even a mayor) and treaties signed by the President and approved by the Senate.

The first half of this book explores the Constitution, judicial decisions, administrative agencies, executive action, and local legislation as they relate to environmental law. The second half is devoted to the major federal statutes.

Municipal Law
Local law (as opposed to federal or state law)

Constitution
1 of 5 sources of legal authority

Legislation
1 of 5 sources of legal authority; also called code or statute; enacted by an elected body (e.g., Congress)

Code
Legislation; also called statute

Statute
Legislation; also called code

Judicial Decisions
1 of 5 sources of legal authority; also called common law, precedent, or case law

Common Law
Judicial decisions; also called precedent

Precedent
Decision in earlier case, similar to present case

Administrative Agencies
1 of 5 sources of legal authority; administers a particular law or program

Regulations
Established by administrative agencies

Executive Action
1 of 5 sources of legal authority; including orders signed by the president or governor

2. Enforcement

There are several ways in which environmental law can be enforced:

a. A **civil** matter is pursued by an individual or group of private people, a business entity, or by governmental body acting in a "private" capacity. If the defendant is found liable (don't use the word guilty!) in a civil environmental lawsuit, the result is an award of damages (money) or a court order, such as an injunction, requiring or prohibiting specific actions. To initiate a civil suit, a party must establish **standing**, by showing that the party has suffered an actual injury as a result of the challenged action and that the injury can be redressed. The requirement of standing means that environmental groups, such as the Sierra Club and EarthFirst!, cannot simply file a lawsuit any time they identify an environmental problem. In a civil case the plaintiff (party who initiates the case) typically has a burden of proving liability by a "preponderance of evidence," meaning "more likely than not."

b. An **administrative action** is pursued by an agency (such as the EPA) and typically results in imposition of fines, issuance of orders, or denials or revocations of permits or licenses.

c. A **criminal** matter is prosecuted by a governmental body, such as the district attorney, and involves a matter of concern to society as a whole, such as burglary or murder. The result may be prison time, probation, even the death penalty, if the defendant is found guilty. The **burden of proof** in a criminal case is "beyond a reasonable doubt," which means that the prosecution has responsibility for producing enough evidence to make guilt almost 100 percent certain. Keep in mind that a single incident can sometimes result in more than one type of action. For example, a person who "dumps" toxic waste may be arrested and tried for a criminal offense and may also be sued by the injured landowner for financial damages.

d. Native American Tribes traditionally kept the peace and administered justice on their homelands by means of a non-adversarial, consensus-based system. In the twentieth century the tribes were encouraged by the U.S. government to set up more formal systems. Many of the Indian nations and Alaskan villages have now enacted their own codes and established their own court systems. While the major federal statutes discussed in the second half of this book specifically address enforcement on tribal lands and often authorize tribal implementation of federal mandates, environmental matters not subject to those statutes (e.g., common law actions, discussed in Chapter 3) can be subject to tribal codes and systems. To see a list of tribal laws relating to environmental issues, visit http://www.tribalresourcecenter.org/legal/details.asp?53. Other areas of law, such as contract law, relate to activities that may or may not involve land. Environmental law is uniquely tied to the land and the tribes are uniquely concerned with land, as evidenced by the existence of the National Tribal Environmental Council, http://www.ntec.org/, and the Native Americans and the Environment project, http://www.cnie.org/NAE/. To learn more about administration of justice on tribal lands and the

Civil Law
Type of law pursued by an individual or group of people, a business, or a governmental body acting in a private capacity; result may be damages or court order

Standing
Right to initiate a lawsuit, depends on whether and how plaintiff has been injured by the challenged action

Administrative Action
A ruling or regulation from an administrative action

Criminal Law
Category of law prosecuted by a governmental body involving a matter of concern to society as a whole

Burden of Proof
Obligation of plaintiff or prosecution to produce sufficient evidence to win case

Tribal Courts
Courts established within
and by Native American
communities

Cite
Verb form of citation (i.e.
to cite)

tribal courts, visit the National Tribal Justice Resource Center website: http://www.tribalresourcecenter.org/aboutus.

Every legal problem is unique. You can memorize the basics of an area of law, such as environmental law, but often you won't know "the answer" to a specific problem when it is presented. To find that answer you will have to research the sources of law to find authority to support your theories. When you find authority, you must be able to understand, analyze, and write about it and **cite** it so that those who read your work can find your sources.

Citation

Citation is a standard system that allows a writer to refer to legal authority so that others can follow the references and find the same authority. Writing by legal professionals is dependent on such references, so it is essential that you learn the abbreviations and rules for citation in your jurisdiction. Different rules apply, depending on the type and source of legal authority being referenced (the types and sources are described in the following sections). Cornell Law School has an excellent online guide to citation, organized by type and source of authority, with lots of helpful examples: http://www.law.cornell.edu/citation/.

B. Steps in Preparing to Research a Legal Issue

Before you start to research a legal problem you will ask yourself several questions:

1. *Is this a matter of local, tribal, state, or federal law?* Environmental problems often implicate state law, federal law, and tribal or local law. You may have to research several bodies of law.

Objective
Not advocating a particular
result

Adversarial
Argues a position

Primary Authority
One of the five sources
of law

Secondary Authority
Material such as text books
and articles that help locate
(finding tools) and understand primary law; form
books, handbooks,
encyclopedias, digests,
etc.; not actual law

2. *What is the desired work product and how much time should be spent on the research?* Your project may be **objective**, such as a memo or report citing authority to analyze a specific situation without arguing a position. On the other hand, you may be working on an **adversarial** memo or brief, arguing a position before a court or other decision-making body.

3. *Does this project require primary authority or secondary authority?* When you are researching a question of law, you will generally be looking for **primary authority** — one of the five sources previously listed. **Secondary authority** is not, itself, the law; it includes text books and scholarly articles that help you understand primary law as well as form books, procedure manuals, and "practice" handbooks that help you accomplish a specific task. Many times a legal problem involves finding the right form or procedure, rather than finding the actual law. Secondary authority also includes material to help you find primary authority when you are using books; these "finding tools," such as digests and encyclopedias, are not necessary when you look for primary law online.

EXHIBIT 1-1

Sources of environmental law are not independent of each other. This statute is implemented by the exhaustive regulations of an administrative agency, the Department of Natural Resources (reproduced, in part, on the next page). In addition, quick computer-assisted legal research (CALR) using a subscription database disclosed three cases concerning the statute.

84.0895, Minnesota Statutes 2006
Copyright © 2006 by the Office of Revisor of Statutes, State of Minnesota.

84.0895 Protection of Threatened and Endangered Species.
   Subdivision 1. **Prohibition.** Notwithstanding any other law, a person may not take, import, transport, or sell any portion of an endangered species of wild animal or plant, or sell or possess with intent to sell an article made with any part of the skin, hide, or parts of an endangered species of wild animal or plant, except as provided in subdivisions 2 and 7.
   Subd. 2. **Application.** (a) Subdivision 1 does not apply to:
      (1) plants on land classified for property tax purposes as class 2a or 2c agricultural land under section 273.13, or on ditches and roadways; and (2) noxious weeds designated pursuant to sections 18.76 to 18.88 or to weeds otherwise designated as troublesome by the Department. (material omitted)
   Subd. 3. **Designation.** (a) The commissioner shall adopt rules under chapter 14, to designate species of wild animal or plant as:
      (1) endangered, if the species is threatened with extinction throughout all or a significant portion of its range;
      (2) threatened, if the species is likely to become endangered within the foreseeable future throughout all or a significant portion of its range; or
      (3) species of special concern, if although the species is not endangered or threatened, it is extremely uncommon in this state, or has unique or highly specific habitat requirements and deserves careful monitoring of its status. (material omitted).
      (b) The range of the species in this state is a factor in determining its status as endangered, threatened, or of special concern. A designation by the secretary of the interior that a species is threatened or endangered is a prima facie showing under this section.
      (c) The commissioner shall reevaluate the designated species list every three years after it is first adopted and make appropriate changes. (material omitted)
   Subd. 4. **Studies.** The commissioner may conduct investigations to determine the status and requirements for survival of a resident species of wild animal or plant.
   Subd. 5. **Management.** (a) Notwithstanding any other law, the commissioner may undertake management programs, issue orders, and adopt rules necessary to bring a resident species of wild animal or plant that has been designated as

EXHIBIT 1-1
(continued)

threatened or endangered to a point at which it is no longer threatened or endangered. (material omitted).

Subd. 6. **Enforcement.** A peace officer or conservation officer, pursuant to chapter 626, may execute a warrant to search for and seize goods, merchandise, plant or animal taken, sold or offered for sale in violation of this section, or items used in connection with a violation of this section. (material omitted).

Subd. 7. **General exceptions.** (a) The commissioner may prescribe conditions for an act otherwise prohibited by subdivision 1 if: (material omitted).

Subd. 9. **Violations.** A violation of this section is a misdemeanor.

EXHIBIT 1-2

This heavily edited list of species was promulgated under the authority of the statute reproduced in Exhibit 1-1, and it doesn't include the plants.

6134.0200 ANIMAL SPECIES.

Subpart 1. Mammals. The scientific names and the common names in this subpart are according to the Revised Checklist of North American Mammals North of Mexico, J. K. Jones, et al., 1992. The following species of mammals are designated as:

A.　Endangered: none.
B.　Threatened: Spilogale putorius, eastern spotted skunk.
C.　Of special concern:
　　(1)　Canis lupus, gray wolf; (material omitted)
　　(13)　Synaptomys borealis, northern bog lemming; and
　　(14)　Thomomys talpoides, northern pocket gopher.

Subp. 2. Birds. The scientific names and the common names in this subpart are according to the American Ornithologists Union Checklist, 1983, and Supplements. The following species of birds are designated as:

EXHIBIT 1-2
(continued)

A. Endangered:
    (1) Ammodramus bairdii, Baird's sparrow; (material omitted)
    (7) Rallus elegans, king rail.
D. Threatened:
    (1) Cygnus buccinator, trumpeter swan;
    (2) Falco peregrinus, peregrine falcon; (material omitted)
    (6) Sterna hirundo, common tern.
H. Of special concern:
    (1) Ammodramus nelsoni, Nelson's sharp-tailed sparrow;
    (2) Asio flammeus, short-eared owl; (material omitted)
    (15) Wilsonia citrina, hooded warbler.

    Subp. 3. Amphibians and reptiles. (material omitted) The following species of amphibians and reptiles are designated as:

A. Endangered:
    (1) Acris crepitans, northern cricket frog; and
    (2) Sistrurus catenatus, massasauga.
D. Threatened:
    (1) Clemmys insculpta, wood turtle;
    (3) Emydoidea blandingii, Blanding's turtle.
G. Of special concern:
    (1) Apalone mutica, smooth softshell; (material omitted)
    (9) Tropidoclonion lineatum, lined snake.

    Subp. 4. Fish. . . . Subp. 6. Mollusks. . . . Subp. 7. Jumping spiders. . . .
    Subp. 8. Butterflies and moths. . . . Subp. 9. Caddis flies. . . .
    Subp. 10. Tiger beetles . . . Subp. 11. Leafhoppers . . . Subp. 12. Dragonflies.
    STAT AUTH: MS s 84.0895

---

    4. *Which of the five sources of law is likely to address the problem?* Because environmental law comes from all five sources, the answer may be that several sources address the problem. Where you start will depend on the factual nature of the problem. For example, if the problem involves water pollution, you might start with the Clean Water Act (CWA). When a statute (like the CWA) governs, often it is written in broad terms (e.g., "If the state fails to act within a reasonable time . . .") and you will need to find cases to provide insight on how courts interpret the terms, such as "reasonable" in specific fact situations. **Statutory interpretation (statutory construction)** is a major function of the courts and a major purpose of legal research. In addition, many of the environmental statutes are administered by agencies, which promulgate regulations concerning compliance with the statute.

Statutory Interpretation
Interpretation of statute's terms; also called statutory construction

Example Statutory Interpretation

Restaurant property was contaminated with petroleum. The county ordered owner to clean up. The owner removed and disposed of tainted soil. Three years later, the owner filed a citizen's suit under the Resource Conservation and Recovery Act (RCRA), 42 U.S.C. §6972(a), against prior owners, seeking to recover cleanup costs. The trial court dismissed the suit, but the court of appeals reversed. The U.S. Supreme Court ruled in favor of the previous owners holding that the RCRA language allowing such a suit if the waste presented an "imminent and substantial endangerment" at the time it was cleaned up made clear that a private party could not recover the cost of a past cleanup and could only bring suit upon allegations that the contaminated site presently posed an imminent endangerment. *Meghrig v. KFC Western, Inc.*, 516 U.S. 479 (1996).

CALR
Computer-assisted legal research system

5. *Where will I do this research?* At some point in your career you will probably learn to use books for legal research, but in this class you will probably complete your assignments using a subscription computer-assisted legal research (**CALR**) system. Your school may provide you with access to WestLaw, Lexis, Loislaw, or some other system. If you do not have access to a subscription CALR system, you can create an account at www.lexisone.com that will allow you to search for judicial decisions from all 50 states and the federal system, going back five years, without paying a fee. You can find statutes on a government-sponsored site, without paying a fee.

6. *How should I describe the problem?* As explained below, you must describe your problem in a few words that can be used in an index or to create a query to use in an online search engine.

Many people use the traditional questions of journalism — who, what, when, where, why, and how — to arrive at their search terms. Choosing terms is difficult because they have to be broad enough that they are likely to appear in most relevant cases and narrow enough that you won't have to read 5,000 cases. Your choice of search terms will depend on whether you are using books or CALR. CALR works well with narrow, specific terms, but if you are using a printed index, you need to think in broader terms.

Example

If you were researching liability for contamination of a water supply with the chemical Benzene, using a print index you would probably start with broad terms, such as "water" and "contamination." The word "Benzene" is likely too specific for a print index. However, using the word "Benzene" in a computerized search would probably get you to the most relevant material quickly. On the other hand, the terms "water and contamination" would probably result in a list with thousands of cases if used in a computerized search.

Another challenge in brainstorming a problem is the unique language of the law. As you take classes and read cases, this will become second nature to you, but it may seem foreign at first. For example, a problem involving marital property might be classified under "husband and wife" in a legal index; a problem involving a

17-year-old might fall into the category "infants." Environmental law has its own vocabulary ("partial, temporary, regulatory taking . . ." huh?) and hundreds of acronyms, such as EPA and CWA.

Here is a sample of how you might "brainstorm" a problem and develop a list of words and phrases that describe the problem:

> Several years ago, Dan Developer bought 50 acres of undeveloped land in Springfield, zoned for residential development at four units per acre. Dan planned to build 200 houses. While Dan was working with architects, engineers, and bankers, but before he obtained any permits for the project, the town decided it had to do more to protect a creek that runs through the property. The town rezoned the land, so that Dan will only be allowed to build 40 houses on the higher land and no houses on the wetlands near the creek. Dan believes that he cannot make a profit by selling only 40 houses, given the cost of putting in roads and other infrastructure. Dan wants to sue to obtain a declaration that he is entitled to build 200 houses.

Who	Town, developer[1]
What	Vested rights[2]
	Loss of profit
Where	Residential Subdivision
	Wetlands
When	Before permits issue
Why	Protect wetlands
How	Rezoning

Identifying **synonyms** and similar terms is an essential part of the process. For example, in the chart, you might insert "builder" next to "developer" and "government agency" or "municipality" or "city" next to "town."

Synonym
Word having same or similar meaning

C. Formulating a Query

If you are going to conduct your search using a computer, you will connect several of your search terms to create a **search query**. The **connectors** describe the relationship between your search terms. All of the major CALR services include some common connectors. Some examples of how they work:

Search Query
Terms and connectors or natural language used in CALR search

- Using "rezoning," and "vested rights" as search terms and entering the query [rezoning & "vested rights"], you get hundreds of cases because the "&" connector only requires that each term appear at some spot in the case. The term "vested rights" is in quotes because some systems require quotes to identify a phrase.

Connector
Symbol describing relationship between CALR search terms

- To narrow the search, use a **"proximity"** or **"near"** connector. Most CALR systems have connectors to require that terms be in the same paragraph [/p], the same sentence [/s], or within a specified number

Proximity Connector
Describes the distance between search terms

---

[1]The terms "Dan Developer" and "Springfield" are obviously too narrow to be used as search terms.
[2]An example of a term that may be unfamiliar, "vested rights" refers to rights that have become definite entitlements at a point in time.

of words of each other [search term /# "search term,"]. You might search [rezoning /25 "vested rights"] to find cases in which the word rezoning appears within 25 words of "vested rights." Failure to include quotes around the phrase "vested rights" might cause the system to read the search as [developer within 25 words of vested **or** rights].

- Suppose that your search pulls up several cases in which a developer challenged a change in the fee structure for permits after rezoning. To eliminate these irrelevant cases, use the **"not" connector** [%], [rezoning/25 "vested rights" % fee].

Not Connector
CALR command to exclude a term

- Still have too many results? Add terms: [rezoning/25 "vested rights"/25 wetlands].
- If you aren't getting enough results, broaden your search to look for [wetlands or creek /25 reclassification or rezoning/25 "vested rights"]. The "or" connector is often used to search for synonyms.

Root Expander
Symbol used to pick up word variations in a computer-based search

- Use **"root expanders"** [!] or [*] to pick up variations such as rezoning or rezoned [rezon!]. To find woman or women you might use a **"wildcard"** [wom*n].

Wildcard
Symbol used to pick up word variations in a computer-based search

If you are not familiar with the connectors and wildcards for your CALR system, you can find its use guide when you sign on, usually by using the HELP tab. Many of the CALR providers have online tutorials you can use even before you sign on. Your instructor will show you how to sign on.[3] In addition, the next chapter specifically describes the steps taken to research particular problems.

Assignment 1-1

Brainstorm the following problems and write a CALR search query for each. Remember, you are not trying to find an answer to the problem at this point, you are only practicing formulating queries.

◆ Jim just signed a five-year lease on a building on the river in Riverside City to operate a pizza restaurant. He plans a large deck overlooking the river, for outdoor dining. He has already begun installing equipment and furniture. Last night the city council approved a permit for a paper mill (Merritt Paper Products) that will operate across the river, upstream about 1/4 mile, in an area zoned for industrial uses. Although the mill will use state-of-the-art technology to prevent air and water pollution, it will emit odors that could be upsetting to diners. Jim wonders whether he has any rights.

---

[3]The examples are "terms and connectors" searches; it is also possible to search using "natural language" on some systems, by entering a question without connectors. A "field search," with which you search or limit the search by names of parties, judges, or lawyers; by citation; or by dates is also possible, but beyond the scope of this book.

◆ Merritt Paper Products began operations in Riverside last year, in compliance with all federal, state, and local laws concerning air quality. Last month, an unusual weather situation brought strong winds out of the east. Prevailing winds are from the west and Riverside rarely experiences strong winds. As a result, the odors from Merritt were carried more than a mile. A child, on the playground at an elementary school about a mile away, experienced a severe asthma attack as a result of inhaling the odors. Emergency workers were delayed in reaching the scene because a tree had fallen across an access road. The child suffered brain damage. Merritt wonders whether it has any liability.

◆ Linda purchased her first home about 18 months ago; a cute brick bungalow previously owned by a nurse, who died last year. Linda bought the house from the nurse's estate. The house was the nurse's only asset and the proceeds from the sale have already been used to pay off the nurse's mortgage, final medical expenses, funeral costs, etc. Last month, when Linda was finally able to afford some landscaping, she discovered that the yard is full of buried medical waste, including syringes, x-ray film, and other dangerous items. Apparently the nurse was responsible for disposing of her employer's (a doctor's office) medical waste and, instead of paying for disposal by a service, simply brought the material home and buried it in her yard. The estimated cost of removing the material, cleaning the yard, and restoring landscaping is close to one million dollars. Linda wonders whether she is liable for the cost.

D.   Primary Authority

Now, an overview of the primary authority you will find when you use CALR. In later chapters, you will use secondary sources.

1.   Statutes

Statutes (also called legislation or code) are enacted by a legislative body (Congress or a state legislature), and most are subsequently **codified** or compiled so that they are organized by **topics**, which are divided into subtopics and sub-subtopics. The EPA website, http://www.epa.gov, includes links to many of the federal statutes that will be discussed in this book.

Codified
Statute entered into a topical system

Topic or **Title**
Generally, statutes are organized by topic; breaking the code into Titles, Acts, Chapters, or Sections

References to U.S. Statutes can be confusing!

The United States Statutes at Large is the official source for laws passed by the U.S. Congress. Entry in Statutes at Large is the second part of a three-part process for publication of federal statutes: 1) slip laws, 2) Statutes at Large (also called session laws), and 3) codification. People will sometimes refer to part of a law using the sections laid out in Statutes at Large, for example, Section 105 of the Comprehensive Environmental Response, Compensation, and Liability Act of 1980 (CERCLA). The codified version of the law, however, begins at 42 U.S.C. §9601, so the U.S. Code citation to the same section is 42 U.S.C. §9605.

To familiarize yourself with the federal statutes you will study in this book, start at the Cornell website, http://www.law.cornell.edu/uscode/.

Scroll down and click Title 42, Public Health and Welfare. If you click Chapter 103, you will find CERCLA, the law referenced above. Notice how many other chapters concern environmental topics.

Topic or **Title**
Generally, statutes are organized by topic; breaking the code into Titles, Acts, Chapters, or Sections

You should also be familiar with the major topics, often called, "**titles**" or "chapters," of the codification of environmental statutes for your state. Knowing the major topics gives you a starting point for statutory research, even if the most recent amendments may not have been "**codified**" (put into the topical system). To find state statutes and look at those topics, start at www.ncsl.org/public/leglinks.cfm. Select your state and "statutes" in the boxes.

Citations to statutes do not use page numbers because the topics can expand or contract. Using references to titles, chapters, acts, sections, or paragraphs eliminates the need to change all references when a law is amended or repealed. For example, section 17 might be one-half page long or it might grow to eight pages long, but it can still be cited as section (§) 17. If section 17 grows to 13 pages, section 18 will begin on a later page, but it can still be called §18. A citation to a statute generally consists of the name of the law, an abbreviation indicating the source (e.g., U.S.C. indicates that the statute was found in U.S. Code; ILCS indicates Illinois Compiled Statutes), and numbers indicating the title, chapter, act, and/or section.

Annotated Statute
Statute with references to articles, cases, and other materials that explain and interpret the law

If you examine an **annotated statute**, the text of the law as enacted by the legislature appears first, followed by references to cases, administrative regulations, law review articles, and other materials that explain and interpret the law. Statutes found on government sites on the Internet are not annotated.

Reading and comprehending statutes takes a lot of practice. Statutes often include nonspecific language, so that courts have discretion to interpret and apply the law. This is necessary because legislation is intended to govern large groups of people or situations; being too specific would create loopholes. Unlike judicial decisions, which deal with specific situations after they have occurred, statutes often govern conduct in advance. Think about the speed limit that applies in bad weather. It is not a specific number; in most states it is "safe for conditions" or a similar description. Stating a specific speed would not govern all possible weather situations that could arise in the future on all possible roads. Statutes may also contain long, confusing sentences. A few tips for reading statutes:

1. *Look at the table of contents for the whole chapter or act* (often located at the beginning of the chapter or act) to get a feel for the law as a whole;
2. *Check whether the act has a "definitions" section* that defines the terms used in the various sections;
3. *Read the sections immediately before and after the section applicable to your research* because they may shed light on the statutory scheme;
4. *Write out the statute and break long sentences into "outline" form* so that you can sort out the "ands" from the "ors."

EXHIBIT 1-3
Major Federal Environmental Statutes

National Environmental Policy Act of 1969 (NEPA)
42 U.S.C. 4321-4347
Chemical Safety Information, Site Security and Fuels Regulatory Relief Act
42 U.S.C. 7412(r)
Clean Air Act (CAA)
42 U.S.C. 7401 et seq. (1970)
Clean Water Act (CWA)
33 U.S.C. 1251 et seq. (1977)
Comprehensive Environmental Response, Compensation, and
Liability Act (CERCLA or Superfund)
42 U.S.C. 9601 et seq. (1980)
Emergency Planning & Community Right-To-Know Act (EPCRA)
42 U.S.C. 11011 et seq. (1986)
Endangered Species Act (ESA)
7 U.S.C. 136; 16 U.S.C. 460 et seq. (1973)
Federal Insecticide, Fungicide and Rodenticide Act (FIFRA)
7 U.S.C. 135 et seq. (1972)
Federal Food, Drug, and Cosmetic Act (FFDCA)
21 U.S.C. 301 et seq.
Occupational Safety and Health Act (OSHA)
29 U.S.C. 651 et seq. (1970)
Oil Pollution Act of 1990 (OPA)
33 U.S.C. 2702 to 2761
Pollution Prevention Act (PPA)
42 U.S.C. 13101 and 13102, et seq. (1990)
Resource Conservation and Recovery Act (RCRA)
42 U.S.C. 321 et seq. (1976)
Safe Drinking Water Act (SDWA)
42 U.S.C. 300f et seq. (1974)
Superfund Amendments and Reauthorization Act (SARA)
42 U.S.C. 9601 et seq. (1986)
Toxic Substances Control Act (TSCA)
15 U.S.C. 2601 et seq.

Assignment 1-2

Find your state's environmental statutes online and bookmark the site on your computer. If you are not already familiar with your online statutes, some helpful starting points include: www.dep.state.pa.us/statelinks.htm, the Pennsylvania Department of Environmental Protection listing of links to state environmental sites, or www.prairienet.org/~scruffy/f.htm.

EXHIBIT 1-4
Example of State Statutes Organized by Topic

From www.ilga.gov/legislation.

Illinois compiled statutes are organized into nine major topics, each of which is divided into chapters. The chapters are divided into Acts, which are further divided into sections. This is a typical scheme of organization for state statutes.

Illinois Compiled Statutes

Information maintained by the Legislative Reference Bureau
Updating the database of the Illinois Compiled Statutes (ILCS) is an ongoing process. Recent laws may not yet be included in the ILCS database, but they are found on this site as Public Acts soon after they become law. For information concerning the relationship between statutes and Public Acts, refer to the Guide.

GOVERNMENT

- CHAPTER 5 GENERAL PROVISIONS
- CHAPTER 10 ELECTIONS
- CHAPTER 15 EXECUTIVE OFFICERS
- CHAPTER 20 EXECUTIVE BRANCH
- CHAPTER 25 LEGISLATURE
- CHAPTER 30 FINANCE
- CHAPTER 35 REVENUE
- CHAPTER 40 PENSIONS
- CHAPTER 45 INTERSTATE COMPACTS
- CHAPTER 50 LOCAL GOVERNMENT
- CHAPTER 55 COUNTIES
- CHAPTER 60 TOWNSHIPS
- CHAPTER 65 MUNICIPALITIES

- CHAPTER 70 SPECIAL DISTRICTS
- CHAPTER 75 LIBRARIES

EDUCATION

- CHAPTER 105 SCHOOLS
- CHAPTER 110 HIGHER EDUCATION
- CHAPTER 115 EDUCATIONAL LABOR RELATIONS

REGULATION

- CHAPTER 205 FINANCIAL REGULATION
- CHAPTER 210 HEALTH FACILITIES

EXHIBIT 1-4
(continued)

- CHAPTER 215 INSURANCE
- CHAPTER 220 UTILITIES
- CHAPTER 225 PROFESSIONS AND OCCUPATIONS
- CHAPTER 230 GAMING
- CHAPTER 235 LIQUOR
- CHAPTER 240 WAREHOUSES

HUMAN NEEDS

- CHAPTER 305 PUBLIC AID
- CHAPTER 310 HOUSING
- CHAPTER 315 URBAN PROBLEMS
- CHAPTER 320 AGING
- CHAPTER 325 CHILDREN
- CHAPTER 330 VETERANS

HEALTH AND SAFETY

- CHAPTER 405 MENTAL HEALTH
- CHAPTER 410 PUBLIC HEALTH
- CHAPTER 415 ENVIRONMENTAL SAFETY
- CHAPTER 420 NUCLEAR SAFETY
- CHAPTER 425 FIRE SAFETY
- CHAPTER 430 PUBLIC SAFETY

HUSBANDRY

- CHAPTER 505 AGRICULTURE
- CHAPTER 510 ANIMALS
- CHAPTER 515 FISH
- CHAPTER 520 WILDLIFE
- CHAPTER 525 CONSERVATION

TRANSPORTATION

- CHAPTER 605 ROADS AND BRIDGES
- CHAPTER 610 RAILROADS
- CHAPTER 615 WATERWAYS
- CHAPTER 620 AIR TRANSPORTATION
- CHAPTER 625 VEHICLES

RIGHTS AND REMEDIES

- CHAPTER 705 COURTS
- CHAPTER 710 ALTERNATIVE DISPUTE RESOLUTION
- CHAPTER 715 NOTICES
- CHAPTER 720 CRIMINAL OFFENSES
- CHAPTER 725 CRIMINAL PROCEDURE
- CHAPTER 730 CORRECTIONS
- CHAPTER 735 CIVIL PROCEDURE
- CHAPTER 740 CIVIL LIABILITIES
- CHAPTER 745 CIVIL IMMUNITIES
- CHAPTER 750 FAMILIES
- CHAPTER 755 ESTATES
- CHAPTER 760 TRUSTS AND FIDUCIARIES
- CHAPTER 765 PROPERTY
- CHAPTER 770 LIENS
- CHAPTER 775 HUMAN RIGHTS

BUSINESS

- CHAPTER 805 BUSINESS ORGANIZATIONS
- CHAPTER 810 COMMERCIAL CODE

> If you click on Chapter 415, Environmental Safety, you will see the list of Acts.

ENVIRONMENTAL SAFETY

- 415 ILCS 5/ Environmental Protection Act.
- 415 ILCS 10/ Local Solid Waste Disposal Act.
- 415 ILCS 15/ Solid Waste Planning and Recycling Act.
- 415 ILCS 20/ Illinois Solid Waste Management Act.
- 415 ILCS 25/ Water Pollutant Discharge Act.
- 415 ILCS 30/ Illinois Water Well Construction Code.
- 415 ILCS 35/ Illinois Water Well Pump Installation Code.
- 415 ILCS 40/ Public Water Supply Regulation Act.
- 415 ILCS 45/ Public Water Supply Operations Act.

EXHIBIT 1-4
(continued)

- 415 ILCS 50/ Wastewater Land Treatment Site Regulation Act.
- 415 ILCS 55/ Illinois Groundwater Protection Act.
- 415 ILCS 57/ Facility Planning Area Rules Act.
- 415 ILCS 60/ Illinois Pesticide Act.
- 415 ILCS 65/ Lawn Care Products Application and Notice Act.
- 415 ILCS 70/ Hazardous Substances Construction Disclosure Act.
- 415 ILCS 75/ Environmental Toxicology Act.
- 415 ILCS 80/ Degradable Plastic Act.
- 415 ILCS 85/ Toxic Pollution Prevention Act.
- 415 ILCS 90/ Household Hazardous Waste Collection Program Act.
- 415 ILCS 95/ Junkyard Act.

- 415 ILCS 97/ Mercury Switch Removal Act.
- 415 ILCS 100/ Response Action Contractor Indemnification Act.
- 415 ILCS 105/ Litter Control Act.
- 415 ILCS 110/ Recycled Newsprint Use Act.
- 415 ILCS 115/ Illinois Pollution Prevention Act.
- 415 ILCS 120/ Alternate Fuels Act.
- 415 ILCS 122/ MTBE Elimination Act.
- 415 ILCS 125/ Environmental Impact Fee Law.
- 415 ILCS 130/ Interstate Ozone Transport Oversight Act.
- 415 ILCS 135/ Drycleaner Environmental Response Trust Fund Act.
- 415 ILCS 140/ Kyoto Protocol Act of 1998

Each Act is further subdivided into sections.

(415 ILCS 5/) Environmental Protection Act.

Title I — General Provisions
Title II — Air Pollution
Title III — Water Pollution
Title IV — Public Water Supplies
Title IV-A — Water Pollution Control and Public Water Supplies
Title V — Land Pollution and Refuse Disposal
Title VI — Noise
Title VI-A — Atomic Radiation
Title VI-B — Toxic Chemical Reporting
Title VI-D — Oil Spill Response
Title VI-D — Right-to-Know
Title VII — Regulations
Title VIII — Enforcement
Title IX — Variances
Title X — Permits
Title XI — Judicial Review
Title XII — Penalties
Title XIII — Miscellaneous Provisions
Title XIV — Used Tires
Title XV — Potentially Infectious Medical Waste
Title XVI — Petroleum Underground Storage Tanks
Title XVII — Site Remediation Program

2. Judicial Decisions

With a few exceptions, print volumes containing judicial decisions (called **reporters**) are not organized by topic and you must use an encyclopedia, digest, or other index to find relevant cases. To avoid this two-step process, CALR is an efficient way of locating judicial decisions. Once you find cases, reading and understanding what you've found requires a solid understanding of court systems.

a. Trial Courts versus Appellate Courts

Most cases enter the legal system when a plaintiff files suit in a **trial court**. As previously noted, the plaintiff must have standing. A trial court is most concerned with **issues of fact**. An issue of fact concerns what happened: Did he dump barrels of chemicals or did someone else do it? Did she purposely falsify the permit application, or was it a typographical error? Trial courts examine evidence and take testimony to make factual decisions. Factual determinations often resolve the case without any need for legal research. For example, in most situations, if she ran the red light she is responsible for the collision. Because factual decisions do not make or interpret the law, most states do not report (publish) trial court decisions; therefore, when you find a reported state court case, it is often a case from an appeals court or the highest court in the system; these courts are concerned with **legal issues**: the appropriate consequences of the facts or how the lower court handled the case. Some federal trial decisions are reported.

When you read a decision from an appeals court or the highest court, remember that the court is not hearing a "new" case, but is reviewing a decision made by a lower court. The appeals court can **affirm**, **reverse**, **remand**, or **modify** the lower court's decision or use some combination of these orders. For example, an appellate court could affirm the trial court's decision that a defendant was responsible for a collision, but find the award of damages unreasonable and reverse and remand on the determination of appropriate damages. If an appellate court determines that a trial court made an error in admitting evidence or making a calculation, the appellate court will generally remand (send the case back to the lower court), because it will not accept evidence or make determinations of fact.

Appeals courts use panels of judges. The decision of the majority governs the outcome of the case (whether to affirm, reverse, or remand) but the other (non-majority) judges may write their opinions. A **dissenting opinion** is written by a judge who disagrees with the **majority decision** (the majority decision is also called the **decision of the court**). A dissenting opinion is not the law, but often provides interesting facts and opinions about the case. A **concurring opinion** is written by a judge who agrees with the majority's decision, but for different reasons.

Reporters
Print volumes that contain judicial decisions

Trial Court
Court in which most cases start, generally concerned with deciding issues of fact

Factual Issues
Trial courts use testimony and evidence to decide facts, i.e. what happened

Legal Issues
Determining appropriate consequences of the facts or whether a trial court handled a case properly

Affirm
Higher court's decision to support or uphold the decision of the lower court

Reverse
Decision to invalidate the decision of the lower court

Remand
Decision to send the case back to the lower court

Modify
Decision to change the decision of the lower court

Dissenting Opinion
Opinion written by a judge who disagrees with the majority; not law but provides interesting facts and opinions about case

Majority Decision
That which governs the outcome of cases; also called decision of the court

Decision of the Court
Majority decision, governs outcome of the case

Concurring Opinion
Written by a judge who agrees with majority decision but for different reasons

EXHIBIT 1-5
A Thought-Provoking Dissent

In the landmark environmental case, *Sierra Club v. Morton*, 405 U.S. 727 (1972), the Supreme Court held that the Sierra Club, as a corporate entity, lacked standing, but that it may sue on behalf of any of its members who had individual standing because the challenged activities affected their aesthetic or recreational interests. Sierra Club lost the case, but established that an environmental group can establish standing in an environmental case by finding, among its membership, a single person with a particularized interest (e.g., one who hikes, hunts, fishes, or camps in or near the affected area). The case is best known for the dissent of Justice Douglas who argued that natural resources ought to have standing to sue for their own protection, stating that: "The critical question of 'standing' would be simplified and also put neatly in focus if we fashioned a federal rule that allowed environmental issues to be litigated before federal agencies or federal courts in the name of the inanimate object about to be despoiled, defaced, or invaded by roads and bulldozers and where injury is the subject of public outrage. Contemporary public concern for protecting nature's ecological equilibrium should lead to the conferral of standing upon environmental objects to sue for their own preservation. . . . Inanimate objects are sometimes parties in litigation. A ship has a legal personality, a fiction found useful for maritime purposes. . . . The ordinary corporation is a 'person' for purposes of the adjudicatory processes. . . . So it should be as respects valleys, alpine meadows, rivers, lakes, estuaries, beaches, ridges, groves of trees, swampland, or even air that feels the destructive pressures of modern technology and modern life. The river, for example, is the living symbol of all the life it sustains or nourishes—fish, aquatic insects, water ouzels, otter, fisher, deer, elk, bear, and all other animals, including man, who are dependent on it or who enjoy it for its sight, its sound, or its life. The river as plaintiff speaks for the ecological unit of life that is part of it. Those people who have a meaningful relation to that body of water—whether it be a fisherman, a canoeist, a zoologist, or a logger—must be able to speak for the values which the river represents and which are threatened with destruction. . . . The voice of the inanimate object, therefore, should not be stilled. That does not mean that the judiciary takes over the managerial functions from the federal agency. It merely means that before these priceless bits of Americana (such as a valley, an alpine meadow, a river, or a lake) are forever lost or are so transformed as to be reduced to the eventual rubble of our urban environment, the voice of the existing beneficiaries of these environmental wonders should be heard. Perhaps they will not win. Perhaps the bulldozers of "progress" will plow under all the aesthetic wonders of this beautiful land. That is not the present question. The sole question is, who has standing to be heard."

b. Reading Cases

The physical layout of cases can be confusing. Depending on your source, publishers' enhancements such as a **synopsis** (summary of the case) and **headnotes** (summaries of individual points made in the case) may or may not be included. If headnotes are included, they may include references to supplemental materials and serve as an outline of the case.

As you read a case, keep a legal dictionary and a piece of paper close by. You will probably have to look up at least a couple of new legal terms with each case you read. You may also want to draw a timeline on a piece of paper so that you can visualize the events before and during the litigation. Judges usually do not give facts in the order in which they occurred (chronological order), which can be confusing. Often the first paragraph in the opinion recites **procedural history**, the court decisions that brought the case to its current position (e.g., "Plaintiff-appellant sought review of summary judgment entered by the Circuit Court of Kendall County. The appellate court, second district, reversed. We granted certiorari . . .") To a beginner this usually makes no sense until the underlying facts are clear. Skip this paragraph, read the underlying facts and do a **timeline**, then go back to the procedural history and add it to the timeline (at the end of the underlying facts, of course).

If there are multiple parties, particularly if the judges refer to those parties as **"appellant"** and **"appellee,"** jot down a quick way of identifying the parties (e.g., you might note that "appellant=employer; appellee = employee"). The appellant is the party bringing the appeal; in other words, this party lost in the lower court. The appellee won in the lower court. Because appellate courts frequently make different rulings on different issues, it is not uncommon for both sides to appeal. For example, the defendant might appeal, arguing that the trial court **"erred"** [made an error] in finding her responsible [**liable**] for harm to property as a result of a release of pollutants. At the same time, the plaintiff might appeal, arguing that the award of $50,000 in damages was insufficient because of the extent of his injuries. Reading an opinion is particularly confusing when the court refers to "plaintiff, cross-appellee," and so on.

One of the most difficult things about reading a judicial decision is that the opinion will contain discussions of several other decisions, made by other courts. The primary function of an appeals court is to review the decisions of lower courts with respect to the case under consideration (also called the **case at hand**). An opinion may contain an extensive discussion of what the court below it did and why that was correct or incorrect.

In addition, the appellate-level court may discuss other cases, decided in the past (precedent), in depth and either **analogize** or **distinguish** those cases — find them similar or different than the case being decided. The court may also discuss the meaning of a statute. It's easy to get lost, and it can be helpful to either take notes or physically mark your copy of the case.

When you find a case online, the body of the case may include numbers spaced at intervals to indicate where the page number would change if you were looking at print material. Sometimes you will want to know the exact page number on which a fact or quote appears in a case (**jump cite**). Online citations to precedent may include links, so that you can click on the citation and see the case being discussed. The first sample case in the next chapter identifies some of these features.

Synopsis
Summary of case, often provided in publishers' enhancements

Headnotes
Summaries of individual points made in the case

Procedural History
The history of the court decisions that have moved the case to its current position

Timeline
A schedule of the times at which certain events took place

Appellant
Party bringing an appeal; lost in the lower court

Appellee
The party that won in the lower court

Err
To make an error

Liable
To be found responsible

Case at Hand
The case under consideration

Analogize
To compare cases and find them similar

Distinguish
To compare cases and find them to be different

Jump Cite
The exact page number on which a fact or quote appears in a case

c. Briefing Cases

Brief
Short case summary

The best way to practice reading and truly understanding cases is to write short case summaries, called **briefs**. Although case briefs are not part of the everyday practice of law, they are the time-honored teaching tool. Law students must brief several cases for each class they attend each day. You can expect to brief many cases while you are in school.

Citation
Address at which authority is found in law books or online

You will find that each instructor has a preferred format for case briefs. Most instructors will want you to put a heading on the brief, including the name, **citation** (its official "address" within law books), and year of the case. You should also include a section for "facts," a statement of the legal issue(s) on appeal, the holding, and a summary of the reasoning. Some instructors also want separate sections reciting the procedural history and the contentions (arguments) of the parties. Be sure that you understand which sections your instructor wants included and your instructor's preferences regarding headings, spacing, and so on.

Facts.   Because a brief should be brief, one page if possible, it is not usually a good idea to copy the facts as stated by the court. Edit out all insignificant facts. To determine whether a fact is significant, ask yourself: "If this fact were changed, would it change the outcome?" For example, assume the case states that the plaintiff was driving her 2005 Ford Mustang to school, on Maple Street, when the defendant ran a red light and caused a collision. Ask yourself: would the result be different if the plaintiff had been driving her 2006 Chevy Aveo to the store on Elm Street when the defendant ran a red light and caused a collision?

Recite the facts in chronological order, as they happened, and in past tense (because the facts are not continuing to occur). Your instructor may want you to include procedural history in the facts; others prefer a separate section. In either case, the procedural history is important and should be included.

Find an easy way to refer to the parties. Using either plaintiff and defendant or the names of the parties (Smith and Jones) can be confusing, particularly if there are several parties. It is often possible to identify the parties by their roles (e.g., landlord-tenant, husband-wife-child, employer-secretary, or buyer-seller).

Issue and Holding.   The issue on appeal is never a factual issue such as "whether the light was red." That may have been the issue at trial, but the trial court made a decision. On appeal, something about how the lower court made that decision is in question. Try to identify the ruling or rulings in question and the arguments made by the parties and you will be able to spot the issue.

Holding
Answer to the legal issue in a judicial decision

The **holding** is the answer to the question posed by the issue. It generally includes this court's disposition of the case (affirm, reverse, etc.) and a short summary of the court's conclusion. For example, if the issue is "whether the trial court erred in refusing to permit testimony of a blind witness," the holding might be "Reversed; a witness may not be considered incompetent to testify based on physical disability alone." Do not accidentally state the holding of a lower court.

Reasoning
Summary of the court's explanation of its decision

Reasoning.   The **reasoning** is a summary of the court's explanation of its decision—the "why" behind the holding. Most instructors prefer that you explain reasoning in your own words. It is almost never sufficient to simply state that the court based its decision on precedent. It is also not helpful to refer to cited cases unless a reader would know what the reference means. Try to explain how the unique facts of this case add to or clarify the law.

Instructors differ on whether dissenting or concurring opinions should be included in a brief. Read these opinions. If they make the facts or the legal arguments more understandable, write a short summary.

E.   In the Field

1.   Employment Opportunities

Many people believe that protection of the environment is the most pressing issue of the twenty-first century and wonder whether they can be part of the solution. In fact, career opportunities that require knowledge of environmental law are at an all-time high. The "In the Field" section of each chapter is intended to introduce you to career opportunities, ethical issues, political issues, and other matters unique to working with environmental law.

Opportunities exist in government, not-for-profit groups, and private industry. All types of skills are required: scientists, lawyers, paralegals, writers, computer specialists, financial specialists, educators, land use planners, insurance specialists,[4] and architects, are all needed. A basic understanding of the structure and terminology of environmental law and how to research most recent developments are essential to people in all of those roles. For example, the Ohio State University website description of the job *Environmental Technician* indicates that the job requires a strong science background: "often you will find candidates with degrees in chemistry or geology who have taken additional courses or a two-year degree in environmental science. Some positions require engineering degrees," but also indicates that a "course of study should include classes that deal with ecology, environmental law, occupational safety, sampling procedures and math, particularly college algebra and statistics. Good computer skills are a must." http://www.ag.ohio-state.edu/~envjobs/job1.htm.

You can start to explore career and internship opportunities immediately. Amherst College has an excellent website concerning environmental careers: www.amherst.edu/~pjpowers/comm/environmental. html. The EPA website, http://www.epa.gov/careers, also has a job-search feature and information about internships. The following pages include descriptions of federal government jobs requiring knowledge of environmental law that were found on www.usajobs.gov.

Assignment 1-3

Find an online posting for a job in the private sector or in state government that requires knowledge of environmental law.

---

[4]Insurance is available to cover environmental claims (e.g., contaminated property) as well as to cover claims of malpractice by environmental professionals.

EXHIBIT 1-6

EPA Paralegal Specialist, GS-950-9/11, CNSL/RGAE
Additional Duty Location Info: 1 vacancy — Kansas City, KS

MAJOR DUTIES:
The full performance level of this position is the GS-12 level. Duties will be commensurate with the grade level to which the successful incumbent is selected. Duties at the full performance level are as follows:

Under the direction of a regional staff attorney, prepares administrative actions under regulatory programs, including drafting correspondence and legal documents; preparation of administrative records; supporting negotiations; coordinate the preparation of the legal documents with the regional attorney and, as appropriate, the regional technical staff.

Assist the regional staff attorney in preparation for administrative and civil litigation including drafting the correspondence, drafting the litigation report consistent with agency guidance, preparation of discovery documents, pleadings, affidavits, motions to dismiss and motions for summary judgment and other documents. Conducts legal research on a variety of legal issues and provides statutory interpretation by researching statutes, legislative history, policy and guidance.

Organizes and maintains files for complex cases. Obtains and reviews records, reports, correspondence and court documents. Evaluates and initiates a comprehensive file system which allows for quick document retrieval. Coordinates with technical staff, contractors, courts and others to obtain documents necessary for a current and accurate file system.

Responsible for answering requests under the Freedom of Information Act (FOIA). Performs analysis, evaluation and review of documents, contracts and coordinates with other office of Regional Counsel personnel, program personnel, and the requestor, as appropriate, while adhering to the procedures specified under FOIA. Provides investigative or technical support in civil/criminal matters. Investigates facts concerning violations of federal environmental statutes. Determines the most effective manner for obtaining factual information and efficiently utilized sophisticated investigative techniques.

Reviews reported case law. Conducts legal research on a variety of legal issues. Provides statutory and regulatory interpretation for Agency personnel by researching statutes, legislative history, regulations and governing policy.

Prepares for, attends and participates in conferences with industry representatives, state or local officials, and federal personnel. Attends deposition, settlement negotiations, pretrial conferences with the federal judge or magistrate and meetings related to cases such as public meetings.

Coordinates with other office of Regional Counsel personnel, program personnel, and the requestor.

EXHIBIT 1-6
(continued)

FAA Environmental Program Specialist

SALARY RANGE: 54,129.00-102,283.00 USD per year
SERIES & GRADE: FV-0028-H/I

OPEN PERIOD:

POSITION INFORMATION:
Full Time Permanent
DUTY LOCATIONS:
1 vacancy-Denver CO

WHO MAY BE CONSIDERED:
All Sources — and employees eligible for FAA Selection Priority Program (SPP)

JOB SUMMARY:
DESTINATION *FAA* — Land the Perfect Job

Business Component: Northwest Mountain Region, Airports Division, Denver Airports District Office

Sample of Duties: The Environmental Program Specialist manages environmental programs in accordance with the National Environmental Policy Act (NEPA) and the Part 150 Noise Compatibility Program for the Airport District . . .
(see Duties tab for more duties)

Knowledge, Skills, Abilities:

1. Knowledge of the National Environmental Policy Act (NEPA) and related laws, regulations and policies.
2. Knowledge of regulations and programs relating to airport noise and land use.
3. Ability to communicate effectively. Describe your experience preparing and communicating information to various audiences.
4. Ability to develop, analyze, refine or implement plans, such as Environmental Assessments (EAs) and Environmental Impact Statements (EISs), to assure that noise, air quality and wetland preservations conform to federal, state and local regulations.
5. Ability to manage and accomplish work through the combined cooperative efforts of others.
6. Knowledge of various airport programs, i.e. Airport Improvement Program, planning, airport construction, safety, in support of the ADO's staff and aviation community.

EXHIBIT 1-6
(continued)

Federal Emergency Management Agency

Department: Department Of Homeland Security

Agency: Homeland Security, Federal Emergency

Management Agency (FEMA)

Job Announcement Number:

MS-06-TRO-1061-MKS

| **Overview** | Duties | Qualifications & Evaluations | Benefits & Other Info | How to Apply |

◄ Back to Search Results

Deputy Environmental Liasion Officer

SALARY RANGE: 62,291.00-80, 975.00 USD per year
SERIES & GRADE: GS-0301-12/12

PROMOTION POTENTIAL: 12

OPEN PERIOD:

POSITION INFORMATION:
Full-Time Temporary
DUTY LOCATIONS:
1 vacancy — Biloxi, MS

JOB SUMMARY:

The specialist serves as a staff resource on environmental/historic preservation issues and compliance requirements to FEMA program staff. The primary responsibility is to assist in implementing compliance with applicable federal environmental laws, including the National Environmental Policy Act (NEPA), the Endangered Species Act, National Historic Preservation Act, and Executive Orders 11988, 11990, and 12898; and others as they pertain to FEMA's disaster programs, including the Public Assistance Program and Hazard Mitigation Grant Program. This includes scoping environmental/historic issues, reviewing grant applications for compliance, providing technical assistance to those involved with grant implementation, and ensuring compliance is sufficiently documented. The work performed by this specialist will assist in the expeditious closeout of disaster operations and grant projects. Provides assistance to program staff members in the ongoing management of environmental/ historic preservation compliance responsibilities for FEMA disaster projects. Manages all aspects of the environmental/historic compliance function in disaster recovery operations. This includes starting the operation, managing staff and the full range of compliance work. Negotiates agreement documents with Federal and State environmental/historic resource agencies and assists in formal consultations with Federal Agencies. Recommends changes in policy, regulations, guidance, and procedures to streamline the environmental/historic preservation compliance for disaster programs.

Knowledge in implementing, in a Federal/State/local context, the requirements of NEPA, and Section 106 of the National Historic Preservation Act and related historic preservation statutes; and familiarity with Endangered Species Act (ESA), Coastal Barrier Resources Act (CBRA), Clean Water ACT (CWA), Coastal Zone Management Act (CZMA), Fish and Wildlife Coordination Act (FWCA), Clean Air Act (CAA), Farmlands Protection Policy Act (FPPA), Migratory Bird Treaty Act, Magnuson-Stevens Fishery Conservation and Management Act, Wild and Scenic Rivers Act, Executive Order 119888 (Floodplains), Executive Order 1190 (Wetlands), Executive Order 12898 (Environmental Justice), and 44 CFR Parts 9 and 10. (Material omitted.)

3. Analytical, critical thinking, organization, and problem solving skills to evaluate environmental/historic compliance support to FEMA disaster programs and to recommend viable solutions to problems.

4. Oral communication and interpersonal skills, to deal effectively with staff and FEMA colleagues, under stressful circumstances; other agencies, states and local governments, and the public; in order to impart information or negotiate conflict resolution.

2. Ethical Issue: Confidentiality

Whatever your career path, you will have to address ethical issues. University of San Diego and University of Charleston have excellent web pages with resources for research on environmental ethics (and other) issues: http://ethics.sandiego. edu/Applied/Environment/index.asp; www.ucwv.edu/academics/majors/ ethics_environmental.aspx.

Some ethical issues are very philosophical in nature. For example, should wildlife habitat be valued more highly than a factory that will provide work for impoverished people? Let's start with a more practical issue. Lawyers and paralegals have a duty of confidentiality. Protection of confidential information against disclosure in litigation is called attorney-client privilege. If you are not familiar with confidentiality and privilege, examine ABA Model Rule 1.6, www.abanet.org/ cpr/mrpc/rule_1_6.html or your state's equivalent (state rules can be found from www.abanet.org/cpr/links.html).

To what extent does privilege extend to other environmental professionals in litigation? The case at the end of this chapter addresses the issue.

> *Related Topics: Can you imagine situations in which a legal professional might want to disregard confidentiality in the context of environmental law?*
> *For additional information, see:*
> *A Lawyer's Perspective on Environmental Reporting Ethics*, S. Longroy, www.ccsb.com/news.php?id=49 2002.
> ABA Memo on Proposed Revisions to Rule 1.6, www.abanet.org/cpr/e2k/e2k-witness_russell.html.
> *Attorney Client Confidentiality in the Criminal Environmental Law Context:*
> *Blowing the Whistle on the Toxic Client*, N. Targ, www.law.pace.edu/pelr/vol14no1f1996/targ.html.

Assignment 1-4

Read the case at the end of this chapter and prepare a case brief. The case involves a contract between a lawyer and a client that is ambiguous and not in compliance with ethical rules. It is intended to show the need for good research and show how precedent is used in deciding cases. While most of the cases presented as samples in this book have been heavily edited, this case has only been slightly edited, so that you can see how cases look when you find them online.

1. Read the case twice before you write anything.
2. Make a timeline showing the chronology: the discovery of contamination, the first suit, the subsequent "Underlying Cases," the settlement, the attempt to obtain compensation from the insurance companies, etc. Keeping the parties straight is a challenge with this case. Consider the following discussion questions:
   a. Traveler's is seeking the privileged material from its own client (Shield is the insured, but has assigned its claims under the policy to the District). Why? What might the insurers hope to find in the reports and memo?
   b. Suppose that Shield had become concerned about contamination before there was any litigation or any threat of litigation and, in an effort to be a "good citizen," had hired Rizzo to assess the situation. Would internal communications among Shield employees and communications between Shield and Rizzo have been protected in subsequent litigation?
   c. The court states that the insurance company can take depositions of Shield employees in an attempt to obtain the desired information without access to the privileged documents. Do those employees have to answer questions relating to pollution caused by their employer? Can they "take the Fifth"?

Key Terms

Administrative Agencies	Jump Cite
Adversarial	Legal Issues
Affirm	Legislation
Analogize	Liable
Annotated Statute	Majority Decision
Appellant	Modify
Appellee	Municipal Law
Brief	Precedent
Burden of Proof	Primary Authority
CALR	Procedural History
Case at Hand	Proximity Connector
Case Law	Reasoning
Citation	Regulations
Cite	Reporters
Civil Law	Remand
Code	Reverse
Codify	Root Expander
Common Law	Search Query
Concurring Opinion	Secondary Authority
Connector	Standing
Constitution	Statute
Criminal Law	Statutory Construction
Decision of the Court	Statutory Interpretation
Dissenting Opinion	Synopsis
Distinguish	Timeline
Err	Title
Executive Action	Topic
Factual Issues	Trial Court
Headnotes	Tribal Courts
Holding	Wildcard
Judicial Decisions	

Review Questions

1. Identify the five sources of environmental law.
2. Is environmental law found in local law, state law, or federal law?
3. Identify three differences between a civil lawsuit and a criminal prosecution.
4. While researching a legal question, you are lucky enough to find an article written by a prominent Harvard professor. The article discusses your precise issue in depth. Is the article primary authority or is it secondary authority?
5. When you find a statute that addresses your issue, you still might have to look for case law. Why?

6. Identify three types of connectors that can be used in a terms and connectors search and describe the functions of wildcards and root expanders.
7. Page numbers are not used in referring to a particular part of a statute. Why?
8. The relevant statute describes "DUI" as being in control of a "vehicle" while intoxicated. Your client was arrested for riding a horse while intoxicated. Describe strategies you would use to determine whether the horse should be considered a "vehicle."
9. Your DUI client is also claiming that he was not intoxicated while riding the horse, but was suffering a reaction to a prescription drug. What type of issue does this present and would legal research be appropriate?

KEY TERMS CROSSWORD

www.CrosswordWeaver.com

ACROSS

5. ! is the root _____
7. _____ history, court decisions that preceded case's current position
11. party who lost in lower court
13. another term for decision of the court
16. _____ lawsuit generally results in award of money
19. to send a case back to lower court
20. uphold lower court decision
24. another word for legislation
26. for a statute to have been entered into topical system
28. * is the _____, used to find variations such as woman/women
29. _____ opinion, agrees with decision but may state different reasons

DOWN

1. issues of _____ dealt with in trial court
2. type of law made by agencies
3. _____ court decisions are often not published
4. connector useful for finding synonyms
6. quotation marks are used for _____ searching
8. IRS is an administrative _____
9. % is the _____ connector
10. _____ authority explains or helps locate the law, but is not actually law
12. / is the _____ or proximity connector
14. _____ statute has references to cases, articles, etc.
15. statutes are organized by _____
17. _____ law comes from one of five sources
18. _____ opinion, by a judge who disagrees
21. change a decision
22. Loislaw automatically retrieves most _____ forms
23. _____ prosecution can result in prison sentence
25. connector that will find terms in case regardless of proximity
26. another word for legislation
27. initials, Loislaw, Lexis are this type of research

DEDHAM-WESTWOOD WATER DIST. v. NAT'L UNION FIRE INS. CO. PITTSBURGH

Superior Court of Massachusetts, at Norfolk
11 Mass. L. Rep. 211 ←
February 15, 2000, Filed

11 Mass. L. Rep. 211 is a citation at which this trial court case can be found in law books.

Shaded material below is a "headnote," added by the publisher to classify the case according to areas of law addressed by the case and summarize/outline the decision. Other headnotes and the court's own footnotes have been eliminated to make the case shorter.

> *Civil Procedure > Discovery > Privileged Matters > Work Product > General Overview* [HN1] Pursuant to *Mass. R. Civ. P. 26(b)(3)*, a document may constitute work product if it is prepared in anticipation of litigation by or for another party or by or for that other party's representative. *Mass. R. Civ. P. 26 (b)(3).*

Defendant, Travelers Indemnity Co. ("Travelers"), moves for an Order compelling non-party witness, Shield Packaging Co., Inc. ("Shield"), to produce for inspection: (1) an investigative report, and (2) memo memorializing interviews with Shield employees. Shield asserts that the documents are not discoverable because they are subject to attorney-client privilege and the work product doctrine. *DENIED.*

Dedham-Westwood Water District ("District"), brought an environmental insurance coverage declaratory judgment action against defendants, including Travelers, for damages related to contamination of the White Lodge Well Field ("Well Field"). The District discovered that two wells were contaminated with volatile organic compounds in 1979. In 1982, the District sued Cumberland Farms, Inc. as the party responsible for the contamination. This litigation lasted for approximately ten years; however, the District was unable to establish its claims. In 1988 a federal district court, found that Shield and the Massachusetts Water Resource Authority ("MWRA") were the likely culpable parties rather than Cumberland.

In 1990, the District instituted a suit against Shield and MWRA ("Underlying Cases"). Simultaneously, the Massachusetts Department of Environmental Protection ("DEP") issued a Notice of Responsibility ("NOR") to Shield requiring it to conduct various environmental site assessments and remedial actions. This process, conducted under the Massachusetts Contingency Plan ("MCP"), continues to this day. Shield hired outside counsel, Nutter, McClennen & Fish, LLP ("Nutter"), and environmental consultants, Rizzo Associates, Inc. ("Rizzo"), to defend the litigation and undertake the MCP. Shield turned to its insurers for defense and indemnification; none of its primary carriers was willing to assume the full defense. Shield and the District, entered a Memorandum of Agreement ("Memorandum") and filed an Agreement for Consent Judgment on January 15, 1992. The Memorandum provided that:

1. Shield's share of damages from contamination of the Well Field would be $9,000,000;
2. Shield and District would file an Agreement for Consent Judgment of $9,000,000;
3. Shield would pay District the total sum of $750,000 over a seven-year period;

4. With the exception of the amount specifically agreed to be paid by Shield, District agreed not to execute or enforce the Judgment entered pursuant to the Agreement;
5. The agreed $9,000,000 Judgment was not intended to determine or operate as admission of Shield's liability with respect to any other proceedings or with respect to any other party;
6. Shield would assign to District its entire right, title and interest in insurance, insofar as policies may provide coverage for the claims asserted by District in the Underlying Cases.

A Final Decree entered in 1993 resulted in dismissal of Underlying Cases. The District filed this case in 1996 against insurance companies in connection with the clean-up . . . claims that it is entitled to coverage under liability insurance policies to Shield.

There were two investigative reports prepared by Shield. The first version prepared by Sgarzi, Shield's Vice President and Corporate Counsel includes information regarding Shield's operations; history of use of 1-1-1 trichloroethane; and groundwater concerns. Although this information may be relevant to the claim that the policies cover Shield's liability, the report is not discoverable. Pursuant to *Massachusetts Rule of Civil Procedure 26(b)(3)*, a document may constitute "work product" if prepared "in anticipation of litigation . . . by or for another party or by or for that party's representative." Protection of attorney work product material is to protect impressions and thought processes of attorneys. Sgarzi created the report because Shield anticipated litigation after the opinion in *Dedham Water Co. v. Cumberland Farms, 689 F. Supp. 1223 (D.Mass. 1988)*. [F]or a document to be covered by the doctrine, it is not necessary that litigation be pending at the time the document is created. The doctrine only requires that litigation be reasonably anticipated in the near future. Shield does not have to demonstrate that the District actually threatened litigation at the time the report was prepared and it is irrelevant that it was not until two years after the decision that the District sued Shield. Shield was aware that District filed suit against Cumberland Farms. The president of Shield, Bates, had been called to testify at trial. Shield was aware of comments made by Judge Tauro in 1988. Additionally, DEP was conducting an investigation that focused on Shield. Sgarzi prepared the report because Shield reasonably anticipated that it might be sued by the District, that the DEP might commence proceedings against it, and that it might be forced to sue its insurance companies to obtain defense and indemnification.

The second report is protected as attorney work product prepared in anticipation of litigation. Changes to the first report were made by Attorney Ryan to provide Rizzo with information to allow them to serve as environmental consultants and litigation consultants in anticipated litigation. Disclosure to Rizzo does not waive work product privilege because Rizzo was specifically retained as a consultant and documents created "by or for" a consultant are shielded from discovery. The report was transmitted to Vice President of Rizzo, by letter indicating that it was confidential work product prepared by Shield for use in defense of anticipated litigation.

The two reports are also shielded from discovery pursuant to the attorney-client privilege. The attorney-client privilege attaches to communication between an attorney and client in confidence, for the purpose of seeking, obtaining or providing legal advice or assistance. The reports were confidentially prepared [to] be turned over to outside counsel for the purpose of obtaining legal advice.

It is irrelevant that the second report was forwarded to Rizzo. Typically, attorney-client privilege is waived when privileged communications are revealed to a third party. However, "disclosure to a third party who is identified with the party claiming the privilege and to whom disclosure is reasonable and necessary in order for all the facts to be made known to the attorney does not waive the privilege." The report was forwarded to Rizzo for the purpose of complying with the DEP NOR and for providing expert consultation for anticipated litigation. Accordingly, disclosure of privileged communications to Rizzo does not waive the attorney-client privilege, and both reports are protected from production.

Travelers claims that it is entitled to discovery of attachments to the reports. However, the attachments are also protected. Sgarzi selected and compiled attachments which, in his judgment, would assist counsel in preparation for anticipated litigation. These compilations were intended to remain confidential; the reports, along with attachments were only revealed to outside counsel and the company president. Therefore, the attachments are protected by the work product doctrine.

Travelers claims that it is entitled to memoranda memorializing interviews between Shield employees and representatives of Shield's outside counsel and Rizzo. The interviews constituted factual discussions relating to Shield's manufacturing operations and waste disposal. The notes of these interviews conducted by counsel are protected from production under the work product doctrine. These notes reflect the attorney's mental impressions, thought processes and opinions. At the time the notes were prepared Shield and its outside counsel were reasonably anticipating litigation. The interviews were part of the process of gathering information to enable Attorney Ryan and Rizzo to effectively counsel Shield in such litigation.

Travelers argues that even if the reports, attachments, and memoranda are protected by attorney-client privilege and/or work product doctrine, they are discoverable because the insurer has a substantial need for them and it is unable without undue hardship to obtain the substantial equivalent by other means. However . . . witnesses who have worked with Shield since the beginning of its operations, including Bates, Sgarzi, and Simpson, are still employed there and are available for depositions. Travelers has not exhausted other means of obtaining substantially equivalent materials . . . its motion is premature and, therefore, must fail.

2

Administrative Agencies
in Environmental Law

A. What's It All About?

In the context of environmental law, the purpose and importance of administrative agencies can be summed up in two words: delegation and regulation. Although administrative law is, in a sense, "third tier law," it is extremely important in environmental law, and, therefore, knowledge of how administrative agencies function is essential to understanding the substance of the law.

CONSTITUTION
The "grandparent" of all American law
created the three branches:

Legislative   Judicial   Executive
Each of the branches can delegate part of its power
to make and/or enforce or implement law to an

Administrative Agency
That can make rules and regulations, conduct investigations, make
adjudicatory decisions, and penalize noncompliance.

---

1. Federal, State, and Local Agencies

Delegation is essential to environmental law because the topic is technical, constantly changing, and enormous. Imagine if Congress had to enact every environmental regulation. Not only would there not be enough hours in a day to accomplish what is necessary, most of our legislators do not have the technical knowledge (biology, chemistry) to make educated decisions. Now suppose that local or state police were given responsibility for testing discharges from factories to ensure that our air and water remain safe.

Agencies concerned with environmental issues exist at the local level (municipal planning and zoning boards, wetlands commissions, open space and preservation departments); the state level; and the federal level. Exhibit 2-1, taken from the EPA website, identifies several relevant federal agencies.

Because there are so many agencies and they do not have identical structures or procedures, this chapter will discuss the procedures and terminology in a general way. In later chapters, discussing substantive environmental law, you will be directed to specific agencies and specific procedures.

EXHIBIT 2-1

Question
Does EPA handle all environmental concerns?

Answer
No, some issues are primarily concerns of other federal, tribal, state or local agencies. EPA also works in partnership with state environmental agencies. Many environmental programs have been delegated to the states and they have primary

---

**EXHIBIT 2-1
(continued)**

---

responsibility for them. Often, it is most appropriate to contact your local (city or county) or state environmental or health agency rather than EPA.

Examples of different situations and who to call include:
The Endangered Species Act is primarily managed by the U.S. Fish and Wildlife Service. EPA's concern with this act is assuring that the use of pesticides does not endanger these species.

Many **wildlife** concerns are **connected with destruction of wetlands**. The U.S. Army Corps of Engineers determines whether an area is a wetland and issues permits for use of such an area. The permit applications are reviewed by the U.S. Environmental Protection Agency under Section 404 of the Clean Water Act. Therefore, initial contact should be made with your nearest Army Corps of Engineers' office. To get the phone number of your local district office, phone 1-800-832-7828 or visit their website at the above link. [You may also visit the Wetlands Oceans and Watersheds Web area for more information about what defines a wetlands.]

For concerns about wildlife such as foxes, birds, prairie dogs, rabbits, etc. that are caused by development and other human encroachment, contact your **state or local wildlife office**. Problems with the environment **inside the workplace,** such as presence or handling of chemicals or noxious fumes, are under the jurisdiction of the Occupational Safety and Health Administration, an arm of the U.S. Department of Labor.

The Consumer Product Safety Commission **is the office that deals with the safety of products used in daily life**. They have information on formaldehyde in mobile homes, fiberglass in insulation and other building materials, the safety of all terrain vehicles, and equipment used for children's safety. The toll free phone number is 1-800-638-2772. This commission is an arm of the U.S. Department of Health and Human Services.

The Food and Drug Administration and EPA have a cooperative arrangement with regard to the Federal Insecticide, Fungicide and Rodenticide Act. FDA is responsible for the safety of food and any substance that is applied to the human body. EPA is responsible for the safe use of pesticides in controlling insects, rodents, fungus, and sanitizers that are used on surfaces. [Licensing of commercial and private pesticide applicators may be handled by state Departments of Agriculture or EPA. You would need to contact your Regional EPA Office for more information.]

Information on gardening or farming in your area is best obtained from your **local Agricultural Extension office,** which can be listed in your local telephone directory under your county offices or your state university listing. **Noise complaints**. EPA no longer regulates most types of noise pollution. You should consult with your local governmental (e.g., city and county) authorities to see if there are local or state laws that might apply to your situation. Dust on Roads is a local issue. You should contact the **local environmental or health agency**. Questions about your local landfill. You should contact your **county environmental agency**.

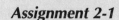

Assignment 2-1

◆ If you have not already done so, visit www.epa.gov/epahome/state.htm and bookmark your state environmental agencies for use in future assignments. If your county or city has a website, determine whether you have local agencies.

◆ If you live or will work near any tribal lands, you should be aware of the interaction between the primary federal environmental agency, EPA, and the tribes. Visit http://www.epa.gov/tribalportal/trprograms/env-programs.htm and note the program-by-program listing, explaining that interaction.

2. The Underlying Statutes

Enabling Act
Law creating administrative agency and defining its powers

Delegation takes the form of an **enabling act (also called an enabling statute)**. The enabling act creates the agency and defines its powers. For example, the Environmental Protection Agency was created when Congress enacted the EPA Reorganization Plan of 1970, 5 U.S.C. §903. Depending on how an agency functions, it may be called a board, a commission, a department, an administration, a bureau, or an agency. Although the differences are important in the study of administrative law, they are not essential to understanding environmental law.

EXHIBIT 2-2

PART OF THE ENABLING ACT FOR THE WISCONSIN DEPARTMENT OF NATURAL RESOURCES

15.34 Department of Natural Resources; Creation.

(1) There is created a department of natural resources under the direction and supervision of the natural resources board.

The responsibilities of the DNR are described in various sections of the state code. To see a direct correlation between an enabling act and an agency's regulations, refer back to Exhibits 1-1 and 1-2, concerning Endangered Species in Minnesota.

Agencies are generally given authority to act **informally** by, for example, issuing permits and licenses for particular functions; processing claims for services or benefits; conducting negotiations or mediation; issuing advisory opinions; and providing information and assistance in compliance with the agency's rules. These activities can usually proceed without need for notice or a hearing.

Informally
Agency action subject to less rigorous procedural requirements

An agency may also be given more formal powers that mirror the powers of the three branches of government: legislative (rule-making); executive (investigation and enforcement); and adjudication (hearings). How the agency exercises some of those powers is governed by an Administrative Procedures Act (APA). The federal **APA**, 5 U.S.C. §§511-599, which governs federal agencies, will be used for illustrative purposes in this book. Each state has its own administrative procedures law to govern its agencies.

APA
Administrative Procedures Act — Federal or state law governing the procedures under which agencies operate

---

Assignment 2-2

Find the Administrative Procedures Act for your state.

B.   Rule-Making

In order to implement broad legislation, agencies establish detailed regulations and rules. Although some agencies use other terms to refer to this exercise of legislative power, the characteristics are more important than the name. A rule or regulation is intended to apply to a large group, rather than an individual, and is directed at future conduct, rather than the past. The rules and regulations of federal agencies are compiled in the Code of Federal Regulations (**CFR**), which can be searched online at www.regulations.gov or www.gpoaccess.gov/cfr. The CFR is organized by agency, so, for example, a citation to 40 C.F.R. XXXX indicates a regulation enacted by the EPA.

CFR
Code of Federal Regulations — Compilation of the rules and regulations of federal agencies

> The problem with terminology and the importance of understanding the nature of the proceedings are demonstrated in the sample case at the end of this chapter. In that case, an agency's decision to issue a permit to allow incineration of chemical weapons is referred to as an "other than contested case" because the permit is viewed as affecting the rights of the public at large, rather than specific individuals. References to a "contested case" indicate that that term is used for decisions involving particular individuals. Another way to look at this is that agency decisions that involve the public or large groups constitute rule-making, whereas decisions that affect specific individuals can be considered adjudication, discussed later in this chapter.

Substantive Rule
Rule that implements statutory directive and has impact outside the agency

Procedural Rule
Governs agencies own actions

Interpretive Rule
Agency's explanation of its actions or statement intended to provide guidance

Federal Register
Daily publication for notice of federal agency rules

Comment
Right of the public to have input in formal rule-making

Rules may be classified as **substantive, procedural,** or **interpretive.** A substantive rule directly implements a statute, creates obligations for people outside the agency, and has the full force of law. Promulgation of substantive rules, therefore, involves the formal rule-making process described below. A procedural rule governs the functions of the agency itself; the process for enactment is less formal. An interpretive rule is the agency's explanation of its actions or a statement intended to provide guidance to the public and is also established by less formal means.

Businesses regulated by environmental agencies must be constantly aware of new rules and of amendments to existing rules that will affect their operations as they are proposed and enacted. Employees of those businesses, consultants, and law firms monitor new developments and must be familiar with the process for enacting substantive rules, which begins with publication of notice of the proposed rule. Notice of new, proposed, and final federal rules is published in the **Federal Register,** which can be accessed online on at www.archives.gov/federal-register. States have equivalent publications.

Publication of notice allows interested parties to **comment** before the rule becomes final. Depending on the type of rule-making and the level of formality, the comments may be made in person, at a hearing, or by mail. To promulgate a substantive rule, the agency generally must engage in formal rule-making and hold an actual hearing. The agency may amend the rule, based on comments, but is not required to do so. The rule must be published again, in its final form.

Assignment 2-3

1. Find an EPA regulation that opened for public comment this week.
2. Search the EPA regulations to find a "nonrule" concerning use of a particular chemical as a de-dusting agent on clay particles that are to be sold as cat litter.
3. Is it possible to submit an electronic comment to an EPA regulation?

C. Executive Functions: Investigation and Enforcement

1. Self-Reporting

Agencies can collect factual information in a variety of ways. Many agencies require regulated businesses to keep specific records and self-report. You may be familiar with this in your personal life. The IRS requires that you report your income, regardless of its source. Your state may require that you have your car's emissions tested.

EXHIBIT 2-3

EXAMPLE OF NOTICE FOR PROPOSED ACTION BY STATE AGENCY
From www.oal.ca.gov/notice/50z-2006.pdf.

CALIFORNIA REGULATORY NOTICE REGISTER 2006, VOLUME NO. 50-Z 1855
PROPOSED ACTION ON REGULATIONS

Information contained in this document is published as received from agencies and is not edited by Thomson West.

TITLE 3. DEPARTMENT OF PESTICIDE REGULATION
Toxic Air Contaminants   DPR Regulation No. 06-005

NOTICE OF PROPOSED REGULATORY ACTION
The Department of Pesticide Regulation (DPR) proposes to amend section 6860 of Title 3, California Code of Regulations (3 CCR). The proposed regulatory action designates the pesticide chemical sulfuryl fluoride as a toxic air contaminant (TAC) in subsection (a) pursuant to Food and Agricultural Code (FAC) section 14023.

SUBMITTAL OF COMMENTS
Any interested person may present comments in writing about the proposed action to the agency contact person named below. Written comments must be received no later than 5:00 p.m. on February 1, 2007. Comments regarding this proposed action may also be transmitted via e-mail <dpr06005@cdpr.ca.gov> or by facsimile transmission at (916) 324-1452. A public hearing has been scheduled for the time and place stated below to receive oral comments regarding the proposed regulatory changes.

DATE: January 31, 2007   TIME: 1:00 p.m.
PLACE: California Environmental Protection
Agency Headquarters Building   Sierra Hearing Room
1001 I Street
Sacramento, California 95814

A DPR representative will preside at the hearing. Persons who wish to speak will be asked to register before the hearing.

Example

When business people refer to the "red tape" or the "bureaucracy" that "burdens" American businesses, they are often referring to the requirements of administrative agencies and, particularly, to the reporting requirements of agencies concerned with environmental matters. Many municipalities, government operations, and private businesses employ full-time environmental compliance officers. In recent years, agencies have made real efforts to lighten that burden. For example, the Texas Commission on Environmental Quality now has a site that allows mandatory reporting of air emissions, recycling, waste reduction, and discharges into water to be done online. www.tceq.state.tx.us/nav/reports/report_data.html.

---

2. Search Warrants and Subpoenas

Agencies can also conduct inspections and examinations on the premises of regulated entities. Some businesses are required to consent to such inspections, in advance, as a condition to obtaining a required license or permit to operate; others comply voluntarily. If a regulated entity objects to inspection, a **search warrant** may issue, if necessary. Many businesses are open to the public and a warrant is not required to search areas open to public observation. Other businesses are so heavily regulated that they fall within an exception to the warrant requirement. Even if the premises is not open to the public and the business is not heavily regulated, there is a low expectation of privacy in a regulated business, and the "probable cause" requirement for obtaining a warrant is less stringent than in a criminal matter or for a search of a home.

Search Warrant
A document issued by a judge or magistrate, authorizing a search

Agencies also have power to issue **subpoenas** ordering individuals to appear and testify or to provide access to records. If the individual refuses to comply, a court can issue a contempt order.

Subpoenas
An order to provide testimony or evidence

There are, of course, limits, on agency power to investigate. Those limits relate to the agency's jurisdiction (the EPA could not investigate a company's records to look for sexual harassment), protection of trade secrets and other privileged information, and Fifth Amendment protection against self-incrimination. The protections of the Fifth Amendment are very limited with respect to required self-reporting.

Example Warrant Requirement

A New York City recycling facility, operating under a permit issued by the New York State Department of Environmental Conservation, was searched by city police, without a warrant. The owner claimed violation of his constitutional rights. In evaluating the claim, a federal trial court stated: "For warrantless inspections to be so authorized, the owner or operator of the commercial premises must be a part of a 'closely regulated industry.' Burger, 482 U.S. at 701 . . . Whether an industry is closely regulated depends on the 'pervasiveness and regularity' of government monitoring, such that the business owner should harbor a lessened expectation of privacy. Id. If the commercial property is utilized in a closely regulated industry, then a warrantless search of it may be deemed reasonable within the meaning of the Fourth

Amendment if three circumstances additionally are established: (1) A 'substantial government interest . . . informs the regulatory scheme pursuant to which the inspection is made'; (2) warrantless inspections are 'necessary to further the regulatory scheme'; and (3) the regulations provide a 'constitutionally adequate substitute for a warrant,' by 'advis[ing] the owner of the commercial premises that the search is being made pursuant to the law and has a properly defined scope, and [by] . . . limit[ing] the discretion of the inspecting officers.' Burger, 482 U.S. at 702-03, 711 . . . This third condition requires that the statutory scheme be 'sufficiently comprehensive and defined that the owner of commercial property cannot help but be aware that his property will be subject to periodic inspections undertaken for specific purposes' and that it limit the 'time, place, and scope' of the regulatory inspections. Id. at 703" *Meserole St. Recycling, Inc. v. City of New York* (S.D.N.Y. 2007).

When a chemical company applied to the New Jersey Department of Environmental Protection (DEP) for a permit to build an industrial wastewater treatment facility, the DEP imposed a condition that the DEP have the right to enter the facility for inspection. The court held that the "pervasive government regulation exception" to the warrant requirement applied because the activity was integrally related to the issue of water pollution and conservation resources, which was an activity that was extensively regulated. Participation in the activity resulted in submission to inspections that are reasonably necessary to the enforcement of water pollution regulations. *In re Dept. of Environmental Protection*, 177 N.J. Super. 304 (1981).

EXHIBIT 2-4

This form and instructions for self-reporting on private water supplies were found at http://www.state.in.us/icpr/webfile/formsdiv/36741.pdf.

DIRECTIONS FOR DESCRIBING, COLLECTING AND MAILING THE SAMPLE

I. DESCRIBING THE SAMPLE

1. The regulations of the Indiana State Department of Health provide that samples of water shall not be examined unless they are collected in containers furnished for that purpose and the description blanks are filled out completely.

II. COLLECTING THE SAMPLE

1. A dechlorinating agent has been added to the bottle. It may appear as a white crystal, a drop of water, or a spot of powder two or three millimeters in diameter. It is sodium thiosulfate. Do not wash or rinse it out. The purpose of the bottles containing thiosulfate is to destroy the chlorine present at the moment the sample is collected. Sodium thiosulfate prevents the killing action of the chlorine on the bacteria while the sample is being transported to the

EXHIBIT 2-4
(continued)

laboratory. Water samples which contain chlorine residuals when they reach the laboratory will not be examined.

2. A sample shall be taken from a tap, such as a faucet, petcock, or small valve. No sample shall be taken from a fire or yard hydrant or a drinking fountain. Kitchen sinks, threaded hose bibs, softened or treated water lines, and spigots with screens or aerators are poor sampling points and should be used only if better sampling points are not available.

3. When the sample is to be collected from a tap, allow the water to run freely for at least five minutes to flush out pipes and fixtures.
   Time by a watch; do not guess.

4. Remove the screw cap being careful not to touch or otherwise contaminate the inside part of the cap or the neck of the bottle itself.

5. Reduce flow of water in tap to a steady stream about the size of a pencil. Fill the bottle exactly to the 100 ml line on the bottle. At this level, there will be 100 ml of water and about 25 ml of air space.

6. Replace the screw cap using the same care as before.

III. MAILING THE SAMPLE

1. Postal authorities require that the sample be packed and mailed in the following manner:
   a. Refold the description form in half lengthwise and wrap it around the bottle. Place the bottle inside the container.
   b. If the return address label (to the State Department of Health) is not already pasted to the package, moisten the back side of the enclosed gummed address label and paste it on the package. Make sure the return address appears on it.

2. Mail the sample immediately after collection. Time of collection of the sample should be governed by the time of mail pickup at the mailing station and the delivery at Indianapolis. The time between the sample collection and the arrival of the sample to the laboratory should not be more than 48 hours, preferably within 30 hours. If the postal service does not give satisfactory service in your area; in the future, you may wish to investigate other means of transporting the samples, such as UPS, Overnight Expresses or by bus.

SDH 44-007　　　　　　　　　　　　　　　State Form 36741 (R4/5-99)

D. Adjudication

1. ADR in Agencies

Many courts now require that litigants participate in alternate dispute resolution (**ADR**) before proceeding to trial. There are many types of ADR; mediation and arbitration are most common. In **mediation**, a third party (the neutral) helps the parties understand each others' positions and interests and facilitates their exploration of possible solutions, but any agreement ultimately comes from the parties. In **arbitration**, the neutral hears both sides and then imposes a decision.

ADR
Alternative Dispute Resolution, resolving conflicts without court involvement

Mediation
Form of ADR in which a neutral party facilitates resolution crafted by parties

ADR can have many advantages: resolution of the dispute often occurs much sooner; it is often less expensive than trial; keeping the conflict out of court can salvage the relationship between the parties; the less-public ADR process can protect the privacy of participants; and the neutral can be an expert in a field that might be a complete mystery to an average judge (for example, having a chemical engineer as an arbitrator in a dispute concerning a chemical spill).

Arbitration
Form of ADR in which neutral party imposes a decision

ADR can also have disadvantages. In recent years, there have been many cases arguing that ADR requirements that deprive parties of their "day in court" are unconscionable. When ADR is mandatory, there is sometimes a backlog and delays.

Like the courts, many agencies now employ ADR. The Administrative Dispute Resolution Act of 1996 (**ADRA**), 5 U.S.C. §571, provides that: "An agency may use a dispute resolution proceeding for the resolution of an issue in controversy that relates to an administrative program, if the parties agree to such proceeding" and provides the rules for agency ADR. The EPA ADR website, http://www.epa.gov/adr/, supports use of ADR in many contexts, including rule making, policy development, administrative and civil judicial enforcement actions, permit issuance, protests of contract awards, administration of contracts and grants, stakeholder involvement, negotiations, and litigation.

ADRA
Federal statute, Administrative Dispute Resolution Act of 1996

Example

From http://www.epa.gov/NE/enforcement/adr/examples.html.

The GE-Pittsfield case, which involved a highly-controversial PCB-contaminated site in western Massachusetts, perhaps best illustrates the diversity of ADR approaches which have been found to be useful to achieve different objectives and to reach different audiences.

First, a team of mediators assisted GE, EPA and eight other agencies in reaching a settlement which addresses GE's liability and provides for remediation of the site. Second, a team of facilitators manages a public dialogue, known as the Citizens' Coordinating Council, in which neighbors, business interests, environmental groups, and other interested parties have an opportunity to raise concerns to GE and the regulatory agencies regarding the site cleanup.

Third, pursuant to the settlement agreement, panels of neutral experts will be engaged to provide neutral opinions on certain specified questions relating to future remedial decisions.

Finally, the consent decree which embodies the settlement contains an ADR provision whereby mediation may be used to resolve disputes arising during the implementation of the settlement. In each of these four ADR applications, the parties consensually tailored the process to meet their specific needs.

2. Hearings

Some agencies hold hearings on individual situations in addition to the hearings held prior to enactment of a rule of general application. These hearings are fairly informal, but they serve a very important role. The individual serving as "judge" is called a hearing officer, examining officer, presiding officer, or an **ALJ** (administrative law judge) and may be an employee of the agency itself. There is no jury and the hearing typically takes place at the agency's offices.

ALJ
Administrative Law Judge; decision maker at agency hearing

The parties are entitled to notice of the details of the hearing in advance and have the right to be represented and to present and challenge evidence. The rules of evidence are very relaxed, compared to rules applied in a trial court, but the parties generally have the right to conduct **discovery** before the hearing to obtain access to the evidence that will be presented. Because many of the issues at agency hearings are highly technical, expert witnesses may be called.

Discovery
Process of obtaining evidence before hearing

The hearing is very important because it may, essentially, serve the role normally served by a trial court, if it meets the constitutional due process requirements of notice, a hearing before an impartial decision maker, and an opportunity to present and challenge evidence. The ALJ serves as finder of fact and generally issues written findings. When a party seeks judicial review of an agency decision, the court may simply review the agency record and not conduct a **de novo** (new) review of the facts. It is essential, therefore, that parties prepare well for adjudication.

De Novo Hearing
Review of evidence and testimony as finder of fact

> In the sample case at the end of this chapter, opponents of the incinerator first claimed that they were entitled to have their opposition treated as "adjudication," rather than as a public hearing. The court rejected the argument, finding that the opponents had no individual rights at stake. Had the matter been handled as an adjudication, the court would not have allowed the opponents to present new evidence in court. Because the opponents were not given full rights to present and challenge evidence, the court held that new evidence should be accepted during judicial review.

An agency's rules may provide for various levels of appeal before a party can seek review in the court system. If such appeals are available, the party is generally required to pursue those appeals before a court will hear the case. This requirement is called **exhaustion of administrative remedies**. A party involved in administrative adjudication (or the representatives of that party) must be thoroughly familiar with the rules for seeking review. The time limits for pursuing appeals before filing in court and for filing in court once administrative remedies have been exhausted can be very short and are rigidly enforced.

Exhaustion of Administrative Remedies
Requirement that a party pursue all levels of administrative review before seeking judicial review

---

Assignment 2-4

◆ Using the site you previously bookmarked or an Internet search for "environmental hearing" and the name of your state, find the procedures or rules for environmental hearings in your state.

◆ If your state agency website includes a search box, enter the term "ADR" or "arbitration" or "mediation" to determine whether your state employs alternate conflict resolution techniques. Using the information you find and/or information found on the EPA website, list three reasons why a situation might NOT be appropriate for ADR, so that the more formal hearing process will be necessary to resolve the dispute.

◆ Examine ADRA and determine whether an arbitration hearing may be conducted by telephone.

E.   Judicial Review of Agency Action

Judicial review is generally[1] available to parties if they have has exhausted administrative remedies and have **standing** in a court of proper **jurisdiction**. The agency's enabling statute generally describes how and where judicial review may take place; if it does not, the APA may govern. Federal courts generally have jurisdiction to hear appeals from federal agencies while state courts hear appeals from state and local agencies. Appeals from most of the federal agencies start in the federal circuit courts of appeal because the "trial" has essentially taken place within the agency hearing.

    Courts are reluctant to interfere with agency discretion and, especially with respect to technical matters within the agency's jurisdiction, tend to defer to the agency. Courts generally will not consider issues or evidence that was not raised in proceedings within the agency. A court will overturn an agency decision if the agency acted **ultra vires** (beyond the authority granted in its enabling act) or did not follow proper procedures. A court may also overturn a decision that is **arbitrary and capricious**, meaning not supported by the facts in the record or by existing law or not supported by substantial evidence. A court will not normally "substitute its judgment" for that of the agency simply because it thinks the agency did not make the best decision or the decision that the court would have made. The sample case at the end of the chapter discusses some of the limitations on judicial review.

Standing
Whether party has suffered an injury sufficient to allow the party to seek review of decision

Jurisdiction
Boundaries of decision makers' powers

Ultra Vires
Beyond the authority granted in enabling act

Arbitrary and Capricious
Decision not supported by the facts or law

---

[1]There are a few enabling acts that prohibit judicial review.

F.   Obtaining Information from Agencies

1.   FOIA and Sunshine Act

FOIA
Freedom of Information
Act — Law requiring that
agencies disclose non-
exempt information upon
request

Agencies collect and compile a tremendous amount of information, which creates conflict between those who want maximum public access to that information and those with an interest in keeping the information private. Several laws found at 5 U.S.C. §552 address that conflict. Federal agencies are regulated by the **Freedom of Information Act** (**FOIA**), which requires those agencies to disclose information that does not fall within listed exceptions. The agencies publish rules for FOIA requests and most agencies have a FOIA officer. In general, the party seeking disclosure must submit a written request that reasonably describes the records being requested and must pay a fee. The agency must respond within ten days by either complying with the request or claiming one of the exemptions.

Vaughn Index
A list of documents withheld

If the agency claims an exemption and internal appeals fail, the party seeking disclosure may seek judicial review. The reviewing court will examine affidavits from the agency and may order the agency to prepare a detailed **Vaughn Index** of documents withheld and the basis for nondisclosure. Parties who are successful in FOIA suits may obtain awards of attorney fees.

Assignment 2-5

Find the EPA FOIA request form online and answer the following:

1. The request must be submitted to a particular office. How are EPA offices organized?
2. Identify the "nine exceptions" that define documents that may be withheld from disclosure under FOIA.
3. Under what circumstances may the EPA request prepayment for a FOIA request?
4. Locate your state's open meetings statute.

Sunshine Law
Requires agencies to
hold meetings open to
the public

Similarly, the **Government in Sunshine Act** requires that agency meetings, with limited exceptions, be announced in advance and open to the public. States have similar laws requiring "open meetings."

Example

If the parameters of what administrative agencies do seem pretty clear to you, think again! Sometimes it's all in how you label a decision. The following example is from Lora Lucero, land use planner, attorney, editor of Planning and Environmental Law, and environmentalist, in Albuquerque. After making a FOIA request to the

New Mexico Department of Transportation NMDOT, Lora learned that the president of Clear Channel had been meeting with staff at NMDOT and the Federal Highway Administration to have "good faith" discussions regarding Clear Channel's implementation of "digital changeable messaging technology" in New Mexico. Clear Channel is a global advertising company that boasts "outdoor advertising is great because you can't turn it off, throw it away, or click on the next page." Lora, and many others, consider billboards akin to "litter on a stick." They believe the LED technology (light-emitting diode) is not merely a nuisance, but a safety hazard, in addition to another unnecessary use of electricity.

When Lora asked NMDOT staff about how the public might weigh in, she was told the public wouldn't have an opportunity unless rule-making occurs. There will be no public notice about the meetings, even if a member of the public specifically requests notice; no opportunity for the public to share evidence about the safety hazards associated with LED signs.

E-mail between Clear Channel and NMDOT (obtained as a result of the FOIA request) disclosed that Clear Channel agreed to prepare a memorandum of understanding (MOU) between the company and NMDOT outlining the meetings. But in response to a second FOIA request for a copy of this MOU, Lora was told it wasn't subject to inspection. NMDOT staff advised Lora to continue making FOIA requests and, perhaps sometime in the future, after the "agreement has been finalized," it might be made available for public inspection.

---

2.   Privacy and Trade Secrets Act

On the other hand, the **Privacy Act** protects records concerning an individual from disclosure and gives the individual the right to see records concerning him or her. The Act includes exceptions, particularly for routine government use. Similarly, the **Trade Secrets Act** protects business secrets from disclosure.

Privacy Act
Law giving individual ability to prevent disclosure of information about the individual

Trade Secrets Act
Protects against agency disclosure of business secrets

G.   In the Field: How Far Can You Go?

In this chapter you've learned about many ways in which you can interact with environmental agencies on behalf of your employer or a client: monitoring rule-making; commenting on pending rules; keeping and submitting required records; monitoring and assisting in ensuring or improving compliance with regulations; participating in inspections; and making FOIA or Privacy Act requests. At what point in dealing with an agency is a lawyer needed? That depends on the agency. Most states have statutes prohibiting unauthorized practice of law and, although "practice of law" is not well defined, it is generally agreed that a non-lawyer cannot represent another person in an adversarial proceeding in court. Many agencies, however, specifically permit representation by a non-lawyer in agency hearings. For a partial listing of those agencies, visit the National Federation of Paralegal Associations website, www.paralegals.org/displaycommon. cfm?an=1&subarticlenbr=334.

EXHIBIT 2-5

10. Appearances
Any party may appear in person or by counsel or other representative. A partner may appear on behalf of a partnership and an officer may appear on behalf of a corporation. Persons who appear as counsel or other representative must conform to the standards of conduct and ethics required of practitioners before the courts of the United States. www.epa.gov/aljhomep/rules/cfr40part7-hearing-procedures.pdf.

Practicing with administrative agencies requires excellent organizational skills and attention to detail. To see an article on the importance of a well-organized administrative record, see http://www.jonesandstokes.com/resource/Admin%20Record%20July03.pdf.

Key Terms

ADR	Interpretive Rule
ADRA	Jurisdiction
APA	Mediation
ALJ	Open Meetings Act
Arbitrary and Capricious	Privacy Act
Arbitration	Search Warrant
Comment	Self-Reporting
CFR	Standing
De novo Hearing	Subpoena
Discovery	Substantive Rule
Enabling Act	Sunshine Law
Exhaustion of Administrative Remedies	Trade Secret Act
Federal Register	Ultra Vires
FOIA	Vaughn Index

Review Questions

1. What is the relationship between the three branches of government and administrative agencies?

2. What are the purposes of an enabling act?

3. What are the three types of rules that can be promulgated by an agency and how do they differ?

4. Identify the process for formal rule-making.

5. What is the CFR?

6. What is the APA?

7. What is an ALJ?

8. When is "exhaustion of administrative remedies" necessary?

9. By what means can an agency obtain information as part of an investigation?

10. What is meant by *de novo* review?

11. Identify reasons why a court might overturn an agency decision.

12. What is FOIA and what is the Privacy Act?

KEY TERMS CROSSWORD

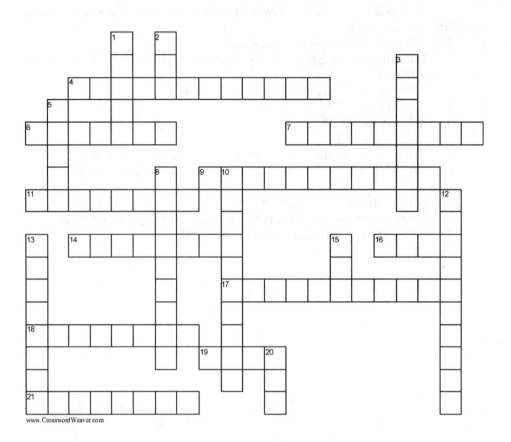

www.CrosswordWeaver.com

ACROSS

4. agency ruling, less formal, gives guidance or explanation
6. act, protects against disclosure of records concerning individuals
7. without basis in fact or law
9. synonymous with rules
11. Federal _____, publication of proposed rules
14. used to compel testimony
16. courts often do not conduct de _____ review of agency decisions
17. agency rule with impact on regulated entities
18. _____ act creates agency
19. initials, requires agencies to disclose records
21. act, requires open meetings

DOWN

1. _____ vires, beyond scope of enabling act
2. abbreviation, federal agency rules published here
3. in many cases an agency does not need a search _____ to inspect
5. _____ Secret Act, protects against disclosure of business secrets
8. agencies can require self-_____
10. _____ of remedies, required for judicial review
12. agency rule governing agency itself
13. before promulgating substantive rule, agency must accept
15. initials, federal statute governing agency procedures
20. initials, hearing officer

Assignment 2-6

Does the tail wag the dog? It might seem so to people not familiar with how administrative agencies operate and how courts view administrative decisions. In the case that follows, the individuals living near a proposed incinerator for chemical weaponry were unhappy when the state environmental agency issued permits. They sought judicial review and undoubtedly wanted the court to look at all of their evidence and decide that the agency was wrong to issue the permit because the burning could endanger their health. Ultimately, they might get part of what they wanted: a chance to present more evidence.

The agency issued the permits after following procedures for an "other than contested case." The procedures for a contested case would have been followed if the rights of a specific person were involved; but in this case, the permits had an impact on every member of the public. Under the procedures the agency followed, the opponents were allowed to participate as members of the public by submitting evidence, but were not allowed to participate more fully by, for example, cross-examining others.

This court first holds that the agency did not make a mistake in following procedures for an "other than contested" case. But, following a kind of "you can't have it both ways" logic, the court concludes that because the opponents were not given full participation rights at the agency level, they are entitled to greater participation in judicial review. If the agency had treated the matter as a contested case and allowed the opponents full discovery and cross-examination at the hearings, the court would not have been required to allow them to supplement the record.

But, once that evidence is reviewed, the court will only determine whether the agency could have reasonably made the decision to issue the permit. The court WILL NOT decide whether it would have been "better" to not grant the permit. This is an example of the ways in which courts defer to agencies.

Read the case to prepare to discuss the following questions. If you are not accustomed to reading cases, you may find the case hard to follow and may have to read it several times.

1. Why not treat it as a contested case? Could the agency have avoided all of this by following contested case procedures to begin with?
2. The court asserts, repeatedly, that the issuance of the permit does not affect a specific party more than others, but is that really accurate? Wouldn't the Army be uniquely affected by the issuance or denial of the permit? Your local building administrator would not normally hold a public hearing before issuing a permit to allow you to remodel your basement, so why, in this case, did issuance of an individual permit require formal rule-making, with notice, comments, and a hearing?
3. What is true of the nature of the agency decision that makes it particularly likely that the court will defer and uphold the issuance of permits?

G.A.S.P. ET AL., APPELLANTS v. ENVIRONMENTAL QUALITY COMM'N OF THE STATE OF OREGON, DEPT. OF ENVIRONMENTAL QUALITY, RESPONDENTS, AND U.S. ARMY, INTERVENOR-RESPONDENT.

Court of Appeals of Oregon
198 Or. App. 182; 108 P.3d 95; March 9, 2005, Filed

Petitioners, environmental organizations and individuals, appeal dismissal of their petition for judicial review of a final order of Environmental Quality Commission (EQC). We hold that petitioners do not have a right to a contested case hearing, but that the trial court's failure to provide an evidentiary hearing requires remand to the trial court.

This case involves Army's application for permits from Department of Environmental Quality (DEQ) and EQC to destroy chemical weapons at Umatilla Army Depot. The Army proposes to burn chemicals and containers in special incinerators . . . it must obtain permits from DEQ and EQC.[n3] EQC must find that the incinerators will meet criteria in ORS 466.055 for facilities that treat or dispose of hazardous waste. One criterion is that it will not have adverse effect on public health or safety, on the environment, or on adjacent lands. Another is that it must use best available technology for treating and disposing of hazardous waste. EQC is required to base its findings on information submitted by the applicant, the DEQ or any other interested party ORS 466.055.

Years passed between when the Army applied and when EQC issued the order that is on review. DEQ hired a firm to examine the proposal; the consultant concluded that the incinerators would not create major adverse effects on public health, safety, or the environment. DEQ made the report and other material public and solicited comments. DEQ held public hearings; EQC conducted work sessions. An Army consultant found that risks of proceeding were less than risks of keeping the material in storage. DEQ received additional comments and materials, supporting and opposing the incinerators; petitioners were among opponents who testified or submitted materials. DEQ's consultant revised its report in light of comments. The Army consultant also responded. EQC issued the permit on conditions. The order was designated an order in other than a contested case; it included findings of fact related to statutory criteria. EQC stated that it was persuaded by reports of DEQ's consultant, information from the Army's consultant, and testimony of an engineering professor. Petitioners sought review under ORS 183.484, which provides for judicial review of final orders in other than contested cases. The court reviewed the EQC record; refused requests to conduct discovery, cross-examine witnesses, or present evidence in addition to the agency record and entered judgment affirming the order in its entirety. Petitioners appeal.

ORS 183.484(5) sets forth criteria for review of an order in other than a contested case:

The court shall remand to the agency if it finds the agency's exercise of discretion to be in violation of a constitutional or statutory provision. The court shall set aside or remand the order if it finds that the order is not supported by

---

[n3] The permits are a hazardous waste storage and treatment permit from EQC and an air contaminant permit from DEQ.

substantial evidence in the record, viewed as a whole, that would permit a reasonable person to make that finding.

[P]etitioners assert that they were entitled to a contested case hearing. If they are correct, the trial court did not have jurisdiction, and we, therefore, would not have jurisdiction. If EQC should have conducted a contested case hearing, petitioners would have had to seek review in this court under ORS 183.482, not in the circuit court under ORS 183.484.

ORS 183.310(2)(a) defines a "contested case" as a proceeding before an agency in which the individual legal rights, duties or privileges of specific parties are required by statute or Constitution to be determined only after an agency hearing at which such specific parties are entitled to appear and be heard; where the agency has discretion to suspend or revoke a right or privilege of a person; for suspension, revocation or refusal to renew or issue a license where the licensee or applicant demands such hearing; or where the agency by rule or order provides for such hearings.

Petitioners assert that the state and federal constitutions require that their individual rights in this proceeding be determined only after a hearing at which they are entitled to appear and be heard. They refer to ORS 466.130, which provides that EQC "shall conduct a public hearing . . . where a proposed hazardous waste disposal site is located . . . applicant may present the application and the public may appear or be represented in support of or in opposition to the application." They argue that decisions under ORS 466.130 require a contested case hearing because the dangers that the incinerator allegedly poses to those who live near it give those persons a legal right to oppose permitting it to operate.

The hearings that ORS 466.130 describes are hearings at which any member of the public may appear. They do not implicate individual legal rights, duties or privileges of specific parties. The purpose is to ensure that EQC has information needed to act in the interest of the public as a whole. It is not EQC's role to adjudicate specific individual rights. The only right that the statute gives is to appear at hearings as part of the public at large. The fact that some, because they live near the depot, may be more concerned about the incinerators than are other members of the public does not give greater rights under the statute. ORS 466.130 is not the source of a statutory right to a contested case hearing.

Petitioners argue that they have a constitutional right to a contested case hearing because incinerating chemicals poses serious dangers to persons who live in the vicinity. They state: "the right to be safe in one's person and home . . . placed in jeopardy by movement, draining, chopping, and burning of deadly chemical warfare agents. . . . the right to be reasonably free from contamination and . . . ingestion or exposure to dangerous chemicals. . . . facility . . . will contaminate air, water, soil, and . . . foods . . . risks associated with . . . releases of chemical warfare agents, dioxins, heavy metals have been inadequately assessed and politically minimized . . . contamination . . . will so threaten or actually contaminate Petitioners' properties that they will be forced to alter their property use." Petitioners' statements are based on evidence that supports their position, much of which they presented to EQC; they do not consider whether other evidence would support other conclusions, let alone show that the record as a whole compels findings they describe. Even if we accepted the statements, they do not indicate that they have a constitutional right to a contested case hearing.

Petitioners assert that the permit will violate Article I, section 10, Oregon Constitution. Section 10 protects the right to a remedy for "injury done" to persons or property, but petitioners have not yet suffered injury and have no present right to a remedy. The protection applies only after injury has occurred; it does not give rights to a proceeding based on speculation about injury they might suffer in the future.

We turn to petitioners' argument under the Due Process Clause of the Fourteenth Amendment. The foundation for determining both a party's due process right to a hearing and the nature of that hearing is the test that the U.S. Supreme Court established in *Mathews v. Eldridge*, 424 U.S. 319 (1976). A court must consider the private interest that will be affected by the official action; the risk of an erroneous deprivation of such interest through the procedures used and probable value of additional or substitute procedural safeguards; and the Government's interests, including the function involved and fiscal and administrative burdens that additional procedural requirement would entail.

In cases holding that there was a due process right to a hearing, the party seeking a hearing had a private interest and was threatened with governmental action that would have affected that interest. Petitioners have not suffered an injury; they are not seeking a governmental benefit, nor are they threatened with governmental action against them. The interests that petitioners assert, and the issues that ORS 466.130 requires EQC to resolve, involve public interest, not private rights. Although those issues may affect some members of the public more than others, nothing in ORS 466.005 to 466.385 creates a private interest in their correct resolution. Petitioners do not identify a constitutionally protected property or liberty interest and were not entitled to a contested case hearing.

Petitioners assert that the trial court erred in not permitting them to introduce evidence in addition to the record before EQC. The statutes do not require an agency in other than a contested case to make a record or to enter findings of fact, while circuit courts routinely make records and find facts; therefore, the "record" to which ORS 183.484 refers, as the basis for judicial review, is the record that the agency and the petitioner make before the circuit court. The proceeding in that court may be the first opportunity that a petitioner has to present evidence. The legislature did not intend to limit the record on review to evidence before the agency. The ability to present evidence in court is significant in light of the "whole record" standard for determining whether substantial evidence supports the agency's findings. In making that decision, the reviewing court must consider evidence that detracts from those findings as well as evidence that supports them. Judicial review may be the first chance for a petitioner to present evidence that would detract from the agency's order, and limiting the record to evidence that was available to the agency would undermine the "whole record" review required by ORS 183.484(4)(c).

Judicial review of a contested case is limited to the record before the agency because, in contested cases, agencies follow trial-like proceedings that culminate in a record and a final order that contains findings of fact and conclusions of law. ORS 183.484 affords parties an opportunity to develop a record like the one developed at an earlier stage in a contested case proceeding. The court's obligation to permit parties to create a complete record on judicial review does not change the court's role in evaluating that record. The purpose is not to find the facts but to decide whether the evidence would permit a reasonable person to make the determination that the agency made.

The court erred in not permitting the parties to make a complete record, including allowing them to present evidence not available when EQC entered its order; that error prejudiced petitioners, who did not have an opportunity directly to challenge evidence on which EQC relied. EQC stated that it relied heavily on the reports of DEQ's consultant and the Army's consultant and on the engineering professor's testimony. Petitioners did not have opportunity to cross-examine the professor or the consultants. The court denied attempts to introduce evidence of events that occurred after EQC entered its order. Without the additional evidence, it is impossible to evaluate the substantiality of the evidence that supports EQC's order. We reverse and remand for that opportunity to occur. We observe, however, that EQC's order is the result of many hearings and contains extensive factual findings. There is a supporting record on eleven computer discs. Petitioners and others participated in creating that record. On remand, the court does not need to create the record from the beginning; the purpose is to supplement the record so that a court may determine, from a complete record, whether EQC's order complies with the requirements of ORS 183.484(5). That determination includes deciding whether there is substantial evidence to support EQC's express findings of fact. ORS 183.484(5)(c).

3

The Courts in Environmental Law

A. Common Law Causes of Action
  1. Trespass
  2. Nuisance
  3. Strict Liability
  4. Negligence
  5. Public Trust Doctrine
  6. Fraud
B. Suing the Government
  1. Sovereign Immunity
  2. Government Property as a Source of Pollution
C. Criminal Prosecution
D. Citizen Suits Under the Statutes
E. SLAPP
F. Assisting in Environmental Litigation
  1. E-Discovery
  2. Litigation Support Software
G. In the Field: Attorneys' Fees

As discussed in other chapters, the courts play a major role in reviewing environmental decisions initially made by administrative agencies, in interpreting and applying environmental statutes, and in resolving constitutional issues relating to the environment. Even before the statutes and the agencies, however, the courts made decisions concerning the environment. While environmental statutes sometimes preempt the right to bring traditional common law claims, the courts and common law continue to play a major role in environmental law. Keep in mind, however, that filing a lawsuit alleging a common law cause of action does not always result in going to court. Many courts now mandate the use of ADR to resolve the conflict before trial.

A.   Common Law Causes of Action

Cause of Action
A recognized basis for a lawsuit

Elements
Facts that must be proven to state claim

Plaintiff
One who initiates the lawsuit

Burden of Proof
The obligation to provide evidence of each element of a claim

Private Attorney General
Theory under which private citizens are allowed to prosecute "citizens' suits"

Statute of Limitations
Law limiting time for filing suit

A **cause of action**[1] is a recognized basis upon which a court can grant an award or enter an order. Some causes of action are created by statute, as discussed later in this chapter, but others exist at common law, meaning they were created by the courts. Every cause of action has **elements**, which are the facts that must be proven by the party (usually the **plaintiff**, who initiated the lawsuit) who has the **burden of proof**. The burden of proof is the plaintiff's obligation to provide enough evidence to establish every element of the claim; in most civil suits that obligation is met by a "preponderance of the evidence." A civil plaintiff need not meet the criminal burden of proof—beyond a reasonable doubt—but need only prove that the assertions are "more likely than not" true.

The plaintiff must have standing. As discussed in later chapters, many of the environmental statutes specify that private individuals may bring suit for violations of the statute; these are called **private attorney general** actions. Plaintiffs alleging common law claims, however, must prove: (1) invasion of a legally protected interest that is (a) concrete and particularized and (b) actual or imminent, not conjectural or hypothetical; (2) a causal relationship between the injury and the challenged conduct; and (3) a likelihood that the injury will be redressed by a favorable decision. Environmental groups, such as the Sierra Club, frequently initiate environmental litigation and, because the club as a corporate entity has not been harmed, must establish that at least one member would have standing.

Every cause of action has a **limitations period (statute of limitations)**, which is the time period within which the suit must be filed. Some causes of action are associated with particular remedies. The most commonly employed common law claims against parties responsible for environmental contamination are trespass, nuisance, strict liability, negligence, and the public trust doctrine. In some situations, environmental contamination may even result in a claim for a breach of contract.

Trespass
To enter or cause entry on to property of another

1.   Trespass

Trespass is the invasion of plaintiff's land by the defendant or an instrumentality controlled by the defendant. For example, if a dry cleaning operation allows its chemicals to spill onto neighboring property, the dry cleaning operation has committed a trespass. The "invading instrumentality" in an environmental case may be capable of great harm, but undetectable to human senses: invisible and not able to be heard, smelled, tasted, or felt.

---

[1]A "cause of action" is sometimes called a "claim for which relief can be granted." If a plaintiff has not articulated a recognized cause of action, the defendant may bring a motion to dismiss the case for "failure to state a claim."

If the trespass is intentional, the plaintiff need not prove harm. The invasion itself is the "harm." A defendant's actions are intentional if he intended the invasion or if he intentionally does an act (e.g., open a valve to allow chemicals to spill on the ground) knowing that the invasion of plaintiff's property is a substantial certainty. If the trespass is a result of negligence (e.g., carelessly fail to completely close a valve on a truck carrying chemicals) the court may require proof of harm.

Example

In the sample case at the end of this chapter, the court found that a property owner was liable for trespass because a "plume" of gasoline-related chemicals traveled, underground, from its gasoline station to a neighbor's property.

---

2. Nuisance

To establish a claim for nuisance, a plaintiff must establish that the defendant unreasonably interfered with use or enjoyment of property in a way that caused substantial harm. Unlike a trespass, which involves an invasion of plaintiff's property, activities that constitute a nuisance generally take place on the defendant's property. For example, the defendant's operation of a quarry on his own property results in noise that disturbs the plaintiff in her home.

> Modern planning and zoning concepts are intended to avoid nuisance problems by providing locations at which necessary, but potentially irritating, uses can operate while keeping incompatible uses apart. Zoning, discussed in another chapter, is the division of land in a municipality into districts in which specified uses are allowed.

Nuisance is a relative concept; whether a particular activity constitutes a nuisance is a matter of degree. A property owner may be disturbed by a neighbor's crying baby or angered by the neighbor's decision to remove grass in favor of a gravel front yard, but these irritations do not rise to the level of nuisance. To determine what is "unreasonable" and "substantial" courts often balance public utility (benefit to society) against the harm. For example, landfills often result in noise, odors, and even vermin, but society needs to dispose of its garbage. Courts also look at what is customary (e.g., a crying baby is customary in a residential neighborhood, a shrieking baboon is not), what would be disturbing to most people, whether the objective could be achieved by a different means (e.g., could runways be aligned so that planes take off over a farm field, rather than over a condominium complex), and which party was "first in time." Some states will not allow a suit by a party that "came to the nuisance" or will at least look at a variety of factors to determine whether relief is appropriate.

Assignment 3-1

---

1. Use CALR to find a case, decided in your state, in which a plaintiff claimed nuisance or continuing trespass based on what could be considered a pollution problem (smoke or other fumes, odor, liquid runoff).

2. Many states now have "right to farm" laws to protect existing agricultural operations from claims of nuisance by residents of new developments. Determine whether your state has such a law.

3. Can businesses that deal with potential contaminants protect themselves from these common law claims by obtaining environmental insurance? Use the Internet to determine what is available.

4. Discuss:
   a. Should parties who "come to the nuisance" always be barred from bringing suit? Can you think of reasons why a use that existed before its neighbors might be considered a nuisance? Other than barring such suits, how could courts strike a balance between the rights of an existing use and the rights of neighboring owners?
   b. If a nuisance is of a continuing nature but is of social value should it be allowed to continue? For example, the quarry is the biggest employer in an isolated town. It cannot operate more quietly or without generating dust and vibration; it cannot relocate. If it closes, the town's economy will be devastated. Should payment of damages suffice?

5. Read and brief the case at the end of the chapter. Answer the following:
   a. Why are the defendant's compliance with the requirements of the state agency and that agency's letter releasing the defendant not sufficient to protect it from liability in this case?
   b. How was the plaintiff able to prove causation?
   c. In this case, the migration of contaminants constituted both a trespass and a nuisance. Is the court's definition of nuisance such that every trespass will also constitute a nuisance?

Private Nuisance
Interference with individual's use or enjoyment of property

Injunction
A court order by which a party is required to perform or abstain from a particular action

Public Nuisance
Interference with use and enjoyment of property common to the public

Equitable Remedy
A court order

A claim of **private nuisance** can result in financial compensation[2] for the harm suffered by the plaintiff or in a court order, such as an **injunction**, requiring the defendant to discontinue actions that interfere with plaintiff's rights. A **public nuisance** action, asserting that the defendant's actions interfere with the rights of the general public, is generally pursued by a governmental body, but can be pursued by a private individual if that individual has suffered an injury different than suffered by most of the public.

---

[2]An award of money, also called damages, is a legal remedy. A court order to do (or not do) something is an **equitable remedy**.

Example

The entire town hears and, to some extent, feels blasting from the quarry. A fine layer of dust over the area often results from the blasting. This is a public nuisance. Lyn, however, has suffered unique injury. Lyn's house is very close to the quarry and Lyn has begun to experience asthma attacks as a result of the blasting. Lyn may be able to bring an action for private nuisance.

Many courts accept a theory of **continuing trespass** or **continuing nuisance.** The theory has interesting consequences with respect to the statute of limitations.

Continuing Trespass or Nuisance
Ongoing trespass or nuisance

Example

In 1947, long before garbage pickup was available in the area, Farmer Todd began burying his nonburnable garbage in a low spot on his land. Over the years, containers with the remnants of oven cleaner, insecticide, paint thinner, nail polish remover, anti-freeze, etc., were thrown in the pile. In 1955 Farmer Todd placed sod over the heap and forgot all about it. As years passed, rain deteriorated the containers and the chemicals gradually seeped into the ground. Eventually they made their way to the water table. In 2007 local landowners learned their wells were contaminated and were able to trace the source to the Todd land. The limitations period for either trespass or negligence is far shorter than 60 years in every state. Yet, in a sense, the contamination occurs every day, as long as the source exists. Should the neighbors be allowed to sue? What if Farmer Todd died in 1968 and the current owner was totally unaware of the dump site? In some states this would be considered a continuing trespass or nuisance and the statute of limitations would not be a problem. The neighbors may have to turn to the Resource Conservation and Recovery Act, discussed in depth in a later chapter, which embodies the common law concepts of nuisance and, in many cases, preempts the existence of that cause of action.

Nuisance law is complicated and has been referred to as a "legal garbage can."[3] The cause of action remains viable in some situations, however, and requires the courts to balance the interests in economic and industrial strength against the need for clean and livable surroundings.

---

[3] *Harrison v. Indiana Auto Shredders Co.*, 528 F.2d 1107 (7th Cir. 1975).

EXHIBIT 3-1

As previously noted, some Native American Tribes have established their own court systems and their own codes and bodies of precedent. This example of a definition of nuisance is from the Oglala Sioux Tribe Law and Order Code http://www.ntjrc.org/ccfolder/oglala_lawandorder25.htm.

SECTION 2. A condition on any tract of real property within an area which is designated an area of population concentration under Section 1 which is unsafe, unsanitary, or an eyesore as the result of abandoned materials or debris of any kinds, including substances that have accumulated as the result of fires, vandalism, or similar causes, affecting the public health, comfort, safety, and welfare, is hereby declared a nuisance.

SECTION 3. Any resident of the Pine Ridge Indian Reservation who believes that a nuisance, as defined in Section 2 exists, may file a complaint to that effect with the Tribal Secretary. The Tribal Secretary shall bring such complaint before the next meeting of the Tribal Executive Committee, which shall determine whether the complaint warrants investigation. If an investigation is ordered, and a nuisance is found to exist, the owner of the tract, his agent, or other persons having an interest therein, shall promptly be order by the Tribal Executive Committee to cause the nuisance to be abated, remedied, or removed, as may be necessary.

Strict Liability
Liability without regard to fault

3. Strict Liability

Strict liability is a cause of action that allows a plaintiff to recover for harm suffered as a result of a defendant engaging in an abnormally dangerous activity, regardless of whether the defendant intentionally caused harm or even was careless. The theory has been applied to some environmental claims because they involve toxic chemicals, radioactive material, explosives, or other products that are unavoidably dangerous. Strict liability is our society's way of placing the risk on those who choose to engage in ultra-hazardous activities, rather than on those who may be harmed as a result of such activities. Strict liability is a "plaintiff-friendly" cause of action because the plaintiff does not have the burden of proving that the defendant did anything "wrong." In considering strict liability environmental claims, courts consider the value of the activity to society and whether the defendant is using state-of-the-art procedures and materials.

Example

Acme has a contract to destroy nerve gas in storage at a weapons plant. Acme is a high-quality operation. The company uses only the highest quality of supplies and equipment; its employees are well trained and careful. During the disposal operation some of the gas escapes (perhaps because of an unexpected weather condition) and injures people in the neighborhood. Acme is not at fault, but may be liable. Consider: if Acme were not liable, how would the injured parties be compensated for their injuries? Acme profits from its operations and has the ability to insure itself, do the injured parties have the same opportunities?

4. Negligence

Negligence is failure to use reasonable care to avoid harm to others. Negligence is not an easy claim for plaintiffs, who have the burden of proving (1) the **duty** of care owed by the defendant (what would have been reasonable); (2) that the defendant breached that duty; (3) that the plaintiff suffered an actual harm; and (4) that the harm was caused by defendant's action or inaction.

If there is a statutory standard governing the defendant, the plaintiff may be able to use that standard to establish the defendant's duty of care under the doctrine of **negligence per se**. In other cases, the plaintiff may have to use expert testimony to establish the standard of care.

It is often particularly difficult to prove the causal link between environmental contamination and illness. In addition, if the carelessness of the plaintiff in any way contributed to the harm, the defendant may assert **contributory negligence** or **comparative negligence**[4] as a defense.

> **Negligence**
> Failure to exercise reasonable care to avoid harm to others
>
> **Duty**
> Element of negligence; obligation to act reasonably to avoid harm to others
>
> **Negligence per se**
> Breach of duty established by statutory standard
>
> **Contributory/ Comparative Negligence**
> Defenses to claim of negligence — plaintiff contributed to injury

---

Example

For many years an electroplating factory simply dumped its untreated waste in a local landfill. Years later, contamination of the municipal well was traced to the landfill. Farmers in the area have had unusually high livestock mortality and have reported the births of several deformed animals. In addition, the area has had a "cluster" of human babies born with cleft palate. There are no existing studies linking the particular chemicals found in the well to those problems. How can the residents prove that the contamination caused the birth defects? The defendant will argue that all of the claimed "harms" can and do happen in the absence of contamination and that they are simply coincidental to the contamination.

A case involving allegations of negligence and strict liability, in connection with the release of a hazardous chemical, is included in Chapter 10, CERCLA.

5. Public Trust Doctrine

The ancient doctrine of public trust holds that certain resources are so valuable that they must be protected for the use of all people. The doctrine was

> **Public Trust Doctrine**
> Certain resources belong to all

---

[4]In some states, any contributory negligence by plaintiff may mean that the plaintiff cannot recover; in other states the court compares the relative negligence of the plaintiff and defendant and reduces the award accordingly.

originally most often applied to navigable bodies of water, but has been applied to fish and wildlife, scenic vistas, and even natural lands.

The doctrine has been applied as a basis for upholding environmental statutes that infringe on private property rights;[5] in suits against governmental bodies to require those bodies to take public trust into account in decision making;[6] and in cases against private owners who attempt to claim ownership of public trust resources.[7] Of course, using the doctrine to sue a governmental body involves special considerations.

Fraud
A false statement of material fact, intended to induce reliance, on which a party does reasonably rely

6. Fraud

In a broad sense, fraud is deception perpetrated for financial gain. While the common law cause of action for fraud differs from state to state, the elements typically include a false statement of material fact, made with intent to deceive (knowledge of falsity), on which the other party reasonable relies, to his or her detriment. The common law cause of action has been used when a seller gives a purchaser misinformation about the environmental status of property. The cause of action has limits, however, and may not be of any use to a buyer in cases where the seller said nothing and did not actively conceal conditions.

In recent years, most states have created a statutory cause of action for failure to disclose material information in the sale of real estate. The law is often codified as part of a Consumer Fraud Act and usually includes a disclosure form to be signed by the seller and provided to the buyer. Recent developments in the law indicate that a seller, particularly a developer, may even have an obligation to inform the buyer of off-site conditions. New Jersey, for example, has a New Residential Construction Off-Site Conditions Disclosure Act.

B. Suing the Government

The common law theories discussed in this chapter can be used in suits against private parties responsible for contamination. Unfortunately, however, responsible private parties cannot always be found or may be without assets to pay damages or remediate the contamination. Can injured parties sue the government? A governmental operation might be the source of contamination or the responsible governmental agency may have simply failed to prevent or remediate an environmental problem. What about suits under the public trust doctrine for making "bad" laws with respect to the environment?

If, in the example involving a contaminated well, the state environmental protection administration had failed to discover the contamination for several years and then failed to order remediation, could the residents sue that agency? As you may have guessed, the answer is "it depends." In some situations there is specific statutory authority for such a suit.

---

[5] *W.J.F Realty Corporation and Reed Rubin v. the State of New York*, 672 N.Y.S.2d 1007 (1998).
[6] *National Audubon Society v. Superior Court*, 33 Cal. 3d 419 (1983).
[7] *Coastal Petroleum v. American Cyanamid*, 492 So. 2d 339 (Fla. 1986).

Example

The Endangered Species Act specifically allows citizens to sue the U.S. Fish and Wildlife Service to cause a species to be "listed." The Service's costs in dealing with these suits and resulting court orders are very high. In 2001 the Bush administration attempted to eliminate funding for dealing with such suits.

---

1. Sovereign Immunity

If there is no specific statutory authority for a suit against the government, the question is whether the government enjoys sovereign immunity for its performance of the function at issue. Under the doctrine of **sovereign immunity** the government cannot be sued without its consent. The federal government has given that consent to some extent, in the **Federal Tort Claims Act (FTCA)**, 28 U.S.C. §1346(b). While the FTCA allows governmental agencies to be held liable for negligent performance of **ministerial** obligations that involve no exercise of discretion, it does not provide for liability based on the performance of functions that involve discretion. Individual states have their own versions of tort claims acts. If a governmental body is failing to enforce environmental statutes, citizens may have another option, a citizens' suit, discussed later in this chapter.

Sovereign Immunity
Government cannot be sued without its consent

(FTCA)
Federal Tort Claims Act— limits sovereign immunity

Ministerial Duty
An obligation that does not involve discretion

2. Government Property as a Source of Pollution

Recent closures of military bases have revealed extensive pollution on government-owned land. Radioactive contamination, leaking underground tanks, dilapidated buildings, asbestos-laden soil and unexploded weaponry are just some of the problems. While the Defense Department does have an Environmental Restoration Program in place, in at least some cases, the department has claimed sovereign immunity with respect to damages.[8]

Federal statutes discussed in later chapters contain waivers of sovereign immunity, but the waivers are not identical and have been interpreted by the courts in different ways. In many cases the government is responsible for compliance with current laws, but is not liable for past noncompliance with environmental laws. Another variable is whether the government still owns the property at issue.

As you might imagine, the issue of federal liability for pollution is very political and the "status quo" is under constant challenge in the courts, legislative bodies, and public opinion. The National Governors' Association, www.nga.org, has taken the position that: "Congress should enact legislation clarifying the CERCLA waiver of sovereign immunity for sites the federal government no longer owns" and that assertion of sovereign immunity by the U.S. Army Corps of Engineers and Department of Defense is "unacceptable."

---

[8]Closure of McClelland Air Force Base, California.

Outside the realm of private lawsuits, the EPA is involved in cleanup of contaminated federal facilities, but does not have the same power with respect to other federal agencies that it has with respect to private entities. To learn the status of property in your state, visit www.epa.gov/fedfac/ff/index.htm.

In low-income neighborhoods near the former Kelly Air Force Base in San Antonio, residents have erected almost 300 purple crosses in front of homes where residents are afflicted with or have died of cancer. They want the Air Force to clean up a plume of toxic chemicals in the groundwater rather than merely preventing the plume from spreading off the base, as proposed. Several federal studies have found no link between pollution and local health problems. However, a recent study by the federal Agency for Toxic Substances and Disease Registry did not rule out the possibility.

To see the Defense Department's information on environmental issues, visit www.denix.osd.mil/denix/Public/Library/Cleanup/CleanupOfc/index.html.

Assignment 3-2

1. Find your state tort claims act.
2. Determine whether your state mandates disclosure in real estate transactions and, if so, whether there is a form to be used for such disclosures.
3. Use the Internet or CALR to find an example of a citizen suing the Fish and Wildlife Service or the EPA.

C. Criminal Prosecution

Most of the environmental statutes discussed in later chapters, such as the Clean Air Act and the Clean Water Act, provide for criminal penalties, including incarceration, for violation. In addition, there have been a few high-profile prosecutions under non-environmental statutes. For example, a film processing company in the Chicago suburbs and several individuals were prosecuted for murder after a worker died as a result of exposure to toxic chemicals, among them, cyanide. The threats of criminal prosecution and of incarceration are important to enforcement. Some large corporations might regard paying fines as just a cost of doing business and easier than preventing or cleaning up pollution, but very few executives would be willing to go to jail for their employers.

D. Citizen Suits Under the Statutes

As discussed, private individuals can seek judicial relief from environmental problems by bringing common law claims or, in some cases, by suing the agency responsible for enforcement. In addition the federal environmental statutes (discussed in later chapters) and some state laws authorize enforcement by **"citizens' suits,"** also called **"private attorney general actions."** The ability to bring a citizens' suit means that the law can be enforced, even if the responsible agency does not have the resources or desire to enforce it.

> **Citizens' Suits/Private Attorney General Actions**
> Private citizens sue to enforce environmental laws

When an environmental statute authorizes citizens' suits, it generally requires notice to the agency with responsibility for enforcement and gives that agency the option of stepping in and bringing enforcement action in lieu of the citizens' action. A private citizen or group cannot profit from an enforcement action; outcomes are generally limited to court orders, but provisions authorizing awards of attorney fees and costs (discussed later in the chapter) make private enforcement financially possible. Citizens' suits can lighten the burden of agencies charged with enforcing environmental statutes and also ensure that those statutes are being enforced regardless of the agency's political agenda or limited resources.

E. SLAPP

As environmental awareness has increased, so has environmental activism. Any proposal for new development is likely to meet with vocal opposition. Existing operations that pollute are often targeted for protests. A few years ago, the developers and businesses began to fight back.

A "strategic lawsuit against public participation" **(SLAPP)** is a lawsuit in which the primary goal of a corporate plaintiff is to stifle or silence a person or a group's challenges to the corporation's actions or plans. Typically, the corporate "SLAPPer" files common law claims such as defamation, conspiracy, abuse of process, or interference with contract.

> **(SLAPP)**
> Strategic Lawsuit Against Public Participation

Protestors often defend themselves under the petition clause of the First Amendment, and the SLAPP is generally dismissed, or summary judgment is entered for the defendant. But the harm has been done. A corporate developer suing a neighborhood activist may have an in-house legal department and can deduct the cost of the lawsuit for income tax purposes. The activist, on the other hand, does not usually have a legal department standing by and cannot treat the costs as a tax deduction or the "cost of doing business." Sometimes activists turn the tables and SLAPP back at the corporation, but the corporation may have already accomplished its goal of silencing the activist. As a result, several states have enacted "Anti-SLAPP" legislation such as the California law shown in Exhibit 3-2.

EXHIBIT 3-2

California Code of Civil Procedure 425.16. (In part)

(a) The Legislature finds and declares that there has been a disturbing increase in lawsuits brought primarily to chill the valid exercise of the constitutional rights of freedom of speech and petition for the redress of grievances. The Legislature finds and declares that it is in the public interest to encourage continued participation in matters of public significance, and that this participation should not be chilled through abuse of the judicial process. To this end, this section shall be construed broadly.

(b) (1) A cause of action against a person arising from any act of that person in furtherance of the person's right of petition or free speech under the United States or California Constitution in connection with a public issue shall be subject to a special motion to strike, unless the court determines that the plaintiff has established that there is a probability that the plaintiff will prevail on the claim. . . .

(c) In any action subject to subdivision (b), a prevailing defendant on a special motion to strike shall be entitled to recover his or her attorney's fees and costs. If the court finds that a special motion to strike is frivolous or is solely intended to cause unnecessary delay, the court shall award costs and reasonable attorney's fees to a plaintiff prevailing on the motion, pursuant to Section 128.5 . . . .

F. Assisting in Environmental Litigation

Environmental lawsuits are notorious for the number of documents involved. Visit http://www.ens-newswire.com/ens/feb2002/2002-02-28-07.asp. Suppose that you were the paralegal responsible for discovery and just "won" access to 7,584 pages of documents relating to energy policy. How would you handle those documents?

Bates Stamping
Numbering of documents, sequentially, chronologically, or by some other method

The documents must be marked with an identification number so that a record can be kept of the document's origin, handling, location, authentication, etc. This is often called **Bates stamping**. Stamping may be done by hand with a device that automatically moves to the next number each time a document is stamped. While hand-stamping is still done, it presents difficulties. You may not have the flexibility to use descriptive numbering. For example, you might want to identify all documents arriving from Tanker Transport as TT-xxxx while identifying all documents received from SuperKlean as SK-xxxx, which would necessitate having special stamps. In addition, you may not want to stamp an original document. You would have to either make a copy (be sure you never remove staples for copying unless an attorney directs you to do so — it could create an impression of tampering), mark the back of the document, or attach and mark a sticker.

There is also the problem of **redacting** any **privileged** material so that it is not accidentally disclosed during **discovery**. When working with hard copy, this is often done by simply using a marker to cover privileged material. Finally there is the problem of filing paper copies so that they are retrievable as needed. Do you file the document by its subject (ownership of the contaminated property vs. source of contamination), its author, its date, or its type (letter, internal memo), or do you make multiple copies and file it in each category, with the resulting waste of resources (bad for the environment). Almost any system of filing hard copies will be inefficient if thousands of documents are involved.

Redact
To remove information, typically due to privilege

Privileged
A right to refuse to provide evidence/testimony, based on a relationship such as attorney-client

Discovery
Pre-trial process of gathering and sharing evidence

1. E-Discovery

Many documents created in today's business world are never printed. They exist in electronic form only. Working in environmental litigation, you are likely to receive electronically stored information (**ESI**) from clients, witnesses, and opposing parties. ESI, which consists of more than traditional documents (e-mail, text messages, websites visited, and much more), has the additional advantage (for the receiving party!) of including metadata: information about history, such as when and on which computer it was created, when it and on which computer it has been altered, and other properties. Keep in mind that discovery is not limited to what is on the computer server or hard drive: cell phones, smart phones, portable computers, and other devices are also subject to discovery.

(ESI)
Electronically stored information

The importance of this data-behind-the-data cannot be overemphasized. The federal rules of evidence[9] provide that ESI is subject to discovery (**e-discovery**), that clients must preserve and produce ESI, that lawyers must request, protect, review and produce ESI, and that courts rectify abusive or obstructive electronic discovery. The emerging field of **computer forensics** enables experts to find documents and e-mails that have been deleted, to determine who had access to information at specific times, and to establish that information has been subject to tampering. Because of fears of accidental **spoliation** of evidence, many firms now **outsource** their computer forensic needs and even their management of information coming in or being produced (sent) as part of discovery.

(E-discovery)
Discovery of ESI

Computer Forensics
Science of discovering the history of electronic information, even if deleted

Spoliation
Destruction, alteration, or mutilation of evidence

Outsource
Sending work to an outside firm

Firms may produce information in electronic form during discovery and/ or may **scan** paper documents as they are received and number them as part of the scanning process. Scanning can even create searchable **OCR** images so that documents can be retrieved by looking for certain words. Scanning documents

Scan
Scanning Conversion of paper documents to electronic images

OCR
Optical Character Recognition, a method of scanning a document that makes it subject to search and alteration

---

[9]Rule 26, see http://www.uscourts.gov/rules/EDiscovery_w_Notes.pdf.

Native Format
Format in which document was created

Image Format
Locked format such as PDF or TIFF

Coding
Process of reviewing documents, summarizing key elements into a structured database format: e.g., date, doc type, Bates no., doc description, to whom, from whom, etc.

Fields
Discrete pieces of information in document or database

Document Unitization
Method of storing documents, can be by page or "as a whole"

Objective Coding
Identifies commonly recognized fields, e.g., date and author

Subjective Coding
Identification of fields requiring knowledge of case

Trial Exhibits
Physical evidence for trial

into certain formats also allows the originator to "lock" the content so that it cannot be altered. A document may arrive in **native format**, such as Word or Word Perfect, and be saved in an **image format**, such as a **PDF or TIFF document.**

Scanning documents into an image format takes away the ability to word-search so scanning generally requires **coding**. For example, a document could be identified by several **fields** that can be searched: date, originator, recipient, subject. Identification of these common fields and the beginning and end of multi-page documents or multi-document sets **(document unitization)** is called **objective coding**. [10] A paralegal or other individual with knowledge of both environmental law and the case at issue may be used for **subjective coding**, which can involve substantive decisions, such as identification of the issue addressed by the document, determination of relevance, and identification of privileged material.

2. Litigation Support Software

Many firms use specialized software, such as Summation or Concordance, to code and organize the documents. Among other features, these programs have the ability to organize and transport documents as needed (e.g., by witness or source, by type of document, or by date); save documents in both OCR format, so that they can be word-searched, and the locked format for sharing with opposing parties; to view and redact from an image; to apply different numbering systems for different purposes (e.g., the number assigned to a document when it is received, another number assigned when it is part of a limited number of documents produced in response to a discovery request); and to create a "slideshow" for using documents as **trial exhibits**.

Because the software is constantly changing, an in-depth discussion would be impractical. To learn more about the software, simply search "litigation support software" on the Internet and visit vendors' websites. For example, you can see an online demonstration of Summation at http://www.summation.com/Solutions/demos.aspx. Most software vendors participate in the annual American Bar Association Techshow — a good source of information about products is http://www.abanet.org/techshow/exhibitors/. For more general information about scanning documents for case files, see http://www.abanet.org/lpm/lpt/articles/tch05061.shtml.

G. In the Field: Attorneys' Fees

American Rule
In most litigation, each party pays its own attorneys and costs

Awards of attorneys' fees and litigation costs in environmental citizen suits enable private citizens to enforce environmental legislation. First introduced in the federal Clean Air Act, attorneys' fee provisions are contrary to the general application of the **"American Rule,"** under which each party pays its own fees and costs. Fee award provisions are now included in virtually all environmental legislation and

---

[10] Documents can be stored and organized according to pages, but the concept of a "page" is often not useful in dealing with documents in image format.

generally allow for prevailing parties to be awarded attorneys' fees when "appropriate." The standard has been routinely applied to award attorneys' fees to prevailing plaintiffs, while defendants have generally been awarded fees only when a suit is deemed frivolous, harassing, or without merit. Courts have wide discretion in determining what is "appropriate."

In addition to paying the actual attorneys' fees, awards (sometimes called **fee reversal**) often include "**costs**," which may include expenses associated with filing the suit, expert witnesses and consultants, and scientific investigation. The award may also include an hourly rate for work done by paralegals, which increases the profit to the prevailing law firm, while, at the same time, keeping the bill to be paid by the nonprevailing party reasonable.

Fee Reversal
Court orders one party to pay other party's legal fees

Costs
Expenses associated with litigation

Attorneys are motivated to hire paralegals not only to get work done efficiently, but also because paralegals are a profit center. Fee reversal cases have made well-educated paralegals a particularly valuable part of an efficient law office. When there is no fee reversal issue, whether the attorney bills the client for paralegal time as a separate item on the bill is purely a private matter; there is no court involved.

Example

Client consults lawyer about conducting an environmental audit to ensure compliance with state rules. Lawyer estimates that the work will take about 10 hours and says "My hourly rate is $250; my paralegal's hourly rate is $80." "WHAT!" client exclaims, "you are going to bill me separately for your paralegal?" Lawyer shrugs and says, "Suit yourself. If you'd prefer to not work with a paralegal I will do all the work myself. Your bill will be about $2,500. If you do work with my paralegal and he does half the work it will be about $1,650." Suddenly, client wants to work with the paralegal.

Why is this arrangement beneficial for the lawyer? The lawyer makes a profit on the paralegal. If the paralegal's salary, benefits, office space, etc., cost the lawyer about $40 an hour, half of the billing rate is profit. In addition, if the lawyer is busy, she can spend the five hours that are "freed up" by the paralegal's work on another client matter. Is there anything unethical about this? No, this is a private contract to which the client has agreed and the lawyer is in business to make a profit, like any other employer.

In a fee reversal case the situation is a little different. The party who ultimately pays the lawyer did not choose the lawyer, did not agree to the hourly rate, and did not have an opportunity to monitor the work as it was done. In order to make sure that the billing is fair, the court making a fee recovery award reviews the bill. If the court determines that the bill was unfair, it will cut the bill. This motivates lawyers to delegate work to those with lower billing rates.

Imagine that the bill submitted to the court included 40 hours of time for summarizing depositions, at $400 an hour. The court might decide that this type of work did not have to be done by a lawyer with a billing rate of $400 and cut the bill to $100 per hour. The firm has learned a valuable lesson: next time use a paralegal for deposition summaries! Most courts not only allow separate billing for paralegals in fee reversal cases, they encourage it by scrutinizing the bill. This is not universally true; always check the precedent in the particular court system.

Of course, unscrupulous lawyers might start including billing for photocopying, filing, and other low-level clerical work as "paralegal work." As a result, many courts scrutinize not only the type of work done, but also the credentials of the paralegals who did the work.

The Colorado Bar Association has a web page describing the responsibilities of an environmental law paralegal: www.cobar.org/index.cfm/ID/106/subID/140/CLAS/Environmental-Paralegal/

Assignment 3-3

- ◆ The attorney general for your state may have a division or department for environmental prosecution and your local states' attorney's office or district attorney's office may have a similar department. Use the Internet to find information about those departments.
- ◆ Use the Internet or CALR to find an example of criminal prosecution by your state for environmental contamination.
- ◆ Determine whether your state has an anti-SLAPP law.
- ◆ Discuss whether the following are beneficial or detrimental to the goal of protecting and improving the environment:

  a. allowing citizens to sue agencies responsible for enforcement of environmental laws
  b. allowing private enforcement of environmental laws by citizen suit against polluters
  c. awarding plaintiffs (but rarely defendants) attorneys' fees and costs in environmental litigation.

Key Terms

American Rule	Costs
Attorneys' Fee Award	Damages
Bates Stamping	Discovery
Burden of Proof	Document Unitization
Cause of Action	Duty
Citizens' Suit	E-discovery
Coding	Elements
Common Law	Equitable Remedy
Computer Forensics	ESI
Continuing Trespass or Nuisance	Fee Reversal
Contributory/Comparative	Fields
Negligence	FTCA

Fraud
Imaged Format
Legal Remedy
Limitations Period
Ministerial Duty
Native Format
Negligence
Negligence Per Se
Nuisance, Private
Nuisance, Public
Objective Coding
OCR
Outsourcing
PDF/ TIFF

Plaintiff
Private Attorney General
Privilege
Public Trust
Redact
Scanning
SLAPP
Sovereign Immunity
Spoliation
Statute of Limitations
Strict Liability
Subjective Coding
Trespass
Trial Exhibits

Review Questions

1. What is a common law cause of action?
2. How does the theory of "continuing trespass" avoid the limitations period?
3. What are the elements of negligence? What is negligence per se?
4. What is the difference between public nuisance and private nuisance?
5. Why do environmental suits authorize awards of attorneys' fees and what benefits result?
6. What is a SLAPP and what is being done to prevent them?
7. What is the difference between trespass and nuisance?
8. Why is strict liability a plaintiff-friendly cause of action?
9. What is sovereign immunity and why does it matter in environmental litigation?
10. What is the public trust doctrine and how is it applied?
11. What is zoning and how does it help prevent nuisance?
12. What is e-discovery and how does it differ from traditional discovery? What features of case management software are particularly helpful in dealing with discovery in environmental litigation?
13. Discuss the reasons for outsourcing projects such as document coding and the reasons why it might be better to keep such projects in-house.

KEY TERMS CROSSWORD

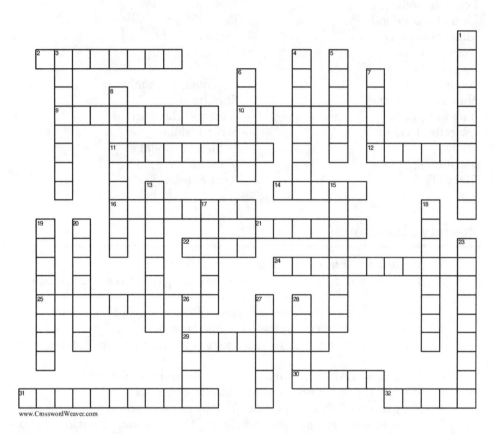

www.CrosswordWeaver.com

ACROSS

2. _____prosecution is possible for environmental violations
9. remedy of court order
10. involves entry on to property of another
11. element of negligence, hard to prove with respect to illness as a harm
12. _____liability does not look at fault
14. an award of money is a_____remedy
16. facts that must be proven to establish a claim
21. PDF and TIFF have this characteristic
22. initials, limits federal sovereign immunity
24. a duty not involving discretion
25. _____per se is proven by showing violation of statutory standard
29. data on the history of a document
30. developer sues protestors, initials
31. period for bringing lawsuit
32. burden of_____, obligation to bring evidence to show elements

DOWN

1. court order to not do something
3. award of attorneys' fees sometimes called fee_____
4. interference with use and enjoyment of property
5. to remove privileged info
6. cause of_____; recognized basis for suit
7. expenses of litigation
8. process of sharing information before trial
13. contributory and comparative negligence are
15. system under which each party pays own attorneys' fees
17. the format in which a document originated
18. _____ suit, also called private attorney general actions
19. sovereign _____; cannot sue government without consent
20. an award of money
23. initiates lawsuit
26. _____law, judge-made
27. identifying fields in a document
28. _____ stamping of documents during discovery

RONALD HOLLAND'S A-PLUS TRANSMISSION & AUTOMOTIVE, INC. v. E-Z MART STORES, INC.

Court of Appeals of Texas 184 S.W.3d 749; November 30, 2005, Filed

Williams operated a convenience store and gas station on land adjacent to Hollands' property. In 1988 Williams removed a 550 gallon underground waste oil storage tank. During removal, the Texas Natural Resources Conservation Commission ("TNRCC") observed leaks in the tank and detected release of an actionable level of TPH (Total Petroleum Hydrocarbons). In 1989 monitoring wells were installed and 250 cubic yards of soil were excavated, with some of the soil being above the action levels. Williams sold its store and underground tank system to Yates, who leased the property to E-Z Mart.

In 1992, during E-Z Mart's operation of the gas station, a gasoline line leak was reported to TNRCC. The line was removed and replaced, soil samples were collected, and 886 cubic yards of soil were disposed of. In 1998, Yates sold his store to E-Z Mart. In 1998 E-Z Mart removed gasoline underground storage tanks and found contamination in excess of action levels. Fifteen groundwater sampling and monitoring events took place. The gradient directs water and other substances from E-Z Mart's property to Hollands' property. According to Extra Environmental, Inc., a company hired by Hollands, a gap between two monitoring wells caused the wells to miss part of a contamination plume that migrated to Hollands' property. Yet, in January 1999, after E-Z Mart completed testing and remedial measures required by TNRCC, TNRCC issued E-Z Mart a standard form letter stating that it concurred with the recommendation that the site had met the closure requirements and that no further corrective action was necessary.

Hollands leased part of the land to Trinity Wireless as a site for a telephone cell tower. In 2001, when Trinity was boring in preparation for construction, an explosion occurred. Trinity hired Drash, an environmental engineering firm, to conduct site assessment. Drash's report revealed the presence of fuel-related constituents, such as Benzene. In 2001, the level of Benzene was eight times the TNRCC action level; in 2004, it was 34 times the action level. According to Drash, because Hollands' land was farmland, never used for gasoline storage or dispensing, fuel-related compounds must have migrated from E-Z Mart's gas station. Extra Environmental concurred. Trinity terminated its lease of the Hollands' property. Hollands filed suit against E-Z Mart. The trial court granted summary judgment in favor of E-Z Mart, dismissing the claims. The Hollands appeal.

Appellees assert that Hollands failed to prove a prima facie case for trespass, nuisance, and negligence; that a claim arising out of the leaks is barred by the TNRCC site-closure letter; and that Hollands failed to prove a cause of action arising out of any other leaks.

While TNRCC has broad authority to impose requirements with regard to contamination, a wrongdoer is not relieved from liability by the Texas Administrative Code, the Water Code, or TNRCC's regulations for contamination of another's land above the state-action level. Although the site-closure letter confirmed that required measures had taken place on the E-Z Mart site, if later contamination is discovered on adjacent property in excess of state-action level the letter does not exonerate appellees from liability for trespass, nuisance, or negligence. TNRCC confirmed that there are no longer actionable levels on the E-Z Mart site, but there is contamination in excess of action levels on Hollands' land.

The elements of negligence are: (1) legal duty owed by one person to another; (2) breach of that duty; (3) the breach was a proximate cause of the injury; and (4) actual injury. Causation cannot be proven by mere speculation. Causation may be proved by expert testimony, if the probability about which the expert testifies is more than coincidence. Hollands have produced sufficient evidence that contaminants migrated from the E-Z Mart site to their land and that contamination increased on their property between 2001 and 2004. Hollands produced CAT-scan aerial photos showing plumes of contamination on their property and the TNRCC's memo which described measures taken on the E-Z Mart site. Hollands also produced a report from Drash, indicating that their property was impacted by petroleum hydrocarbons released from the E-Z Mart site and the affidavit of expert Gary Eaves, Ph.D., who affirmed that he had reviewed: San Antonio Testing Lab reports of core samples of soil gathered in 2004, showing that Hollands' property was contaminated by actionable levels of hydrocarbons in both water and soil; series of aerial photographs of Hollands' property taken using Multiple-Image Spectral Scanning Analysis, showing underground gasoline plumes emanating from the E-Z Mart site to Hollands' land; and results from a PID detector, showing positive results for organic vapors found associated with gasoline. Relying on the data, Eaves concluded that contamination on Hollands' land came from the E-Z Mart site. Eaves ruled out all other potential sources of contamination. Looking at this evidence in the light most favorable to Hollands, there is more than a scintilla of evidence on causation to support their claim.

In Texas, nuisance involves a condition which substantially interferes with use and enjoyment of land by causing unreasonable discomfort or annoyance to persons of ordinary sensibilities attempting to use and enjoy it. A nuisance may occur in one of three ways: (1) physical harm to property, such as encroachment of a damaging substance or by the property's destruction; (2) physical harm to a person on his property, such as by an assault to his senses or by other personal injury; and (3) emotional harm to a person from deprivation of enjoyment of property, such as by fear, apprehension, offense, or loss of peace of mind. To be actionable, "a defendant must generally engage in one of three kinds of activity: (1) intentional invasion of another's interest; (2) negligent invasion of another's interests; or (3) other conduct, culpable because abnormal and out of place in its surroundings, that invades another's interest." Hollands' evidence of negligence also supports a claim of nuisance. The evidence shows that contaminants migrated from the E-Z Mart site subsoil and interfered with use and enjoyment of Hollands' land.

Trespass to real property requires a showing of an unauthorized physical entry onto the plaintiff's property by some person or thing. The entry need not be in person but may be made by causing or permitting a thing to cross the boundary of a property. Hollands produced evidence to raise a fact question regarding unauthorized entry of contaminants onto their property. Hollands' evidence of contamination exceeding state action levels, combined with reports from various environmental companies and experts pointing to the E-Z Mart site as the source of contamination, is evidence in support of the trespass claim.

4

The Constitution and the Executive in Environmental Law

A. Constitutional Issues

Americans take their property ownership rights very seriously and attempts to regulate the use of property to protect the environment have been met with constitutional challenges. What gives the federal government the power to regulate an owner's use of property? Our federal government is a government of limited powers and the powers specified to Congress do not include the power to regulate the use of land. In addition, might regulation of the uses of property amount to a deprivation of property in violation of the Fifth Amendment?

EXHIBIT 4-1

UNITED STATES CONSTITUTION, AMENDMENT V

No person shall be held to answer for a capital, or otherwise infamous crime, unless on a presentment or indictment of a Grand Jury, except in cases arising in the land or naval forces, or in the Militia, when in actual service in time of War or public danger; nor shall any person be subject for the same offense to be twice put in jeopardy of life or limb; nor shall be compelled in any criminal case to be a witness against himself, **nor be deprived of life, liberty, or property, without due process of law; nor shall private property be taken for public use, without just compensation.** (Emphasis added.)

---

1. Federal Power

a. Commerce Clause

Commerce Clause
Basis for most federal regulation of the environment

The daily lives of most Americans are governed primarily by state and local (or tribal) law; the federal government has limited powers and cannot regulate without a constitutional basis. The basis for most federal regulation of the environment is found in the **Commerce Clause**. Article 1, Section 8 of the Constitution gives Congress power "To regulate Commerce with foreign Nations, and among the several States, and with the Indian Tribes." The constitutional basis for a challenge to federal authority to regulate is generally the **Tenth Amendment**, which provides that "powers not delegated to the United States . . . are reserved to the States respectively, or to the people."

The last 40 years have seen enactment of a tremendous body of federal environmental law. There are three possible sources of federal authority for these enactments: Either the activity regulated clearly has substantial effect on interstate commerce (e.g., air pollution), or the statute specifies that it reaches only activities in, or affecting, interstate commerce, or Congress makes specific findings that the regulated activity affects interstate commerce.

> "[T]he grant of authority to Congress under the Commerce Clause, though broad, is not unlimited." *Solid Waste Agency of Northern Cook County v. U.S. Army Corps of Engineers,* 531 U.S. 159 (2001) (the SWANCC case).

While the courts generally rule in favor of federal authority to regulate private landowners to protect the environment, the trend has not been unchallenged. One very controversial issue has been the authority of the U.S. Army Corps of Engineers (the Corps) to regulate isolated wetlands (not directly connected to navigable water) under the Clean Water Act (CWA). The issue is important to developers and to farmers dealing with seasonal ponds, drainage ditches, intermittently dry streams, prairie potholes and other wet areas that may be adjacent to other waters. If the federal government asserts jurisdiction farming and development activities may be substantially restricted. Unfortunately, as of the writing of this book, the issue has not been clearly resolved.

EXHIBIT 4-2

SHORT HISTORY OF A CONTROVERSY — "WATERS OF THE UNITED STATES"

In simple terms, the CWA (discussed in depth in a later chapter) prohibits discharge of pollutants (including fill material) into the "navigable waters of the United States" without a permit issued through the Corps. Since 1975 the Corps has asserted jurisdiction over "other waters," such as streams, wetlands, and ponds if the use or destruction of those areas could affect interstate commerce. The jurisdiction of the Corps expanded with court decisions in the 1970s and 1980s, and the Corps asserted authority to regulate isolated wetlands, not adjacent to the waters of the United States, if there was a link between the wetland and interstate commerce.

In the mid-1980s the Corps took the position that the use of waters by migratory birds could support its exercise of jurisdiction. The U.S. Court of Appeals for the Seventh Circuit upheld the Corps position in the SWANCC case, which involved an abandoned gravel pit planned for use as a solid waste disposal site. Excavation trenches on the land had created permanent and seasonal lakes that had become home to migratory birds and endangered species. The Corps refused to issue a permit to fill some of the ponds for the landfill use. In 2001 the Supreme Court reversed and held that the "migratory bird rule" exceeded the authority given the Corps under the CWA. The Court did not address the Corps's jurisdiction under the Commerce Clause and several questions remained unanswered. Might a sufficient basis for jurisdiction exist if the isolated wetland is used for recreational purposes by interstate travelers or used for industrial purposes by an interstate business? What if the wetland is habitat to an endangered species?

In 2006 the Court further "muddied the waters" in its decision in *Rapanos v. United States*, which involved two Michigan owners, prevented from developing their properties without CWA permits. One owner had a tract that abutted, but was hydrologically distinct from, a ditch that connected to a drain that connected to a creek that connected to Lake St. Clair. The other land was more than 10 miles from the nearest navigable water, but drained to a ditch that emptied into a creek that flowed to a navigable river. The federal appeals court ruled in favor of the Corps. The Supreme Court vacated the decisions, but did not render a majority

**EXHIBIT 4-2
(continued)**

opinion. Justice Scalia's plurality (four Justices) opinion took the position that "waters of the United States" includes only relatively permanent standing or continuously flowing bodies of water that are ordinarily called "streams," "oceans," or "lakes," and that a wetland may not be considered "adjacent to" remote waters of the United States based on a hydrological connection alone. Justice Kennedy's narrower concurring opinion took the position that jurisdiction could extend to waters with a significant nexus to navigable waters, but that the lower court had not considered all the factors relevant to determining whether such a nexus exists. Justice Kennedy would have the Corps consider the goals and purposes of the CWA and make the determination on a case-by-case basis.

Some states have decided that their isolated waters should have as much protection as their flowing waters. Following the SWANCC decision the New Mexico Water Quality Control Commission amended the state's definition of "surface waters" to indicate that the state's power over waters within its boundaries was not constrained by the federal Commerce Clause, but extends to all surface waters situated wholly or partly within or bordering upon the state. The decision noted that more than 80 percent of the state's waters are non-perennial and that the Supreme Court decision supported protection of isolated waters by state, rather than federal, authority. The Supreme Court subsequently decided *Rapanos*, indicating that federal jurisdiction is limited to "relatively permanent" bodies of water. The appeals court upheld that definition, rejecting an argument that the new definition could be applied improperly to "virtually any land feature" over which water passes and leaves a mark. The court acknowledged than an exception for "private waters that do not combine with other surface or subsurface water" will present fact-sensitive questions, but stated that the law is not impermissibly vague in all applications. *New Mexico Mining Association v. Water Quality Control Commission,* Court of Appeals of New Mexico, Decided May 10, 2007.
Stay tuned . . . .

Assignment 4-1

◆ Use CALR or the Internet to determine how "waters of the United States" cases have been decided since the *Rapanos* decision.
◆ Use CALR or the Internet to determine the status of proposed legislation to clarify the jurisdiction of the Corps.

Can Congress regulate the states themselves as it regulates private landowners? The answer, as with so many legal questions, is "it depends." Specifically, it depends on whether Congress is attempting to regulate the state "as a state," in a way that impairs the state's ability to exercise sovereign powers, or is only attempting to regulate the state in its performance of a nonsovereign function. For example, a state might operate a fleet of vehicles that pollute the air just as privately owned vehicles would do; the federal government could regulate that enterprise. In other cases the answer depends on the technique used by Congress to coerce state participation in a federal program. While Congress may not "commandeer the legislative process of the states by directly compelling them to enact and enforce a federal regulatory program,"[1] it may "encourage" participation, for example by use of its Spending Power or by the "threat" of preemption, discussed in the next section.

State regulation may be precluded even if Congress has not enacted law on a particular subject. The **Dormant Commerce Clause** may result in invalidation of a law that discriminates against out-of-state interests, unless the state can show that the law advances a legitimate state or local interest that cannot be met by a reasonable nondiscriminatory alternative. State and local waste disposal laws favoring local businesses have been struck down, despite claims that such laws were necessary to preserve dwindling landfill space and to minimize the burden on natural resources. While state and local *regulatory authorities* may not discriminate against out-of-state waste, a state or local governmental body, acting as the owner or operator of a waste disposal, may do business with anyone it chooses, without regard to interstate commerce discrimination constraints. This is known as the **market participant exception**.

Dormant Commerce Clause
Basis for invalidation of state/local laws that discriminate to favor local interests or impact interstate commerce, even if Congress has not regulated the subject

Market Participant Exception
Government acting as owner or operator of waste disposal facility may discriminate against out-of-state waste

Dormant Commerce Clause

Where did it get that name?

If Congress has the power to regulate in a particular area, but has not chosen to exercise that authority, that authority lies "dormant," but it still exists.

The Dormant Commerce Clause may apply if a state or local law interferes with interstate commerce, even if it does not discriminate in favor of local interests. Courts apply a balancing test in such situations. For example, when Chicago banned the use of detergents containing phosphates, the ban did not favor local interests. The ban did burden interstate commerce by affecting sales in other states, but the court concluded that the burden was slight and was outweighed by the city's interest in decreasing algae.[2]

---

[1] *New York v. United States*, 505 U.S. 144 (1992).
[2] *Proctor & Gamble v. Chicago*, 509 F.2d 69 (7th Cir. 1975).

EXHIBIT 4-3

This case summary, written by the author for the American Planning Association publication, *Planning and Environmental Law*, is reprinted with permission from the editor, Lora Lucero. To see the full text, http://www.law.cornell.edu/supct/html/05-1345.ZS.html.

Because of environmental concerns and problems in dealing with private waste management companies, the counties requested and New York State created the Association to manage all solid waste (Pub. Auth. Law §2049). Private haulers can pick up trash, but the Authority sorts, processes, and disposes of the waste and provides services such as recycling, composting, and household hazardous waste disposal. The Authority collects "tipping fees" from haulers to cover costs. A tipping fee is, literally, a fee for tipping the contents of a garbage truck onto the Authority's property. The counties are responsible for the difference between the Authority's operating costs and the amount it takes in from tipping fees. The Authority's tipping fees are significantly higher than what is charged on the open market. The counties enacted "flow control" ordinances that require that all solid waste generated within the counties be delivered to the Authority and that all private haulers obtain permits from the Authority. An association of private waste management companies sued under 42 U.S.C. §1983, alleging Commerce Clause violations. A federal trial court enjoined enforcement of the flow control laws, but the Second Circuit reversed. On remand, the trial court ruled in favor of the counties and the Second Circuit affirmed.

The Supreme Court granted certiorari and affirmed, with Chief Justice Roberts delivering the opinion of the Court. The "dormant" Commerce Clause is an implicit restraint on state authority in regulating commerce; if a law discriminates between in-state and out-of-state economic interests, it will be upheld only if the state can show that it had no other means to advance a legitimate local purpose. The ordinance at issue favors a state-created public benefit corporation over private businesses, but does not distinguish between in-state and out-of-state private businesses. Compelling reasons justify treating such a law differently than a law that favors particular businesses over their competitors; any other conclusion would result in judicial interference in the functions of state and local governments. The burden of the extra expense is being borne by those who vote in local elections, not by out-of-state interests, and any incidental impact on out-of-state interests is outweighed by local interests in the environment.

In concurring opinions, Justices Scalia and Thomas expressed doubts about the constitutional basis of the "negative" Commerce Clause and indicated that the theory should not be employed or expanded as a basis for striking state laws. Justices Alito, Stevens, and Kennedy, dissenting, argued that the Court's decision in *C&A Carbone, Inc. v. Clarkstown*, 511 U.S. 383 (1994), invalidated an identical flow-control ordinance and that the public/private benefit distinction was illusory and unprecedented. *United Haulers Assoc., Inc. v. Oneida-Herkimer Solid Waste Management Authority, Supreme Court of the United States [highest court]*, Decided April 30, 2007.

Some legal scholars question the constitutional bases of the dormant or "negative" Commerce Clause and argue that the Constitution does not specify that the states are prohibited from regulating in an arena that Congress has left unregulated, even if that regulation has an impact on interstate commerce. Recent case law (see Exhibit 4-3) indicates a tendency to apply the doctrine sparingly.

After reading the case summary, discuss whether the flow control law actually does have an impact on out-of-state businesses and whether the private/public distinction should make a difference.

b. Preemption

Preemption
Federal law overrides state law; state law overrides local law

Implied. Under the Supremacy Clause of the Constitution federal law "trumps" state and local law that conflicts with or interferes with federal law. Preemption can also be implied if the federal law is so pervasive that there is no room for state or local regulation, but if a federal law does not clearly state its preemptive effect, courts tend to try to avoid preemption. Often the state or local law is stricter than the federal law and does not, therefore, interfere with the federal law. Some federal laws even include a **savings clause** that expressly preserves state and local rights to regulate.

Savings Clause
Statutory provision preserving state or local law against preemption

Explicit. Congress can explicitly preempt state and local laws when it enacts new laws. Federal environmental laws rarely directly and totally preempt state and local laws, however, because Congress recognizes the need to tailor environmental decisions to local conditions and the need to use local technical resources and personnel. Typically Congress successfully coerces state participation in federal environmental programs by offering technical and financial assistance to state agencies; by threatening to cut off federal funding; by threatening to increase regulatory burdens on businesses in uncooperative states; or by giving the states a level of autonomy in making decisions about implementation and enforcement.

When Congress does preempt state authority, it tends to limit the preemption to what is necessary to serve an important national need. For example, under the Clean Air Act (CAA), the federal government establishes, monitors, and enforces pollution standards for new cars. The reason is clear: It would be impractical to have 50 unique sets of emission standards. Even in such a case, however, Congress may offer the states some decision-making role. Under the CAA the states may adopt the stricter "California standards." Another example of substantial federal preemption with respect to environmental regulation is the labeling of pesticides. Federal law regulates the labeling, but the states are free to regulate use.

Federal and state governments share power over many pollution programs, although state preferences are often secondary to federal policy and standards. In these programs, the federal agency's role is to set substantive standards for environmental quality or pollution emissions, to review and approve state regulatory programs designed to implement and enforce those standards, and to oversee state implementation and enforcement. The federal agency maintains authority to resume implementation and enforcement if state efforts fall below a minimum threshold. For example, under the CAA, EPA defines nationally uniform "air quality" standards for common pollutants that each state is expected to attain within stated time limits. EPA reviews state programs to determine whether the states are qualified to implement and enforce the federal standards. After EPA approves a state program, the state agency issues all air pollution permits, monitors compliance, and enforces permit and other regulatory violations. EPA's primary role is to ensure that the state permit requirements meet federal standards and that the state agency takes appropriate enforcement actions. States are not required to participate, but are disinclined to surrender the power involved in implementing the program and setting enforcement priorities.

In other cases, the federal and state governments have parallel programs. For example, the National Environmental Policy Act (NEPA) requires a federal agency to prepare an environmental impact statement whenever it makes a decision that may significantly affect the environment (e.g., to issue a development permit). Several states have similar requirements for state agencies. In large development projects requiring both federal and state permits (or funding), both levels of government will participate in environmental analysis of the project. Similarly, states are free to adopt their own programs to preserve wetlands and endangered species.

In the pollution statutes, Congress usually permits states to adopt standards that supplement or even supersede federal standards. Under the CAA, states adopt water quality standards separately for each body of water and those standards are enforced along with federal industry-wide effluent standards. The polluter must meet the stricter standard. Similarly, the CAA permits states to adopt stricter pollution standards (except for new cars). In addition, most federal pollution statutes permit state suits based on nuisance and other state causes of action.

To the extent not preempted by federal law, the states and local governmental bodies have authority to protect the environment as part of their "police power." **Police power** is the inherent right of government to make laws to protect the public health, safety, and general welfare.

Police Power
Inherent right of government to protect health, safety, and welfare

2. Eminent Domain/Inverse Condemnation

Having considered which government can regulate to protect the environment, let's consider how far that regulation can go. Environmental regulation at any level often reduces the profit that an owner can derive from her land and, in some cases, renders all or part of the land unusable.

Eminent Domain
Governmental power to take property for public purpose by paying just compensation; also called condemnation

If a governmental body wants to take ownership of property for environmental purposes, it may be able to do so if it has the power of **eminent domain**. For example, a county might initiate **condemnation** proceedings to acquire land for a park and wildlife sanctuary. The county would obtain title to the land and pay the former owner **just compensation**. Problems arise when the government does not exercise eminent domain, but the owner believes that his land has been **"taken"** as a result of other governmental action and claims **inverse condemnation**.

Just Compensation
Must be paid in exercise of eminent domain

Inverse Condemnation
Government "takes" property without instituting eminent domain or paying just compensation

The law of inverse condemnation is very complicated and is constantly evolving in the courts. The following discussion is not intended to give a thorough understanding of takings law, but only to familiarize you with the issues and terminology.

As a starting point, remember that the government cannot take what the owner does not have. One of the first questions in a takings analysis is whether the "right" that was taken was ever within the owner's "bundle of rights." A landowner does not have a right to use property in a way that is injurious to others, so a law prohibiting an activity that would constitute a nuisance does not result in a taking.

There are several theories of inverse condemnation, including claims of **per se taking**. A claim of per se taking is based on physical occupation; the government has taken physical possession of property, has given itself the right to take possession, or has denied the owner access, without paying for the privilege. For example, a city decides to build a series of levees to prepare an area for industrial development; the change in the contours of surrounding property causes owner's land to flood. City builds a runway next to owner's house; the intrusion of noise, fumes, and vibration render the property uninhabitable.

Per Se Taking
Physical occupation of or exclusion of owner from land

EXHIBIT 4-4

Every state has a statute describing condemnation procedures.

Georgia Code
Copyright 2006 by The State of Georgia

TITLE 22. **EMINENT DOMAIN**
CHAPTER 1. GENERAL PROVISIONS
O.C.G.A. §22-1-2 (2006)

§22-1-2. Nature of Right of Eminent Domain; Property to be Put to Public Use
(a) The right of **eminent domain** is the right of the state, through its regular organization, to reassert, either temporarily or permanently, its dominion over any portion of the soil of the state on account of public exigency and for the public good. Thus, in time of war or insurrection the proper authorities may possess and hold any part of the territory of the state for the common safety. Notwithstanding any other provisions of law, neither this state nor any political subdivision thereof nor any other condemning authority shall use **eminent domain** unless it is for public use. Public use is a matter of law to be determined by the court and the condemnor bears the burden of proof.

(b) All condemnations shall not be converted to any use other than a public use for 20 years from the initial condemnation. . . .

Regulatory Taking
Regulation of land goes "too far" and takes property rights

Ripeness
Requirement that plaintiff exhaust other possibilities before litigation

Claims that do not involve any physical occupation of property are known as **regulatory takings claims**. Claims of regulatory taking must be **ripe**. For litigation in state court, that generally means that the owner has obtained a final agency decision that spells out what can and cannot be done with the property. In federal court litigation involving allegations that a state or local agency caused a taking, the owner must first seek redress through state administrative agencies and, often, through state courts before a claim can be brought into federal court.

Example

Variance
An exception to zoning laws

Landowner is denied a building permit because the house he proposes to build is within 50 feet of wetlands and the ordinance calls for a 50-foot setback. Landowner cannot file suit until he has attempted to obtain a **variance** or tried other ways of placing the house on the land.

Categorical Taking
Regulation takes away all economically viable use of property

A claim of **categorical taking** requires proof that the imposition of a regulation totally deprived an owner of all economically viable use of property. Even if the owner is deprived of all beneficial use of property, the court will consider whether the use was ever within the owners' "bundle of rights."

Example

A subdivision was created 50 years ago by filling swamp land near the coast. There have been serious problems with septic systems on lots on which houses were built. The owner of a vacant lot is denied a permit to build a house and install a septic system. The owner may not be able to build anything, but the owner does not have the "right" to create a nuisance or a health hazard; no taking has occurred.

The court may also have to wrestle with defining "the property." For example, in order to protect the water table in a particular area, a county enacts an ordinance that requires a minimum one-acre lot to build any structure. If there is no possibility of a variance and if the law does not protect preexisting lots, the owner of a one-half acre lot might be deprived of all beneficial use. But what if the owner holds title to three one-half acre lots, adjoining each other?

More commonly, however, regulations deprive an owner of some, but not all uses, and the court will consider a variety of factors, including the economic impact of the governmental action, the owner's "investment-backed expectations," and the nature of the governmental action.

Example

A sophisticated developer buys 100 acres containing substantial wetlands at a price lower than would normally be paid for such a large parcel. Although the zoning would normally permit three houses per acre, the developer finds that he will be allowed to build only 90 houses, less than one-third of what he planned, because of the wetlands. It is likely that no taking has occurred. The developer should have realized that the property would not be able to be developed at high density and, therefore, he did not have reasonable investment-backed expectations. The nature of the governmental action, protecting important environmental resources, and the overall impact, which allows the developer to build a substantial number of houses, indicate that the regulation did not go "too far."

Conditional approvals of development may also be challenged as takings. For example, a city agrees to approve a plan for a subdivision on the condition that the developer dedicate a public park on the land. In such cases, courts will look at whether the condition furthers a legitimate governmental purpose and whether the condition is roughly proportional to the need created by the activity being permitted. Let's assume that the subdivision will provide housing for about 700 people and that the city does not have adequate park space. Requiring the developer to provide a park that would accommodate 700 people would not constitute a taking; the development created the need. On the other hand, requiring the developer to dedicate a park to accommodate 2,000 people might be an unconstitutional **exaction.**

Exaction
Requirement that developer make dedication as a condition to approval

---

EXHIBIT 4-5

Many states now have statutes requiring analysis of governmental action, in an effort to avoid inverse condemnation and/or laws requiring compensation for reductions in value attributable to governmental actions.

From Texas Government Code http://tlo2.tlc.state.tx.us/statutes/gv.toc.htm

§2007.043. Takings Impact Assessment.
(a) A governmental entity shall prepare a written takings impact assessment of a proposed governmental action described in Section 2007.003(a)(1) through (3) that complies with the evaluation guidelines developed by the attorney general under Section 2007.041 before the governmental entity provides the public notice required under Section 2007.042.
(b) The takings impact assessment must:
(1) describe the specific purpose of the proposed action and identify:
(A) whether and how the proposed action substantially advances its stated purpose; and
(B) the burdens imposed on private real property and the benefits to society resulting from the proposed use of private real property;
(2) determine whether engaging in the proposed governmental action will constitute a taking; and
(3) describe reasonable alternative actions that could accomplish the specified purpose and compare, evaluate, and explain:
(A) how an alternative action would further the specified purpose; and
(B) whether an alternative action would constitute a taking.
(c) A takings impact assessment prepared under this section is public information.

Assignment 4-2

1. Determine whether your state has a statute dealing with inverse condemnation.
2. Use CALR to find and brief a case from your state dealing with inverse condemnation.

---

3. Fourth Amendment

Enforcement of environmental laws requires investigation. When an investigation involves a search or seizure, it implicates the Fourth Amendment. The legal tools (search warrants, subpoenas, self-reporting requirements) used by administrative agencies conducting investigation are discussed in another chapter. Those working in the field of environmental law must be aware of the "physical tools" as well as the legal tools.

Administrative agencies and criminal prosecutors have, in recent years, acquired new "remote-sensing" tools to assist in investigating environmental violations.

In 1986 the Supreme Court[3] upheld the EPA's use of an aerial mapping camera to photograph a chemical manufacturing facility. The facility was heavily secured at ground level, but was at least partially open to observation from the air. The Court stated that: "When Congress invests an agency with enforcement and regulatory authority, it is not necessary to identify explicitly each and every technique that may be used in the course of executing the statutory mission" and rejected an argument that EPA misappropriated trade secrets, stating that the government took the photos in navigable airspace to regulate, not to compete with the company. The warrantless search did not violate the Fourth Amendment because the company did not have an expectation of privacy against technology readily available to the public. Lower court cases, not concerning environmental enforcement, have upheld the use of thermal imaging without a warrant.

GIS
Geographic Information System — mapping based on database

The federal government and many state governments also use **Geographic Information Systems (GIS)** to monitor environmentally sensitive areas. GIS is essentially a computerized mapping system based on a database; the environmental data on which a GIS is based may take the form of aerial photography, satellite imagery, or maps based on these data sources. For example, GIS may be used to monitor deterioration of wetlands on private property through "before" and "after" photographs.

Seizure
Forcible taking of property by a law enforcement official

Those working in the field must also be aware of the way in which courts interpret the word **"seizure"** for purposes of the Fourth Amendment. While the common understanding of the word involves taking physical possession, courts take a broader view. As demonstrated by the case at the end of the chapter, a seizure can occur when the government asserts control over property or causes others to

---

[3] *Dow Chemical v. United States*, 476 U.S. 227 (1986).

EXHIBIT 4-6

UNITED STATES CONSTITUTION, AMENDMENT IV

The right of the people to be secure in their persons, houses, papers, and effects, against unreasonable searches and seizures, shall not be violated, and no Warrants shall issue, but upon probable cause, supported by Oath or affirmation, and particularly describing the place to be searched, and the persons or things to be seized.

---

do so, even if the control does not totally displace the owner. A seizure may also occur if the government prevents the owner from exercising control.

4. Equal Protection and Due Process

The Fourteenth Amendment to the Constitution extends the due process protections created by the Fifth Amendment with respect to actions by the federal government to actions by the states. The Fourteenth Amendment creates our equal protection rights. While a thorough exploration of those rights is beyond the scope of this book, a basic understanding of the concepts and vocabulary is essential. Property owners frequently allege due process and equal protection violations in challenging environmental and zoning laws.

Procedural due process[4] is required when the government (remember, these constitutional protections do not apply to private actors) acts to deprive a person of life, liberty, or property. Property means much more than physical property, such as land, and includes "legal entitlements." So, for example, a developer who has obtained all necessary permits and approvals to construct a building has a "property interest" in the right to build; an environmental agency could not step in and prevent construction without extending the developer due process. Note that this does not necessarily mean that the owner cannot be deprived of that right, only that he is entitled to due process.

Procedural Due Process
Entitlement to notice and hearing before deprivation of constitutional right

What is due process? In simple terms, it consists of notice and a hearing before an impartial decision maker. The "level" depends on the nature of the deprivation. For example, in most states a 14-year-old is legally entitled to a free education; if he is threatened with a 3-day suspension for smoking in the boys' room, he is entitled to due process because that would be a deprivation of property. The deprivation, however, is not very significant, so the notice might consist of a letter sent to the parents and the hearing might be a meeting in the dean's office. On the other hand,

---

[4]Substantive due process, a complex and ambiguous concept concerning protection of our essential rights against unwarranted governmental intrusion, is less frequently raised in environmental cases and is beyond the scope of this book.

EXHIBIT 4-7

UNITED STATES CONSTITUTION, AMENDMENT XIV

Section 1. All persons born or naturalized in the United States, and subject to the jurisdiction thereof, are citizens of the United States and of the state wherein they reside. No state shall make or enforce any law which shall abridge the privileges or immunities of citizens of the United States; nor shall any state deprive any person of life, liberty, or property, without due process of law; nor deny to any person within its jurisdiction the equal protection of the laws.

---

a defendant charged with a serious crime is threatened with a serious deprivation of liberty. His notice is likely to consist of an arrest, with full Miranda warnings; his hearing may be a jury trial with the protections of the rules of evidence. Zoning and environmental regulations provide for notice and a hearing appropriate to the decision being made.

Equal Protection
Requirement that government justify unequal treatment of similarly situated parties

Does the **equal protection** clause require that the government always treat people equally? Of course not! Suppose that a city is hiring bus drivers. Does it have to give equal consideration to an applicant who is legally blind? The government is, however, required to justify unequal treatment of similarly situated individuals. The justification is weighed against the classification that was the basis for the unequal treatment.

Classification	economic	mid-level: illegitimacy, gender	suspect: race, fundamental rights, religion
Justification	rational basis	substantial relationship to governmental interest	compelling interest

In the zoning[5] and environmental arenas most unequal treatment is based on an economic classification. For example, a city may have a regulation that requires that liquor stores close between the hours of midnight and 10:00 A.M., while allowing other retail operations to remain open 24 hours. On its face, the ordinance discriminates among different types of businesses. Liquor store owners might bring a **facial challenge** to the ordinance, but they are likely to lose. This is an economic classification, essentially based on a business decision. It is at the lowest end of the justification spectrum and the city need only have a rational reason for its decision. Perhaps the city council believes that having liquor stores

Facial Challenge
Challenge to the constitutionality of a law as written

Spot Zoning
Creates an "island" of inconsistently zoned land

---

[5]In zoning law, a claim of **spot zoning** is a claim that a piece of property was zoned differently, essentially creating an "island" of differently zoned property. This is discussed in another chapter.

close during the night will reduce crime or reduce public intoxication. The city does not have to be able to prove that its strategy will actually work. Courts tend to defer to legislative decisions concerning economic regulation.

On the other end of the spectrum, when a governmental body makes a distinction based on race or a fundamental right, such as religion, it must be able to prove a compelling justification. The court will subject that justification to strict scrutiny.

Example

Four years ago Metropolis granted a variance from its wetlands protection ordinance to allow construction of a Catholic church that would encroach by 10 feet into the 100-yard required setback from a creek. This year a group of African-American Muslims applied for a variance to build a Mosque on property bordering a creek. The application is denied and the group files suit.

- The laws concerning wetlands setbacks and variances do not make any reference to religion — they are not discriminatory on their face. This will be a challenge to the laws **as applied** to a specific situation.
- The court will have to determine whether the groups were similarly situated. Perhaps the property owned by the Catholic church has an irregular shape so that no building could be built without a variance, while the Mosque property was large enough to accommodate the building without encroachment on the setback.
- If the groups were similarly situated, the city will have to prove a compelling reason for denying the application. The court will subject that reason to strict scrutiny to determine whether it is related to a legitimate governmental purpose and whether that purpose could have been achieved by nondiscriminatory means.

As Applied
Challenge to constitutionality of a law as applied to particular situation

---

How would the Muslim group in the example enforce its rights under the constitutional equal protection provisions? The mechanism is often a suit under a federal statute, such as the Fair Housing Act, 42 U.S.C. §§1364(a), (b), the Religious Land Use and Institutionalized Persons Act, 42 U.S.C. §2000, or the federal civil rights statutes, 42 U.S.C. §1981 or 42 U.S.C. §1983, which state: **"Every person who, under color of any statute,** ordinance, regulation, custom, or usage, of any State or Territory or the District of Columbia, subjects, or causes to be subjected, any citizen of the United States or other person within the jurisdiction thereof to the **deprivation of any rights, privileges, or immunities secured by the Constitution and laws, shall be liable** to the party injured in an action at law, suit in equity, or other proper proceeding for redress, except that in any action brought against a judicial officer for an act or omission taken in such officer's judicial capacity, injunctive relief shall not be granted unless a declaratory decree was violated or declaratory relief was unavailable." (emphasis added). Note that the statute does not indicate whether the deprivation of rights must have been intentional. As discussed later in this chapter, however, in some cases proof of intent is required.

Assignment 4-3

Read the case at the end of the chapter and answer the following:

1. The property owner brought a Fourth Amendment claim; describe the nature of the "seizure" at issue.
2. The court held that the owner could pursue more than one constitutional claim in a single suit and points out that the legal theories for the Fourth Amendment claim and the inverse condemnation claim are different. Given the facts in this case, are the allegations for the two claims significantly different?
3. Why did the court refuse to consider whether the owner had a legitimate claim of inverse condemnation?
4. Do you think a taking did occur? What type of a taking would it be? Does it matter that the owner was not deprived of her entire lot or that the "invasion" has been relatively short term? Do you think the owner should be able to obtain an award of damages if the defendants correct the situation and she regains total control of her property?

Executive Order
Order by president or governor, often implementing a statute or governing operation of executive agencies

B. Executive Orders

Other than the power to veto legislation, the power of the executive is not clearly defined and its exercise is sometimes very controversial. In fact, the Constitution and the federal statutes do not describe or define the President's power of executive order at all. There have been few court decisions, which have given only the imprecise guidance that executive orders should only be used in connection with power given to the President by the Constitution or a statute enacted by Congress. As a result, many executive orders are directed at those working in the executive branch. Exhibit 4-9 reproduces parts of an order concerning environmental issues and the executive branch. Other orders implement discretionary powers given by Congress. For example, President Clinton used the presidential power to designate national monuments (Antiquities Act of 1906, 16 U.S.C. §§431-433) in a very controversial way.

In 2001, during the last days of his administration, President Clinton announced new protections for nearly 60 million acres of federally controlled forest lands. Like the previous Democrat to hold the office (Jimmy Carter), Clinton left office with a flood of executive orders, many dealing with environmental protection, knowing that the incoming Republican administrations would be more focused on economic development and energy exploration. While incoming administrations can, with effort, sometimes "undo" the effect of such orders, it is not as simple as "flipping a switch." For example, depending on what has been done pursuant to the order, studies and/or hearings might be required to "undesignate" national monument land. It is also possible for Congress to pass a law overriding an executive order or to refuse to fund the mandates of the order.

Assignment 4-4

Determine whether the governor of your state has signed any executive orders relating to the environment.

C.   In the Field: Environmental Justice

Constitutional Issues Addressed by Executive Order

The following material was researched and organized by Samira Qureshi, Paralegal, BA, Political Science and Economics, McGill University; MA, Literature University of Toronto; BVC Elgin Community College.

"Give Me Liberty, I've Already Got Death" was a message displayed in 1978 by a resident of Love Canal. Love Canal is now a toxic ghost town, its residents evacuated in 1978 due to mismanagement of a toxic waste site. In the 1950s Hooker Chemical Company used the Love Canal as an industrial dump. After operations finished, the company covered the site and sold the land for one dollar. The working class town of Love Canal was built on this dump site. In August of 1978, corroding waste-disposal drums could be seen breaking up through the ground in backyards. The drum containers, which held 82 different compounds, 11 of them suspected carcinogens, had been rotting and leaching their contents into the backyards and basements of 100 homes and a public school built on the banks of the canal. Trees and gardens were turning black and dying. One entire swimming pool had been popped up from its foundation, afloat on a small sea of chemicals. Children returned from play with burns on their hands and faces. Many see it as the most appalling environmental tragedy in American history.

> For a more detailed history of the Love Canal tragedy and an overview of the state's response, visit www.health.state.ny.us/nysdoh/lcanal/lctimbmb.htm.

EXHIBIT 4-8

From www.epa.gov/fedrgstr/eo/index.html.

Selected Presidential Documents or Executive Orders
The executive orders listed below are found in EPA's Federal Register environmental documents collection and are available here for quick access. For a more in-depth listing of executive orders, please visit the U.S. National Archives & Records Administration (NARA) site at www.archives.gov/federal-register/executive-orders/disposition.html.

Executive Order 13211 — Actions Concerning Regulations That Significantly Affect Energy Supply, Distribution, or Use
[Federal Register: May 22, 2001 (Volume 66, Number 99)]

Executive Order 13175 — Consultation and Coordination With Indian Tribal Governments
[Federal Register: November 9, 2000 (Volume 65, Number 218)]

Executive Order 13158 — Marine Protected Areas
[Federal Register: May 31, 2000 (Volume 65, Number 105)]

Executive Order 13101 — Greening the Government Through Waste Prevention, Recycling, and Federal Acquisition
[Federal Register: September 16, 1998 (Volume 63, Number 179)]

Executive Order 13045 — Protection of Children From Environmental Health Risks and Safety Risks
[Federal Register: April 23, 1997 (Volume 62, Number 78)]

Executive Order 12988 — Civil Justice Reform
[Federal Register: February 7, 1996 (Volume 61, Number 26)]

Executive Order 12986 — International Union for Conservation of Nature and Natural Resources
[Federal Register: January 22, 1996 (Volume 61, Number 14)]

Executive Order 12898 — Federal Actions to Address Environmental Justice in Minority Population and Low-Income Populations
[Federal Register: February 11, 1994 (Volume 59, Number 32)]

Executive Order 12866 — Regulatory Planning and Review
[Federal Register: September 30, 1993 (Volume 58)]

Executive Order 12630 — Governmental Actions and Interference with Constitutionally Protected Property Rights
[Federal Register: March 15, 1988 (Volume 53)]

EXHIBIT 4-9
Executive Order 13423 of January 24, 2007

Strengthening Federal Environmental, Energy, and Transportation Management

By the authority vested in me as President by the Constitution and the laws of the United States of America, and to strengthen the environmental, energy, and transportation management of Federal agencies, it is hereby ordered as follows:

Section 1. *Policy*. It is the policy of the United States that Federal agencies conduct their environmental, transportation, and energy-related activities under the law in support of their respective missions in an environmentally, economically and fiscally sound, integrated, continuously improving, efficient, and sustainable manner.

Sec. 2. *Goals for Agencies*. In implementing the policy set forth in section 1 of this order, the head of each agency shall:

(a) improve energy efficiency and reduce greenhouse gas emissions of the agency, through reduction of energy intensity by (i) 3 percent annually through the end of fiscal year 2015, or (ii) 30 percent by the end of fiscal year 2015, relative to the baseline of the agency's energy use in fiscal year 2003;

(b) ensure that (i) at least half of the statutorily required renewable energy consumed by the agency in a fiscal year comes from new renewable sources, and (ii) to the extent feasible, the agency implements renewable energy generation projects on agency property for agency use;

(c) beginning in FY 2008, reduce water consumption intensity, relative to the baseline of the agency's water consumption in fiscal year 2007, through life-cycle cost-effective measures by 2 percent annually through the end of fiscal year 2015 or 16 percent by the end of fiscal year 2015;

(d) require in agency acquisitions of goods and services (i) use of sustainable environmental practices, including acquisition of biobased, environmentally preferable, energy-efficient, water-efficient, and recycled-content products, and (ii) use of paper of at least 30 percent post-consumer fiber content;

(e) ensure that the agency (i) reduces the quantity of toxic and hazardous chemicals and materials acquired, used, or disposed of by the agency, (ii) increases diversion of solid waste as appropriate, and (iii) maintains cost effective waste prevention and recycling programs in its facilities;

(f) ensure that (i) new construction and major renovation of agency buildings comply with the *Guiding Principles for Federal Leadership in High Performance and Sustainable Buildings set forth in the Federal Leadership in High Performance and Sustainable Buildings Memorandum of Understanding (2006)*, and (ii) 15 percent of the existing Federal capital asset building inventory of the agency as of the end of fiscal year 2015 incorporates the sustainable practices in the Guiding Principles;

EXHIBIT 4-9
(continued)

(g) ensure that, if the agency operates a fleet of at least 20 motor vehicles, the agency, relative to agency baselines for fiscal year 2005, (i) reduces the fleet's total consumption of petroleum products by 2 percent annually through the end of fiscal year 2015, (ii) increases the total fuel consumption that is non-petroleum-based by 10 percent annually, and (iii) uses plugin hybrid (PIH) vehicles when PIH vehicles are commercially available at a cost reasonably comparable, on the basis of life-cycle cost, to non-PIH vehicles;

(h) ensure that the agency (i) when acquiring an electronic product to meet its requirements, meets at least 95 percent of those requirements with an Electronic Product Environmental Assessment Tool (EPEAT)-registered electronic product, unless there is no EPEAT standard for such product, (ii) enables the Energy Star feature on agency computers and monitors, (iii) establishes and implements policies to extend the useful life of agency electronic equipment, and (iv) uses environmentally sound practices with respect to disposition of agency electronic equipment that has reached the end of its useful life.

Sec. 3. *Duties of Heads of Agencies.* In implementing the policy set forth in section 1 of this order, the head of each agency shall:

(a) implement within the agency sustainable practices for (i) energy efficiency, greenhouse gas emissions avoidance or reduction, and petroleum products use reduction, (ii) renewable energy, including bioenergy, (iii) water conservation, (iv) acquisition, (v) pollution and waste prevention and recycling, (vi) reduction or elimination of acquisition and use of toxic or hazardous chemicals, (vii) high performance construction, lease, operation, and maintenance of buildings, (viii) vehicle fleet management, and (ix) electronic equipment management;

(b) implement within the agency environmental management systems (EMS) at all appropriate organizational levels to ensure (i) use of EMS as the primary management approach for addressing environmental aspects of internal agency operations and activities, including environmental aspects of energy and transportation functions, (ii) establishment of agency objectives and targets to ensure implementation of this order, and (iii) collection, analysis, and reporting of information to measure performance in the implementation of this order;

(c) establish within the agency programs for (i) environmental management training, (ii) environmental compliance review and audit, and (iii) leadership awards to recognize outstanding environmental, energy, or transportation management performance in the agency;

(d) within 30 days after the date of this order (i) designate a senior civilian officer of the United States, compensated annually in an amount at or above the amount payable at level IV of the Executive Schedule, to be responsible for implementation of this order within the agency, (ii) report such designation

---

EXHIBIT 4-9
(continued)

---

to the Director of the Office of Management and Budget and the Chairman of the Council on Environmental Quality, and (iii) assign the designated official the authority and duty to (A) monitor and report to the head of the agency on agency activities to carry out subsections (a) and (b) of this section, and (B) perform such other duties relating to the implementation of this order within the agency as the head of the agency deems appropriate;

(e) ensure that contracts entered into after the date of this order for contractor operation of government-owned facilities or vehicles require the contractor to comply with the provisions of this order with respect to such facilities or vehicles to the same extent as the agency would be required to comply if the agency operated the facilities or vehicles;

(f) ensure that agreements, permits, leases, licenses, or other legally-binding obligations between the agency and a tenant or concessionaire entered into after the date of this order require, to the extent the head of the agency determines appropriate, that the tenant or concessionaire take actions relating to matters within the scope of the contract that facilitate the agency's compliance with this order; [material omitted, to see the entire order visit http://a257.g.akamaitech.net/7/257/2422/01jan20071800/edocket.access.gpo.gov/2007/pdf/07-374.pdf]

The story of Love Canal left many questions unanswered. Were there more, unidentified, "toxic towns" remaining; were other contaminated towns, like Love Canal, populated by working-class citizens? The answers were not surprising: Low-income communities and minority communities bear a disproportionate burden of toxic contamination, either through production and release of hazardous chemicals or through the location of waste management facilities.[6] Race and income level are the determining factors for predicting where locally unwanted land uses go. The problem may have many origins, ranging from the fact that land is generally less expensive in such communities to the inability of the residents to stay informed and protect themselves by means of the political process. In wealthier communities, **NIMBYs** have greater resources to prevent development of undesirable land uses. Some argue that the disparity is unconstitutional, citing the Equal Protection Clause and 42 U.S.C. §1983 (discussed earlier in this chapter).

NIMBY
Not In My Backyard; a person who opposes undesirable land uses in his or her community

---

[6]See www.epa.gov/compliance/resources/faqs/ej/index.html.

In 1994, President Clinton issued Executive Order 12898, requiring that each federal agency prioritize environmental justice by identifying and addressing disproportionately high and adverse human health or environmental effects of its programs, policies, and activities on minority populations and low-income populations. What is environmental justice? The United States Environmental Protection Agency defines it as the "fair treatment for people of all races, cultures, and incomes regarding the development of environmental laws, regulations and policies."

The EPA began to address environmental justice concerns even before the Order. Major components of EPA strategy include: (1) public participation and accountability, partnerships, outreach, and communication with stakeholders; (2) health and environmental research; (3) data collection, analysis, and stakeholder access to public information; (4) American Indian and indigenous environmental protection; and (5) enforcement, compliance assurance, and regulatory reviews. The EPA established the National Environmental Justice Advisory Council (NEJAC) in 1993 to provide independent advice to the EPA on matters relating to environmental justice. It consists of 25 members appointed from stakeholder groups including community-based organizations; business and industry; academic and educational institutions; state and local government agencies; tribal government and community groups; nongovernmental organizations and environmental groups.

In its Strategic Plan for Fiscal Years 2006-2010, the EPA established eight national environmental principles and set targets, committing to environmental justice. It identified strategies to measure outcomes and ensure that its resources reach disproportionately burdened communities. The priorities are:

- Reduce asthma attacks
- Reduce exposure to air toxics
- Ensure that fish and shellfish are safe to eat
- Ensure that water is safe to drink
- Ensure compliance with environmental laws
- Revitalize brownfields (abandoned or underused, contaminated industrial or commercial property) and other contaminated sites
- Initiate collaborative problem solving
- Reduce the incidence of elevated blood lead levels.

The EPA and others believe that environmental justice is best achieved by public participation. Citizens can start by identifying their state's environmental agency to discern whether the state has authority to administer any programs under national environmental laws (discussed earlier in this chapter). If a state has chosen the EPA to administer an environmental program, then key decisions about permits and approvals are made at the EPA regional office. If a state has elected to seek "primacy" or program delegation, key decisions about permits are made by the state. A state's decision to seek program delegation provides a great opportunity for input because the EPA approves the adequacy of the state's program. Citizens can identify program weaknesses and file petitions with the EPA for withdrawal or modification of their state program if they believe that the state is failing to address environmental justice.

The EPA is developing a handbook on civil participation (see www.epa.gov/compliance/resources/faqs/ej/index.html) and has established a Community Small Grants Program to provide financial assistance to help communities, grass-roots organizations, and other nongovernmental organizations become knowledgeable about environmental justice.

Example: Environmental Justice

At a public hearing held regarding the permitting of an Exxon chemical facility in Alsen, Louisiana, a member of an environmental group, charged: "Alsen is probably one of the best examples of environmental racism in the nation. The problem here goes far beyond mere environmental justice concerns. It is a case of outright discrimination. Many do not like to hear the term racism brought up today, claiming that that is all in the past. Unfortunately, Alsen has been forced to continue to endure the racist actions of the past. The decision to industrialize Alsen was not made by the people of Alsen. In fact, because of their race, the people of Alsen were deliberately and systematically denied the right to participate in government and shape their own destinies. Now, Alsen is told it must live with these racist decisions. This is clearly an injustice, and is unamerican [sic]." The court responded that it "is unfortunate that the original zoning placed this industrial complex next to [the community of] Alsen. The fact that it was done a long time ago, doesn't make any difference in considering environmental justice because a lot of things were done a long time ago that were not right. . . . Placing this industrial area in the neighborhood of the Alsen community does not appear to be intentionally racist. It's between a railroad and a river in a relatively rural area. Exxon has used a plant facility that was already in existence. They're actually putting out less pollution than the plant that was there previously. Considering the other policy considerations, should Exxon locate this some place where there is an area where there is no pollution? That's not a particularly good idea. Should they locate it in another industrial area? Well, that only moves the problem to somebody else's city. Overall, in the balance, I cannot find that DEQ abused its discretion in putting [the Exxon plant] in an industrial area at the site of a prior plant that actually probably produced more pollution than the system that's been proposed." *N. Baton Rouge Environmental Ass'n v. Dept. of Environmental Quality*, 805 So. 2d 255 (La. App. 2001).

To see a petition submitted to the EPA by opponents of the facility, visit/ www.epa.gov/Region7/programs/artd/air/title5/petitiondb/petitions/exxon_petition1998.pdf.

In 1998, African Americans sued the city of Dallas, alleging that the city allowed illegal dumping and failed to use its zoning and land use powers to protect them, in violation of their equal protection rights. The facts are complicated, but individuals were ultimately convicted for illegal dumping—as of the time of the civil trial against the city, the city had not cleaned up the dump site. There was evidence that city contractors had contributed to the illegal dumping. The court held that to prevail the plaintiffs had to prove three factors: (1) the action was the result of an official agency decision; (2) the City intended to discriminate against plaintiffs based on race; and (3) the action violated the Equal Protection Clause. The court found that the action was the result of an agency decision, and that "the City's efforts to stop the illegal dumping at Deepwood were inconsistent, inadequate, and largely ineffective," but that the residents did not show that "these failures were the result of a widespread practice attributable to the City Council or to the Board of Adjustment of not using the City's zoning land use power to protect African American neighborhoods." The court acknowledged that it was bewildered by the city's inability to protect its citizens, but stated that the city's procedures in dealing with the situation did not differ from those followed in other situations. Ruling in favor of the city, the court held that the plaintiffs had not shown **discriminatory intent or purpose**. *Cox v. City of Dallas,* affirmed, 430 F.3d 734 (5th Cir. 2005), cert. denied, 126 S. Ct. 2039 (2006). www.ca5.uscourts.gov/opinions/pub/04/04-11304-CV0.wpd.pdf.

Assignment 4-5

Discuss the policy reasons behind a decision like that in the Cox case (above). Consider:

◆ Potential costs to already-strapped governing bodies
◆ Could the residents have filed a citizens' suit?
◆ Does the reasoning in the Baton Rouge case apply? The garbage has to go somewhere.

From the EPA Environmental Justice Page, www.epa.gov/compliance/environmentaljustice/index.html. Determine which EPA regional office covers your state (Where You Live tab) and use the Frequently Asked Questions tab to identify some common environmental problems.

Key Terms

As-applied Challenge
Categorical Taking
Commerce Clause
Condemnation
Dormant Commerce Clause
Eminent Domain
Equal Protection
Exaction
Executive Order
Facial Challenge
GIS
Inverse Condemnation
Just Compensation
Market Participant Exemption

NIMBY
Per Se Taking
Police Power
Preemption
Procedural Due Process
Regulatory Taking
Remote-sensing Technology
Ripeness
Savings Clause
Spot Zoning
Takings Clause
Tenth Amendment
Variance

Review Questions

1. How is the power of executive order normally used?
2. Identify instances in which the use of executive order is controversial.
3. Which part of the Constitution provides the basis for most federal environmental regulation?
4. Describe the controversy surrounding federal regulation of isolated wetlands.
5. How does Congress "coerce" state participation in federal programs?
6. Describe how the state and federal governments share power with respect to some environmental programs.
7. What is the difference between eminent domain and inverse condemnation?
8. How can a regulatory taking occur?
9. Describe how new technology is being used in environmental investigation and enforcement.
10. What is meant by "property" in the due process clause and what are the requirements of procedural due process?
11. Explain how the government is required, by the equal protection clause, to justify unequal treatment.

KEY TERMS CROSSWORD

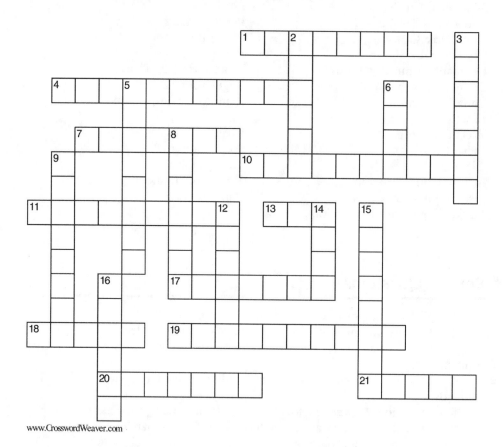

www.CrosswordWeaver.com

ACROSS

1. requirement that plaintiff exhaust other possibilities before suit
4. _____ taking, denies all economically viable use
7. procedural due process requirement
10. federal law overrides state and local
11. can issue executive orders
13. initials for mapping/database system
17. _____ domain, for public purpose
18. Amendment reserves power to states
19. _____ taking, regulation goes too far
20. to exercise eminent domain
21. _____protection; from 14th Amendment

DOWN

2. _____power, right of government to protect health, safety, welfare
3. _____ commerce clause, Congress has not acted but state law discriminates
5. requirement that developer dedicate
6. _____ compensation, must be paid in condemnation
8. _____ condemnation, regulatory taking
9. exception to zoning law
12. per se _____. physical occupation of land
14. _____ zoning creates an "island"
15. clause that is basis for most federal regulation of environment
16. procedural due process requirement

SHIRLEY PRESLEY, Plaintiff-Appellant v. CITY OF CHARLOTTESVILLE; RIVANNA TRAILS FOUNDATION, Defendants-Appellees.

United States Court of Appeals for the Fourth Circuit
464 F.3d 480
September 22, 2006, Decided

Presley, a resident of Charlottesville, Virginia, brought this *42 U.S.C. §1983 (2000)* action against the City and Rivanna Trails Foundation ("RTF"), a nonprofit corporation. She alleges that, without her consent, the Defendants conspired to publish a map that showed a public trail crossing her yard and that, even after Defendants realized their error, they did not correct it but criminally prosecuted her when she herself took measures to prevent trespasses on her property. Presley asserts that Defendants' actions violated her *Fourth Amendment* and due process rights. The district court granted motions to dismiss Presley's complaint for failure to state a claim upon which relief could be granted. For the reasons that follow, we affirm in part, reverse in part, and remand for further proceedings.

Presley's home and yard are less than an acre on the Rivanna River. In 1998, without having obtained her consent, RTF began distributing a map that displayed a public trail, the Rivanna trail, crossing her property. The City publicized the map on its website. Relying on the map, members of the public began traveling across Presley's yard, leaving behind trash, damaging vegetation, and sometimes even setting up overnight camp sites. Initially, Presley did not realize the extent of the intrusion because she was caring for her ailing husband in a nursing home. After her husband's death in 2001, however, Presley began complaining to RTF and the City about the trespasses. Although the Defendants acknowledged their error, they assertedly neither changed the map nor stopped its distribution. Rather, several RTF officials and members of the city council met with Presley and asked her to give Defendants an easement across her property in exchange for favorable tax treatment and other favors (but not compensation). Presley refused.

Intrusions by trespassers persisted and became more severe. Presley called the police, who responded regularly, but could not stem the tide. Presley then posted over one hundred "no trespassing" signs, all of which were defaced and destroyed. Finally, Presley installed razor wire along the perimeter. City responded by revising an ordinance to prohibit Presley's protective measures and bringing a criminal prosecution against her for violating that ordinance. The prosecution was later dismissed. When Presley filed this action in 2005, the City and RTF had not amended the map. Presley alleges that Defendants engaged in conspiracy to violate her rights and that Defendants' actions constitute an unreasonable *Fourth Amendment* seizure and deprive her of due process rights under the *Fourteenth Amendment*.

The *Fourth Amendment's* protections against unreasonable seizures extend to real property. *See, e.g., United States v. James Daniel Good Real Property, 510 U.S. 43, (1993)* (*Fourth Amendment* applies to seizure of land with a house). The district court held that Presley's claim was foreclosed because it "merely amount[ed]" to a *Fifth Amendment* takings claim. But the Supreme Court has considered multiple constitutional claims based on the same facts: "[c]ertain wrongs affect more than a single right and, accordingly, can implicate more than one of the Constitution's commands." *Soldal v. Cook County, 506 U.S. 56 (1992)*. The Court has rejected the argument that, on the basis of a single set of facts, a plaintiff could only assert violation of one constitutional provision, holding that the plaintiff could simultaneously bring a due process claim and a *Fourth Amendment* claim.

Even if the same appropriation constitutes both a seizure and a taking, legal differences separate a *Fourth Amendment* seizure claim from a *Fifth Amendment* takings claim. To prevail on a seizure claim, a plaintiff must prove that the government *unreasonably* seized property. *Soldal, 506 U.S. at 71*. To make out a takings claim, a plaintiff must demonstrate that the government took property *without just compensation. Williamson County Reg'l Planning Comm'n v. Hamilton Bank, 473 U.S. 172, (1985)*. Because the legal elements of a seizure claim and a takings claim differ, there is no danger that one constitutional provision will subsume the other. Put simply, that Presley may have a claim under the *Fifth Amendment's Takings Clause* does not bar her from bringing a *Fourth Amendment* seizure claim.

The district court alternatively held that no seizure had occurred because Presley was not "completely deprived . . . of her possessory interests in her property." But a deprivation need not be this severe to constitute a seizure; the *Fourth Amendment* also governs temporary or partial seizures. *See United States v. Place, 462 U.S. 696 (1983)*. The Supreme Court has held that a seizure of property occurs whenever "there is some meaningful interference with an individual's possessory interests in that property." *United States v. Jacobsen, 466 U.S. 109 (1984)*. Presley has alleged an "interference with" her "possessory interests" that is clearly "meaningful"; indeed, this interference has assertedly been disruptive, stressful, and invasive. Her complaint states that she has been deprived of the use of her property due to the regular presence of a veritable army of trespassers who regularly traverse her yard, littering, making noise, damaging her land, and occasionally even camping overnight. This constant physical occupation certainly constitutes a meaningful interference with Presley's possessory interests in her property.

It is private individuals, not City officials, who have actually interfered with Presley's interests. Although private actions generally do not implicate the *Fourth Amendment*, when a private person acts as an agent of Government or with participation or knowledge of any governmental official, the person's acts are attributed to government. The government need not compel nor even involve itself directly in the person's actions. Several factors combine to convince us that Defendants did more than adopt a passive attitude toward the underlying private conduct and that the acts of private persons are attributable to Defendants. Defendants knew that their map was erroneous. They also knew that the map would encourage public use of the trail; this was the map's purpose. Defendants also knew that the City's involvement would communicate to trail users that there were no legal barriers to their use of the entire trail, including the portion that cut through Presley's property. Defendants assertedly did nothing to correct their error, and, when Presley attempted to protect her own property, the Defendants initiated a meritless criminal prosecution to force her to take down the razor wire. *Fourth Amendment* is implicated when government officials prevent lawful resistance against seizures effected by private persons. These factors are clear indices of encouragement, endorsement, and participation, and suffice to implicate the *Fourth Amendment*.

Although Presley's *Fourth Amendment* claim survives Defendants' motion to dismiss, her procedural due process claim does not. Assuming that Presley suffered a deprivation, the district court correctly recognized that because the only deprivation that she has alleged is effectively a physical taking, an inverse condemnation action for just compensation (available under state law) provides all the process to which she is due. A taking differs from other deprivations, both in its importance to governance and in additional procedural protections provided whenever a taking occurs. When the facts establish a taking (regardless of whether plaintiff has alleged one), the owner of taken property is constitutionally entitled to two protections not afforded to others suffering property deprivations: the government must demonstrate that the taking was for a public use, and the government must afford the owner just compensation. A century of precedent has created a distinct body of law for cases in which the challenged deprivation is a physical taking. Under these precedents, government entities need not provide a hearing before they physically take property, so long as the taking is for a public use. Nor need the government provide notice before a physical taking. Rather, in the takings context, the *Due Process Clause* only entitles property owners to adequate notice prior to a judicial condemnation or just-compensation proceeding. *See Schroeder v. City of New York, 371 U.S. 208.* Thus, when a government entity condemns land, notice must precede the initiation of judicial proceedings that will determine the value of that land, regardless of whether those proceedings occur before the government takes physical possession of the land. But the government need not provide notice prior to a physical taking that, as here, is not itself preceded by *any* judicial process.

Rather, when the alleged deprivation is effectively a physical taking, procedural due process is satisfied so long as private property owners may pursue meaningful post-deprivation procedures to recover just compensation. These well-established principles govern the case at hand. If we accept Presley's factual allegations, as we must at this stage in the proceedings, then the City has physically taken, and therefore deprived Presley of, some of her property. Nevertheless, Presley cannot show that she was denied adequate procedures to obtain just compensation. Under Virginia law, aggrieved property owners may file an inverse condemnation action pursuant to Virginia's declaratory judgment statute. (*Va. Code Ann. §8.01-184* (West 2000)). If they prevail, they may obtain a court order requiring that the relevant governmental body comply with Virginia's established procedures for determining compensation. Because Virginia law provides an adequate procedure for obtaining compensation for a taking — a procedure readily available to Presley — Presley has alleged no denial of procedural due process. One final note: Our holding today may seem to raise the specter of government entities deciding to physically take property (for which no predeprivation process is due) rather than pursuing the more gruelling path of condemnation proceedings. But what condemnation proceedings lack in procedural ease, they gain in security. While a taking by physical invasion, being completely efficacious to acquire title, might be thought preferable to the administrative difficulties attendant upon formal condemnation proceedings, there are of course overpowering reasons to prefer the latter. Properly conducted, the formal proceeding can, and typically does, dispose of all issues and conclude all persons in a setting chosen by the condemning authority. Taking by physical invasion on the other hand simply exposes the government to continued "inverse condemnation" actions by various claimants proceeding as and when they will. *AFFIRMED IN PART, REVERSED IN PART, AND REMANDED.*

5

Protection of the Environment at the Local and International Levels

A. Zoning and Environmental Sustainability
    1. Permitted, Conditional, and Nonconforming Uses
    2. Comprehensive Plans
    3. Flaws in the Plan
    4. Process of Local Regulation
    5. Trends in Land Use Regulation
B. International Law
    1. The United Nations and Related Organizations
    2. Other Organizations
    3. Native American Tribes
C. In the Field: Planners

A. Zoning and Environmental Sustainability

In a sense, zoning and planning at the local level are first-level environmental regulations. Planning and zoning concern development of land for a variety of uses and, while some people think of environmental protection and development as incompatible, each must accommodate the other. Think of it this way: Would you oppose construction of a factory on a previously undeveloped meadow, which has served as a sanctuary for wildlife? Would it change your mind to learn that the factory is the only hope for alleviating unemployment in an economically depressed area? Wouldn't it be nice if we could have both the factory and the wildlife sanctuary? Very few land uses are inherently "bad," and many of the uses that create the most environmental problems are essential to society.

Environmental Footprint
Measures impact of development on nature

Sustainable Development
Development that meets today's needs while preserving the ecosystems for future generations

The two uses, a factory and a sanctuary, might be able to coexist, if the factory's **environmental footprint** is carefully controlled. The term **sustainable development** describes growth and development with an environmental footprint that meets today's needs while preserving the ecosystems for future generations. The concept is so important that the EPA devotes part of its website to it, http://www.epa.gov/sustainability/index.htm.

Sustainable development crosses disciplinary lines. For example, the National Science Foundation has an Environmental Sustainability Program that "supports engineering research with the goal of promoting sustainable engineered systems that support human well-being and that are also compatible with sustaining natural (environmental) systems—which provide ecological services vital for human survival." Business Week has invited its readers "to imagine a world in which socially responsible and eco-friendly practices actually boost a company's bottom line." Many companies and governmental bodies have sustainability policies in place.

How do we measure the environmental footprint and determine whether development is sustainable? Different methodologies are used, but in general the analysis measures human demands on nature and consumption of natural resources with the earth's capacity to regenerate. This can be done by calculating the biologically productive land and marine area required to produce the resources a population consumes and to absorb the corresponding waste, using prevailing technology. This calculation can be applied to almost any activity: building a factory, manufacturing a product, or driving of a car. The Wausau Paper Company even released a brochure on sustainability for art directors involved in advertising![1]

There have been studies of the average per capita footprint of people living in different countries. As you might imagine, the footprint of a resident of the United States is quite large when compared to the footprint of people in many other nations where people have what we would consider a lower standard of living. These studies are controversial, however, and questions remain unanswered: how to account for nuclear power (many studies consider it to have the same ecological footprint as fossil fuel), which data sources are used, how to account for regional differences within a country, how space for biodiversity should be included, and how imports and exports should be accounted for.

Calculate your own footprint at http://www.earthday.net/footprint/info.asp. For more information about measuring and comparing environmental footprints, visit http://www.footprintnetwork.org/, http://www.sustainablesonoma.org/keyconcepts/footprint.html, and http://www.sustainablemeasures.com/Indicators/IS_EcologicalFootprint.html.

---

[1]http://www.wpprintingandwriting.com/assets/environment/SustainabilityBrochure_LO-RES.pdf.

All of the factors that go into calculating the footprint of a local activity also have global implications. Overpopulation, global warming, and marine pollution affect every person on the planet. This chapter starts by looking at local-level regulation and finishes with a discussion of international efforts.

At the local level, careful planning and zoning of the "built environment" are essential to controlling the footprint of a building or a use and to promoting sustainable development. Zoning is the division of a municipality into districts to keep incompatible uses apart and the regulation of the physical attributes of uses, such as building size and height, siting on the lot, parking requirements, yard size, and required **easements**.

1.   Permitted, Conditional, and Nonconforming Uses

A zoning ordinance typically identifies districts and the uses **permitted by right** in those districts. For example, the R-1 district might permit single-family housing, while the R-2 district permits duplex housing and the R-3 district permits apartment housing; the C-1 district might permit small retail stores, while the C-2 district permits "big-box" retailers. The ordinance may also provide for **special uses** or **conditional uses**, permitted if they meet certain conditions. For example, a building for religious worship might be allowed in an R-1 district if it meets conditions relating to lot size, availability of parking, **setbacks and buffering**, and hours of operation. The ordinance may also define permitted **accessory** uses. For example, a day care operation for care of no more than three children might be an accessory use in a residential district. In addition to regulating the use of property, zoning ordinances often regulate the **subdivision** of land — the division of a large parcel into smaller parcels.

Zoning did not take root in the United States until the twentieth century. New York City passed the first major zoning ordinance in 1916, but many communities did not follow suit for many years. A few municipalities still do not impose zoning restrictions. As a result, there are many **nonconforming uses**. For example, a small factory might exist, surrounded by houses, in an area now zoned for residential use. Such a use is generally considered to be **grandfathered** and is allowed to continue, but is not allowed to expand or change. The owner is said to have a **vested right** to continue the use until it is abandoned or terminated. Whether the use may be resumed if destroyed by fire or other causes beyond the control of the owner differs from state to state.

If land cannot be used for the purposes for which it is zoned, the owner may apply for a variance from dimensional restrictions or use limitations. Laws governing variances differ from state to state, but the applicant is generally required to prove that some unique feature of the property (e.g., its shape or topography) makes its use, as zoned, impractical or impossible.

2.   Comprehensive Plans

Municipalities have the power to zone only if that power is granted by the state constitution or by statute. Because zoning does infringe on the rights of property owners, it must be reasonable and it must be done with the purpose of serving the public health, safety, and welfare. Exhibit 5-1 is an Ohio statute authorizing counties to zone. Note the reference to a comprehensive plan. Zoning is

Easement
A limited right to use property of another

Permitted
Use identified as allowed in zoning district

Special Use
See conditional use

Conditional Use
A use that is permitted in a zone if it meets certain conditions

Setback
Distance between lot line and structure

Buffering
Shielding one use from another, often by landscaping

Accessory Use
Use incidental to main use

Subdivision
Creation of smaller lots from larger tract

Nonconforming Use
Use that existed before zoning restrictions and does not comply with those restrictions

Grandfathered
Use that existed before zoning restrictions can continue

Vested Right
An absolute, legally recognized right

Comprehensive Plan
Plan for community's future development

invalid if it is arbitrary, and by preparing a well-researched **comprehensive plan**, with input from the community, the community can avoid arbitrary zoning.

Example

Metropolis zones a large area for construction of single-family housing except for one parcel, right in the center of the residential area, which it zoned for a retail store. By coincidence the parcel singled out for different use is owned by one of the richest families in town. The family made its fortune running convenience stores. This appears to be **spot zoning**, which creates an "island" of different use. Unless there is a reasonable basis for the distinction, it may be arbitrary.

Spot Zoning
Zoning inconsistent with surrounding property

Elements
Parts of a comprehensive plan

In many communities a comprehensive plan is far more than a map of future land development. It may include plans for many other **elements** of development, such as transportation and roads, parks and recreation, affordable housing, services (library, fire and police protection, etc.) or economic development.

EXHIBIT 5-1

TYPICAL ZONING ENABLING LANGUAGE

§xxxx. County regulation of land use in unincorporated territory; landscaping and architectural standards.

(A) Except as otherwise provided in this section, in the interest of the public health and safety, the board of county commissioners may regulate by resolution, **in accordance with a comprehensive plan**, the uses, location, height, bulk, number of stories, and size of buildings and other structures, including tents, cabins, and trailer coaches, percentages of lot areas that may be occupied, set back building lines, sizes of yards, courts, and other open spaces, the density of population, the uses of buildings and other structures, including tents, cabins, and trailer coaches, and the uses of land for trade, industry, residence, recreation, or other purposes in the unincorporated territory of the county . . . For all these purposes, the board may divide all or any part of the unincorporated territory of the county into districts or zones of such number, shape, and area as the board determines. All such regulations shall be uniform for each class or kind of building or other structure or use throughout any district or zone, but the regulations in one district or zone may differ from those in other districts or zones.

Nothing in this act allows or shall be construed to allow any county or township authority to establish a minimum price for a house or lot.

Assignment 5-1

1. Find your state statute concerning comprehensive plans. Does it describe the elements that must be included? Does it require communities to enact and update comprehensive plans?
2. Find your local zoning ordinance online; does it define "conditional or special use," "nonconforming use," or "variance"?
3. Does your state have a statute concerning redevelopment of brownfields (described below)?

3. Flaws in the Plan

Zoning and planning laws have been criticized, not only because they infringe on the rights of property owners, but because they sometimes preserve some of a community's worst traits. Representatives of Barrington Hills, an affluent Chicago suburb, were once quoted in a newspaper as saying that the village's five-acre minimum lot size kept out the "riff-raff." In addition to having an **exclusionary** impact, such zoning is bad for the environment because it necessitates the use of private cars and private yards rather than public open space.

Exclusionary
Zoning that excludes unpopular uses

To some extent, property owners can control the uses of property around them by means of **covenants**, promises recorded against the title to property, typically by a common owner before the property is subdivided. Lots in a residential subdivision might, for example, be subject to covenants requiring that houses be of a specified size and design and not be used for any purpose other than a dwelling.

Covenant
A promise or prohibition recorded against the title to land

Most people recognize the need for nuclear or coal-fired power plants, sewage treatment facilities, landfills, crematoriums, and similar uses, but they want them to be located far from their own homes. Those who object to such uses near their homes are sometimes called **NIMBYs** (Not In My Back Yard). Because of resistance to the location of some uses, in some states municipalities are prohibited from totally excluding legitimate uses, such as landfills. In many states local regulation of uses such as landfills is limited under principles of preemption.

NIMBY
Not In My Backyard, opponents of unpopular uses

4. Process of Local Regulation

The process of zoning and planning varies from state to state and sometimes from municipality to municipality within the state. Understanding the process in the relevant jurisdiction is essential and may require examination of the state zoning and planning enabling statutes as well as local code.

Some land use matters begin at a **ministerial** level. For example, the building official may be required to issue a building permit if the application meets code

Ministerial
Duties that do not involve discretion

Discretion
The ability to exercise judgment in performing duties

specifications. Other decisions may involve **discretion**. In some communities such decisions start out with a body that is advisory in nature. For example, a planning and zoning board may make recommendations to the decision-making body (in some cases the city or county council). In other communities, the application goes straight to a decision-making body. In most municipalities there is a level of review available from both ministerial and discretionary decisions before judicial review is possible.

A municipality's land use decisions can, obviously, have a huge impact on neighboring municipalities. Whether municipalities are required to consult or cooperate with neighboring governments differs from state to state. To prevent "NIMBY mentality," achieve some uniformity, and meet larger state goals, some states have created statewide boards of review. For example, Oregon has its Land Use Board of Appeals, see Exhibit 5-2.

EXHIBIT 5-2

From http://www.oregon.gov/LUBA/about_us.shtml.

About Us
Welcome to the Land Use Board of Appeals

Vision
The Land Use Board of Appeals (LUBA) was created by legislation in 1979 (ORS Chapter 197) and has exclusive jurisdiction to review all governmental land use decisions, whether legislative or quasi-judicial in nature.

Prior to LUBA's creation, land use appeals were heard by the Land Conservation and Development Commission (LCDC) and the circuit courts. LUBA was created to simplify the appeal process, speed resolution of land use disputes and provide consistent interpretation of state and local land use laws. The tribunal is the first of its kind in the United States.

The governor appoints the three-member board to serve four-year terms. The appointments are confirmed by the Oregon Senate. The board members must be members of the Oregon State Bar.

Mission Statement
LUBA was created to:

- *simplify the appeal process;*
- *speed resolution of land use disputes; and*
- *provide consistent interpretation of state and local land use laws.*

---

5. Trends in Land Use Regulation

Concerns about the environment and the desire to promote sustainable development have motivated many current trends in land use regulation:

- Desire to reduce use of vehicles has led to more **mixed-use development**, so that people can live, shop, and even go to work without relying on private cars. Mixed use developments are often **planned unit developments (PUD)** or **floating zones**[2] for which some of the usual restrictions on one-lot-at-a-time development, such as setback and density requirements, are relaxed in favor of creative use of open space, communal recreation areas, pedestrian-friendly design, and other innovations.

- Desire to preserve open space in large parcels, which are better for the environment than individual yards, has led to increasing popularity of **cluster** or **zero lot line development**. Individual houses are grouped together to allow for larger expanses of open space.

- Incentives, such as reduced property taxes, are being offered to owners who grant open space, agricultural, or **conservation easements**, under which they enter contracts promising not to develop the property.

- In some communities owners can **transfer development rights**. An owner, entitled, under existing zoning, to build 26 houses on his land along the lakeshore might be persuaded to build only 10 houses if he could sell his "right" to build 16 houses to an inland owner. The result will be fewer houses on the environmentally sensitive lake and improved views of and public access to the lake.

- Many communities now offer incentives, especially tax breaks and financing, to those willing to redevelop environmentally contaminated **brownfields** or to commit to **infill development** — reuse of property in an already developed urban area rather than construction on previously undeveloped land.

- Some municipalities are implementing **performance or incentive zoning**, which allows the developer to choose from a menu of municipal goals. For example, a developer who includes affordable housing and preservation of an open meadow in his subdivision plan might be allowed to build at a higher density.

Assignment 5-2

---

1. Find the statutes enacted by your state dealing with landfills, also called solid waste disposal facilities. Does state government preempt most regulation of landfills, or do local governments have authority to restrict the location, size, etc.?

---

[2]A floating zone or PUD is a designation that can be applied to property meeting certain qualifications, upon application by developer, but the designation is not typically identified to specific property on zoning maps.

Mixed Use
Uses normally separated, such as commercial and residential, combined in a development

PUD
Planned Unit Development, a zoning designation that can be applied to allow creative development of a large tract

Floating Zone
A zone that can be applied to property that meets criteria

Cluster Development
Structures are grouped together so that open space is in large parcels

Zero Lot Line
Buildings are clustered without setbacks

Conservation Easements
Include agricultural and open space easements — give owners tax breaks for covenant not to develop

Transfer Development Rights
Ability to transfer right to develop a particular density to another owner

Brownfields
Contaminated property

Infill
Development of property in an already developed area

Performance or Incentive Zoning
Developer is offered breaks on zoning requirements in return for meeting municipal goals

2. Read the case at the end of the chapter and answer the following:
   a. Why did the company initially not want public participation?
   b. Do you see any way that the court could have concluded that the landfill would be a public utility?
   c. What purpose is served by the award of attorneys' fees and the dismissal of the SLAPP (strategic lawsuit against public participation) claim?
   d. The state seems to share regulatory authority over landfills with local governments; what is the role of each?

EXHIBIT 5-3

HOW IT WORKS IN THE FICTIONAL TOWN, CUMBERLAND

1. Comprehensive Plan contains a broad overview of plans for future development. Cumberland's Housing Element, adopted in 1970 and amended most recently in 2005, states:

Location. Infill development and redevelopment, as well as new conservation developments, will receive preference. In order to maximize compatibility with public transit and minimize auto use, housing within one mile of major transit service, a job hub, or town center provides a future market for transit. The project may be within two miles of a rail transit station if provisions are made to provide ongoing shuttle service to the future residents. Major transit service is defined as a bus or rail stop with peak period wait times of no more than 30 minutes. Major transit service also includes funded, but not yet built, fixed rail stations.

Land Use. New developments that aim to cluster housing in an efficient manner, in context with the surrounding community, to preserve natural resources and open space will be given priority attention. Higher densities and mixed uses are particularly appropriate near transit stations to reduce the growth of traffic congestion on local and regional roads.

2. The Zoning Map and Zoning Code are very specific and detailed.
The low-rise residential districts comprise the majority of the land area of Cumberland. These districts include the Residence A-1, A-2, B, B-1, C and C-1 districts. Most one, two and three family buildings in the City are located in these districts. Zoning requirements for these areas can be found in the following sections of the Zoning Ordinance:

- Dimensional Requirements are located in Article 5,000, Table 5-1.

EXHIBIT 5-3
(continued)

- Use Regulations are located in Article 4.31, Residential Uses.
- Parking Regulations are located in Article 6.36.1, Residential Uses-Parking.

3. Implementation. In 1972, When Cumberland first zoned the Aspen neighborhood, near the train station, it was designated for low-rise residential use. Permitted uses include single- and two-family (duplex) dwellings. A pharmacy that already operated in the area is allowed to continue as a nonconforming use. A day-care home, for care of no more than ten children, is a conditional use, allowed if the applicant can meet conditions relating to traffic safety and buffering. One lot backs up to the train station and has remained vacant for years because of noise and dust. The owner applies for a variance, to use the lot as a parking facility for the station; he argues that the lot's unique location makes it unsuitable for residential use. The town will attempt to preserve the integrity of its plan, even if it imposes some hardship on the individual owner. Whether he obtains a variance will likely depend on whether residential use of the property is economically viable.

B.   International Law

Pollution does not respect international boundaries. Because local, state, and federal efforts with respect to the environment can be undermined by pollution from other nations, the EPA's Office of International Affairs (**OIA**) works to connect EPA initiatives to projects of other nations. The OIA has entered into several specific agreements with the governments of our neighbors, Mexico and Canada, as well as with nations on the other side of the world. The OIA focuses on issues—such as marine pollution or long-range transport of pollutants—that only sustained international cooperation can help solve.

OIA
EPA Office of International Affairs

It is difficult to discuss the substance of international environmental law because treaties and agreements imposing controls on the ecology are often focused on other concerns, such as public health, transportation, or economic development. In addition, relevant **treaties** and agreements may be bilateral, involving only two countries, regional, or multilateral; many grew out of meetings such as the 1972 United Nations Convention on the Human Environment held in Stockholm, Sweden (known as the Earth Summit); the 1992 United Nations Conference on Environment and Development, held in Rio de Janeiro, Brazil, and the 2002 conference, known as the World Summit on Sustainable Development (WSSD), held in Johannesburg, South Africa.

Treaties
International agreements

Agreements and treaties are supplemented by **protocols**, which are like "mini-agreements" concerning details of implementation. International environmental law also includes the decisions of international courts and tribunals. While there are few such decision makers and they have limited authority, their decisions are influential. The tribunals include the International Court of Justice, www.icj-cij.org/; the European Court of Justice, http://curia.europa.eu; and, to some extent the World Trade Organization www.wto.org/english/thewto_e/whatis_e/tif_e/disp1_e.htm.

Protocols
Sub-agreements to implement international treaties

Detailing the scope of each treaty or agreement is beyond the scope of this text, but in addition to being aware of the work of the OIA, you can become familiar with the major organizations that produce material or provide access to the relevant agreements.

1.   The United Nations and Related Organizations

Divisions of the **United Nations (UN)** and agencies related to the UN produce material relevant to international environmental law that can be accessed from the UN web page, www.un.org. Resources include a subscription database of treaties, http://untreaty.un.org. Divisions and related organizations able to provide information on specific topics include:

UN
United Nations, responsible for much environmental use

a.   The UN Environment Programme, www.unep.org.
b.   The Climate Change Secretariat, www.unfccc.de. The site includes an overview of climate change, documents of the various conferences, identification of agencies and groups, communications, and technical papers.
c.   The UN Commission on Sustainable Development and the Division for Sustainable Development, www.un.org/esa/sustdev/csd.htm and www.un.org/esa/sustdev/dsd.htm. The Commission's definition of sustainable development refers to methods of development intended to relieve

poverty, create equitable standards of living, satisfy the basic needs of all people, produce sustainable economic growth, and establish sustainable political practices, while taking the steps necessary to avoid irreversible damage to the natural environment. Sustainable development looks at long-term results, rather than short-term benefits.

d. The Convention on Biological Diversity Clearinghouse, www.biodiv. org/chm/, a network of parties working to implement the United Nations Convention on Biological Diversity.

e. The Food and Agriculture Organization, www.fao.org, has a mandate to raise levels of nutrition and improve agricultural productivity.

f. The Convention on Prevention of Marine Pollution, www. londonconvention.org.

g. UN Development Programme, www.undp.org.

h. The Global Environment Facility, www.gefweb.org, funds efforts to address ozone depletion, global warming, loss of biodiversity and pollution of international waters.

i. The World Conservation Union, www.iucn.org/themes/law, compiles treaty information.

j. The World Health Organization, www.who.int, has a section on protection of the human environment, www.who.int/phe/en.

k. The World Meteorological Organization, www.wmo.ch, provides information on world climate and atmospheric conditions.

2. Other Organizations

The **European Union (EU)** has a Directorate-General for the Environment, http://ec.europa.eu/dgs/environment/index_en.htm, a European Environment Agency, www.eea.europa.eu, and a database of treaties and other documents, www.eel.nl. The Organization of American States has an Office for Sustainable Development and the Environment, www.oas.org/usde.

EU
European Union; responsible for some environmental treaties

The **World Trade Organization (WTO)** is the only global international organization dealing with trade between nations. At its heart are WTO agreements, negotiated and signed by the bulk of the world's trading organizations; several of those agreements include provisions concerning the environment. For example, in November 2007, Brazil and Peru proposed that biofuels and organic food products be considered as environmental goods subject to certain tariff cuts or elimination.

WTO
World Trade Organization

The North American Free Trade Agreement (**NAFTA**) came into effect on January 1, 1994 and establishes a set of rules for trade between the United States, Mexico, and Canada. Many people believe that NAFTA has had a major environmental impact in Mexico.

NAFTA
North American Free Trade Agreement

Assignment 5-3

◆ How could a treaty concerning commerce cause air and water pollution? Do an Internet search and write or orally present an explanation of the environmental impacts of NAFTA.

◆ Visit the EPA site on treaties, http://www.epa.gov/ebtpages/intetreatinorthamericanfreetradeagre.html.
◆ Examine the Great Lakes Water Quality Agreement. Does the agreement address the discharge of waste from ships on the lakes?

EXHIBIT 5-4

From www.bls.gov/oco/ocos057.htm.

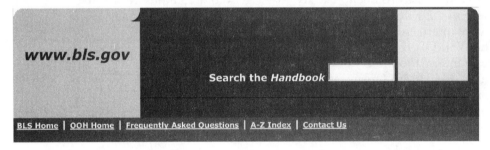

Urban and Regional Planners

Local governments employ 7 out of 10 urban and regional planners.

Most entry-level jobs require a master's degree; bachelor's degree holders may find some entry-level positions, but advancement opportunities are limited.

Most new jobs will be in affluent, rapidly growing urban and suburban communities.

Planners develop long- and short-term plans to use land for the growth and revitalization of urban, suburban, and rural communities, while helping local officials make decisions concerning social, economic, and environmental problems. Because local governments employ the majority of urban and regional planners, they often are referred to as community, regional, or city planners.

Planners promote the best use of a community's land and resources for residential, commercial, institutional, and recreational purposes. Planners may be involved in various other activities, including making decisions relating to establishing alternative public transportation systems, developing resources, and protecting ecologically sensitive regions. Urban and regional planners address issues such as traffic congestion, air pollution, and the effects of growth and change on a community. They may formulate plans relating to the construction of new school buildings, public housing, or other kinds of infrastructure. Some planners are involved in environmental issues ranging from pollution control to wetland preservation, forest conservation, and the location of new landfills. Planners also may be involved in drafting legislation on environmental, social, and economic issues, such as sheltering

EXHIBIT 5-4
(continued)

the homeless, planning a new park, or meeting the demand for new correctional facilities.

Planners examine proposed community facilities, such as schools, to be sure that these facilities will meet the changing demands placed upon them over time. They keep abreast of economic and legal issues involved in zoning codes, building codes, and environmental regulations. They ensure that builders and developers follow these codes and regulations. Planners also deal with land-use issues created by population movements. For example, as suburban growth and economic development create more new jobs outside cities, the need for public transportation that enables workers to get to those jobs increases. In response, planners develop transportation models and explain their details to planning boards and the general public.

Before preparing plans for community development, planners report on the current use of land for residential, business, and community purposes. Their reports include information on the location and capacity of streets, highways, airports, water and sewer lines, schools, libraries, and cultural and recreational sites. They also provide data on the types of industries in the community, the characteristics of the population, and employment and economic trends. Using this information, along with input from citizens' advisory committees, planners design the layout of land uses for buildings and other facilities, such as subway lines and stations. Planners prepare reports showing how their programs can be carried out and what they will cost.

Planners use computers to record and analyze information and to prepare reports and recommendations for government executives and others. Computer databases, spreadsheets, and analytical techniques are utilized to project program costs and forecast future trends in employment, housing, transportation, or population. Computerized geographic information systems enable planners to map land areas, to overlay maps with geographic variables such as population density, and to combine or manipulate geographic information to produce alternative plans for land use or development.

Urban and regional planners often confer with land developers, civic leaders, and public officials and may function as mediators in community disputes, presenting alternatives that are acceptable to opposing parties. Planners may prepare material for community relations programs, speak at civic meetings, and appear before legislative committees and elected officials to explain and defend their proposals.

In large organizations, planners usually specialize in a single area, such as transportation, demography, housing, historic preservation, urban design, environmental and regulatory issues, or economic development. In small organizations, planners do various kinds of planning.

3. Native American Tribes

Federal environmental laws apply to Native American reservations when Congress has specifically indicated that tribes are subject to particular laws. Many federal environmental laws give the EPA authority to approve tribal management of federal environmental programs, similar to the EPA's oversight and approval authority with respect to state administration of these laws. If there is no EPA-approved program for tribal administration, most environmental laws give the federal government enforcement jurisdiction on reservations.

Federal environmental laws that permit the EPA to authorize tribal management include the Clean Air Act, the Clean Water Act, and the Safe Drinking Water Act. The EPA has also exercised this authority with respect to the Resource Conservation and Recovery Act and the Toxic Substance Control Act and has established a limited tribal role in administration of the Federal Insecticide, Fungicide and Rodenticide Act, the Emergency Response and Community Right to Know Act, and the Comprehensive Environmental Recovery, Compensation and Liability Act. All of these laws are discussed in later chapters.

A tribe seeking to administer federal environmental law must apply for "treatment-as-a-state" status and provide the EPA with details concerning the regulatory program it intends to implement, including the scope of jurisdiction the tribe seeks for the program. The application can result in a jurisdictional battle between the applicant tribe and the state, with respect to people who live on reservations, but are not members of the tribe.

The EPA has several web pages: www.epa.gov/opptintr/tribal/index.html, excellent background and training material, www.epa.gov/indian/resource/resource.htm, and even a newsletter devoted to tribal issues, www.epa.gov/opptintr/tribal/pubs/tribalpilot1a.pdf.

C. In the Field: Planners

Planners
A professional involved in zoning and planning of land uses

At the local level much of the important work in planning and zoning is done by **planners**. Planners play an important role in protecting the environment by establishing rules so that flourishing businesses can coexist with a healthy natural environment.

Exhibit 5-4 contains the U.S. Bureau of Labor Statistics description of the job of planner. For more information about the fields of planning and zoning, visit www.planning.org. Exhibit 5-5 contains two job notices found on the site in 2007.

EXHIBIT 5-5

Environmental Planner,   Entry Level Position   Company/Agency:

Job Category: **Environmental Planning**
Salary Range: **Open**   Experience Required: **1 Year**
Job Description
XXX has an immediate opening for an entry-level Environmental Planner in our . . . CA, office.

Responsibilities include, but are not limited to:

—Assisting in research for CEQA, NEPA, and planning documents,

—Preparing or assisting in preparation of sections for CEQA, NEPA, and planning documents,

—Assisting in coordination with sub-consultants and project team members,

—Assisting in research and coordination with regulatory agencies, and

—Assisting Project Manager with budget and schedule tracking and project management duties.

A BS (MS preferred) in Urban or Environmental Planning, Environmental Studies, or related field required. The successful candidate must have good communication skills, particularly as related to writing. Experience and/or familiarity with CEQA/NEPA requirements is a plus. Strong analytical skills required. One year of work experience preferred. Experience developing environmental documents for the Bureau of Reclamation and the Army Corps of Engineers a plus.

Job#   Environmental Planner
Mid Level Position   Company/Agency:
Job Category: **Environmental Planning**   Salary Range: **Open**
Experience Required: **3-5 Years**

Job Description
XXX is a diversified environmental, transportation, and community planning organization with California offices in . . . and an office in . . . Colorado. The staff includes experts in environmental analysis, transportation planning and engineering, biology and wetlands, habitat restoration, resource management, geographic information systems (GIS), community and land planning, landscape architecture, archaeology and paleontology, noise, and air quality.

We are recognized as innovators in the field of environmental impact assessment, and we have developed a reputation among clients and professional peers in both the public and private sectors as being thorough, innovative, and objective.

EXHIBIT 5-5
(continued)

XXX is seeking an Environmental Planner with 4-6 years of consulting experience to develop technical sections for, and coordinate or manage preparation of, environmental assessments/documents, technical studies, and other similar reports in support of project managers and Principals in Charge; and conduct literature searches and field studies. Ability to work with clients, agency representatives, and other professional team members. Assume project manager responsibilities for small- to medium-sized projects.

BS/BA in environmental or urban planning field. Working knowledge of CEQA/NEPA; local, regional, state, federal requirements; and other environmental, entitlement, and planning regulations/laws. Excellent writing, research, interpersonal communication, and time management skills required.

Our greatest asset is our employee ownership. We take great pride in our work, and provide an environment in which each person can grow professionally. We are always looking for talented, dedicated professionals to join our team. We offer excellent compensation and benefits, including competitive pay; medical, dental, vision, group life, and long-term disability insurance plans; vacation, sick, and holiday pay, an Employee Stock Ownership Plan (ESOP); and a Profit Sharing and Savings Plan (with 401k and company match).

Key Terms

Accessory Use	NAFTA
Brownfields	NIMBY
Buffering	Nonconforming Use
Cluster Development	OIA
Comprehensive Plan	Permitted
Conditional Use	Planner
Conservation Easements	PUD
Covenant	Protocols
Discretion	Setback
Easement	Special Use
Elements	Spot Zoning
Exclusionary	Subdivision
EU	Transfer Development Rights
Floating Zone	Treaties
Grandfathered	UN
Incentive Zoning	Vested Right
Infill	Zero Lot Line
Ministerial	Zoning
Mixed Use	

Review Questions

1. Describe some current trends in zoning and how they may contribute to protecting the environment.
2. What are the sources of international environmental law and which major bodies are involved with international environmental law?
3. How does a nonconforming use differ from a conditional use and from a variance?
4. Describe how a conservation easement can work to protect the environment.
5. How can zoning have a negative impact on a community?
6. What is the purpose of a comprehensive plan?
7. What is a vested right?

KEY TERMS CROSSWORD

www.CrosswordWeaver.com

ACROSS

3. distance between lot line and structure
7. splitting a large parcel into smaller tracts
11. right to use part of another's property
13. contaminated property
15. _____ impact, keeps people out
16. _____ zoning, allows developer to choose from goals, more flexible
17. _____ a use that is allowed if it meets criteria
19. owners can sometimes _____ development rights
20. parts of comprehensive plan
21. authorization to have a use or structure inconsistent with zoning

DOWN

1. an owner may have a _____ right to continue the use of property
2. initials, usually a mixed use development
3. zoning that creates an island
4. _____ plan, basis for zoning
5. _____ development, keeps open space together by having smaller yards
6. a noncompliant use may be allowed to continue because it is _____
8. redevelopment of city lots
9. initials, lawsuit by developers against opponents
10. protecting one use from another, e.g., by landscaping
12. decision not involving discretion
14. a use that existed before zoning prohibited the use
18. initials, people who oppose unpleasant uses

EARTHRESOURCES, LLC v. MORGAN COUNTY et al.
(two cases).

Supreme Court of Georgia, 281 Ga. 396
November 30, 2006, Decided

Georgia Advance Headnotes

(1) Energy & Utilities Law. Administrative Proceedings. Public Utility Commissions. Trial court was correct in holding that a privately-owned landfill is not a public utility. A prior Supreme Court holding alone was sufficient to exclude the Department of Natural Resources from the role of a state regulatory commission regulating and controlling public utilities and, therefore, to exclude plaintiff's landfill from the category of public utility.

(2) Real & Personal Property Law. Zoning & Land Use. Zoning Generally. Since plaintiff's landfill could not meet the definition in a county's zoning ordinance, the trial court did not err in granting the county summary judgment on an issue, and, since that designation was central to plaintiff's claim of entitlement to verification of zoning compliance, the trial court did not err in granting summary judgment to the county as to all of plaintiff's substantive claims.

(3) Administrative Law. Governmental Information. Public Meetings. Evidence made it plain that notice sufficiently complied with a statute. The record established without question that notice of a meeting was posted in a timely fashion at the offices of a board of commissioners (Board), which was designated as the regular meeting place of the Board, and that the notice properly advised the public that a meeting would be held at an alternate site.

(4) Administrative Law. Governmental Information. Public Meetings. There was no allegation, much less evidence, that a technical violation of an agenda-posting requirement deprived plaintiff of a fair and open consideration of its request or in any way impeded the remedial and protective purposes of the *Open Meetings Act*. Under the unusual circumstances of the case, in which plaintiff first advocated a closed meeting and later objected to permitting public participation in the consideration of its request, the posting of the agenda at the regular meeting place of a board of commissioners rather than at the actual meeting site was sufficient compliance with a statute's requirements.

(5) Constitutional Law. Fundamental Freedoms. Freedom to Petition. Coverage of the anti-SLAPP statute plainly does not extend to protecting those who abuse the judicial process. The trial court was correct in holding the anti-SLAPP statute inapplicable to a county's claim for attorney fees pursuant to *OCGA §9-15-14.*

(6) Civil Procedure. Costs & Attorney Fees. Attorney Fees. Since there was neither evidence nor statutory or case law in support of plaintiff's claim that its landfill would be a public utility, and case law made it clear that plaintiff's proposed landfill could not fit that role, the trial court's award of attorney fees was affirmed.

EarthResources, LLC purchased property in Morgan County zoned for agriculture and sought verification of zoning compliance so it could pursue a state permit to build a landfill. See *OCGA §12-8-24 (g)*. EarthResources asserted its plans met zoning requirements because its landfill would be a public utility and public utility structures were permitted under the zoning ordinance then in effect. When the Board of Commissioners denied the verification, EarthResources filed a complaint. The trial court granted Morgan County's motion for summary judgment. In response to Morgan County's subsequent motion for attorney fees under *OCGA §9-15-14*, EarthResources, pursuant to *OCGA §9-11-11.1*, the anti-SLAPP (Strategic Lawsuits Against Public Participation) statute, filed a motion to dismiss the motion for attorney fees. The trial court granted Morgan County's motion and awarded it attorney fees. EarthResources appeals the grant of summary judgment against it, the award of attorney fees, and denial of its anti-SLAPP motion to dismiss.

Central to EarthResources' assertion that it was entitled to verification of compliance were claims that its landfill would be a public utility and the zoning provision that public utilities were permitted in areas zoned for agriculture. Absent a finding that its landfill would be a public utility, the claim to verification of zoning compliance is without basis. Morgan County's zoning ordinance in effect when EarthResources sought verification defined public utility as follows: "Entities engaged in regularly supplying the public with some commodity or service which is of public consequence or need, regulated and controlled by a state or federal regulatory commission and which may have the power of eminent domain." EarthResources bases its claim on the facts that its corporate charter identifies it as such, that it would supply a service the public needs, and that landfills are regulated by the Environmental Protection Division of the Georgia Department of Natural Resources. The trial court held that a privately-owned landfill is not a public utility. We agree.

Accepting for the purpose of argument that the proposed landfill would provide a needed public service, the landfill still fails to meet an essential part of the definition, that it be "regulated and controlled by a state or federal regulatory commission." In considering the authority to regulate public utilities, this Court has held that "the Public Service Commission, rather than any other agency of the executive branch, has authority to regulate public utilities." *Lasseter v. Ga. Public Svc. Comm., 253 Ga. 227 (1984)*. That holding excludes the Department of Natural Resources from the role of a state regulatory commission regulating public utilities and, therefore, excludes EarthResources' landfill from the category of public utility.

EarthResources contended it was denied due process in the hearing before the County Board in that the Board limited the time for EarthResources to argue its position and refused to consider printed material provided by EarthResources at the hearing before voting to deny the verification. On appeal, EarthResources offers no argument or authority on these issues. EarthResources claimed that the decision of the Board was invalid because the meeting violated the *Open Meetings Act*, *OCGA §50-14-1*. On appeal, EarthResources argues that notice of the meeting was insufficient because the notice was posted at the regular meeting place, but the meeting was conducted at a different location.

Notice of the time and place of meetings subject to the *Open Meetings Act* is controlled by *OCGA §50-14-1 (d)*, which reads in pertinent part as follows: Every agency shall prescribe the time, place, and dates of regular meetings of the agency. Such information shall be available to the general public and a notice containing such information shall be posted and maintained in a conspicuous place available to the public at the regular meeting place of the agency. Meetings shall be held in accordance with a regular schedule, but nothing in this subsection shall preclude an agency from canceling or postponing any regularly scheduled meeting.

Whenever any meeting required to be open to the public is to be held at a time or place other than at the time and place prescribed for regular meetings, the agency shall give due notice thereof. "Due notice" shall be the posting of a written notice for at least 24 hours at the place of regular meetings and giving of written or oral notice at least 24 hours in advance of the meeting to the legal organ in which notices of sheriff's sales are published in the county where regular meetings are held. . . .

The record in this case establishes that notice of the meeting was posted in a timely fashion at the offices of the Board, which was the regular meeting place of the Board, and that notice properly advised that the May 2005 meeting at which EarthResources' request was denied would be held at an alternate site. There is no evidence that any other site had been designated as regular meeting place. The notice sufficiently complied with the statute. Under the unusual circumstances of the present case, in which EarthResources first advocated a closed meeting and later objected to permitting public participation, we consider the posting of the agenda at the regular meeting place of the Board, rather than at the actual meeting site to be sufficient compliance with the statute's requirements.

We agree with the trial court that the anti-SLAPP statute does not apply to the County's claim for attorney fees. The General Assembly enacted the anti-SLAPP statute to encourage Georgians to participate in matters of public significance through the exercise of constitutional rights of freedom of speech and the right to petition government for redress of grievances. *Georgia Community Support & Solutions v. Berryhill, 275 Ga. App. 189 (2005)*. EarthResources had a full and public consideration of its grievance before a court and lost that case on the lack of merit in the essential claim. But the anti-SLAPP statute was not intended to immunize from the consequences of abusive litigation a party who "has asserted a claim . . . with respect to which there existed such a complete absence of any justiciable issue of law or fact that it could not be reasonably believed that a court would accept the asserted claim. . . ." *OCGA §9-15-14 (a)*. The anti-SLAPP statute extends to " 'abusive litigation that seeks to chill exercise of certain *First Amendment* rights' based upon defamation, invasion of privacy, breach of contract, and intentional interference with contractual rights and opportunities arising from speech and petition of government." *Browns Mill Dev. Co. v. Denton, 247 Ga. App. 232 (2000)*. It does not extend to protecting those who abuse the judicial process. The award of attorney fees to Morgan County was based on finding that EarthResources' claim "that its landfill is a public utility is unsupported by any authority whatsoever and lacks common sense" and a conclusion that the claim lacked any justiciable issue of law or fact and it could not be reasonably believed that a court would accept that claim. Since there is neither evidence nor statutory or case law in support of EarthResources' claim that its landfill would be a public utility, and the case law cited above in the discussion of the merits of EarthResources' claim makes it clear that EarthResources' proposed landfill could not fit that role, the trial court's award of attorney fees is affirmed. *Judgments affirmed. All the Justices concur.*

6

Due Diligence in Transactional Law

A. Due Diligence: What and Why

The Comprehensive Environmental Response, Compensation, and Liability Act of 1980 (**CERCLA**), 42 U.S.C. §9601 (discussed in depth in a later chapter), identifies **potentially responsible parties (PRPs)**, liable for the cost of cleanup,

CERCLA
Comprehensive Environmental Response, Compensation and Liability Act, describes who is liable for contamination

PRP
Potentially Responsible Party, possibly liable for contamination

Retroactive
Applying to a period prior to enactment

Joint and Several Liability
Each debtor is responsible for the entire amount of the debt

Strict Liability
Liability without regard to fault

Secured Creditors
Hold a special assurance of payment, such as a mortgage, lien, or other collateral

Innocent Landowner
Not involved in contamination, may have defense under CERCLA

Bona Fide Prospective Purchaser
Buyer who conducts AAI before purchasing may have CERCLA defense

Contiguous Property Owner
Owner of property touching contaminated property, may have CERCLA defense

Brownfields Program
Cleanup of contaminated property

Due Diligence
Careful inquiry

regardless of whether the PRP has any fault with respect to the contamination. Under Section 107 of CERCLA, PRPs include: (1) the current owner and operator; (2) any owner or operator at the time of disposal of any hazardous substances; (3) any person who arranged for the disposal or treatment of hazardous substances, or arranged for the transportation of hazardous substances for disposal or treatment; and (4) any person who accepts hazardous substances for transport to the site and selects the site.

CERCLA liability is **retroactive**: A party may be held liable even if the hazardous substance disposal occurred before CERCLA was enacted in 1980. Liability is **joint and several**; if two or more parties are responsible for the contamination at a site any one or more of the parties may be held liable for the entire cost of the cleanup, unless a party can show that the injury or harm at the site is divisible. Most states have laws that have parallel provisions.

The potential for **strict liability** prevented the desirable redevelopment of contaminated property and was a threat to both purchasers and lenders, who could become owners of contaminated property by foreclosure.[1] In response to the concerns of those groups, Congress amended the law in 1986 and again in 2002, to include and clarify defenses for **secured creditors**, **innocent landowners**, **bona fide prospective purchasers**, **contiguous property owners**, and **brownfields programs.** Simply put, **due diligence** is the careful inquiry and/or procedures (diligence) required (due) to secure protection from liability.

Due diligence is normally required in commercial (business property) transactions. Many title insurance policies for residential transactions include an endorsement to protect lenders against environmental liens. More importantly, the EPA "Policy Towards Owners of Residential Property at Superfund Sites" states that the agency will not take enforcement actions against residential owners who did not actively contribute to the release of hazardous substances and who are cooperative with cleanup efforts.

Nonetheless, the future may hold potential problems for residential owners whose property has been used for methamphetamine production. Contamination from a meth lab can spread throughout a structure and, without being readily detectable, have a severe impact on current and future inhabitants. In 2008 Congress enacted Public Law 110-143, the "Methamphetamine Remediation Research Act," to require the EPA to develop guidelines for detection and cleanup.

1. Secured Creditors

To protect lenders who foreclose on contaminated property, CERCLA[2] excludes from the definition of an "owner or operator" any "person, who, without

---

[1] Foreclosure is the process by which a lender takes possession of property that has been used to secure the debt (e.g., by mortgage) after the borrower/owner fails to make required payments.
[2] Section 101(20)(A).

participating in the management of a . . . facility, holds indicia of ownership primarily to protect his security interest in the . . . facility." Avoiding participation in management of the borrower is essential to avoiding liability. The EPA provides guidelines. Before foreclosure, participating in management includes controlling environmental compliance and handling or disposal of hazardous substances or controlling other operations at a level similar to that of a manager of the facility. A lender **does not** participate in management by:

- Having ability to influence or the unexercised right to control facility operations
- Acting or failing to act before the security interest in the facility was established
- Holding, abandoning, or releasing a security interest
- Monitoring or inspecting the facility
- Including a term relating to environmental compliance in the credit agreement
- Monitoring or enforcing terms of credit or security interest
- Requiring response to a release or threatened release of a hazardous substance
- Providing advice to a borrower to prevent default or loss of property value
- Changing the terms of the loan or security interest
- Exercising remedies for breach of the loan or security agreement
- Conducting a response action under CERCLA that does not rise to the level of participating in management

After foreclosure, a lender who did not previously participate in management may generally maintain business activities; wind up operations; undertake a response action under CERCLA; sell, re-lease, or liquidate the facility; or take actions to preserve, protect, or prepare the property for sale. After foreclosure, the lender must attempt to sell, re-lease, or otherwise divest itself of the property at the earliest practicable, reasonable time using commercially reasonable means.

There is a similar exemption for **fiduciaries**, who act on behalf of others. Trustees, executors, and other administrators can take specified non-negligent actions without incurring personal liability.

Fiduciary
One who acts on behalf of another, such as a trustee

2. Innocent Landowners and Contiguous Property Owners

The "innocent landowner" defense[3] is available to an owner of contaminated property, and the contiguous property owner defense is available to an owner whose property is contaminated by releases migrating from adjoining property not held by the same owner, if the party asserting the defense:

- Is not otherwise a PRP or affiliated with a PRP
- Conducted **all appropriate inquiry (AAI)** into the previous ownership and uses of the property consistent with good commercial or customary practices in an effort to minimize liability before acquiring the property

AAI
All appropriate inquiry for defense to CERCLA liability

---

[3] 42 U.S.C. §§9601(35)(A)(i) and 9607(b)(3).

- Cooperates with response agencies
- Complies with land use restrictions and does not impede the effectiveness or integrity of institutional controls
- Provides required notices concerning releases
- Takes reasonable steps to stop continued releases, prevent future releases, and limit exposure to the hazardous substances

3. Bona Fide Prospective Purchasers

Prior to the 2002 "Small Business Liability Relief and Brownfields Revitalization Act," a person who purchased property with knowledge of the contamination was subject to "owner or operator" liability under CERCLA. After January 2002, prospective landowners may purchase property with knowledge of contamination and obtain some protection from liability, if they meet the same pre- and post-purchase requirements as an innocent landowner or contiguous property owner.[4] Like an "innocent owner," a "bona fide prospective purchaser" has the burden of establishing that all disposal occurred before the facility was acquired.

4. Brownfields Programs

A defense is also available to those who have conducted or are conducting response actions at "eligible response sites"[5] in compliance with a "state program that specifically governs response actions for the protection of public health and the environment." The definition of an "eligible response site" includes "brownfield sites." The definition of a brownfield site is very broad and includes property with real or perceived contamination with specified exclusions.

EXHIBIT 6-1

CERCLA, Selected Sections
42 USCS §9607 Liability

(a) Covered persons; scope; recoverable costs and damages; interest rate; "comparable maturity" date. Notwithstanding any other provision or rule of law, and subject only to the defenses set forth in subsection (b) of this section —

(1) the owner and operator of a vessel or a facility,

(2) any person who at the time of disposal of any hazardous substance owned or operated any facility at which such hazardous substances were disposed of,

---

[4] 42 U.S.C. §9607(r).
[5] §§101(41); 101(39).

EXHIBIT 6-1
(continued)

(3) any person who by contract, agreement, or otherwise arranged for disposal or treatment, or arranged with a transporter for transport for disposal or treatment, of hazardous substances owned or possessed by such person, by any other party or entity, at any facility or incineration vessel owned or operated by another party or entity and containing such hazardous substances, and

(4) any person who accepts or accepted any hazardous substances for transport to disposal or treatment facilities, incineration vessels or sites selected by such person, from which there is a release, or a threatened release which causes the incurrence of response costs, of a hazardous substance, shall be liable for —

(A) all costs of removal or remedial action incurred by the United States Government or a State or an Indian tribe not inconsistent with the national contingency plan;

(B) any other necessary costs of response incurred by any other person consistent with the national contingency plan;

(C) damages for injury to, destruction of, or loss of natural resources, including the reasonable costs of assessing such injury, destruction, or loss resulting from such a release; and

(D) the costs of any health assessment or health effects study carried out under section 104(i) [42 USCS §9604(i)].

(b) Defenses. There shall be no liability under subsection (a) of this section for a person otherwise liable who can establish by a preponderance of the evidence that the release or threat of release of a hazardous substance and the damages resulting there from were caused solely by —

(1) an act of God;

(2) an act of war;

(3) an act or omission of a third party other than an employee or agent of the defendant, or than one whose act or omission occurs in connection with a contractual relationship, existing directly or indirectly, with the defendant (except where the sole contractual arrangement arises from a published tariff and acceptance for carriage by a common carrier by rail), if the defendant establishes by a preponderance of the evidence that (a) he exercised due care with respect to the hazardous substance concerned, taking into consideration the characteristics of such hazardous substance, in light of all relevant facts and circumstances, and (b) he took precautions against foreseeable acts or omissions of any such third party and the consequences that could foreseeably result from such acts or omissions; or

(4) any combination of the foregoing paragraphs.

(e) Indemnification, hold harmless, etc., agreements or conveyances; subrogation rights.

EXHIBIT 6-1
(continued)

(1) No indemnification, hold harmless, or similar agreement or convey-ance shall be effective to transfer from the owner or operator of any vessel or facility or from any person who may be liable for a release or threat of release under this section, to any other person the liability imposed under this section. Nothing in this subsection shall bar any agreement to insure, hold harmless, or indemnify a party to such agreement for any liability under this section.

. . .

(q) **Contiguous** properties.

(1) Not considered to be an owner or operator.

(A) In general. A person that owns real property that is **contiguous** to or otherwise similarly situated with respect to, and that is or may be con-taminated by a release or threatened release of a hazardous substance from, real property that is not owned by that person shall not be considered to be an owner or operator of a vessel or facility under paragraph (1) or (2) of subsection (a) solely by reason of the contamination if—

(i) the person did not cause, contribute, or consent to the release or threatened release;

(ii) the person is not—

(I) potentially liable, or affiliated with any other person that is potentially liable, for response costs at a facility through any direct or indirect familial relationship or any contractual, corporate, or finan-cial relationship (other than a contractual, corporate, or financial rela-tionship that is created by a contract for the sale of goods or services); or

(II) the result of a reorganization of a business entity that was potentially liable;

(iii) the person takes reasonable steps to—

(I) stop any continuing release;

(II) prevent any threatened future release; and

(III) prevent or limit human, environmental, or natural resource exposure to any hazardous substance released on or from property owned by that person;

(iv) the person provides full cooperation, assistance, and access to persons that are authorized to conduct response actions or natural resource restoration at the vessel or facility from which there has been a release or threatened release (including the cooperation and access necessary for the installation, integrity, operation, and maintenance of any complete or partial response action or natural resource restoration at the vessel or facility);

EXHIBIT 6-1
(continued)

(v) the person—

(I) is in compliance with any land use restrictions established or relied on in connection with the response action at the facility; and

(II) does not impede the effectiveness or integrity of any institutional control employed in connection with a response action;

(vi) the person is in compliance with any request for information or administrative subpoena issued by the President under this Act;

(vii) the person provides all legally required notices with respect to the discovery or release of any hazardous substances at the facility; and

(viii) at the time at which the person acquired the property, the person—

(I) conducted all appropriate inquiry within the meaning of section 101(35)(B) [42 USCS §9601(35)(B)] with respect to the property; and

(II) did not know or have reason to know that the property was or could be contaminated by a release or threatened release of one or more hazardous substances from other real property not owned or operated by the person.

(B) Demonstration. To qualify as a person described in subparagraph (A), a person must establish by a preponderance of the evidence that the conditions in clauses (i) through (viii) of subparagraph (A) have been met.

(C) **Bona fide prospective purchaser**. Any person that does not qualify as a person described in this paragraph because the person had, or had reason to have, knowledge specified in subparagraph (A)(viii) at the time of acquisition of the real property may qualify as a **bona fide prospective purchaser** under section 101(40) [42 USCS §9601(40)] if the person is otherwise described in that section.

(D) Ground water. With respect to a hazardous substance from one or more sources that are not on the property of a person that is a **contiguous** property owner that enters ground water beneath the property of the person solely as a result of subsurface migration in an aquifer, subparagraph (A)(iii) shall not require the person to conduct ground water investigations or to install ground water remediation systems, except in accordance with the policy of the Environmental Protection Agency concerning owners of property containing contaminated aquifers, dated May 24, 1995.

(2) Effect of law. With respect to a person described in this subsection, nothing in this subsection—

(A) limits any defense to liability that may be available to the person under any other provision of law; or

EXHIBIT 6-1
(continued)

(B) imposes liability on the person that is not otherwise imposed by subsection (a).

(3) Assurances. The Administrator may—

(A) issue an assurance that no enforcement action under this Act will be initiated against a person described in paragraph (1); and

(B) grant a person described in paragraph (1) protection against a cost recovery or contribution action under section 113(f) [42 USCS §9613(f)].

(r) Prospective purchaser and windfall lien.

(1) Limitation on liability. Notwithstanding subsection (a)(1), a **bona fide prospective purchaser** whose potential liability for a release or threatened release is based solely on the purchaser's being considered to be an owner or operator of a facility shall not be liable as long as the **bona fide prospective purchaser** does not impede the performance of a response action or natural resource restoration.

CERCLA includes other exemptions, for discrete groups. In addition, liability is sometimes avoided by bankruptcy. These issues are discussed in Chapter 10.

B. Securing Protection from Liability

In examining the defenses available to innocent landowners, contiguous owners, and bona fide prospective purchasers, you will notice that they involve common elements: cooperation with cleanup efforts and efforts to prevent future releases after contamination is discovered, and, before acquiring ownership, "all appropriate inquiry" (AAI) to discover contamination.

While parts of the "post-discovery" obligations are straightforward, others are not so clear. Whether an owner is providing required notices, complying with land use restrictions, not impeding controls in place on the property, and complying with information requests, is objectively ascertainable. On the other hand, determining whether a party is "cooperating with cleanup efforts," and taking "reasonable" or "appropriate" steps to prevent future releases can be troublesome.

The pre-acquisition requirement of AAI has, historically, been less than clear. In November 2006, new EPA standards for conducting AAI became effective. To understand those standards, you must first understand the process, which includes the contract between the parties and environmental assessment. To what extent is the owner required to disrupt his business operation, move his equipment and materials, and physically assist with the process of cleanup? How much does the innocent owner have to spend to stabilize the site and prevent exposure or worsening of conditions? These issues have not been explored in great detail in the courts. The EPA's "policies and guidance" page, www.epa.gov/superfund/policy/index.htm, can be of some help.

An owner or purchaser may be able to obtain a **"comfort letter"** or "status letter" concerning the property. Regional EPA offices may issue such letters, often before a property is sold, to help the prospective purchaser, seller, or lender determine the condition of the property. To see an EPA memo concerning comfort letters, visit www.epa.gov/compliance/resources/policies/cleanup/rcra/comfort-rcra-brwn-mem.pdf. For an example of a regional office's policy, visit www.epa.gov/ne/brownfields/guidance/comfort.htm.

Comfort Letter
An advisory letter from the EPA, concerning the status of property

1. Terms of Contract/Lease

A prospective purchaser of commercial or industrial property generally makes an offer to purchase, contingent on satisfactory environmental assessment. This gives the buyer an "out" if the property's environmental status is risky. The **contingency** may also be desirable to the seller, who may not want to proceed with the sale and give up control of the property, knowing that there will be liability for cleanup in the future. The contingency clause should provide adequate time for a thorough environmental assessment, should state which party will order and pay for the assessment, and should be very specific about why and how a party may terminate the agreement, as well as about confidentiality.

Contingency
Contract condition, may give a party an "out"

Environmental assessment is important in transactions other than purchase of real estate, particularly in contracts for financing and leases. Consider: Might the tenant under a long-term commercial lease use or store chemicals that could result in contamination that would linger long after the end of the lease? What about the landlord's liability for harm to the tenant's employees or property as a result of existing contamination? Depending on the circumstances, a lease should address:

- Warranties — does the landlord warrant that the property is not contaminated; does the tenant warrant that it will not use or store toxic materials?
- Responsibility for required remediation and standards for remediation
- Responsibility for fines and penalties imposed by governmental bodies
- Insurance or bonding to cover potential financial liabilities

2. Transaction Screen/Phase I Assessment

In order to limit costs, environmental assessment is generally conducted in phases. A prospective purchaser, with no reason to believe the property is contaminated, might start by obtaining a **transaction screen** or a **Phase I assessment**. In fact, a Phase II Assessment would likely not be possible at the outset, without any knowledge of the types of contaminants that might be present. On the other hand, a company buying an old gas station may suspect the presence of petroleum contamination and may want to order a Phase II Assessment immediately.

Transaction Screen
Lowest level of environmental assessment, not always conducted by professionals

Phase I Assessment
Environmental assessment without sampling, indicates what further testing may be needed

Commercial
Not residential, ASTM
standards apply to
commercial property

ASTM
American Society for
Testing and Materials

What goes on in the various phases? Historically, the phases have been based on uniform standards for **commercial**[6] transactions, issued by the American Society for Testing and Materials (**ASTM**). In preparation for issuing the 2006 AAI regulation, the EPA worked with ASTM so that the ASTM standard is in full compliance with the AAI regulation and the AAI regulation makes reference to the ASTM standard.

A **transaction screen** is a minimal assessment, typically consisting of interviews with site owners and occupants, a site visit, and a limited review of governmental and historical records to identify uses of the property and of neighboring properties. Past uses are often the biggest indicator of possible contamination. History of use as a gasoline station, a plant for the manufacture of insecticide, or paint factory should sound a warning bell! A transaction screen is not always conducted by environmental professionals; the buyer or the buyer's legal counsel may do the work. A transaction screen would be inadequate inquiry for many transactions, but its low cost may make it attractive in low risk situations. For example, a lender making a small loan to finance the purchase of a fairly valuable property may be willing to rely on a transaction screen because, in the worst case scenario, the lender could abandon the property and take a loss on the loan rather than foreclose and take ownership of the contaminated property.

When a professional environmental assessment is desired, the consulting firm chosen to conduct the investigation and prepare the report should be chosen with care. The consulting firm and the report must be credible in court if contamination is discovered after the client assumes ownership. The EPA's AAI regulations address qualifications, as do many state regulations.

EPA definition of environmental professional includes individuals who:

- Hold a current Professional Engineer's or Professional Geologist's license or registration from a state, tribe, or U.S. territory and have the equivalent of three (3) years of full-time relevant experience; or
- Be licensed or certified by the federal government, a state, tribe, or U.S. territory to perform environmental inquiries as defined in Sec. 312.21 and have the equivalent of three (3) years of full-time relevant experience; or
- Have a Baccalaureate or higher degree from an accredited institution of higher education in science or engineering and the equivalent of five (5) years of full-time relevant experience; or
- Have the equivalent of ten (10) years of full-time relevant experience.

The definition of "relevant experience" is "participation in the performance of environmental site assessments that may include environmental analyses, investigations, and remediation which involve the understanding of surface and subsurface environmental conditions and the processes used to evaluate these conditions and for which professional judgment was used to develop opinions regarding conditions indicative of releases or threatened releases . . . to the subject property."
From http://www.epa.gov/EPA-WASTE/2005/November/Day-01/ f21455.htm.

---

[6]A commercial transaction involves property not for one to four units of totally residential use.

Other factors that should be considered in retaining an environmental professional include whether the firm's experience is relevant to the particular property and particular contamination suspected and the firm's insurance coverage.

Assignment 6-1

Determine whether your state has a property transfer act that requires sellers to disclose certain environmental information. While such disclosures do not satisfy AAI standards for the buyer, they may save the buyer the cost of environmental assessment.

A Phase I assessment generally involves a records review, site visit, interviews, and a formal report completed by an environmental professional. Its primary purpose is to determine what will be required for "appropriate inquiry," although it is also useful to the potential buyer in assessing whether the property will be usable for its intended purpose and its value. It does not generally include sampling or testing of samples from the site. If the Phase I assessment identifies potential problems, the parties may want to proceed to Phase II assessment; the Phase I findings should provide guidelines to "map" the Phase II assessment.

EXHIBIT 6-2

TYPICALLY INCLUDED IN PHASE I ENVIRONMENTAL ASSESSMENT

Interviews

Contact past and current owners and occupants and government officials to identify:

- previous environmental assessments
- notices of code violations
- storage tank registrations
- environmental permits
- safety plans in use at the site
- community right-to-know plans
- environmental violation notices

**EXHIBIT 6-2
(continued)**

- geo-studies
- material safety data sheets

Records Review

To identify past uses of the site and of neighboring properties (contamination migrates):

- title/property tax records kept by the county
- operating and/or financial statements
- fire insurance maps, aerial maps, and other historic maps
- city records and street directories
- newspaper archives
- list of past tenants
- historical information at local libraries and historical societies
- records of federal, state, and local environmental agencies (using a FOIA request, if necessary), e.g., EPA list of Superfund sites

Many of these records can be found online.

Site Visit

To observe and record:

- topography and drainage
- wetlands
- surrounding uses
- storage tanks
- visible discharges and discoloration, odors
- utilities
- presence of materials such as asbestos, lead paint, PCBs
- presence of waste disposal

---

3. Phase II/Phase III Assessment

Phase II assessment builds on information developed during a transaction screen and/or Phase I assessment and includes analysis of sub-surface soil and/or groundwater. Because it is focused on concerns identified in earlier assessment, there is no standard approach to a Phase II analysis. While a Phase II assessment can generally confirm or exclude the presence of contamination, it is not intended to identify the exact nature or extent of contamination. Phase II assessments often take longer than expected because the consultants find unexpected conditions that make testing difficult.

The Phase II report may reveal no contamination or, if it confirms the presence of contamination, it may be used to determine whether cleanup is appropriate. If additional information is needed concerning the extent of contamination, a Phase III assessment may be ordered. The nature of a Phase III assessment depends on the particular property and what was discovered in Phase II assessment.

4. Working with Environmental Assessment Reports

In ordering and/or examining an environmental assessment report:

- Be sure that the consultant understands the purpose for which the report is being prepared; different analysis is required, for example, when a change in use is planned.
- If your firm orders a report, you may want to review a draft before the final report is issued.
- Read the report with a critical eye, especially if it was prepared at a "bargain price."
- Note the date of the report; under ASTM standards a Phase I report is good for only 180 days after completion.
- Note the consultant's statement about standards employed in preparing the report, particularly in states that have unique standards for "innocent purchaser" status under state law.
- Pay particular attention to any **exculpatory** or limiting language with which the consultant attempts to limit its own liability.
- Note any statement about who is entitled to rely on the report.
- Identify information gaps. Does the report detail review of records, interviews, and a site visit?
  - Who was interviewed? For example, if employees were interviewed, how long have they worked at the site? Are better sources of information available?
  - How detailed is the summary of site inspection? Does it include comments about the geology, the presence of storage tanks, septic systems, etc.? Is there any discussion of surrounding properties?
  - Did review of records go back to the earliest developed use of the property? If not, why not? Were records on surrounding properties checked?
  - Are copies of relevant documents attached to the report?

Exculpatory
A clause that absolves a party from responsibility for damages

A report in compliance with ASTM standards may discuss "activity and use limitations" that affect the property. Those limitations identify physical or legal restrictions on use or access to reduce potential exposure to contamination or prevent interference with effective cleanup. The limitations may be **engineering controls** concerning physical modifications, such as paving over a contaminated site, or they

Engineering Controls
Physical modification of property

Institutional Controls
Limits on use of property

Indemnification
Promise to reimburse for costs/losses

Hold Harmless
See indemnification

Occurrence Policy
Insurance looks at date of event causing liability to determine coverage

Claims-Made Policy
Insurance looks at date of injury to determine coverage

may be **institutional controls**, limiting use or access to the site, such as a recorded covenant[7] prohibiting use of groundwater at the site.

Can the parties avoid the consequences of the reported results by contractual means? Perhaps. The parties may provide for **indemnification** in their contract; one party (typically the seller) agrees to reimburse the other (also called "**hold harmless**") for specified liabilities. The value of such a provision, of course, depends on the financial stability of the party making the promise. Parties outside the contract are not bound by such a provision. For example, if seller agrees to indemnify buyer, and contamination is later discovered, buyer is not protected from liability, but only has the right to sue seller to recover losses. The fact that seller is not financially able to compensate buyer does not protect buyer from liability.

Environmental insurance is now available, usually to cover cost of remediation above a specified "cap," or to protect against tort claims by outside parties. If the parties rely on insurance, in addition to the stability of the insurer and policy limits, they should consider whether they are getting an **occurrence policy**, under which the date of the conduct giving rise to the claim determines whether the loss was within the policy period, or a **claims-made policy**, under which the date of injury or damage determines whether a claim is within the period covered by a policy.

Practice Tips

Site assessment standards do not call for evaluation of matters outside CERCLA. For example, a site assessment will not address radon, mold, lead paint, asbestos, health, or building code issues.

Clients may resist environmental assessment by outside consultants, not only because of the cost and fear of what may be disclosed, but also because they may not wish to have plans to buy/sell property made public.

A seller may want to order and pay for environmental assessment in order to retain control over the report. If your firm represents the buyer, make sure that the report indicates that it is for the benefit of the buyer as well as the seller and is sufficiently detailed to establish due diligence.

C. Environmental Compliance Programs

Aside from any duty to disclose to potential buyers, property owners and the operators of businesses have obligations to report contamination to state and federal authorities under a variety of laws. Many businesses have voluntary environmental compliance programs or environmental management systems in order

---

[7]A covenant is recorded against the title to real estate and includes promises concerning the use of land.

to ensure the accuracy of those and other public reports. Such programs can also help meet the obligations of boards of directors to ensure that companies comply with the law, minimize the liability of management and employees, minimize penalties for noncompliance, enhance image with the public and investors, and avoid the possibility of whistle-blowers. While some companies have taken a "see no evil" approach in the past, many states now have statutory environmental audit privileges that provide protection from prosecution for environmental violations discovered during a voluntary audit, if the company acts promptly to address the problem. Such a state law may not provide immunity from federal prosecution and penalties.

Definitions

Audit Privilege makes voluntary internal corporate environmental **audits** privileged or secret.

    Immunity makes a corporation immune from criminal and civil penalties for self-disclosed violations of environmental regulations.

Audit
Procedure to determine environmental compliance

Immunity
Protection from prosecution

Assignment 6-2

Do your state statutes establish a privilege or immunity for voluntary environmental audits?

    Some people believe granting audit privilege might actually discourage corporations from remediating contamination by allowing them to hide their failures from regulatory and public scrutiny, gaining an unfair competitive advantage over corporations that comply with environmental laws.

    The EPA policy encourages environmental audits and first issued an audit policy in 1986. The policy specifically: (1) encourages regulated entities to develop, implement and upgrade environmental auditing programs; (2) discusses when the EPA may or may not request audit reports; (3) explains how EPA enforcement activities may respond to business efforts to assure compliance through auditing; (4) endorses environmental auditing at federal facilities; (5) encourages state and local environmental auditing initiatives; and (6) outlines elements of effective auditing programs. The EPA does not routinely request environmental audit reports, but may do so during investigations and private parties may seek disclosure in citizens' suits and other litigation. The policy does not provide that the EPA will forgo inspections, reduce enforcement responses, or offer other incentives in exchange for implementation of environmental auditing. The 1986 Policy remains in effect, but there have been later developments.

A 1991 EPA "Policy on the Use of Supplemental Environmental Projects in EPA Settlements" indicates that certain types of environmental auditing projects can reduce the amount of a civil penalty in settlement with the agency, if the business agrees to provide the EPA with a copy of the audit report. Usually, the company must also agree that it will correct the problems. In addition, the EPA's 1992 "Procedures to Implement the Guidelines of the U.S. Sentencing Commission for Organization Defendants" addresses the use of environmental auditing in sentencing; auditing can be imposed as a condition of probation. The Sentencing Guidelines contain provisions for the imposition of measures that can be characterized as auditing and a sentencing court can consider the existence of an effective environmental auditing program in imposing a sentence.

In 1995 the EPA revised its audit policy to "enhance the protection of human health and the environment" and encourage greater compliance with environmental laws and regulations. Incentives are available to those who voluntarily discover violations, promptly disclose violations in writing, and timely correct those violations as part of systematic, objective and periodic environmental auditing. Some penalties are reduced for qualifying disclosures and corrections; the EPA will not recommend criminal prosecution and will refrain from routine requests for audits if conditions of the 1995 policy are met. In 1995 the EPA established the Audit Policy Quick Response Team to ensure consistent application of the self-policing policy across the country. In 1997, the EPA established a separate Voluntary Disclosure Board to review possible criminal violations that are disclosed under the policy.

D. Environmental Inspections

Businesses subject to environmental regulation are also subject to inspections and should have checklists of steps to take in the event of an inspection. That checklist should include a call to legal counsel in addition to calls to senior officials in the company.

While some inspections are unannounced, in most cases the company will be notified in advance. Upon receiving notice of the pending inspection, an individual within the regulated company should obtain information about dates and times of inspection; the members of the inspection team; whether other agencies will be involved; and whether the business is expected to accommodate the inspectors with office space and equipment or with respect to personal needs. With that information, a memo can be sent to appropriate employees, indicating how they should prepare. The memo should remind employees to answer inspectors' questions honestly, but briefly, limiting their answers to their knowledge of the specific topic under discussion.

The memo should also detail the itinerary for the inspection. The schedule will typically include an opening meeting between the inspectors and company officials, breaks for meals, office time (during which inspectors can work on their notes, etc.), a daily de-briefing of escorts, and a closing meeting at the end of the inspection. If the daily de-briefing is thorough, the company may be able to address some of the inspectors' concerns in the closing meeting. A company employee should reserve rooms and order supplies in advance.

If the inspectors have indicated in advance that they will want to review specific records, those records should be retrieved and made accessible for inspection. Employees should make sure that any other relevant log books, equipment maintenance records, and environmental reports are up-to-date and accessible. The company may also want to prepare handouts for its own employees and the inspectors, including the itinerary for the inspection, information about the individuals with whom the inspectors will be interacting, an overview of the company's environmental program, and other relevant information.

The company should appoint knowledgeable escorts for inspectors, who will accompany the inspectors and provide necessities such as hardhats, a facilities map, cameras, badges, and other equipment. Each escort should:

- Plan a route, make sure that he has access to all areas, and identify key personnel in each area;
- Ensure that a qualified operator will be available to demonstrate any equipment or systems;
- Take thorough notes and take pictures of anything that the inspectors photograph;
- Prepare a summary at the end of each day for the benefit of company officials and attorneys;
- Never leave the inspectors unattended;
- Answer any questions honestly, but briefly;
- Attempt to arrange for immediate correction of any violations noted during the inspection; and
- Offer and attempt to find the answer to any question the escort is unable to answer.

E. In the Field

1. Professional Profile

Connie S. Kubajak has recently joined the Naperville, Illinois firm of Dommermuth, Brestal, Cobine & West, Ltd. She has a Bachelor of Science degree in Mechanical Engineering from the University of Illinois, a Master of Business Administration degree from Roosevelt University, and a Paralegal Certificate from Elgin Community College. After working 20 years in the manufacturing

industry, she decided to pursue a second career in law. She has worked as a paralegal for 5 years.

"People sometimes think of environmental law as an area you don't need to study unless you plan to go into that specific arena. I disagree. My first position in the legal field was with a small general practice firm, where I found myself doing 'due diligence' for real estate transactions. It's all connected."

Although Connie has been employed at general practice law firms, her duties have been focused primarily on land use and real estate related transactions and litigation, all of which often require the research, interpretation, and application of environmental laws. She reviews commercial real estate contracts and financing agreements with respect to sellers' warranties and representations as well as provisions regarding due diligence and environmental testing and documentation requirements for both parties.

"Every so often a case presents itself in which the purchaser or seller was not so diligent in determining the condition of the property prior to sale. In these cases, litigation arises and affords an opportunity to examine the applicable environmental laws," according to Ms. Kubajak. Connie had an opportunity to research and apply the "innocent landowner" provisions of Illinois law while assisting in the defense of clients named as third-party defendants in an action involving the sale of vacant land that turned out to be significantly contaminated.

Connie finds the investigation of the historical uses of properties through such research tools as ASTM Standard Records, aerial photographs, and the EPA event database particularly interesting. Since, as the old saying goes, land is a commodity that "they aren't making any more of," it is fascinating to see how the uses of a particular parcel have changed over the course of many years.

2. Whistleblowers

An environmental whistleblower is an employee who reports concerns about violations of environmental laws. These employees frequently face retaliation by employers. Do they have any protection? Yes, according to the website of the U.S. Occupational Safety and Health Administration, www.osha.gov:

What environmental laws with whistleblower protections does OSHA enforce?

OSHA administers the whistleblower provisions of the following environmental laws.

Note that complaints must be reported to OSHA within 30 days of the alleged retaliation.

- Asbestos Hazard Emergency Response Act
- Clear Air Act
- Comprehensive Environmental Response, Compensation and Liability Act
- Federal Water Pollution Control Act
- Safe Drinking Water Act
- Solid Waste Disposal Act
- Toxic Substances Control Act

Other laws exist to protect workers against retaliation for reporting safety and health concerns, including concerns about asbestos in schools. Information on the whistleblower provisions of other laws enforced by OSHA can be obtained as described below.

What actions of retaliation do the whistleblower provisions prohibit?

Employer retaliation against employees who exercise their legal rights under these employee protection statutes is prohibited. Such discrimination may include the following actions:

- Blacklisting
- Demotion
- Discharge
- Disciplinary actions (such as assigning to undesirable shifts, denying overtime or promotion, disallowing benefits, or reducing pay or hours)
- Failure to hire or rehire
- Harassment
- Suspension

Governmental employees do not necessarily have the same protections, according to Public Employees for Environmental Responsibility, www.peer.org.

In addition, Congress included certain whistleblower protections in the Sarbanes-Oxley corporate governance reform legislation in 2002.

Sarbanes-Oxley

SEC. 1107. RETALIATION AGAINST INFORMANTS.
    (a) IN GENERAL — Section 1513 of title 18, United States Code, is amended by adding at the end the following:
    (e) Whoever knowingly, with the intent to retaliate, takes any action harmful to any person, including interference with the lawful employment or livelihood of any person, for providing to a law enforcement officer any truthful information relating to the commission or possible commission of any Federal offense, shall be fined under this title or imprisoned not more than 10 years, or both.

Assignment 6-3

Read the case abstract at the end of the chapter, keeping in mind that the court is not deciding whether the builder or previous owners might be liable to the homeowners. The only issue is whether the environmental consultants might be liable to the builder. The environmental consultants were not hired or paid by the builder and, in fact, were likely not aware of the builder's plans. The court is nonetheless allowing the builder's claim to go forward. We don't know whether the builder will obtain an award against PBS&J, but PBS&J will have to continue to fight the claim. Do you think this is right?

What factors are most relevant?

Key Terms

AAI	Fiduciary
ASTM	Hold Harmless
Audit	Immunity
Bona Fide Prospective Purchaser	Indemnification
Brownfields Program	Innocent Landowner
CERCLA	Institutional Controls
Claims-Made Policy	Occurrence Policy
Comfort Letter	Phase I
Commercial	Phase II/III
Contiguous Property Owner	Privilege
Contingency	PRP
Due Diligence	Strict Liability
Engineering Controls	Transaction Screen

Review Questions

1. What is the EPA position with respect to voluntary environmental audits?
2. What are the characteristics of a transaction screen, a Phase I assessment, and a Phase II assessment?
3. Identify the PRPs who may be held liable under CERCLA; what is meant by joint and several liability with respect to those parties and what is meant by retroactive liability?
4. What is a comfort letter?
5. Identify groups with possible defenses to liability under CERCLA.
6. How can a lender protect itself from liability if it secures a loan by a mortgage on contaminated property?
7. How is "innocent landowner" status established?
8. How can a company prepare for an environmental inspection?
9. How can a prospective buyer protect himself at the contract stage?
10. What is the difference between engineering controls and institutional controls?
11. Identify records that should be searched and people who should be interviewed as part of due diligence. What should be checked at a site visit?
12. What is a whistleblower and what protection is available?

KEY TERMS CROSSWORD

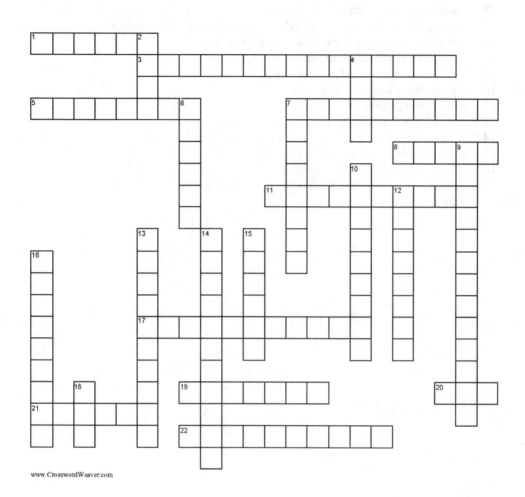

www.CrosswordWeaver.com

ACROSS

1. _____ made insurance policy
3. agreement to reimburse other party
5. hold _____, to indemnify
7. owners of _____ property have been granted some protection from liability
8. some states protect a voluntary environmental _____ from disclosure
11. conducted during assessment
17. _____ controls include paving over contamination
19. reviewed during assessment
20. initials, EPA standard for environmental assessment
21. initials, law that creates owner liability
22. type of insurance, looks at date of conduct giving rise to liability

DOWN

2. should be visited during assessment
4. initials, historically set standards for environmental assessment
6. transaction _____, lowest level of investigation
7. a restriction recorded against title to property
9. _____ controls, include limiting use
10. a protection against disclosure
12. protection against prosecution
13. ASTM standards apply to _____ transactions
14. a contract clause that may give a party an "out"
15. environmental assessment is typically conducted in _____
16. due _____ is required to avoid liability for contamination
18. initials, current owner may be a _____ even if not at fault for contamination

BONNIEVIEW HOMEOWNERS ASSOCIATION, LLC, et al., Plaintiff v. WOODMONT BUILDERS, LLC, et al., Defendants

U.S. District Court for the District of New Jersey,
Unpublished, 2006 U.S. Dist. LEXIS 47414
July 11, 2006, Decided

Plaintiffs, Bonnieview Homeowners Assoc., LLC, 15 homeowners in Montville Township, New Jersey, learned that their properties were contaminated by substances left over from pesticides used many years earlier when the properties formed one parcel operated as an apple orchard. Plaintiffs seek damages because the contamination was not discovered and/or disclosed to them prior to purchasing the property.

Plaintiffs filed suit against Woodmont Builders and previous owners of the lots, ("Builders"), the real estate brokerage that arranged sale of the property, (Montville Township), and environmental consulting firms that assessed the land, PBS&J, Princeton Hydro, LLC, and Maser. In previous decisions, the Court dismissed Plaintiffs' claims against the environmental consulting firms for failure to file an Affidavit of Merit in accordance with *N.J.S.A. 2A:53A-26q*. However, the Court declined to dismiss Builders' cross-claims asserting that PBS&J's negligent Phase I environmental assessment was the cause of their failure to inform Plaintiffs of the contamination. Princeton Hydro also filed a cross-claim against PBS&J. Presently before the Court is PBS&J's motion for summary judgment dismissing those cross-claims. The motion will be denied as to Builders and granted as to Princeton Hydro's cross-claim.

Plaintiffs live on land that, until its subdivision, was part of the 131-acre Bonnieview Farms, an apple orchard prior to 1970. In 1970, the property was purchased and left undeveloped until the mid-1990's, when the buyers contracted with Woodmont Builders to subdivide the land for residential development; Woodmont would obtain governmental approvals and build and sell the houses. Before August 1997, Woodmont submitted a plan and preliminary subdivision application to build 47 one-family residences. However, the Township planned to acquire the tract and preserve it as open space for recreational use. The Township applied to the Morris County Open Space and Farmland Preservation Trust Fund for assistance, noting that the site had formerly been an "Orchard Farm" and contained "Large Apple, Oaks and Maple trees." The County approved a grant of $500,000 toward the purchase; the county required Phase I environmental assessments of any property financed through the Trust Fund and entered into a contract for assessment of the tract.

In April 1998, PBS&J completed Phase I assessment and sent a report to the County, noting that the objectives of a Phase I assessment are "to determine if current or past land use practices have adversely impacted the site, to identify any other potential environmental concerns, and to determine if additional field investigations are warranted." PBS&J noted "[t]his report was prepared to satisfy the requirements of most lending institutions for a 'Phase I Environmental Audit'" and was "based on the guidelines established by the American Society of Testing and Materials, the Federal National Mortgage Association ('Fannie Mae'), the Federal Home Loan Board, and the New Jersey Department of Environmental Protection's Technical Requirements for Site Remediation (N.J.A.C. 7:26E)." PBS&J

stated that no sampling is conducted at the Phase I level and listed limitations of a Phase I study: 1. No attempt was made to verify compliance of current or former landowners with Federal, State or local environmental regulations. 2. A review of Federal and State database information was conducted on material provided in Appendix B. . . . accurate evaluation of all potential environmental concerns cannot be made without more comprehensive investigation which may require soil and/or water analyses. This environmental assessment should not be regarded as assurance that environmental concerns beyond those which could be determined within the scope of work of this investigation are not present at or near the site. This report is for exclusive use of the County, as it applies to an evaluation of the property. It has been prepared in accordance with generally accepted practices in environmental assessments. . . .

Its report recognized that the site "was forested (orchards) naturally occurring" and noted that there was evidence of a former "tree nursery." The assessment designated three areas of concern: (1) an area containing aboveground storage tanks and drums of varying sizes; (2) an area containing debris (abandoned autos, tires, and construction debris); and (3) concrete foundations appearing to have underground storage tanks. While none of the observed debris was considered hazardous, additional material in lower layers could be classified as such. No sampling is recommended for this area at this time; however, when the debris is removed, lower layers should be carefully examined. PBS&J recommended use of ground penetrating radar to determine presence of underground storage tanks. PBS&J did not discover the preexisting environmental contamination caused by the use of pesticides in the orchard many years earlier.

The Planning Board denied the subdivision application, presumably because it intended to acquire and preserve the land as open space. Woodmont filed suit, contesting the denial. In 1998 the Township agreed to permit Woodmont to subdivide 30 acres and build 25 residential lots. Woodmont agreed to sell 100 acres to the Township for open space and to remove debris discovered during Phase I assessment. Woodmont represented that it did not have "any knowledge as to the presence of any kind of hazardous substance or the like." Township forwarded a copy of PBS&J's Phase I assessment to Woodmont, which forwarded to First Union Bank in an attempt to obtain financing. Woodmont did not obtain PBS&J's permission to use the report in this manner and ended up financing with Valley Bank, which did not require a Phase I report.

Township hired Princeton Hydro to inspect to ensure that the debris had been cleaned up on land intended to be used as open space. Princeton Hydro represented that the property had been cleared. Later, the Township was notified by a resident who had been walking in the open space that debris noted in PBS&J's report remained. The Township Engineer recommended subsurface soil testing at each area of concentrated debris. Township hired Maser to perform testing in summer 2000. Maser did not complete its testing on the 100 acres until 2002 and reported unsafe levels of lead, arsenic, DDT, and other contaminants in the soil, associated with orchard use. Maser advised that "[b]ased on the historical aerials, MC believes the 25-lot residential subdivision under construction may also have been part of the same orchard and may contain constituents elevated above the [Residential Direct Contact Soil Cleanup Criteria]. . . . Township Board of Health involvement may be warranted to advise the public. In 2003, Township informed Plaintiffs that it was suing the Defendants for failing to clean up, that soil testing on their property was complete, and that the residential lots contained levels of contaminants exceeding NJDEP limits.

In September, 2003, Plaintiffs filed the Complaint in this case. PBS&J has moved for summary judgment dismissing Builder's cross-claims, arguing that it owed no duty to Builders and that dismissal of the cross-claims would not prejudice the remaining co-defendants in their ability to obtain the benefit of the New Jersey Comparative Negligence Act.

The question of whether a duty exists in a particular case is a question of fairness and policy that implicates many factors. Among these factors, the foreseeability of injury to others from defendant's conduct is the most important. The "foreseeability" factor does not, by itself establish the existence of a duty, but it is a crucial element. The court must identify, weigh, and balance several factors which include: the relationship of the parties, the nature of the attendant risk, the opportunity and ability to exercise care, and the public interest in the proposed solution. While there is a connection between the concept of foreseeability and other factors, foreseeability of harm is susceptible to an objective analysis, while the resolution of fairness and policy is a much less certain determination. The magnitude and likelihood of potential harm are objectively determinable, but the propriety of imposing a duty of care is not.

It is well settled that although an environmental consultant must conform to a standard of care possessed by members of the profession in good standing, it only owes a duty to those persons who fall normally and generally within a zone of risk created by the tortious conduct and is therefore foreseeable. This does not require a specific forecasting of particularly identifiable victims. That a plaintiff may be found within a range of harm emanating from tortfeasor's activities is more significant than whether the parties stand in a direct contractual relationship. Lack of privity is no bar to recovery. In the instant case, PBS&J's duty then turns on whether or not it was foreseeable that the Phase I assessment would be transferred to, and relied upon by the owner of the property in giving assurances to buyers.

The Builders argue that PBS&J's duty of care extended to all parties who had a proprietary interest in the Property (the Township and Builders) because it was foreseeable that those parties would rely on the Phase I Assessment; that the scope of work required PBS&J to identify "recognized environmental conditions" at Bonnieview Farms, so PBS&J's duty extended to all parties with a proprietary interest in the property. The extension of PBS&J's duty then turns on whether or not it was foreseeable that the Phase I assessment would be transferred to, and relied upon by the owner of the property in giving assurances to buyers.

The duty to foresee . . . should be commensurate with the degree of responsibility which the engineer has agreed to undertake. *224 N.J. Super. at 694.* The Court must consider the original purpose of the Phase I assessment in deciding whether PBS&J's duty extended beyond the County. The purpose of the Phase I assessment was to "determine if current or past land use practices have adversely impacted the site, to identify any other potential environmental concerns, and to determine if additional field investigations are warranted." PBS&J performed the assessment for the County to ensure that the land, the purchase of which was financed in part by the County, was free from contamination, and to advise if further testing would be necessary. The purpose behind the County's Phase I requirement was to prevent the expenditure of public funds on contaminated property. Open space acquisition and preservation exists in the County to "assure

Morris County's longstanding tradition of maintaining a high quality of life through the acquisition of open space, recreational lands, and areas of environmental significance." Upon taking on the responsibility to perform the assessment, PBS&J representatives knew that the Phase I was being performed as a precursor to the sale of the property. PBS&J was properly on notice that the property in question would be sold once its assessment was completed, and that the assessment was to be used in conjunction with the sale. PBS&J agreed to undertake the responsibility "to determine if current or past land use practices have adversely impacted the site."

PBS&J argues that the duty it undertook when it performed Assessment for the County did not extend to a commercial developer not in contemplation of PBS&J when it undertook the work. The report itself states that "[t]his report is for the exclusive use of the County of Morris . . . as it applies to an evaluation of [specific lots]" and that it was "based on the guidelines established by the American Society of Testing and Materials . . . and the New Jersey Department of Environmental Protection's Technical Requirements for Site Remediation (N.J.A.C. §7:26E)." N.J.A.C. §7:26E includes guidelines for Phase I environmental assessment consistent with the ASTM E1527.

ASTM E1527-97 states: 4.5.4 Comparison With Subsequent Inquiry — It should not be concluded or assumed that an inquiry was not appropriate inquiry merely because the inquiry did not identify recognized environmental conditions in connection with a property. Environmental Site Assessments must be evaluated based on the reasonableness of judgments made at the time and under the circumstances in which they were made. Subsequent environmental site assessments should not be considered valid standards to judge the appropriateness of any prior assessment based on hindsight, new information, use of developing technology or analytical techniques, or other factors.

PBS&J has pointed to evidence that NJDEP set up an Historic Pesticide Contamination Task Force in 1997. Its final report relating to "findings and recommendations for the remediation of historic pesticide contamination" was issued in March 1999, after issuance of PBS&J's Phase I Report. PBS&J also pointed to evidence that in 1998 "[h]istoric pesticides just wasn't a typical issue that was being identified," and "[a]t that time, it wasn't generally looked at as an area of concern, and even when those rules were promulgated . . . there was no mechanism to make someone sample farm fields, or orchards . . . and there still isn't." Further, a Phase I Assessment has a limited life span. As stated in P 46 of ASTM E1527-97: 4.6 Continued Viability of Environmental Site Assessment — An environmental site assessment meeting or exceeding either Practice E1528 or this practice and completed less than 180 days previously is presumed to be valid. An environmental site assessment meeting or exceeding either practice and completed more than 180 days previously may be used to the extent allowed by 4.7 through 4.7.5.

Builders have no evidence to establish that they undertook any of these steps before relying upon the 1998 Assessment when they purchased and developed the property. The 180 day period of presumed validity of PBS&J's Report elapsed as of October 1998. Woodmont sent a copy of that Report to First Union on March 25, 1999. Woodmont closed on the 30-acre parcel and obtained its construction financing in late June 2000. PBS&J has substantial evidence that it was not negligent and that either the Builders did not rely on the Phase I Report, or if they did rely on the Report, their reliance was not reasonable. Negligence, reliance and the reasonableness of any reliance raise issues of fact and cannot be decided on a motion for summary judgment. The Court is not prepared, with the complex state of the record, to hold that PBS&J owed no duty of care to Builders. The 180-day limitation on the reliability existed primarily to guard against new contamination that might affect a property after an assessment. See ASTM E1527-97, 4.6 through 4.72. Due to its historical use as an orchard, Bonnieview Farms was contaminated long before its assessment. Further, although PBS&J believed that Bonnieview Farms was going to be preserved as open space and not converted into a residential development, it was not unreasonable to anticipate that at least some of the property would be devoted to residential use.

PART II

◆ ◆ ◆

THE STATUTES

◆ ◆ ◆

7

National Environmental Policy Act (NEPA)

A. Overview

NEPA, 42 U.S.C. §4321 et seq., was enacted to serve as a national "charter" for environmental planning; its focus is on planning, not on specific results. NEPA is procedural, not substantive, in nature. It includes no scientific standards. To promote a national policy of preventing damage to the environment, NEPA establishes a process that must be followed by federal agencies in making decisions that have the potential to have a significant impact on the environment. The process requires that the agency:

1. Identify and analyze environmental consequences of proposed action in detail comparable to economic and operational analysis;
2. Identify and assess reasonable alternatives to the proposed action;
3. Document environmental analysis and findings; and
4. Make environmental information available to public officials and citizens before the agency makes a decision.

CEQ
Council of Environmental Quality — Responsible for overseeing NEPA and establishing regulations

NEPA establishes the **Council on Environmental Quality (CEQ)**, responsible for oversight of the NEPA process and for reporting to the President and Congress on the status of the environment. CEQ promulgates regulations for implementation of NEPA, which can be found at 40 C.F.R. 100-1508 (www.nepa.gov/nepa/regs/ceq/toc_ceq.htm).

1. Agencies' Actions that May Trigger Review

An action may trigger NEPA if it involves federal funding or the decision of a federal agency to issue a permit or a license, even if the project is primarily undertaken by private interests. What about actions of the EPA itself? Some EPA actions are considered exempt from the requirements of NEPA because it is assumed that the EPA takes environmental consequences into account in all of its decision making. The EPA is, however, required to comply with NEPA procedures in conducting its research and development activities, facilities construction, wastewater treatment construction grants under Title II of the Clean Water Act (CWA), EPA-issued National Pollutant Discharge Elimination System (NPDES) permits for new sources, and for certain projects funded through EPA annual Appropriations Acts.[1] The CWA and NPDES systems are discussed in later chapters.

Sometimes whether NEPA compliance is required depends on who "makes" the decision, as demonstrated by the 2004 Supreme Court decision in *Department of Transportation v. Public Citizen*.[2] After the North American Free Trade Agreement (NAFTA — discussed in Chapter 5) became law, the President stated he would lift a ban on Mexican trucks operating in the United States following preparation of new regulations. The Federal Motor Carrier Safety Administration (FMCSA) proposed new regulations to govern Mexican trucks. It determined that the likely effects of the regulations — primarily arising from increased roadside inspections of Mexican trucks — were minor, and, pursuant to NEPA, issued a finding of no significant impact (FONSI), determining that no environmental impact statement (EIS) was required. Environmental groups challenged the FONSI, contending FMCSA should have considered the environmental impact of increased cross-border traffic from Mexican trucks. The U.S. Supreme

---

[1] http://www.epa.gov/compliance/nepa/epacompliance/index.html.
[2] 541 U.S. 752.

Court held that an increase in cross-border operation of Mexican trucks, with a correlating increase in emissions, is not a legal "effect" of the agency's rulemaking, so the agency action did not violate NEPA. The Court reasoned that FMCSA had no authority to consider environmental impacts; its statutory mandate requires it to issue operating permits for any carrier that meets its safety and financial responsibility requirements. It has no power to authorize or prevent cross-border operations. Because only the President possesses this power, the agency had no discretion to prevent entry of Mexican trucks. Under NEPA regulations, the agency properly determined it was required only to consider whether inspection-related emissions would occur from roadside inspections, as an EIS considering the purported effects of the regulations would serve no purpose under NEPA.

Example

Agency Actions Requiring NEPA Review Fit Into Four General Categories

Type of Action	Example
Federal funding	Construction of a highway with federal funding
Issuance of federal permit	Issuance of a CWA (Clean Water Act) permit to allow filling of wetlands for construction of a road
Actions involving federal land, facilities, or equipment	Oil and gas exploration on national park land
Federal agency rulemaking	FEMA (Federal Emergency Management Agency) makes major changes to its flood insurance program

NEPA requires agencies to analyze reasonably foreseeable international effects of actions proposed to occur within in the United States.[3] NEPA can apply to actions that take place outside the United States. For example, NEPA applied to actions undertaken by the National Science Foundation in the Antarctica.[4]

---

2. State and Local Laws

Only environmentally significant federal projects invoke NEPA. Private, state government, and local government actions are not covered. Many states have, however, enacted their own versions of NEPA to cover state and local projects. For example, California has the California Environmental Quality Act (CEQA), summarized on the web page reproduced as Exhibit 7-1.

---

[3] http://www.nepa.gov/nepa/regs/transguide.html.
[4] *Environmental Defense Fund v. Massey*, 986 F.2d 528 (D.C. Cir. 1993).

Assignment 7-1

Determine whether your state has a statute requiring environmental review of projects involving state or local government.

EXHIBIT 7-1

From www.ceres.ca.gov/topic/env_law/ceqa/summary.html.

THE CALIFORNIA ENVIRONMENTAL QUALITY ACT

- The basic goal of the California Environmental Quality Act (CEQA) (Pub. Res. Code §21000 *et seq.*) is to develop and maintain a high-quality environment now and in the future, while the specific goals of CEQA are for California's public agencies to:
  1) identify the significant environmental effects of their actions; and,
  2) avoid those significant environmental effects, where feasible; or
  3) mitigate those significant environmental effects, where feasible.
- CEQA applies to "projects" proposed to be undertaken or requiring approval by State and local government agencies.

  "Projects" are activities which have the potential to have a physical impact on the environment and may include the enactment of zoning ordinances, the issuance of conditional use permits and the approval of tentative subdivision maps.

- Where a project requires approvals from more than one public agency, CEQA requires ones of these public agencies to serve as the "lead agency."
  A "lead agency" must complete the environmental review process required by CEQA. The most basic steps of the environmental review process are:
  1) Determine if the activity is a "project" subject to CEQA;
  2) Determine if the "project" is exempt from CEQA;
  3) Perform an Initial Study to identify the environmental impacts of the project and determine whether the identified impacts are "significant".

B. The Process

Federal agencies must integrate NEPA into their planning at the earliest possible stage by identifying the purpose and need for a proposed project, possible alternatives, and environmental impacts. After the agency makes those initial determinations, it must classify the project.

1. Classifications

The regulations require that agencies categorize proposed actions according to the level of environmental analysis required. The categories are: **categorical exclusion (CE)**, applied to actions that do not normally have potential for significant impact and that do not require detailed environmental assessment; **environmental assessment (EA)**, applied when the proposed action does not fit an existing CE or if its potential for environmental impact is unknown; and **environmental impact statement (EIS)**, for proposed actions that will have a significant impact.

As shown in Exhibit 7-2, categorical exclusions may be established by statute or by agency rule. If a project fits within a categorical exclusion, the agency may have to prepare a form to document the classification, but typically goes no further in analyzing environmental impacts.

The agency will prepare an EA if:

1. The project's potential for significant environmental impacts is unknown.
2. A categorical exclusion applies, but unusual circumstances exist. For example, an oil exploration activity involving less than five acres, described as a categorical exemption on Exhibit 7-2, might encroach on significant archaeological sites.
3. A categorical exclusion does not apply, but the agency does not believe that the project will have significant environmental impacts.

If the project will have a significant impact, the agency will begin the EIS process without considering a CE or and EA.

2. Environmental Assessment

An EA is a concise public document that serves to provide sufficient evidence and analysis for determining whether to prepare an EIS or a **Finding of No Significant Impact (FONSI)**. The EA must include brief discussions of the need for the proposed action, alternatives, the environmental impacts of the proposed action and its alternatives, and a list of agencies and persons consulted. The EA must focus on environmental issues and be concise, objective, and well balanced so that the public can understand the basis for the agency's decision to prepare an EIS or a FONSI. If potentially adverse environmental impacts are identified for an action or group of related actions, the EA must discuss any reasonable alternative courses of action that offer less environmental risk or

---

CE
Categorical exclusion—Applied to actions that do not normally have potential for significant impact and that do not require detailed environmental assessment

EA
Environmental Assessment—Applied when the proposed action does not fit an existing CE or if its potential for environmental impact is unknown

EIS
Environmental Impact Statement, for proposed actions that will have a significant impact on the environment

FONSI
In an EA, a Finding Of No Significant Impact

EXHIBIT 7-2
Categorical Exclusions

FROM THE ENERGY POLICY ACT OF 2005.

Sec. 390. Nepa Review.

(a) NEPA REVIEW. — Action by the Secretary of the Interior in managing the public lands, or the Secretary of Agriculture in managing National Forest System Lands, with respect to any of the activities described in subsection (b) shall be subject to a rebuttable presumption that the use of a categorical exclusion under H. R. 6 — 155 the National Environmental Policy Act of 1969 (NEPA) would apply if the activity is conducted pursuant to the Mineral Leasing Act for the purpose of exploration or development of oil or gas.

(b) ACTIVITIES DESCRIBED. — The activities referred to in subsection (a) are the following:

(1) Individual surface disturbances of less than 5 acres so long as the total surface disturbance on the lease is not greater than 150 acres and site-specific analysis in a document prepared pursuant to NEPA has been previously completed.

(2) Drilling an oil or gas well at a location or well pad site at which drilling has occurred previously within 5 years prior to the date of spudding the well.

(3) Drilling an oil or gas well within a developed field for which an approved land use plan or any environmental document prepared pursuant to NEPA analyzed such drilling as a reasonably foreseeable activity, so long as such plan or document was approved within 5 years prior to the date of spudding the well.

(4) Placement of a pipeline in an approved right-of-way corridor, so long as the corridor was approved within 5 years prior to the date of placement of the pipeline.

(5) Maintenance of a minor activity, other than any construction or major renovation or a building or facility.

From the U.S. Forest Service Handbook, www.fs.fed.us/im/directives/fsh/ 1909.15/1909.15_30.doc.

The following categories of routine administrative, maintenance, and other actions normally do not individually or cumulatively have a significant effect on the quality of the human environment (sec. 05) and, therefore, may be categorically excluded from documentation in an EIS or an EA unless scoping indicates extraordinary circumstances (sec. 30.3) exist:

1. Orders issued pursuant to 36 CFR Part 261 — Prohibitions to provide short-term resource protection or to protect public health and safety. Examples include but are not limited to:

   a.   Closing a road to protect bighorn sheep during lambing season.

   b.   Closing an area during a period of extreme fire danger.

that are environmentally preferable to the proposed action. The EA may also discuss possible **mitigation measures** — measures that can be taken to reduce the harm to the environment.

Mitigation Measures
Measures that can be taken to reduce the harm to the environment

If more than one federal agency is involved in a project, a **lead agency** is designated to supervise preparation of the environmental analysis. Federal agencies, together with state, tribal, or local agencies, may act as joint lead agencies. Lead agencies must identify any cooperating agencies that may ultimately be involved in the proposed action, including issuance of any required permits. Once cooperating agencies have been identified they have specific responsibilities under NEPA. A lead agency will sometimes engage an outside contractor to assist in the preparation of an EIS; if it does so, it must avoid possible conflicts of interests.

Lead Agency
Agency responsible for EIS preparation

Assignment 7-2

1. From the Department of Energy website, www.doe.gov, enter in the SEARCH box environmental assessment nepa weapons fonsi
   Click on one of the links and examine an EA that was prepared for a DOE project involving materials that might be used in making weapons of mass destruction.
   Report to your class:

   ◆ An overview of the project
   ◆ Alternatives considered by the department
   ◆ A summary of DOE's analysis of the possibility of accidents or sabotage
   ◆ Who was consulted in preparing the EA

2. Read the case at the end of this chapter and discuss:

   ◆ In what way was the EA inadequate?
   ◆ What is your opinion of the court's decision to defer to the agency on the issue of earthquake safety?
   ◆ What was the problem with the FOIA requests?
   ◆ Do you think that a facility like this is a good idea for a highly populated, earthquake-prone area? Do you think that the court thinks it is a good idea? If not, why doesn't the court "just say no" to the plans?

EXHIBIT 7-3
Environmental Assessment Letter and Policy Statement

October 2, 2003

Keith Dohrmann
Conservation and Recreation Division
Iowa Department of Natural Resources
Wallace State Office Building
502 E. 9th
Des Moines, IA 50319-0034

Dear Mr. Dohrmann:

The city of Truesdale, Iowa is an unsewered city. USDA Rural Development is considering funding a new central wastewater collection and treatment system. The treatment site has not been selected and we wish to consider any endangered species in the area when planning the system. We therefore request any information the state has on endangered species within 1-mile of the city so we may consider any impacts this potential project may have on them.

Please submit any comments within 30 days to:

James Carroll
USDA Rural Development
210 Walnut, rm 873
Des Moines, Iowa 50309

Sincerely,

James A. Carroll., P.E.
State Engineer

POLICY

It is the policy of USDA-Rural Development and the Iowa Department of Economic Development not to approve or fund any proposals that, as a result of their identifiable impacts, direct or indirect, would lead to or accommodate the irreconcilable impact on the assessment categories listed in this document. The only exception to this policy is if the approving official determines that there is no practicable alternative to the proposed actions, the proposal conforms to the planning criteria, and the proposal includes all practicable measures for reducing the impact in accordance to the corresponding federal regulation.

Many samples of EAs are available on the Internet, but they are too long to reproduce in this text. The letter and policy statement reproduced above are part of a 96-page EA available at http://www.iowalifechanging.com/community/downloads/sampleEA.pdf. A shorter sample is available at http://www.eqb.state.mn.us/resource.html?Id=17303. To see the sample FONSI prepared for the construction of a visitor education center for Old Faithful at Yellowstone National Park, visit http://www.nps.gov/yell/parkmgmt/upload/ofvecfonsi.pdf.

3. Environmental Impact Statements

If an EIS is required, the responsible agency publishes **notice of intent (NOI)** in the Federal Register, indicating intent to prepare a **draft environmental impact statement (DEIS)** and the date and place of any **scoping meetings**, to permit interested members of the public and other agencies to participate.

NOI
Notice Of Intent — published in Federal Register before preparation of DEIS

DEIS
Draft Environmental Impact Statement

a. Scoping

Scoping is intended to inform and actively involve interested parties; during the process all potentially significant environmental impacts and project alternatives are identified and discussed and insignificant issues are eliminated — the "scope" of the EIS is defined. During scoping all relevant federal, state, and local legislation, executive orders, and agency regulations are identified. Scoping generally involves public hearings, but in some cases the public is invited to submit comments by other means. Scoping may have also been conducted in connection with preparation of an EA.

Scoping
Process of evaluating the purpose, impacts, and alternatives for a project

> Examples of federal laws that may be relevant to a given project include the Fish and Wildlife Coordination Act, the Clean Air Act, the Clean Water Act, the Endangered Species Act, the National Historic Preservation Act, the Wild and Scenic Rivers Act, the Farmland Protection Policy Act, Executive Order 11990 (Protection of Wetlands), and Executive Order 11998 (Floodplain Management).

While permit applicants often feel that projects conceived and developed by private parties should not be questioned or second-guessed by the government, the scoping process must identify reasonable alternatives to such projects. Reasonable alternatives include those that are practical or feasible from the technical and economic standpoint and using common sense rather than simply desirable from the standpoint of the applicant. NEPA does not require examination of purely conjectural possibilities; there is no need to disregard the applicant's purposes and needs and the common sense realities of a given situation in the development of alternatives.

The agency must look at the **cumulative impact** of the project: the impact on the environment that results from the incremental impact of the action when added to other past, present, and reasonably foreseeable future actions regardless of what agency or person undertakes such other actions. Cumulative impact can result from individually minor but collectively significant actions taking place over a period of time.

Cumulative Impacts
Impact of action when considered with other past, present, or future actions

Tiering
Preparing sequential EISs
for different phases of an
action

b. Tiering

Tiering refers to the process of addressing a broad, general program, policy, or proposal in an initial EIS and analyzing a narrower site-specific proposal, related to the initial program, plan, or policy in a subsequent EIS. Tiering can eliminate repetitive discussions and allow focus on the actual issues ripe for decisions at each level of environmental review. While tiering is not required and is not appropriate for all projects, it can be useful in certain situations. For example, assume that a federal agency adopts a formal plan that will eventually be executed throughout a particular region and later proposes a specific activity to implement the plan in specific area. Both actions need to be analyzed under NEPA and both may be subject to the EIS requirement. The agency can either prepare two EISs, with the second repeating much of the analysis and information found in the first, or can tier the two documents. If tiering is employed, the site-specific EIS contains a summary of the issues discussed in the first statement and the agency will incorporate by reference discussions from the first statement. The second, site-specific statement, would focus primarily on the issues relevant to the specific proposal and would not duplicate material found in the first EIS.

Assignment 7-3

1. From the EPA Federal Register page, www.epa.gov/fedrgstr/index.html, find a NOI published within the last six months and report to the class.
2. You are a paralegal working for the State Environmental Protection Agency (SEPA) (make up an address), which is the lead agency for the Little City Wastewater Treatment Works project, proposed by the Little City Redevelopment Association (make up an address). As required by state law, Little City submitted a permit application and an environmental checklist. Little City anticipated a determination that its project would have no significant environmental impact, but SEPA has concluded that the project may have an impact on an archaeological site important to a local tribe. It is possible that the impact could be avoided by changing the location of a parking lot. SEPA has decided to let the applicant resubmit before making a determination concerning significant environmental impacts. Write a letter explaining the situation to Marty Ceithaml, the attorney representing Little City. For some guidance on such letters, you may look at http://www.ecy.wa.gov/programs/sea/sepa/handbk/hbappd.html# earlynotice. Be sure to indicate your title and not give legal advice!

---

c. Contents

During scoping, a statement of "purpose and need" for the project is developed and refined. For example, a highway construction might be intended to alleviate specified traffic problems. Several potential alternatives are developed to satisfy the purpose and need. Criteria and measures are developed, based on project goals, to evaluate and screen those alternatives to a small number of alternatives that best meet the project's purpose and need. This screening process is repetitive and includes technical analysis and review and feedback from the public and local agency representatives. A detailed environmental analysis is conducted for the alternatives that survive the screening process. The detailed impact analysis includes a comprehensive list of environmental resources and transportation facilities. Once impacts are identified, potential mitigation measures are proposed for each alternative to minimize or avoid project impacts. Finally, a DEIS is prepared.

Typical Draft Environmental Impact Statement

- Executive Summary
- Description of Proposed Project or Decision
- Purpose and Need of Proposed Action
- Significant Issues or Sensitive Receptors
  - What will be impacted the most?
  - What are the most important impacts?
- Alternative Development — Are there better ways to meet the Purpose and Need?
- Financial Assessment of Alternatives
- Affected Environment — Existing Conditions
  - *Environmental Data — Surface and Ground Water, Air, Vegetation, Wildlife, Fish, Habitat Quality or Condition*
- Environmental Consequences — Prediction of Environmental Impacts
- Mitigation — What Will Be Done to Reduce or Prevent Impacts?
- Summary of Public and Agency Involvement

The DEIS is distributed to the public and agencies for review and comment over a 45-day period. A public hearing is held during the 45-day comment period.

The **final EIS (FEIS)** incorporates public comments and the agency's response to comments received on the DEIS. The FEIS presents the **Locally Preferred Alternative (LPA)** recommended for the project and commits to mitigation measures and any interagency agreements. The FEIS is made available for a final review to allow the public to provide final comments. Following the FEIS comment period, the agency may issue a **record of decision (ROD)**, which formally approves the LPA. To see a sample EIS visit http://www.mt.blm.gov/ea/ohv/index.html.

FEIS
Final Environmental Impact Statement

LPA
Locally Preferred Alternative; the alternative chosen for pursuing a project subject to NEPA

ROD
Record Of Decision, approves project after EIS

Typical Final Environmental Impact Statement

- Information from DEIS
- Changes Made to DEIS

- Responses to Comments on the DEIS
- Additional Information Supplementing the DEIS

A supplemental EIS may be required if the agency makes substantial changes in the proposed action relevant to environmental concerns, or when there are significant new circumstances or information relevant to environmental concerns bearing on the proposed action and is optional when an agency otherwise determines to supplement an EIS.

d. Role of the EPA

The EPA has a unique role in the NEPA environmental review process because a lead agency developing an EIS is required by the act to consult with any federal agency that has jurisdiction by law or special expertise with respect to any environmental impact involved. The EPA has a broad range of environmental responsibilities and expertise and is, therefore, virtually always involved in this consultation process.

In addition, Section 309 of the Clean Air Act (CAA) requires the EPA to "review and comment in writing on the environmental impact of any matter relating to duties and responsibilities granted pursuant to this chapter or other provisions of the authority of the Administrator contained in any legislation or regulation" proposed by an agency of the federal government as well as any major federal action to which the National Environmental Policy Act applies. This section of the CAA also requires that the Administrator make a finding as to whether the proposed federal action is satisfactory from the standpoint of public health, welfare, and environmental quality. When the Administrator makes a finding that the proposed federal action is unsatisfactory from the standpoint of public health, welfare, or environmental quality, he or she is required to publish this finding and refer the matter to the CEQ. The EPA's findings are published in the Federal Register as shown in Exhibit 7-4.

The EPA may also review other environmental documents, such as EAs. Federal agencies need to formally file all EISs with EPA Headquarters so the EPA can announce its availability in the Federal Register for public comment as shown in Exhibit 7-4. The EPA guidelines for filing an EIS are at http://www.epa.gov/compliance/resources/policies/nepa/fileguide.html.

e. In the Field

i. Who Can Work on an EIS?

If you are not pursuing a degree in chemistry or biology and are not planning to go to law school, you might wonder whether you would ever have any involvement in the environmental review process. The answer is yes. You will find a paralegal and an individual with a degree in education on the list of preparers for the EIS available at www.fakr.noaa.gov/sustainablefisheries/crab/eis/final/Chapter5.pdf.

If you find yourself working in such a position, you will find many resources on the Internet. For example, at www.ecy.wa.gov/PROGRAMS/sea/sepa/

handbk/hbappd.html, the state of Washington has samples of letters that can be used in the environmental review process. To see a sample of an actual EIS, visit www.fws.gov/midwest/planning/craborchard/FinalEIS.html.

EXHIBIT 7-4
EPA: Availability in the Federal Register for Public Comment

FR Home
About the
Site
FR Listserv
FR Search
Contact Us
Selected
Electronic
  Dockets
Regulatory
Agenda
Executive
Orders
Current Laws
  and
Regulations

Environmental Impacts Statements; Notice Of Availability

[Federal Register: February 2, 2007 (Volume 72, Number 22)]
[Notices]   [Page 5049-5050]
From the Federal Register Online via GPO Access [wais.access.gpo.gov]
[DOCID:fr02fe07-60]

ENVIRONMENTAL PROTECTION AGENCY [ER-FRL-6683-6]
Environmental Impacts Statements; Notice Of Availability Responsible Agency: Office of Federal Activities, General Information (202) 564-7167 or http://www.epa.gov/compliance/nepa/.

Weekly receipt of Environmental Impact Statements Filed 01/22/2007 Through 01/26/2007 Pursuant to 40 CFR 1506.9.

EIS No. 20070019, Draft EIS, FHW, TX, Grand Parkway/State Highway 99 Improvement Project, Segment G, from Interstate Highway (IH) 45 to U.S. 59, Funding, Right-of-Way Grant, U.S. Army COE Section 404 Permit, Harris and Montgomery Counties, TX, Comment Period Ends: 04/27/2007, Contact: Donald Davis 512-536-5960.

EIS No. 20070020, Final EIS, AFS, AK, Tuxekan Island Timber Sale(s) Project, Timber Harvesting, Implementation, Coast Guard Bridge Permit, U.S. Army COE Section 10 and 404 Permits, Tongas National Forest, Thorne Bay Ranger District, Thorne Bay, AK, Wait Period Ends: 03/05/2007, Contact: Forrest Cole 907-228-6200.

EIS No. 20070021, Draft Supplement, BLM, MT, Montana Statewide Oil and Gas, Development Alternative for Coal Bed Natural Gas Production and Amendment of the Powder River and Billings Resource Management Plans, Additional Information Three New [[Page 5050]] Alternatives, Implementation, U.S. Army COE Section 404 Permit, NPDES Permit, Several Cos, MT, Comment Period Ends: 05/02/2007, Contact: Mary Bloom 406-233-2852. This document is available on the Internet at: http://www.blm.gov/eis/mt/milescity_seis/.

EIS No. 20070022, Final EIS, AFS, MN, Echo Trail Area Forest Management Project, Forest Vegetation Management and Related Transportation System, Superior National Forest Land and Resource Management Plan, Implementation, Lacroix Ranger District and Kawishiwi Ranger District, St. Louis and Lake Counties, MN, Wait Period Ends: 03/05/2007, Contact: Carol Booth 218-666-0020.

EXHIBIT 7-4
(continued)

EIS No. 20070023, Final EIS, AFS, WA, Buckhorn Access Project, To Utilize the Marias Creek Route to Construct and Reconstruct Roads, Funding, NPDES Permit and U.S. Army COE Section 404 Permit, Okanogan and Wenatchee National Forests, Tonasket Ranger District, Okanogan County, WA, Wait Period Ends: 03/05/2007, Contact: Phil Christy 509-486-5137. This document is available on the Internet at: http://www.fs.fed.us/r6/oka/projects. EXIT Disclaimer
(material omitted)

Amended Notices
EIS No. 20060414, Draft EIS, USA, CO, Pinon Canyon Maneuver Site (PCMS) Transformation Program, Implementation, Base Realignment and Closure Activities, Fort Carson, Las Animas, Otero and Huerfano Counties, CO, Comment Period Ends: 02/16/2007, Contact: Karen Wilson 703-602-2861.
Revision to FR Notice Published 10/13/2006: Reopening Comment Period from 01/11/2007 to 02/16/2007. (Material omitted)

Dated: January 29, 2007.
Robert W. Hargrove, Director, NEPA Compliance Division, Office of Federal Activities. [FR Doc. E7-1727 Filed 2-1-07; 8:45 am [BILLING CODE 6560-50-P

Environmental Impact Statements and Regulations; Availability of EPA Comments

[Federal Register: February 2, 2007 (Volume 72, Number 22)] [Notices]
[Page 5048-5049]
From the Federal Register Online via GPO Access [wais.access.gpo.gov]
[DOCID:fr02fe07-59]
ENVIRONMENTAL PROTECTION AGENCY   [ER-FRL-6683-7]
Environmental Impact Statements and Regulations; Availability of EPA Comments

Availability of EPA comments prepared pursuant to the Environmental Review Process (ERP), under section 309 of the Clean Air Act and Section 102(2)(c) of the National Environmental Policy Act, as amended. Requests for copies of EPA comments can be directed to the Office of Federal Activities at 202-564-7167. An explanation of the ratings assigned to draft environmental impact statements (EISs) was published in FR dated April 7, 2006 (71 FR 17845).

Draft EISs

EXHIBIT 7-4
(continued)

EIS No. 20060355, ERP No. D-MMS-A02244-00, Outer Continental Shelf Oil & Gas Leasing Program: 2007-2012, Exploration and Development Offshore Marine Environment and Coastal Counties of AL, AK, DE, FL, LA, MD, MS, NJ, NC, TX and VA. Summary: EPA expressed environmental concerns about cumulative impacts and mitigation. Rating EC2.

EIS No. 20060378, ERP No. D-NPS-A84030-00, Programmatic — Service-wide Benefits Sharing Project, To Clarify the Rights and Responsibilities of Researchers and National Park Service (NPS) Management in Connection with the Use of Valuable Discoveries, Inventions, and Other Developments, across the United States. Summary: EPA does not object to the preferred alternative. Rating LO.

ii.   Professional Profile

Dan Pava works as an environmental planner at the Los Alamos National Laboratory, reviewing large projects to assure that they comply with federal environmental laws, including the National Environmental Policy Act (NEPA).

He obtained an undergraduate degree in physical geography, which required a variety of science courses ranging from geology to meteorology to biology. According to Dan, "These were in most cases not advanced courses, but they have provided me with a practical and fundamental understanding of natural systems upon which human societies depend and interact. Planning has been my career of choice for 25 years. I became a planner because this is a profession where you can make a difference by improving the quality of life. I had always been passionate about environmental protection but also concerned that people have the opportunities to better their lives. I started in planning working as an intern in a municipal planning office while still pursuing my master of community and regional planning and master of public administration. I believe that ecology is the economy of living systems, upon which all our other pursuits depend. The future of planning will be based upon sustainable design and systems that mitigate humanity's impacts by how we live, work, house, transport, communicate and recreate."

Example of Dan's work: After Cerro Grande Fire in May 2000 and the events of September 11, 2001, the Department of Energy recognized a need to re-evaluate the issue of public and worker traffic along trails within Laboratory boundaries. As part of the Ecology Group, Dan worked on environmental assessment of management of about 20 trails on the Laboratory's land. According to Pava, workers and the general public have used some of the trails for hiking for more than 50 years. Some of the trails within the Laboratory are maintained in a limited fashion while many others have become subject to unchecked erosion or other hazards to the environment and users.

Key Terms

CE	Lead Agency
CEQ	LPA
Cumulative Impacts	Mitigation
DEIS	NOI
EA	ROD
EIS	Scoping
FEIS	Tiering
FONSI	

Review Questions

1. What are the three classifications that may be applied to a project to determine the level of environmental review?
2. When a project under review has been proposed and planned by a private company and NEPA review is required only because that company needs a permit from a federal agency, is that agency precluded from considering alternatives for the project?
3. What types of actions are subject to NEPA review?
4. What is scoping? What is tiering?
5. What is the role of the EPA with respect to EISs?
6. How are categorical exemptions established?
7. Where do regulations concerning NEPA come from?
8. What is meant by cumulative impacts?
9. Does NEPA require that every project be designed to have the least-possible environmental impact?

KEY TERMS CROSSWORD

www.CrosswordWeaver.com

ACROSS

2. environmental _____, step between CE and EIS
5. _____agency, responsible for coordinating EIS
7. DEIS is made available for public _____
11. many _____ have laws similar to NEPA
12. _____ EIS, prepared before final
13. lead agency identifies _____ agencies
14. the process of exploring issues and alternatives before preparing EIS
15. initials, determination in EA that EIS is not needed
16. one EIS builds on another

DOWN

1. initials, approves project after EIS
3. measures to reduce impact
4. initials, published in Federal Register before preparation of EIS

6. locally preferred _____ may be approved after EIS
7. _____ exclusion; pre-determined to have no significant environmental impact
8. federal _____ of a project may trigger NEPA
9. _____ impacts from past and future projects must be considered
10. initials, makes regulations for NEPA

TRI-VALLEY CARES et al., Plaintiffs-Appellants v. DEPARTMENT OF ENERGY et al., Defendants-Appellees

UNITED STATES COURT OF APPEALS FOR THE NINTH CIRCUIT
Uunpublished 203 Fed. Appx. 105; 2006 U.S. App. LEXIS 25724
October 16, 2006

Plaintiffs Tri-Valley Cares, Nuclear Watch of New Mexico, and individuals (collectively, "Tri-Valley") appeal the district court's order granting summary judgment in favor of Defendants United States Department of Energy and its auxiliaries (collectively, "DOE"). On appeal, Tri-Valley makes three specific arguments concerning the proposed construction of a federal government biological weapons research laboratory near San Francisco. First, Tri-Valley asserts that the DOE failed to comply with the National Environmental Policy Act of 1969, *42 U.S.C. §§4321-4370* ("NEPA"), by issuing a Finding of No Significant Impact ("FONSI") after analyzing the project in an Environmental Assessment. According to plaintiffs, the proposed research laboratory may have a significant effect on the human environment and, accordingly, the DOE must prepare an Environmental Impact Statement. Second, Tri-Valley claims that, under the Freedom of Information Act, *5 U.S.C. §552* ("FOIA"), DOE failed timely to provide non-exempt documents. Third and finally, plaintiffs claim that the district court improperly struck portions of plaintiffs' extra-record declarations.

If an Environmental Assessment demonstrates that substantial questions are raised about the environmental effects of a proposed agency action, a FONSI may not be issued and the agency must prepare a full Environmental Impact Statement. *Found. for N. Am. Wild Sheep v. U.S. Dep't of Agric., 681 F.2d 1172, 1178 (9th Cir. 1982)*. Plaintiffs challenge the DOE's Environmental Assessment due to its alleged failure to assess fully and correctly potentially significant effects on public health and safety (such as fire, earthquake, and terrorist attacks), uncertain effects posing substantial risks, significant precedential effects, significant cumulative effects, and public controversy.

Review of agency action under the Administrative Procedure Act, *5 U.S.C. §706(2)*, is "highly deferential." *Friends of the Earth v. Hintz, 800 F.2d 822, 831 (9th Cir. 1986)*. Although Tri-Valley raised some substantial questions about the validity of DOE's substantive conclusions,[1] this court may not substitute its judgment for the reviewing agency's. *Laguna Greenbelt, Inc. v. U.S. Dep't of Transp., 42 F.3d 517, 523 (9th Cir. 1994)* (per curiam). [HN4] NEPA is a procedural statute that " 'does not mandate particular results,' but 'simply provides the necessary process' to ensure that federal agencies take a 'hard look' at the environmental consequences of their actions." *Muckleshoot Indian Tribe v. U.S. Forest Serv., 177 F.3d 800, 814 (9th Cir. 1999)* (per curiam) (quoting *Robertson v. Methow Valley Citizens Council, 490 U.S. 332, 350, 109 S. Ct. 1835, 104 L. Ed. 2d 351 (1989))*. With the exception of the lack of analysis concerning the possibility of a terrorist attack, we hold that the DOE did take a "hard look" at the identified environmental concerns and that the DOE's decision was "fully informed and well-considered." *Save the Yaak Comm. v. Block, 840 F.2d 714, 717 (9th Cir. 1988)* (internal quotation marks omitted).

---

[1]We note in particular the DOE's minimal assessment of earthquake risks despite the presence of known, active faults that run directly under nearby Berkeley/Alameda County, California.

Concerning the DOE's conclusion that consideration of the effects of a terrorist attack is not required in its Environmental Assessment, we recently held to the contrary in *San Luis Obispo Mothers for Peace v. Nuclear Regulatory Commission, 449 F.3d 1016 (9th Cir. 2006)*. In Mothers for Peace, we held that an Environmental Assessment that does not consider the possibility of a terrorist attack is inadequate. *Id. at 1035.* Similarly here, we remand for the DOE to consider whether the threat of terrorist activity necessitates the preparation of an Environmental Impact Statement. As in Mothers for Peace, we caution that there "remain open to the agency a wide variety of actions it may take on remand [and] . . . [w]e do not prejudge those alternatives." Id.

1. Plaintiffs requested many documents pursuant to FOIA, and all of the requested documents have been produced. Eventual production, "however belatedly, moots FOIA claims." *Papa v. United States, 281 F.3d 1004, 1013 (9th Cir. 2002)* (internal quotation marks omitted). No exception to the mootness doctrine applies because there is no evidence of bad faith or a recurring pattern of FOIA violations by the DOE. See generally *Biodiversity Legal Found. v. Badgley, 309 F.3d 1166, 1174 (9th Cir. 2002)* (holding that an agency which exhibited a recurring pattern of correcting regulatory violations immediately after the commencement of litigation could be challenged, as an exception to the mootness doctrine). The district court properly concluded that the DOE's response to Tri-Valley's FOIA requests was adequate, see *Zemansky v. EPA, 767 F.2d 569, 571 (9th Cir. 1985)* ("In demonstrating the adequacy of the search, the agency may rely upon reasonably detailed, nonconclusory affidavits submitted in good faith."), and that the often considerable delay was not due to bad faith.

2. The district court did not abuse its discretion by excluding certain extra-record declarations submitted by Tri-Valley. See *Sw. Ctr. for Biological Diversity v. U.S. Forest Serv., 100 F.3d 1443, 1447 (9th Cir. 1996)* (holding that a district court's decision to exclude extra-record evidence is reviewed for abuse of discretion). Judicial review of agency action is generally limited to review of the administrative record, *5 U.S.C. §706; Animal Def. Council v. Hodel, 840 F.2d 1432, 1436 (9th Cir. 1988)*, and extra-record materials are allowed only in certain circumstances. The district court, after conducting a thorough and detailed analysis of each of the fifteen declarations submitted by Tri-Valley, allowed three declarations in whole and four declarations in part, and excluded eight declarations. The district court found that the excluded declarations contained impermissible legal conclusions, opinions from lay witnesses, or political statements; raised only remote and highly speculative consequences, *Presidio Golf Club v. Nat'l Park Serv., 155 F.3d 1153, 1163 (9th Cir. 1998)*; improperly raised information that became available after the agency decision-making process, *Northcoast Envtl. Ctr. v. Glickman, 136 F.3d 660, 665 (9th Cir. 1998)*; or were cumulative, id. The district court properly excluded the declarations based on these legally valid reasons and therefore did not abuse its discretion. AFFIRMED in part, REVERSED in part and REMANDED for further action consistent with this decision. The parties shall bear their own costs on appeal.

8

The Air We Breathe

A. Overview of the Clean Air Act

The Clean Air Act, 42 U.S.C. §§7401-7671 (**CAA**) is federal law, first adopted in 1963 and most recently amended in 1997; EPA regulations for implementing the

Act are at 40 C.F.R. 50-95. Because of its evolution through many amendments, the CAA is a complicated "patchwork" of programs, rather than a cohesive, logical scheme. A single source of pollution may be covered by a number of programs. Trying to get the "big picture" with respect to the CAA can be very frustrating. Exhibit 8-1 is a map of the major sections of the CAA and (roughly) of the organization of this chapter. Refer back to the chart while reading the chapter; it should help you see the "forest" as well as the "trees." Keep in mind that the CAA applies to the entire country, but much of the implementation and enforcement is left to the states.

To better organize your thoughts as you study this chapter, make notes categorizing each new concept according to:

- Whether the concept or program relates to the *technology* required of the pollution source, to the *quality of ambient air* (the air in a defined area), or to the *quality of air being discharged* by a particular source;
- Which *specific pollutants* are regulated;
- Does application of the concept or program depend on whether the area has *attained or not attained* existing standards;
- Whether the program or regulation applies only to *major sources*, as defined by the volume of emissions;[1]
- Whether the concept or program applies to *existing sources or to new sources;* and
- Whether the concept or program applies *to stationary sources*, such as factories, to *mobile sources*, such as vehicles, *or other sources*, such as consumer products.

1. Enforcement Options

The CAA establishes **criminal penalties** for violations, including jail terms, and authorizes the EPA to pursue civil suits for injunctions or monetary remedies. Such civil and criminal cases go through the courts. Without having to go through the courts, the EPA can issue **administrative citations** (like a traffic ticket) for minor violations and assess fines. For more significant violations, the EPA can initiate **administrative enforcement** actions, hold hearings, and impose more substantial financial penalties, without having to go through the courts. The EPA can also pay a bounty to anyone who provides information that leads to a conviction or a penalty for violation of the Act. The CAA also permits **citizens' suits** against violators and against agencies that fail to fulfill their obligations.

Major Source
A source of emissions, so classified because of the volume of its emissions

Stationary Sources
Sources of pollution that are not mobile, such as factories

Mobile Sources
Vehicles and fuel

Administrative Citation/ Enforcement
Methods of enforcing pollution laws that do not necessitate resorting to the courts

Citizens' Suits
Also called private attorney general actions; a statute provides for enforcement by private citizens

---

[1]To make understanding of the CAA even more complicated, the definition of "major source" is not the same for every program.

EXHIBIT 8-1
CAA Map

CAA Section	Statutory Directive	Action/Regulation
§7407	Divide U.S. into air quality control regions to determine attainment of NAAQS	40 C.F.R. part 81
§7409	Establish National Ambient Air Quality Standards (NAAQS)	EPA has established primary and secondary NAAQS for "criteria" pollutants: carbon monoxide; lead; ground-level ozone; nitrogen dioxide; particulate matter; sulfur oxides. 40 C.F.R. part 61
§7410	Each state must enact State Implementation Plan (SIP) to meet NAAQS goals, to be approved by EPA	40 C.F.R. parts 51, 52
§7411	EPA must set standards for new or modified stationary sources of pollution	EPA has established emissions levels and requires permits for major new sources and for modifications of existing nonmobile sources of pollution. New Source Performance Standards (NSPS) are based on categories and employ lowest achievable emission rates (LAER). 40 C.F.R. part 60
§7412	EPA must regulate hazardous air pollutants (HAPs)	Statute initially identified 189 HAPs. EPA is to identify major and area sources of HAPs and develop National Emission Standards for Hazardous Air Pollutants (NESHAPS) for all industries that emit one or more in significant quantities. Sources must use Maximum Available Control Technology (MACT) to reduce pollutant releases; major sources must obtain an operating permit. 40 C.F.R. part 63
§§7470-7492	EPA must protect air quality in areas that meet NAAQS	Prevention of Significant Deterioration (PSD) program
§§7501-7509	EPA must deal with areas that fail to meet NAAQS	Special provisions deal with nonattainment for each of the six criteria pollutants; areas are classified by level of nonattainment. Areas may be denied federal assistance if nonattainment persists.
§§7521-7554	EPA must set emissions standards for moving sources	EPA has established standards for fuel and fuel additives and emissions from vehicles and engines. www.epa.gov/otaq/

EXHIBIT 8-1
(continued)

CAA Section	Statutory Directive	Action/Regulation
§7651	Sets goals for reduction of sulfur dioxide (SO2) and nitrogen oxides to reduce acid deposition (acid rain)	EPA Acid Rain Program includes: Phased tightening of restrictions on fossil fuel power plants; continuous emission monitoring (CEM) requirements; Allowance trading system — utility units are allocated allowances based on historic fuel consumption and a specific emissions rate. Allowances may be bought, sold, or banked. Regardless of allowances, a source may not emit at levels that would violate limits set under §§7407-7509. www.epa.gov/airmarkets/progsregs/arp/basic.html; 40 C.F.R. part 72
§7661	Permits required for major industrial sources	Operating permits, CAAPPs
§7671	Control pollutants that deplete stratospheric ozone.	EPA has specific regulatory programs for motor vehicle air conditioning systems, stationary refrigerant systems, phase-outs of certain products, recycling, labeling requirements, and more. See www.epa.gov/ozone/title6/index.html; 40 C.F.R. part 82

2. Other Relevant Laws

OSHA
Occupational Safety and Health Administration — Concerned with indoor air pollution

The CAA is concerned with outdoor air pollution. Indoor pollution in the workplace is regulated under the **Occupational Safety and Health Administration Act (OSHA).** Specific industries may also be subject to other federal laws. For example, air pollution from hazardous waste facilities is regulated by the Resource Conservation and Recovery Act (RCRA), discussed in another chapter; the Emergency Planning and Community Right to Know Act, also discussed in another chapter, requires that certain toxic air emissions be reported to state and federal authorities. Many states also have state laws relevant to air pollution that supplement the state role under the CAA. The CAA allows individual states to have stronger pollution controls, but states are not allowed to have weaker pollution controls than those set for the whole country.

Assignment 8-1
OSHA Requirements

◆ Find the National Institute for Occupational Safety and Health Guide to Chemical Hazards online.
◆ Find the OSHA Guide to Hazard Chemical Communication.

EXHIBIT 8-2
MSDS

MSDS
Material Data Safety Sheet, contains information about safe handling and disposal of potentially hazardous substances

A Material Safety Data Sheet (MSDS) is created to provide workers and emergency personnel with the proper procedures for handling or working with a particular substance; they are not generally intended for or provided to consumers, who only handle the substance occasionally. Consumers interested in the safety and environmental characteristics of substances can consult the U.S. National Library of Medicine Household Products Database, http://household-products.nlm.nih.gov/.

An MSDS is generally two to five pages long and includes physical information such as melting point, boiling point, and flash point; toxicity characteristics, health effects, and first aid; and handling procedures, reactivity, storage, disposal, protective equipment, and spill/leak procedures. OSHA has a suggested format on its website. Much information about preparing or reading an MSDS can be found on the Internet; a good starting point is www.ilpi.com/msds/faq/parta.html.

Several laws mandate creation of an MSDS in certain circumstances. The Occupational Safety and Health Administration requires an MSDS under 29 C.F.R. 1910.1200 to ensure that employers communicate adequate information to employees. In addition, the EPA may require an MSDS under the Community Right to Know Law and similar state and local laws may contain similar requirements.

B. Major Sections of the CAA

1. Division of United States into Regions

Pursuant to the CAA the United States is divided into **air quality control regions (AQCRs)**; a state may contain several AQCRs, as shown in Exhibit 8-3. The stringency of regulations applicable to a business that is a source of air pollution may depend on the region in which it is located. The boundaries of the

AQCR
Air quality control region

regions, therefore, have economic ramifications. The level of regulation can have an impact on an area's ability to attract new businesses.

Regulation of air quality is complicated by the fact that pollution travels from its source across county lines, state lines, and even international borders. Weather and geography determine where pollution goes and how bad it is, so, while individual states generally handle cleanup planning and implementation, governing bodies must cooperate to solve the problem. The CAA provides for **interstate commissions** on air pollution control; interstate issues are discussed in more depth later in this chapter.

Interstate Commissions
Established by the EPA to provide a forum for cooperation

EXHIBIT 8-3

By visiting any EPA regional website, you can find air quality maps such as the one below, which was found on the Region 9 website.

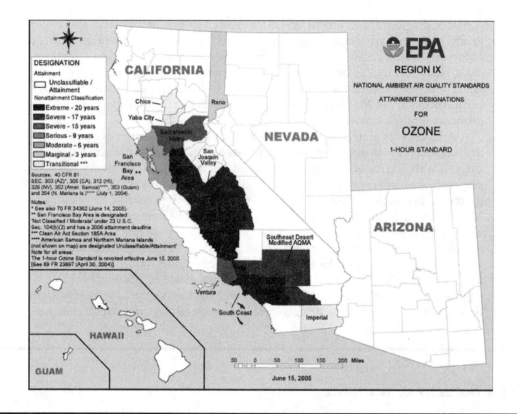

2. NAAQS

The EPA has identified **criteria pollutants** and set a national standard for each, so that people in all states have the same environmental protection with

Criteria Pollutants
Lead, smog, carbon monoxide, nitrogen dioxide, sulfur oxides, and particulate matter, regulated by NAAQS

respect to those pollutants. The standards are **National Ambient Air Quality Standards (NAAQS).** The pollutants are called criteria pollutants because the EPA develops health-based criteria for setting permissible levels; secondary standards (see Exhibit 8-4) are intended to prevent environmental and property damage. In establishing NAAQS, the EPA *does not* consider the cost of achieving the standards. The EPA is to review and, if necessary, revise the NAAQS every five years. The current criteria pollutants are:

- Carbon monoxide, usually a byproduct of combustion
- Lead (disappearing since its mandatory removal from gasoline)
- Ground-level ozone (ozone in the stratosphere protects the environment, but at ground level it combines with other pollutants and creates **smog**)
- Nitrogen dioxide, usually a byproduct of combustion
- Particulate matter, such as dust, ash, dirt
- Sulfur oxides

While the EPA first set deadlines for achievement of NAAQS in the early 1970s, many areas are still not in compliance. The EPA works with the states to identify areas that do not meet the standards. There are monitoring stations in every major urban area and at other locations across the country. Areas that do not comply with NAAQS are called **nonattainment zones** with respect to a pollutant and are classified by the level of pollution; for example, smog nonattainment has five classifications, from marginal to extreme. As discussed later in this chapter, regulation of criteria pollutants depends on whether an area is in **attainment** or not; in nonattainment areas cleanup goals are based on the degree of nonattainment.

3. SIPs §7410

States take the lead in carrying out the CAA with respect to stationary sources because problems and solutions associated with stationary sources require special understanding of local industries, geography, housing patterns, etc. Each state is required to develop a state implementation plan (**SIP**), which is a collection of regulations with a goal of reducing each pollutant to below the NAAQS level. SIP requirements for nonattainment areas (**NAAs**) are more stringent. States must involve the public, and provide opportunities to comment, in the development of the SIP.

The EPA must approve each SIP, and if a SIP is not acceptable, the EPA can take over enforcing the Act in that state. Because the EPA itself has limited resources, it is more likely to impose sanctions on states that have not developed acceptable SIPs. A state can lose federal highway funds for failure to correct deficiencies in its SIP. The EPA assists states by providing scientific research, expert studies, and money to support clean air programs. EPA **control technology guidelines (CTGs)** are available to both the regulators and regulated businesses. The EPA's approval of a SIP means that the EPA can enforce the provisions of that SIP. When the EPA requires amendment of a SIP, it is referred to as a "SIP call."

NAAQS: Primary and Secondary
National Ambient Air Quality Standards for levels of criteria pollutants: primary are concerned with health criteria; secondary with property damages and other concerns

Smog
Also called ground-level ozone; one of the criteria pollutants

Nonattainment Zones
Areas not in compliance with NAAQS

Attainment
Description of an area that is in compliance with NAAQS

SIP
State Implementation Plan for achieving attainment with respect to NAAQS

Control Technology Guidelines
Provided by EPA to assist regulated entities

EXHIBIT 8-4

From www.epa.gov/air/criteria.html.

National Ambient Air Quality Standards (NAAQS)

The Clean Air Act, which was last amended in 1990, requires the EPA to set **National Ambient Air Quality Standards** (40 C.F.R. part 50) for pollutants considered harmful to public health and the environment. The Clean Air Act established two types of national air quality standards. *Primary standards* set limits to protect public health, including the health of "sensitive" populations such as asthmatics, children, and the elderly. *Secondary standards* set limits to protect public welfare, including protection against decreased visibility, damage to animals, crops, vegetation, and buildings.

The EPA Office of Air Quality Planning and Standards (OAQPS) has set National Ambient Air Quality Standards for six principal pollutants, which are called "criteria" pollutants. They are listed below. Units of measure for the standards are parts per million (ppm) by volume, milligrams per cubic meter of air (mg/m^3), and micrograms per cubic meter of air ($\mu g/m^3$).

National Ambient Air Quality Standards

Pollutant	Primary Stds.	Averaging Times	Secondary Stds.
Carbon Monoxide	9 ppm (10 mg/m^3)	8-hour[1]	None
	35 ppm (40 mg/m^3)	1-hour[1]	None
Lead	1.5 $\mu g/m^3$	Quarterly Average	Same as Primary
Nitrogen Dioxide	0.053 ppm (100 $\mu g/m^3$)	Annual (Arithmetic Mean)	Same as Primary
Particulate Matter (PM$_{10}$)	Revoked[2]	Annual[2] (Arith. Mean)	
	150 $\mu g/m^3$	24-hour[3]	

EXHIBIT 8-4
(continued)

Pollutant	Primary Stds.	Averaging Times	Secondary Stds.
Particulate Matter (PM$_{2.5}$)	15.0 μg/m^3	Annual[4] (Arith. Mean)	Same as Primary
	35 μg/m^3	24-hour[5]	
Ozone	0.08 ppm	8-hour[6]	Same as Primary
	0.12 ppm	1-hour[7] (in limited areas)	Same as Primary
Sulfur Oxides	0.03 ppm	Annual (Arith. Mean)	——
	0.14 ppm	24-hour[1]	——
	——	3-hour[1]	0.5 ppm (1300 μg/m^3)

[1]Not to be exceeded more than once per year.

[2]Due to a lack of evidence linking health problems to long-term exposure to coarse particle pollution, the agency revoked the annual PM$_{10}$ standard in 2006 (effective December 17, 2006).

[3]Not to be exceeded more than once per year on average over 3 years.

[4]To attain this standard, the 3-year average of the weighted annual mean PM$_{2.5}$ concentrations from single or multiple community-oriented monitors must not exceed 15.0 μg/m^3.

[5]To attain this standard, the 3-year average of the 98th percentile of 24-hour concentrations at each population-oriented monitor within an area must not exceed 35 μg/m^3 (effective December 17, 2006).

[6]To attain this standard, the 3-year average of the fourth-highest daily maximum 8-hour average ozone concentrations measured at each monitor within an area over each year must not exceed 0.08 ppm.

[7](a) The standard is attained when the expected number of days per calendar year with maximum hourly average concentrations above 0.12 ppm is ≤ 1, as determined by appendix H. (b) As of June 15, 2005 EPA revoked the 1-hour ozone standard in all areas except the fourteen 8-hour ozone non-attainment Early Action Compact (EAC) Areas.

EXHIBIT 8-5

CONTENTS OF AN APPROVED SIP

To see another example of an approved SIP, visit http://yosemite.epa.gov/r10/airpage.nsf/webpage/SIP+-+WA+Table+of+Contents?OpenDocument.

IMPLEMENTATION PLAN FOR THE CONTROL OF AIR POLLUTION IN THE STATE OF IDAHO

Chapter I — Introduction

Chapter II — Administration

Chapter III — Emissions Inventory

Chapter IV — Air Quality Monitoring

Chapter V — Source Surveillance

Chapter VI — Emergency Episode Plan

Chapter VII — Approval Procedures for (New and Modified Facilities)

Chapter VIII — Nonattainment Area Plans

VIII-a — Silver Valley Nonattainment Plan

VIII-b — Lewiston Nonattainment Plan

VIII-c — Transportation Control Plan for the carbon monoxide of Ada County (Chapter VIII — Nonattainment Area Plans (cont.))

VIII-c — Transportation Control Plan for the carbon monoxide of Ada County VIII-d — Pocatello TSP Nonattainment Plan

VIII-e — Soda Springs Nonattainment Plan

VIII-f — Pinehurst PM10 Nonattainment Plan

VIII-g — Northern Ada County/Boise PM10 Nonattainment Plan

VIII-h — Fort Hall PM Nonattainment Area Plan (FIP)

VIII-i — Sandpoint PM10 Nonattainment Area Plan VIII-j — Ada County/Boise Idaho PM10 Maintenance Plan

Chapter IX — Reserved

Chapter X — Plan for Maintenance of National Ambient Air Quality Standards for Lead Small Business Assistant Program

Because attainment of NAAQS did not occur as planned, the 1990 amendments to the Act added requirements. SIPs now include programs for issuing operating permits to existing stationary sources that emit pollutants at a specified level. Operating permits, discussed further in a later section, include information on which pollutants are being released, how much may be released, and steps the source is taking to reduce pollution, including technology requirements and plans to monitor the pollution. This section will focus on the terminology associated with the sources and the applicable standards.

Assignment 8-2

1. Read the case summarized in Exhibit 8-6.

   ◆ If there is no question that the distribution center is an "indirect source" and that indirect sources do require permits under the Wisconsin SIP, why was the claim dismissed?
   ◆ What is the underlying conflict that might make the permitting authority willing to allow construction of the facility without stringent review?
   ◆ What does the case tell you about the discretion granted to states with respect to achieving the goals of the CAA?

2. Although the EPA has been regulating criteria pollutants for more than 30 years, many urban areas are classified as nonattainment for at least one pollutant. It has been estimated that about 90 million Americans live in nonattainment areas. How is your state doing?

   ◆ Visit http://epa.gov/air/data/geosel.html and identify areas in your state that are in nonattainment.
   ◆ Find the contact information for the individual responsible for monitoring air quality in your state.
   ◆ From the search box at www.epa.gov, enter the name of your state and "state implementation plan approval." Determine when your SIP was most recently revised.
   ◆ Start at the website for the regional office of the EPA that covers your state (find the regional website from www.epa.gov/epahome/whereyoulive.htm), then click AIR. From this page you should be able to find the SIP for your state. Try to find a permit for a specific facility (e.g., a large factory) in your area.

---

4. Areas of Attainment; Areas of Nonattainment

The operating permit for an existing **major source** located in a *nonattainment* area is subject to **reasonably achievable control technology (RACT)** standards. Federal law does not define RACT; states define and require RACT in their SIPs. Under RACT standards, a source may not be required to spend more than a predetermined "reasonable" amount to control emissions.

RACT
Reasonably Available Control Technology — standard for existing sources in nonattainment areas

---

EXHIBIT 8-6

VILLAGE OF OCONOMOWOC LAKE v. DAYTON-HUDSON CORP.

U.S. DISTRICT COURT FOR THE EASTERN DISTRICT OF WISCONSIN, 1993 U.S. Dist. LEXIS 20058 (1993)

Plaintiffs claim that construction of a distribution center for Target Stores violates the Clean Air Act because pollution permits have not issued. The claim must be dismissed.

Plaintiffs claim that when the center becomes operational, trucks and employee vehicles traveling to and from it will emit at least 300 tons of nitrogen oxides, as well as 260 tons of carbon monoxide per year. Because nitrogen oxides combine with other matter to form ozone, plaintiffs say, operation of the center will increase the level of ozone pollution in southeastern Wisconsin, where the ozone level exceeds applicable NAAQS. Plaintiffs contend that the CAA and Wisconsin's SIP, require [a permit application] prior to construction of the center, treating the center as a "major emitting facility" or "major stationary source" being constructed in an NAAQS "nonattainment area."

The Wisconsin Department of Natural Resources described the center as a "minor, new, attainment air pollution source." Issuance of the permit was not, therefore, subject to the more stringent standards applicable to a major emitting facility or major stationary source in a nonattainment area. See Wis. Stat. §144.393; *42 U.S.C. §7503*(a).

Plaintiffs' suit is brought pursuant to Section 304(a)(3) of the CAA, which provides that "any person may commence a civil action . . . against any person who proposes to construct or constructs any new or modified major emitting facility without a permit required under" parts C or D of the Act. *42 U.S.C. §7604*(a)(3). Defendants contend that the citizen-suit provision is inapplicable because the center is not a facility for which a permit is required under parts C or D of the CAA. The CAA does not itself require a permit for a facility like the center. Permits are required only for a "major emitting facility" or "major stationary source," both of which refer to a "stationary . . . source" of pollution. *42 U.S.C. §7602*(j). "Stationary source" is defined to mean "any source of an air pollutant except those emissions resulting directly from an internal combustion engine for transportation purposes or from a nonroad engine or nonroad vehicle." *42 U.S.C. §7602*(z). Because the center will cause only the excepted type of emission, it cannot be a major emitting facility or major stationary source within the meaning of the CAA. Thus, the CAA does not by its own terms require a permit for the center.

The exception for internal combustion engines is consistent with Sect.110 of Part A, *42 U.S.C. §7410*, which sets conditions to federal approval of SIPs and provides that the EPA may not require that a SIP include a program for determining whether an "indirect source" of pollution would contribute to nonattainment of an NAAQS. "Indirect source" is defined as "a facility, building, structure, installation, real property, road, or highway which attracts, or may attract, mobile

---

**EXHIBIT 8-6
(continued)**

---

sources of pollution." The center falls within this definition and, therefore, the EPA could not have required Wisconsin to include in its SIP a program under which a permit for the center would have been necessary.

Plaintiffs point out, however, that although Wisconsin was not required to adopt an "indirect source review program," it has chosen to do so, and the program, along with the rest of the Wisconsin SIP, has been approved by the EPA in accordance with the CAA. As a result, plaintiffs contend, the requirements of the SIP have become, in effect, the requirements of the CAA. Thus, if the SIP requires a major-source permit prior to construction of the center, then the permit is also required under the CAA, and so the citizen-suit provision applies. The difficulty is that the pertinent citizen-suit provision refers only to permits "required under" Parts C or D of the Act, and nothing in those parts purports to incorporate by reference the permit requirements of an approved SIP. This is significant, because when Congress intended to allow civil actions or enforcement actions based on noncompliance with the terms of an SIP, as opposed to the terms of the CAA, it made that clear. Under a separate citizen-suit provision, for example, a federal suit may be brought against "any person . . . alleged to be in violation of . . . an emission standard or limitation under this Act," and such a standard is defined to include a "standard, limitation, or schedule established . . . under any applicable State implementation plan." *42 U.S.C. §§7604*(a)(1), 7604(f)(4). The provision upon which plaintiffs rely refers only to permits required under Parts C and D, it cannot afford a basis for challenging the failure to obtain a permit required under a SIP. Because that is the nature of the claim, the court lacks jurisdiction to hear it, and it must be dismissed.

---

5. New Sources

While existing sources may be required to obtain operating permits and meet the RACT standard, new sources of emissions are the primary focus of efforts to bring NAAs into attainment and of **prevention of significant deterioration (PSD)** in attainment areas. New major sources of emissions must submit to **new source review (NSR)** and a obtain permit before construction begins.

Since it began regulating emissions, Congress has been concerned that requiring existing businesses to revamp facilities to achieve state-of-the-art pollution control would be economically devastating and has, therefore, applied different standards to new sources of pollution. Any change in the physical plant or in the method of operation of a major source[2] that results in an increase in the amount of

PSD
Prevention of Significant Deterioration — emissions standard for sources in attainment areas

NSR
New Source Review

---

[2]For purposes of NSR, a "major source" is defined by its potential to emit and the level of nonattainment in the area.

pollution or release of a different type of pollutant can subject the facility to a higher level of regulation. Economists and business people often argue that the new source review policies actually motivate businesses to retain older, less efficient equipment rather than go through the stringent review process.

A source's classification as major or minor, like the question of whether a change in operations or physical plant constitutes a modification or simply routine maintenance, repair, and replacement, has tremendous implications for the source. As a result, the time period used for measuring baseline emissions, the methodology for projecting future emissions, and the question of whether a single facility can "average out" all of its emissions (sometimes referred to as the "bubble concept") are often points of contention.

> Note: The case summarized in Exhibit 8-6 involved an allegation that the distribution center should have been subject to the NSR. Because NSR is an extremely difficult process, the applicant sought, and was granted, a permit for a **minor source** — not subject to NSR. Similarly, in the UDigg example at the end of the chapter (Exhibit 8-12), the paralegal was happy to learn that the new ethanol facility planned by the client would likely not be a major source subject to NSR.

NSR (pre-construction) permits are issued by state or local pollution authorities, or, in some cases, the EPA. A state or local agency may have its program for NSR approved by the EPA as part of its SIP or the EPA may delegate authority for new source review. An applicant for a new source permit must first identify and quantify projected emissions of pollutants and must analyze alternative configurations and processes for the project as well as environmental control plans.

Keep in mind that a new source construction permit is not the same as an operating permit, issued to an existing source. New source permits specify what construction is allowed, what emission limits must be met, and often how the source must be operated. For example, the permit may specify that the source have stacks of heights that the permit agency used in its analysis of the source. Some limits in the permit may be there at the request of the source itself, to avoid being classified at a level subject to more stringent requirements. To assure that sources follow the permit requirements, permits also contain monitoring, record-keeping, and reporting requirements.

BACT
Best available control technology; a standard for new sources

In attainment areas, PSD rules apply. Those rules create classifications, based on the source's maximum theoretical emissions: major sources, natural minor sources, synthetic minor sources, and de minimis sources. The PSD rules require use of **best available control technology (BACT)** to limit emissions of criteria pollutants and other pollutants; the determination of BACT takes into account economic, energy, and environmental factors. Because BACT is determined on a case-by-case basis by the states (with oversight by the EPA), it may or may not be more stringent than NSPS (defined below) for the facility.

LAER
Lowest Available Emissions Rate — standard for new sources in nonattainment area

A new or modified major source proposed for a nonattainment area (one that will emit more than the threshold amount of a criteria pollutant) must control emissions at the **lowest achievable emission rate (LAER)**. The LAER rules are the most stringent SIP standards. The applicant must show that it is in compliance with regulations at any facilities it is already operating within the state and that the benefits of the proposed project will outweigh the environmental costs.

The applicant is also required to **offset** the project's emissions by closing or reducing emissions at an existing source. The applicant can buy or trade with other sources — allowance and trading programs are discussed in more detail later in this chapter. An offset must be real and legally enforceable. It cannot be accomplished by looking only at potential emissions. For example, a factory might have a permit that allows emission of 200 tons per year of a certain pollutant, but it actually emits only 150 tons of the pollutant per year. The factory cannot sell the 50 tons of unused potential as an offset.

Offsets
Part of market-based regulation; source increasing emission of one pollutant can offset by reduction of another

In addition, new and modified sources may be subject to **new source performance standards (NSPS)**. As shown by Exhibit 8-7, NSPS are industry-specific and, unlike the standards contained in SIPs, NSPS are established by the EPA and are uniform across the country. Application of NSPS does not depend on whether the new source is located in a nonattainment area. NSPS may include standards for pollutants other than criteria pollutants, including HAPs, described in the next section. As shown by the exhibit, NSPS standards can be numerical, for example, "particulate matter in excess of 0.15 kg per metric ton of feed," or, if numerical standards are not feasible, the standards may contain descriptions of equipment or operations.

NSPS
New Source Performance Standards

Assignment 8-3

◆   Determine how new source permitting is handled in your area. Visit www.epa.gov/nsr/where.html.
◆   Many states provide guidance concerning the meaning of PSD, RACT, and BACT. An example of guidance on PSD, from the Iowa Department of Natural Resources, can be found at www.iowadnr.com/air/prof/const/files/psd_guidance.pdf. Try to find a governmental resource that describes how PSD, RACT, or BACT are applied in your state.

---

6.   Hazardous Air Pollutants §7412

There is more to air pollution than the criteria pollutants. The EPA has had authority to regulate hazardous air pollutants **(HAPs)** since 1970, but only regulated seven substances prior to the 1990 CAA amendments. As a result, Congress identified 189 HAPs in the 1990 amendments and directed the EPA to develop emission standards for sources (**national emission standards for hazardous air pollutants, NESHAPs**). The EPA is to revise the list every eight years; existing sources may be subject to lower standards than new sources. NESHAPs are nationwide and do not depend on attainment status.

HAPs
Hazardous Air Pollutants — approximately 189 substances Congress has required the EPA to regulate

NESHAPs
National Emissions Standards for Hazardous Air Pollutants

EXHIBIT 8-7
Example of Sections of NSPS

From www.epa.gov/epacfr40/chapt-I.info/.

Title 40: Protection of Environment

    PART 60 — STANDARDS OF PERFORMANCE FOR NEW STATIONARY SOURCES

Subpart F — Standards of Performance for Portland Cement Plants

§60.60 Applicability and designation of affected facility.

    (a) The provisions of this subpart are applicable to the following affected facilities in portland cement plants: Kiln, clinker cooler, raw mill system, finish mill system, raw mill dryer, raw material storage, clinker storage, finished product storage, conveyor transfer points, bagging and bulk loading and unloading systems.

    (b) Any facility under paragraph (a) of this section that commences construction or modification after August 17, 1971, is subject to the requirements of this subpart.

§60.62 Standard for particulate matter.

    (a) On and after the date on which the performance test required to be conducted by §60.8 is completed, no owner or operator subject to the provisions of this subpart shall cause to be discharged into the atmosphere from any kiln any gases which:

        (1) Contain particulate matter in excess of 0.15 kg per metric ton of feed (dry basis) to the kiln (0.30 lb per ton).

        (2) Exhibit greater than 20 percent opacity.

    (b) On and after the date on which the performance test required to be conducted by §60.8 is completed, no owner or operator subject to the provisions of this subpart shall cause to be discharged into the atmosphere from any clinker cooler any gases which:

        (1) Contain particulate matter in excess of 0.050 kg per metric ton of feed (dry basis) to the kiln (0.10 lb per ton).

        (2) Exhibit 10 percent opacity, or greater.

    (c) On and after the date on which the performance test required to be conducted by §60.8 is completed, no owner or operator subject to the provisions of this subpart shall cause to be discharged into the atmosphere from any affected facility other than the kiln and clinker cooler any gases which exhibit 10 percent opacity, or greater.

Based on the statutory factors set forth in CAA §183(e)(2)(B), the EPA developed the following eight criteria for ranking consumer and commercial products:

1. Utility
2. Commercial demand
3. Health and safety functions
4. Emissions of highly reactive VOC
5. Availability of alternatives
6. Cost-effectiveness of controls
7. Magnitude of annual VOC (volatile organic compound) emissions
8. Regulatory efficiency and program considerations

NESHAPs for major sources in specified industries are based on **maximum available control technology (MACT).** Nonmajor sources of HAPs, called **area sources,** may also be subject to NESHAPs. Examples of area sources include wood-burning stoves, gas stations, and dry cleaning operations. Because cars are mobile sources, subject to another section of the Act, they are not subject to NESHAPs.

MACT
Maximum Available Control Technology — basis of NESHAPs for major sources

Area Sources
Nonmajor sources that may be subject to NESHAPs

The EPA is attempting to achieve compliance with trading and incentives-based programs. If a source wants to increase the amount of a particular HAP released from its factory, it may choose to offset the increase so that total HAP releases from the factory do not go up. In the alternative, the factory could install pollution controls to keep HAPs at the required level. If a source reduces its releases of a HAP by about 90 percent before the EPA regulates the chemical, the source will get extra time to finish cleaning up the remaining 10 percent.

Another aspect of dealing with HAPs concerns accidental releases. The 1984 disaster in Bhopal, India, involving accidental release of methyl isocyanate gas from a Union Carbide India Limited pesticide plant is estimated to have killed more than 2,000 people. Since then, the EPA has required that businesses develop risk management plans to prevent accidental releases of highly toxic chemicals. The CAA establishes the Chemical Safety Board to investigate and report on accidental releases of hazardous air pollutants from industrial plants.

Assignment 8-4

◆ Visit www.csb.gov/index.cfm and determine whether the Chemical Safety Board is currently investigating any incidents in your area.
◆ Examine 42 U.S.C. §7412. Find the definition of "major source." Find the section dealing with new and existing sources. The section states that standards for existing sources may be lower than standards for new sources, but may not be lower than . . . what?

◆ Visit the list of 188 regulated pollutants at www.epa.gov/ttn/atw/ 188polls.html and the list of industries required to comply with NESHAPs at www.epa.gov/ttn/atw/ mactfnlalph.html.
1. Determine whether the manufacture of vitreous bathroom fixtures is subject to any NESHAPs and, if so, find the NESHAPs.
2. Find the applicable NESHAPs for dry cleaning operations.

Acid Deposition/Acid Rain
Mixture of wet and dry deposits from the atmosphere, with higher-than-normal levels of nitric acids and sulfuric acids

7. Acid Rain

"Acid rain," also called **acid deposition**, is a broad term referring to a mixture of wet and dry deposition (deposited material) from the atmosphere that contains higher-than-normal amounts of nitric and sulfuric acids. The precursors, or chemical components, of acid rain are from natural sources, such as volcanoes and decaying vegetation, and from man-made sources, primarily sulfur dioxide (SO_2) and nitrogen oxides (NO_x) resulting from fossil fuel combustion. In the United States, roughly 2/3 of all SO_2 and 1/4 of all NO_x come from electric power generation that relies on burning fossil fuels, like coal.

To deal with acid rain, the EPA is using cap and trade programs, under which emission allowances are used to achieve compliance with emission reduction requirements. Sources can choose how to reduce emissions, including whether to buy additional allowances from other sources that reduce emissions. When the Acid Rain Program began in 1995, some sources pursued significant early reductions by reducing emissions more than required in the first phase in order to build a large allowance bank for use to meet the tighter requirements of the second phase, which began in 2000. The programs involve:

Caps
Limits on emissions

- An emissions "**cap**" limiting the total amount of pollution that can be released from all regulated sources (e.g., power plants); the cap is set lower than historical emissions in order to reduce emissions.
- Allowances: Each source is given authorization to emit a fixed amount of a pollutant; all of the allowances issued total the cap or less than the cap. The EPA sometimes keeps some of the allowances to use as incentives for sources that install new, cleaner equipment or switch to a renewable energy source. The EPA also auctions allowances, so that there is always a public source of allowances available. The allowances are sometimes purchased by public interest groups so that they are not available to sources of emissions.
- Allowance trading: Sources can buy or sell their allowances on the open market. Because the total number of allowances is limited by the cap, emission reductions are assured.
- Measurement: Tracking of all emissions.
- Compliance: At the end of each compliance period, each source must own at least as many allowances as its emissions. Regardless of how many allowances a unit holds, it may not emit at levels that would violate any other state or federal requirements.

Assignment 8-5

Visit www.epa.gov/airmarkets/trading/buying.html. Write a short report on how a business or environmental group could purchase allowances.

The Program requires sources to install **Continuous Emissions Monitoring Systems (CEMS)** to continuously measure and record emissions and to report hourly emissions on a quarterly basis to the EPA. Information is available to the public at http://cfpub.epa.gov/gdm/.

CEMS
Continuous Emissions Monitoring System — required to check compliance with emissions allowances

At the end of each year, each source has a 60-day grace period to buy SO_2 allowances, if necessary, to cover emissions for the previous year. At the end of the grace period, the allowances a source holds must equal or exceed the annual SO_2 emissions recorded by its monitoring system and verified by EPA. Remaining allowances may be sold or banked for use in future years. If annual emissions exceed the number of allowances held, the source must pay a penalty and must offset the excess SO_2 emissions by surrendering future year allowances in an amount equivalent to the excess.

8. Operating Permits

As you have seen, an operation may be subject to more than one of the programs intended to deal with air pollution. For instance, an electric power plant may be covered by the acid rain, hazardous air pollutant, and nonattainment (smog) parts of the Clean Air Act; the detailed information required by all these separate sections will be in one place — on the source's **operating permit, also called a Title V Permit**. A Title V operating permit (sometimes called a **CAAPP — Clean Air Act Program Permit**) should not be confused with a permit for construction of a new source, described in a previous section.

Operating Permit
Also called a Title V Permit, issued to an existing source

Under the CAA amendments of 1990, states were required to establish programs to issue, review, and renew permits to operate for their most important or "major" sources of air pollution. These Title V permits encompass all Clean Air Act requirements that apply to a source, but a permit itself imposes no new requirements concerning the level or type of emissions; the primary purpose of the permits is to require sources to self-examine for compliance. An operating permit typically does require monitoring, testing, record-keeping, reporting, and annual certification of compliance.

Issuance of an operating permit by a state requires public notice, notice to other states within 50 miles of the source (air quality does not respect state boundaries), and a period for comments as well as review by the EPA. A permit is valid for up to five years. Significant revisions to a permit require compliance with notice and comment procedures.

The operating permit may reflect flexible programs, called market or **market-based** approaches that were established by the 1990 amendments. As discussed in a previous section, the acid rain program offers businesses choices as to how they reach their pollution reduction goals and includes pollution allowances that can be

Market-based
EPA's preferred approach to regulation; includes incentives for earlier compliance, allowance trading programs

---

EXHIBIT 8-8
Who Needs a Permit?

Because permitting is generally handled at the state level, SIPs differ in how they attempt to achieve NAAQS, and states may have their own laws, more stringent than federal law, this book cannot tell you exactly which businesses need operating permits. Certainly a huge, coal-burning, electric power plant needs a permit. But a small, local auto body shop may also need a permit. Determine whether your state has a site similar to the site below, maintained by the Illinois Environmental Protection Agency.

Office of Small Business — Publications

Does My Business Need An Air Pollution Control Permit?

Table of Contents

- State Construction Permits
  - Does My Business Need a Construction Permit?
    - Step 1 — Does my business have an emission source?
    - Step 2 — Does my emission source fit within any of the exemptions from the state permit requirements?
    - Step 3 — For an existing emission source, have you made any modifications that trigger the construction permit requirement?
    - Step 4 — If new equipment or modifications cause increased emissions that are at a major source level, are any other regulations triggered?
- State Operating Permit
  - Does My Business Need an Operating Permit?
    - 1. Will you need an air pollution operating permit for your emission source?
    - 2. What Type of Operating Permit Is Required?
      - Lifetime State Operating Permit
      - Clean Air Act Permit Program
      - Federally Enforceable State Operating Permit

---

traded, bought, and sold. Similarly, a source of criteria pollutants might be allowed to expand or change its operation in a way that increases emission of one criteria pollutant, if it is able to **offset** the increase by obtaining a reduction in emission of the pollutant (the reduction must be greater than the increase being offset) at another location within the nonattainment area. The amendments also included economic incentives for cleaning up pollution sooner rather than later. For instance, gasoline refiners can get credits if they produce cleaner gasoline than required, and they can use those credits when their gasoline doesn't quite meet later cleanup requirements.

EXHIBIT 8-9
Review of Stationary Source Concepts

BACT? RACT? What's up with that?

Your head may be spinning by now, so let's put it in a framework based on whether you are working with an existing source or a new or modified source of emissions.

1. Existing Major Sources
    a. Must have CAAPS permit, good for no more than five years
    b. If in NAA, subject to RACT
    c. Must comply with NESHAPs (even if not a major source), which may be different for existing sources than for new
    d. If it produces energy by burning fossil fuels, may be subject to Acid Rain Program (CEMS, trading allowances)
2. New or Modified Sources
    a. Preconstruction review:
        1. If in NAA, NSR with LAER and offsets
        2. If in attainment area, PSD
    b. Must comply with NESHAPs, even if not major
    c. If it produces energy by burning fossil fuels, may be subject to Acid Rain Program (CEMS and trading allowances)

---

9. Protection of the Stratospheric Ozone Layer

Deterioration of the ozone layer is likely causing **climate change (global warming)**, skin cancers and cataracts, harm to agriculture, and damage to plant life. Despite efforts described below, ozone destruction will likely continue, due to ozone-destroying chemicals already in the stratosphere and those that continue to arrive.

The United States banned chlorofluorocarbons (**CFCs**) as propellants in aerosol cans in 1978 and was among the nations that ratified the Montreal

Climate Change/Global Warming
Climate change assumed to result from destruction of stratospheric ozone layer

CFCs
Chlorofluorocarbons-responsible for damage to stratospheric ozone

Protocol in 1987. The EPA subsequently began the phase-out of other "nonessential" ozone-destroying chemicals. Consumer products containing CFCs and other ozone-destroying chemicals are being reformulated and products containing environmentally friendly alternatives are being labeled as such. The EPA has plans for regulation of hair sprays, paints, foam plastic products (such as disposable Styrofoam coffee cups), carburetor and choke sprays. The EPA also has a number of voluntary programs. For a summary of those programs, visit www.epa.gov/climatechange/policy/neartermghgreduction.html.

Kyoto Protocol
International treaty intended to deal with climate change (global warming)

In 1997 a group of interested nations negotiated the **Kyoto Protocol** with the goal of "stabilization of greenhouse gas concentrations in the atmosphere at a level that would prevent dangerous anthropogenic interference with the climate system." As of 2006, more than 160 countries, not including the United States, had ratified the treaty.

Before April 2007, the EPA had taken the position that additional steps toward dealing with global warming should primarily be the responsibility of the President and Congress. The EPA's position on ozone-depleting omissions may change as a result of the case summarized in Exhibit 8-10.

Assignment 8-6

1. Research the Kyoto Protocol and prepare a report. Describe how the treaty differentiates between developed and nondeveloped nations. How did the differential treatment serve as a basis for some nations' refusal to ratify? What is the counter-argument to the claim that the treaty is unfair in placing a greater burden on developed nations? How many nations have now ratified?

2. Find an EPA ruling concerning phase-out/substitution of Styrofoam. This will be a two-step process. First, find the scientific name for Styrofoam (using any search engine) then search the EPA site using that scientific name.

3. Read the case summarized in Exhibit 8-10 and answer the following:

   ◆ Is the Court ordering the EPA to regulate greenhouse gases?
   ◆ Which particular source of greenhouse gases is at issue in the case?
   ◆ Do you see a conflict between the Department of Transportation's mileage regulations and the ability of the EPA to regulate emissions?

4. Environmental law is a constantly changing field. Being able to work successfully in the field requires the ability to keep up with the changes. What has the EPA done in response to the Supreme Court decision in *Massachusetts v. EPA*? Research and write a report.

EXHIBIT 8-10

The Supreme Court weighed in on EPA discretion in regulating emissions in 2007, in *Massachusetts v. Environmental Protection Agency*. To see the entire opinion, visit www.supremecourtus.gov/opinions/06pdf/05-1120.pd.

Courtesy of Lora Lucero, editor of Planning and Environmental Law.

After the U.S. declined to enter into the Kyoto Protocol for reducing greenhouse gas emissions, a group of environmental organizations petitioned the EPA to regulate such emissions from new motor vehicles under §202 of the CAA. That section provides that the EPA shall regulate emission of "any air pollutant" from new motor vehicles which, in the judgment of the EPA administrator, contributes to air pollution reasonably anticipated to endanger public health or welfare. The EPA received more than 50,000 comments during its rule-making process and a report was prepared, concluding that accumulation of greenhouse gases is causing temperatures to rise. The EPA nonetheless denied the petition, stating that it lacked authority to regulate greenhouse gases and that if it had authority, it would be unwise to exercise it at that time. The groups sought review, joined by local governments and several states. The Court of Appeals denied review.

The United States Supreme Court reversed and remanded. Justice Stevens wrote the opinion for the 5-4 majority. First, the Court held that Massachusetts has standing to challenge the EPA's refusal to promulgate regulations, relying heavily on the "special solicitude" owed the Commonwealth. Massachusetts owns substantial land and has suffered direct and substantial harms resulting from climate change because "the rising seas have already begun to swallow Massachusetts' coastal land." The Court noted that the state itself cannot "invade Rhode Island to force reductions in greenhouse gas emissions" or negotiate treaties and is acting to secure federal protections for its citizens, not to protect its citizens from federal laws. Although the harms from global warming are widely shared, Massachusetts has a substantial interest in the outcome of the litigation. The fact that regulation of emissions from new vehicles will not halt or reverse climate change does not justify the EPA's refusal to act.

After concluding that Massachusetts has standing, the Court acknowledged that review of the statutory issues is narrow. The Court distinguished a challenge to EPA's denial of rule-making petitions from an agency's refusal to initiate enforcement proceedings which are not ordinarily subject to judicial review. Although EPA concluded the CAA did not authorize it to regulate greenhouse gas emissions, the Court disagreed and noted that the statute is unambiguous and covers "any" physical or chemical substance that enters the ambient air. There is no indication that Congress intended to limit the EPA's ability to regulate greenhouse gases; the EPA cannot "shirk" its duties based on the fact that regulating emissions would overlap the authority of the Department of Transportation to regulate mileage standards. The Court also rejected the reasons EPA claimed for its refusal to regulate greenhouse gas emissions: that by regulating greenhouse gas emissions it would interfere with the President's negotiations with other nations and non-regulatory programs to promote reduction of emissions. The Court noted that the EPA did not argue that greenhouse gases do not present a danger. The agency can only avoid promulgating regulations, Justice Stevens wrote, "if it determines that greenhouse gases do not contribute to climate change or if it provides some reasonable explanation as to why it cannot or will not exercise its discretion to determine whether they do."

Dissenting Justices acknowledged that global warming may be the "most pressing environmental problem of our time," but concluded the challenges were nonjusticiable and the grievances should properly be redressed by Congress and the Chief Executive.

10. Mobile Sources

Today's cars produce 60 to 80 percent less pollution than cars in the 1960s. More people are using mass transit. Leaded gas has been phased out. Motor vehicles are, nonetheless, responsible for the release of more than half of hazardous pollutants. The EPA imposes standards to limit harmful emissions from vehicles when they are running and evaporative emissions when they are not. The EPA's Transportation and Air Quality Program, at www.epa.gov/otaq/index.htm:

- Regulates tailpipe emissions from mobile sources;
- Imposes performance standards on the mechanical parts of vehicles;
- Regulates the fuels used to operate mobile sources; and
- Encourages use of public transit to minimize emissions.

Regulated "mobile sources" include cars and light trucks, large trucks and buses, off-road recreational vehicles (such as dirt bikes and snowmobiles), farm and construction equipment, lawn and garden equipment, marine engines, aircraft, and locomotives.

a. Tailpipe Emissions

The CAA initially set the first federal tailpipe standards, but granted California, which has some of the worst air quality in the country, authority to set its own emission standards. Beginning in 1990, other states have been allowed to adopt the California program as their own (and several have done so), but are prohibited from setting their own emission standards. The 1990 amendments also require inspection and maintenance programs in nonattainment areas. Some states already had emission inspection programs in place, but now must meet federal standards. Federal and California standards limit exhaust emissions of five pollutants: hydrocarbons, nitrogen oxides, carbon monoxide, particulate matter (diesel vehicles only), and formaldehyde. The standards regulate emissions from cars and "light-duty trucks," which includes sport utility vehicles (SUVs), pickups, and minivans.

Tier 1/Tier 2
Federal standards for vehicle emissions

The federal **Tier 1** standards, phased in between 1994 and 1997, allowed SUVs, minivans, pickup trucks, and diesel vehicles to pollute more than gasoline cars. Between 1997 and 2004, the National Low-Emission Vehicle Program reduced emissions by means of cooperation between government and vehicle manufacturers. In 2004, the EPA began phasing in **Tier 2** standards, which include a fleet averaging program. Manufacturers can produce vehicles with emissions ranging from relatively dirty to zero, but the mix of vehicles a manufacturer sells each year must have average emissions below a specified value. The CAA, unlike the Energy Policy Act (discussed in another chapter), does not mandate use of alternative fuel vehicles (AFVs), but the Tier 2 standards create an environment favorable to AFVs. Tier 2 provides automakers with flexibility for meeting the standards and is a cost-effective method of reducing overall pollution from automobiles.

EPA Description of Tier 2

From www.epa.gov/orcdizux/regs/ld-hwy/tier-2/index.htm.

The Tier 2 Vehicle and Gasoline Sulfur Program is a landmark program that affects every new passenger vehicle and every gallon of gasoline sold in the U.S. By designing cleaner cars that run on cleaner fuels the result is cleaner air. The program is a series of "firsts." For the first time:

◆ SUVs, pickups, vans, and even the largest personal passenger vehicles are subject to the same national emission standards as cars;
◆ vehicles and the fuels they use are treated as a system, so the cleaner vehicles will have the low-sulfur gasoline they need to run their cleanest;
◆ new emission standards apply to all light vehicles, regardless of whether they run on gasoline, diesel fuel, or alternative fuels.

The LEV (low emission vehicle) programs adopted by states following California standards are fleet average programs, like the federal Tier 2 standards. Manufacturers can certify vehicles to one of several emissions categories as long as the average hydrocarbon emissions of all new vehicles sold meets a specified standard. This standard becomes more stringent each year, forcing manufacturers to move toward a cleaner overall mix of vehicles. California's authority to enact more stringent regulations can have an interesting impact on manufacturers, which normally oppose more stringent federal regulation. When the EPA proposed new rules for emissions from small engines in April 2007, some manufacturers actually favored the change because California had already enacted the rule, so they had to comply with the more stringent standards for equipment sold in that state.

NEWS FLASH: In *Center for Biological Diversity v. National Highway Traffic Safety Admin. (NHTSA)*, the third "global warming" case decided by federal courts in 2007, public interest groups, states, and cities sued NHTSA, the agency that sets vehicle mileage requirements under the Energy Policy and Conservation Act, 49 U.S.C. §32901. Note that these standards relate to mileage rather than emissions, which are the subject of EPA regulations. The plaintiffs characterized an increase in required corporate average fuel economy (CAFE) mileage for "light trucks" to 23.5 miles per gallon by 2010 as "trivial." The category includes many top-selling sport utility vehicles, minivans, and pickup trucks and is currently required to achieve average fuel economy of 22.2 mpg.

In November 2007, the Ninth Circuit Court of Appeals held that NHTSA acted arbitrarily in implementing the Act's mandate that CAFE standards "be the maximum feasible average fuel economy level." While NHTSA is not prohibited from using a cost-benefit analysis to set standards, it cannot "put a thumb on the scale by undervaluing the benefits and overvaluing the costs of more stringent standards" as it did by failing to monetize the benefit of carbon emissions reductions. The agency's failure to close the "SUV loophole" was also called arbitrary: "NHTSA's decision runs counter to the evidence showing that SUVs, vans and pickup trucks are manufactured primarily for the purpose of transporting passengers and are generally not used for off-highway operation." The court further held that the NHTSA must consider first-ever fuel economy requirements on heavy pickup trucks, weighing 8,500 to 10,000 pounds. Finally, the court held that NHTSA must prepare an environmental impact statement pursuant to the NEPA. The CAFE standard will affect the level of greenhouse gas emissions and global warming. The environmental assessment prepared by the agency inadequately assessed cumulative impacts and considered an inadequate range of alternatives.

b. Performance Standards

Before a manufacturer may sell a regulated vehicle, it must apply for an EPA Certificate of Conformity and demonstrate that emissions standards will be met for the prescribed "useful life." The useful life period can range from 10 years or 100,000 miles for passenger cars and up to 365,000 miles for heavy truck engines. Manufacturers must also generally ensure that vehicle emission control systems operate in-use as they do during testing. The EPA also monitors compliance with new on-board diagnostic system requirements for most cars and trucks, which are designed to detect and alert the operator to certain emissions systems failures. In addition, manufacturers must notify EPA when substantial numbers of defects occur in a vehicle's emissions control system.

The EPA usually discovers violations by spot testing vehicles, notifications from the manufacturers, or information from a variety of other sources such as state inspection stations. In addition to penalties, EPA may seek recall of vehicles (where a notice is sent to vehicle owners to bring their vehicles in for free repair) or other measures.

c. Fuels

EPA regulations require that each manufacturer or importer of gasoline, diesel fuel, or a fuel additive have its product registered before introduction into commerce. In some cases, the EPA requires testing for possible health effects.

Among other requirements, the EPA requires that gasoline contain a certified detergent to reduce emissions, has banned lead in gasoline since 1995, and requires gasoline to meet volatility standards to decrease evaporative emissions. Gas stations in nonattainment areas are required to install vapor recovery nozzles on gas pumps. As an example of the overlap between programs, in 2007, the EPA finalized a NESHAP limiting the benzene content of gasoline to reduce toxic emissions from passenger vehicles and gas cans. To see the EPA standards for fuels and additives, visit www.epa.gov/otaq/fuels.htm and www.epa.gov/nvfel/ (the National Vehicle and Fuel Emissions Laboratory).

d. Mass Transit

Although the 1990 amendments called for state and regional transportation plans in "conformity" with SIPs, court decisions and budget problems have delayed the process. Nonetheless, some nonattainment metropolitan areas have changed or will have to change their transportation policies, discourage unnecessary auto use, and encourage efficient commuting (van pools, HOV (high-occupancy vehicle) lanes, etc.) in order to reduce their level of nonattainment.

For information about public transportation and the environment, far beyond the scope of this book, visit www.fhwa.dot.gov/environment/conform.htm. The "vehicle fleet" provisions of the 1990 Amendments are also beyond the scope of this chapter, but interested students can easily research those requirements on the Internet.

C. In the Field: Working with the CAA

While the number of programs enforced under the CAA, the different standards, and the overlap of programs may make you hope that you never encounter a CAA issue in your career, keep in mind that "thar's gold in them-thar acronyms." Do a quick search of a job site, such as Monster or Careerbuilder, or just use a search site, such as Google, and enter a CAA term, such as "Title V Permit" or "NESHAPs." You will be amazed at the number of jobs that refer to knowledge of those terms and at the high salaries attached to those jobs. Some of these jobs require engineering or science degrees; many do not.

So, if you don't have a scientific background, how can you determine the relevant scientific requirements and whether a facility is in compliance? Companies operating in regulated industries or producing potentially regulated products often rely on professional associations to keep up with legal requirements. For example, manufacturers of outdoor power equipment may opt for membership in the Outdoor Power Equipment Institute, www.opei.org; those who manage vehicle fleets and must be aware of emissions rules might refer to http://fleetowner.com/about/. A dry cleaning establishment might join an organization such as www.sda-dryclean.com/. Careful searches of the EPA website will also result in a wealth of information, as shown in Exhibit 8-11, from www.epa.gov/OMSWWW/equip-ld.htm.

Policies for Operating a CAA-Regulated Facility

- ◆ Check regularly to be sure you have all required permits. If you buy or sell a business, do not assume that permits can be transferred.
- ◆ Avoid revision of the permit. Write the permit application as broadly as possible to allow flexibility in methods of operation or use of different chemicals. Once you have a permit, do not assume that you can change the way you operate or replace equipment without invalidating the permit.

◆ Having a permit and permit compliance are two different things. Have a system in place for ensuring that key people know what the permit requires and regularly check for compliance.

◆ The law changes. Do not assume that the future will be like the past or present.

EXHIBIT 8-11
Resources

The EPA has many web pages to assist the public with compliance issues.

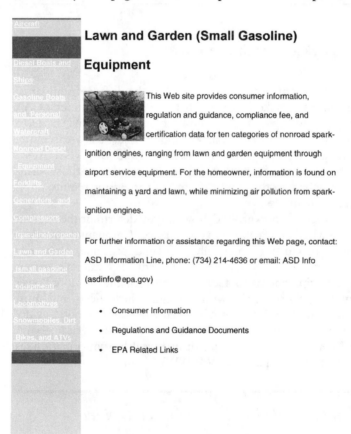

Lawn and Garden (Small Gasoline)

Equipment

This Web site provides consumer information, regulation and guidance, compliance fee, and certification data for ten categories of nonroad spark-ignition engines, ranging from lawn and garden equipment through airport service equipment. For the homeowner, information is found on maintaining a yard and lawn, while minimizing air pollution from spark-ignition engines.

For further information or assistance regarding this Web page, contact: ASD Information Line, phone: (734) 214-4636 or email: ASD Info (asdinfo@epa.gov)

- Consumer Information
- Regulations and Guidance Documents
- EPA Related Links

In addition, the EPA Technology Transfer Network has a Clean Air Technology Center that can be researched to determine current standards: www.epa.gov/ttn/catc/.

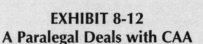

EXHIBIT 8-12
A Paralegal Deals with CAA

Author's note:

Writing about the CAA nearly defeated me! My goal, as a teacher, is not only that the students "know" the material, but that they understand it. It should make sense and they should be able to visualize how the information will fit into their careers. After I finished the chapter, I gave it to my paralegal, Samira, for her comments. Samira pulled a "Dr. Phil" and told me to "get real." I told Samira to help me get real by creating a scenario so that students can follow it through the process. In developing this "walk through the process" we had substantial help from the Iowa DNR. The e-mails are real and only slightly edited; some agency personnel were shy about having their real names appear in print.

SCENE ONE: I FOUGHT THE LAW AND THE LAW WON

It was busy day at Vietzen and Associates, with faxes ringing and clients calling for updates on their files when a message from the secretary caught Ms. Vietzen's eye. The message was from UDigg, LLC, the firm's biggest client, so Ms. Vietzen immediately returned the call, with her paralegal, Lisa, listening to the speaker phone and taking notes. Motivated by gas prices approaching $4 per gallon in the Chicago area and bad news about the impact of global warming, the company is planning to build an ethanol plant in Iowa City, Iowa, and has already acquired land and zoning approvals. The company is working with a consulting firm of engineers and is modeling the plant after an existing plant in Coon Rapids, Iowa.

Ms. Vietzen assigned this file to Lisa at once and advised her, "Deal with this, I'm swamped!" Lisa had joined the firm two months earlier, fresh out of college. She had a paralegal certificate. She had no real environmental law experience but had taken an environmental law course. After Ms. Vietzen assigned her the file, Lisa "wigged out." She kept thinking that UDigg was a major client and she could really mess things up!! After ten minutes of hyperventilating, she finally calmed down and made a checklist. She remembered a few concepts from her class; she knew she had to find out whether Iowa has an approved SIP and whether the area was in attainment. She also decided to educate herself about ethanol plants, so that she would be able to discuss the project with the client.

A quick visit to www.epa.gov revealed that Iowa has an approved SIP and that the IDNR administers the program. According to www.epa.gov/air/data/geosel, Iowa has no nonattainment zone. The site tested for carbon monoxide, nitrogen dioxide, ozone, sulfur dioxide, particulate (less than both 2.5 and 10 micrometers) and lead.

Just a few minutes on the Internet, searching [Iowa ethanol air permit] led to a website that provided Lisa with much-needed background information. From the www.iowa.gov website:

EXHIBIT 8-12
(continued)

AIR QUALITY

Standard Air Construction Permit

The type of air quality permits needed for an **ethanol** processing facility is determined by the potential emissions from the facility. Construction permits must be applied for and obtained prior to beginning construction. There are several activities and processes that **ethanol** plants typically require construction permits for, including:

- Grain receiving, grinding/milling, grain transfer, grain storage and distillation,
- **Ethanol** storage tanks, boilers, additive storage tanks, fermenters, and diesel fire pump,
- Cooling tower, **ethanol** truck loadout, **ethanol** rail loadout,
- Drying of distillers dried grains (DDGS), DDGS storage, DDGS loadout, methanators, and
- If burning coal, coal receiving, storage, conditioning, and fly-ash handling.

Some emission control options that an **ethanol** plant will need to consider are thermal oxidizer on DDGS dryers, flares on **ethanol** loadouts, particulate filters on grain bins, and at a minimum low NO_x (nitrogen oxides) burners in any boilers. If burning coal, then fluidized bed, selective non-catalytic reduction (SNCR), lime injection and a baghouse should be considered.

Prevention of Significant Deterioration (PSD) Permit

If the **ethanol** plant's potential emissions are above the federal Prevention of Significant Deterioration (PSD) thresholds, PSD construction permits are needed. The threshold of concern is 100 tons per year. (A threshold is the point at which the quantity or type of pollutant emitted requires securing a PSD permit.)

Specific types of pollutants that an **ethanol** facility would need to consider installing pollution controls for, in order not to exceed PSD thresholds, include volatile organic compounds (ozone), and NO_x (nitrogen oxides). The average IDNR time to approve a PSD permit is six to nine months. The ability of IDNR to approve a PSD permit within six months is predicated on a number of criteria. Public notice and holding a public hearing are built into this timeframe. For more information on IDNR guidelines see http://www.iowadnr.com/air/prof/const/const.html.

Lisa next found the permit for the Coon Rapids plant at http://www.iowadnr.com/air/prof/oper/tv/final/07-TV-001.pdf and printed it for future reference. After a thorough examination of the Iowa Department of Natural Resources website, she jotted down the information and wrote a memo.

EXHIBIT 8-12
(continued)

TO: L Vietzen   From: Lisa Walker
DATE: April 21, 2007
CLIENT: UDigg, LLC (contact G Bushney)
FILE: 07-843-3221   Building Ethanol Plant

Our first step on this project will be to determine whether this plant will qualify for "standard" construction permits. If its potential emissions will exceed PSD limits, we will have to follow the more rigorous PSD permit process, which starts with a pre-application meeting required of all Greenfield Ethanol Plant PSD projects. The meeting would most probably be at the site of the facility and would include a tour of the area and/or the processes involved.

The following information would need to be submitted to the Department of Natural Resources (DNR) at least one week prior to the meeting: an agenda of items for discussion; a list of people who will attend; an executive summary of the project; anticipated emission rates and controls; location of the proposed facility and of any nearby facilities that are under common control or will provide support; analysis of MACT/NSPS applicability (will a Title V permit be required); modeling protocol if modeling is required; plans for pre-construction monitoring if existing data is insufficient; and whether we want the EPA involved in the meeting.

The following items will be discussed at the pre-application meeting: required application forms; the permitting process; site-specific issues; acceptable/anticipated control measures; local air quality concerns; pre-construction monitoring and dispersion modeling; modeling protocol; additional impact analysis; identification of examples of similar permits; BACT; monitoring, testing, record-keeping; economic feasibility; communication expectations, procedures, and responsibilities; confidentiality; applications formatting and copies; allowable pre-permit activities; timeline for review; and DNR policy for determining priority for the project.

The pre-application meeting itself should be scheduled no earlier than three months prior to permit application submittal. The application itself should be nearly complete before attending the pre-application meeting. The DNR will send all appropriate people based on the information submitted prior to the meeting and will also coordinate with EPA and the local agency if their attendance is applicable.

EXHIBIT 8-12
(continued)

After Attorney Vietzen reviewed the memo, she sent Lisa a brief note:

Lisa,

I appreciate your work on this, but before we get back to the UDigg folks, we need a bit more information:

1. What is a Greenfield Ethanol Plant? Are there other types? Would the UDigg project be a Greenfield project?

2. Before we jump the gun and assume that we have to go the PSD route, let's check with some agency folks and see if we might qualify for standard permits.

3. What the heck is modeling protocol?

Lisa was already on top of things and responded:

TO: L Vietzen   From: Lisa Walker
DATE: April 21, 2007
CLIENT: UDigg, LLC (contact G Bushney)
FILE: 07-843-3221   Building Ethanol Plant

Greenfield Ethanol Plants.

Internet research on ethanol plants indicates that there are two types of ethanol. Conventional ethanol and cellulosic ethanol both produce the same ethanol but use different feedstock and processes. Conventional ethanol is derived from grains such as corn, wheat or soybeans. Corn, the predominant feedstock, is converted to ethanol in either a dry or wet milling process. In dry milling operations, liquefied corn starch is produced by heating corn meal with water and enzymes. A second enzyme converts the liquefied starch to sugars, which are fermented by yeast into ethanol and carbon dioxide. Wet milling operations separate the fiber, germ (oil), and protein from the starch before it is fermented into ethanol.

Cellulosic ethanol is produced from cellulosic biomass feedstock including agricultural plant wastes like cereal straws or sugarcane bagasse, plant wastes from industrial processes like sawdust and paper pulp, and energy crops grown specifically for fuel production, such as switchgrass. www.Harvestcleanenergy.com. A given volume ethanol requires 27 volumes of switchgrass compared to 3.6 volumes of corn grain!

Greenfield ethanol plants seem to use corn ethanol. According to the Alternative Energy Sources website, a new ethanol plant will be built in Ogden, Iowa. AES describes itself as operating "greenfield" sites including constructing, owning and operating fuel-grade ethanol plants. After reviewing the permit for the plant in Coon Rapids, it seems that it produced conventional ethanol.

EXHIBIT 8-12
(continued)

Modeling protocol? Modeling protocol is one of the items to be discussed at the pre-application meeting. They don't really define what modeling protocol is, unless they have specific plant model specifics that need to be adhered to. I believe that knowing that the UDigg plant will be modeled after the Coon Rapids plant will be helpful.

SCENE TWO: WE GET BY WITH A LITTLE HELP FROM OUR FRIENDS

Later, Lisa got the following e-mails from her boss. Ms. Vietzen had contacted IDNR.

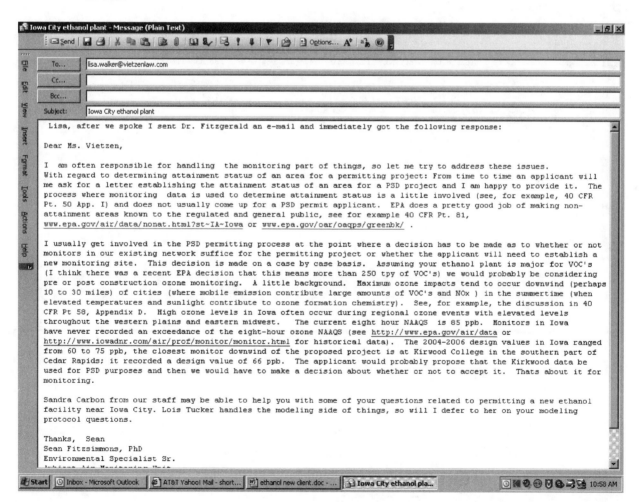

EXHIBIT 8-12
(continued)

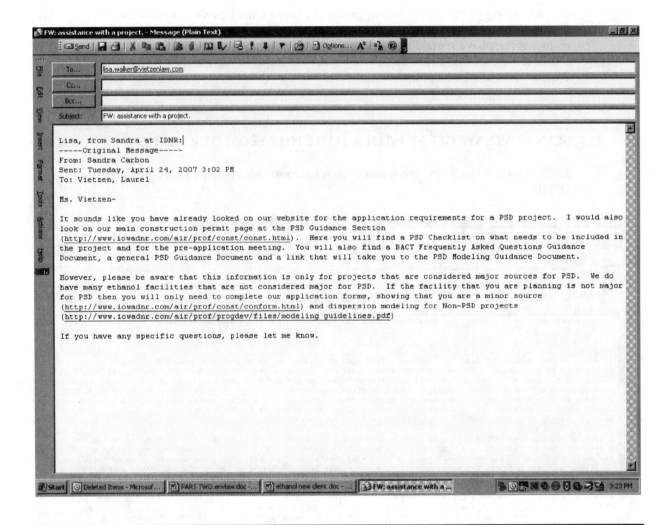

EXHIBIT 8-12
(continued)

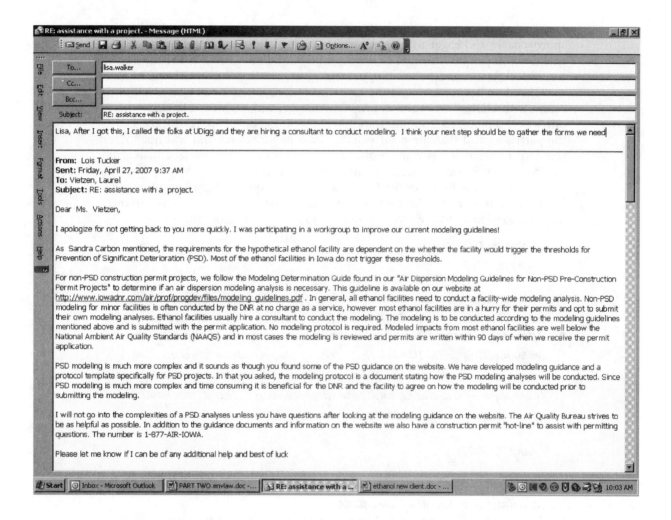

To... lisa.walker

Cc...

Bcc...

Subject: RE: assistance with a project.

Lisa, After I got this, I called the folks at UDigg and they are hiring a consultant to conduct modeling. I think your next step should be to gather the forms we need

From: Lois Tucker
Sent: Friday, April 27, 2007 9:37 AM
To: Vietzen, Laurel
Subject: RE: assistance with a project.

Dear Ms. Vietzen,

I apologize for not getting back to you more quickly. I was participating in a workgroup to improve our current modeling guidelines!

As Sandra Carbon mentioned, the requirements for the hypothetical ethanol facility are dependent on the whether the facility would trigger the thresholds for Prevention of Significant Deterioration (PSD). Most of the ethanol facilities in Iowa do not trigger these thresholds.

For non-PSD construction permit projects, we follow the Modeling Determination Guide found in our "Air Dispersion Modeling Guidelines for Non-PSD Pre-Construction Permit Projects" to determine if an air dispersion modeling analysis is necessary. This guideline is available on our website at http://www.iowadnr.com/air/prof/progdev/files/modeling_guidelines.pdf . In general, all ethanol facilities need to conduct a facility-wide modeling analysis. Non-PSD modeling for minor facilities is often conducted by the DNR at no charge as a service, however most ethanol facilities are in a hurry for their permits and opt to submit their own modeling analyses. Ethanol facilities usually hire a consultant to conduct the modeling. The modeling is to be conducted according to the modeling guidelines mentioned above and is submitted with the permit application. No modeling protocol is required. Modeled impacts from most ethanol facilities are well below the National Ambient Air Quality Standards (NAAQS) and in most cases the modeling is reviewed and permits are written within 90 days of when we receive the permit application.

PSD modeling is much more complex and it sounds as though you found some of the PSD guidance on the website. We have developed modeling guidance and a protocol template specifically for PSD projects. In that you asked, the modeling protocol is a document stating how the PSD modeling analyses will be conducted. Since PSD modeling is much more complex and time consuming it is beneficial for the DNR and the facility to agree on how the modeling will be conducted prior to submitting the modeling.

I will not go into the complexities of a PSD analyses unless you have questions after looking at the modeling guidance on the website. The Air Quality Bureau strives to be as helpful as possible. In addition to the guidance documents and information on the website we also have a construction permit "hot-line" to assist with permitting questions. The number is 1-877-AIR-IOWA.

Please let me know if I can be of any additional help and best of luck

EXHIBIT 8-12
(continued)

Lisa gained an important insight from this: Agency personnel are generally very approachable and eager to help. They have a lot of expertise and do not mind dealing with people who don't know as much. She knew that in the future she would feel very confident about approaching agency employees with questions.

Based on her research and the input from the agency, Lisa began communicating with UDigg's consultant, project manager, and engineers. Because everyone was well prepared, communication went well. In consultation with the DNR, the parties agreed that the plant will not be a major source and will qualify for standard construction permits, rather than PSD review. Ms. Vietzen instructed Lisa to start work on the necessary application forms.

Lisa found the forms for the Minor Source Emissions Inventory, mentioned by Ms. Carbon, at www.iowadnr.com/air/prof/emiss/emiss.html. The site is extremely helpful and includes lots of practical information about filling out the forms.

Notes to File
May 1, 2007

- *The application will require multiple forms and will go through several levels of agency review. DNR has a flow chart of the review process online.*
- *After 4/29 meeting with Ms. Vietzen regarding the application forms, set a meeting with UDigg's engineer. The application forms require very specific technical info. There are questions about the number of stacks; the height of the stacks; and even if there were "control" stacks just in case one of the regular stacks were to get obstructed.*

May 7, 2007

- *Met with UDigg engineer, Elise Peters, who assisted in the detailed calculations of potential emissions.*
- *Iowa DNR will conduct tests again after the plant is up and running, to check actual emissions.*
- *It was very impressive that every function of the plant was so well planned, with back up plans just in case. I never realized that there was so much care given to every industrial endeavor!*
- *Prepared drafts of application forms, forwarded to Ms. V and Ms. Peters for review.*

EXHIBIT 8-12
(continued)

AIR QUALITY BUREAU
7900 Hickman Rd., Suite 1
Urbandale, IA 50322

IOWA DNR Emission Inventory Questionnaire

Form INV-1 Facility Identification

☐ YES ☐ NO - *Would you like an instruction book mailed to you for the next inventory cycle?*

1) Application Type	Initial **X**	Supplemental ☐
2) Facility Number		
3) Company/Facility Name	UDigg, LLC	
4) Emission Year	2008	
5) Facility Street Address	1200 Warski Road	
6) Facility City	Iowa City	IA
7) Zip Code	52241	
8) Facility Contact Person	George Bushney	
9) Facility Contact Phone Number	847-555-1234	
10) Mailing Street/PO Box	P.O.Box 29	
11) Mailing City	Industrial City	
12) State	Illinois	
13) Zip Code	60060	
14) Parent Company / Owner Name		
15) Parent Company / Owner Mailing Address		
16) City		
17) State		
18) Zip Code		
19) Parent Company Contact/Agent		
20) ParentCompanyContactPhone		
21) Standard Industrial Classification (SIC)	2869	
22) Activity Description	Industrial Organic Chemicals	

23) SECONDARY ACTIVITIES

SIC	
Activity Description	
SIC	
Activity Description	

24) PLANT LOCATION

Latitude	
Longitude	

Key Terms

Acid Deposition
Acid Rain
Administrative
Citation
Enforcement
Allowance-trading
AQCR
Area Sources
Attainment
BACT
CAAPP
Caps
CEMS
CFCs
Criteria Pollutants
Global Warming
HAPs
Kyoto Protocol
LAER
MACT

Major Source
Market-based Approach
Mobile Sources
MSDS
NAAQS:
    Primary and
    Secondary
NSR/NSPS
NESHAPs
Offsets
Operating Permit
OSHA
PSD
RACT
SIP
Smog
Stationary Sources
Stratospheric Ozone
Tier 1/Tier 2
Title V Permit

Review Questions

1. Identify the enforcement options available under the CAA. What is the main advantage of administrative enforcement?
2. Which law/administrative agency regulates indoor air pollution? What is an MSDS and who is it intended to protect?
3. What impact does the division of the country into air quality regions have on the economy?
4. What is the impact of stricter regulation of new sources?
5. What are criteria pollutants and how do they relate to NAAQS?
6. What is the difference between primary NAAQS and secondary NAAQS?
7. By what means does the CAA attempt to achieve attainment of NAAQS?
8. How might a state be sanctioned for failing to develop an adequate SIP?
9. Why might an existing source of emissions limit upgrades and changes at its facility?
10. What are the three types of requirements for new stationary sources?
11. To what situations do BACT, LAER, and PSD apply? What do those initials stand for? Which is the most stringent?
12. By what means does the EPA deal with pollution from motor vehicles? What are the Tier II regulations?

13. What are NESHAPs? Are new sources treated differently with respect to NESHAPs, and does it matter whether the source is in an attainment area? Are NESHAPs applicable only to major sources?
14. Explain the acid rain trading allowances program. What other market-based incentives exist to help improve air quality?
15. An existing stationary source, making no changes, is not subject to NSR or NSPS, but it still must have a permit. What type of permit will it have and what types of standards/limitations will be contained in that permit?

KEY TERMS CROSSWORD

www.CrosswordWeaver.com

ACROSS

2. _____ pollutants include lead, smog, carbon monoxide, nitrogen dioxide, sulfur oxides, and particulate matter
7. a pollution source may be stationary or _____
8. In SIPs for attainment areas, this standard applies (initials)
9. must submit implementation plans for dealing with criteria pollutants
12. abbreviation—standards for criteria pollutants
14. The EPA favors _____-based approaches to decreasing pollution
15. initials, one of the standards for new sources in nonattainment areas
16. agency that deals with indoor pollutants
18. Regulation of pollution from mobile sources involves regulation of this
19. _____NAAQS are based on health criteria
20. a _____ suit is possible if the agency fails to enforce pollution laws
21. Initials, 189 were identified by Congress for regulation

DOWN

1. an administrative _____ is like a traffic ticket for violating environmental regulations
3. existing major sources in nonattainment areas standard (initials)
4. the EPA sets these, as part of acid rain program
5. abbreviation, manufacturer provides this to inform workers about handling dangerous chemicals
6. regulation of criteria pollutants depends on whether region is in _____
10. also called ground-level ozone
11. initials, a standard for hazardous pollutants
13. regulation of acid rain involves trading these
17. _____ protocol, a treaty dealing with global warming

9

◆ ◆ ◆

Water

◆ ◆ ◆

A. Overview: Riparian Rights and Public Trust

As with air pollution, the issue of water pollution is complicated by the nature of the resource. Water exists in many forms: **surface water**, such as lakes, ponds, and

Surface Water
Water above ground

227

Navigable
Capable of navigation

Ground Water
Water beneath the surface

Riparian Rights
Rights of adjoining land-
owners to use a body of
water

Littoral Rights
Rights of owners of lake
frontage

Prior Appropriation
Doctrine for allocation of
water rights in some states

Public Trust Doctrine
Theory that resources are
held in trust for public use

rivers; it may be **navigable** or may be confined to a single owner's property; **ground water** is beneath the surface of the earth. Water travels across jurisdictional lines and may be polluted by indirect means, such as acid rain. While concerns about air focus on quality, concerns about water involve both quality and availability. Like regulation of air pollution, regulation of water pollution has evolved so that the law appears to be a patchwork of programs, rather than a cohesive whole. In addition to the Clean Water Act, 33 U.S.C. §1251 et seq., federal statutory law includes the Safe Drinking Water Act, 42 U.S.C. §300, the Coastal Zone Management Act, 16 U.S.C. §301, the Oil Pollution Act,[1] 33 U.S.C. §2701, and the Ocean Dumping Ban Act, 16 U.S.C. §§1431 et seq., 1447 et seq.; 33 U.S.C. §§1401 et seq., §§2801 et seq.[2] There are also common law concepts, such as the doctrine of **riparian rights**, and various state and local laws.

Under the riparian rights doctrine, all owners of property adjacent to a body of water own property under the navigable water, generally to the center of the stream, and have the right to make reasonable use of the water. The owners of property abutting a nonflowing body, such as a lake, have similar rights, known as **littoral rights**. What is "reasonable" use depends on the impact of the use on other riparian owners and on the general public. Because of the public trust doctrine, discussed below, many states restrict the rights of riparian owners to withdraw water and to install structures in the water. If a riparian owner does have the right to withdraw water and there is not enough water to satisfy all users, allotments are generally fixed in proportion to frontage on the water source.

In several western states, however, water rights are allocated under the principle of **prior appropriation**, under which the right to use water is established according to the "first in time, first in right" theory. The doctrine treats water rights as a resource unrelated to land. In those states water rights can be sold, independently of the land, and can even be mortgaged. Some states have "dual systems," in which both the riparian rights doctrine and the prior appropriation doctrine apply to water rights. States can have different systems and it is important to know the law for your jurisdiction. For example, California's system might be appropriately called a "plural system"; water rights are use rights and all waters are the property of the state. A water right in California is a property right allowing the use of water, but it does not involve ownership of the water.

At the same time, the constitutions of most states provide state government with authority over navigable waters and that authority must be exercised consistently with the **public trust doctrine** (discussed in a previous chapter). Under that doctrine, the government is obligated to protect the quality of the water, public access, and uses, such as navigation and recreation. The public's right to access the shore, balanced against the rights of the riparian owner, can lead to complex issues that are resolved differently in different states. For example, in Wisconsin, a person has the right to walk along the shore of a flowing stream and a riparian owner may not install barricades to prevent such access, but a nonowner's placement of a "crawdad trap" under the water along the shore would constitute trespass.

---

[1] The statute is beyond the scope of this book, but you should be aware of its existence. The law improved governmental response to oil spills and requires both businesses and government to establish contingency plans.

[2] Among other things, this law regulates ocean dumping, http://epw.senate.gov/mprsa72.pdf.

EXHIBIT 9-1

States are increasingly restricting riparian rights to protect the public interest in waterways. For example, some states limit a riparian owner's rights.

From http://www.legis.state.wi.us/rsb/stats.html.

30.133 Prohibition against conveyance of riparian rights.

(1) Beginning on April 9, 1994, no owner of riparian land that abuts a navigable water may convey, by easement or by a similar conveyance, any riparian right in the land to another person, except for the right to cross the land in order to have access to the navigable water. This right to cross the land may not include the right to place any structure or material in the navigable water.

From www.leg.state.nv.us/NRS/NRS-445A.html#NRS445ASec170.

NRS 445A.170 Permit or written permission required from State Department of Conservation and Natural Resources.

1. It is unlawful for any person, firm, association or corporation to:
   (a) Construct a pier, breakwater or marina in or to alter the shoreline of Lake Tahoe;
   (b) Remove gravel, sand or similar material from Lake Tahoe; or
   (c) Deposit any fill or deleterious material in Lake Tahoe, without first having secured written permission from the State Department of Conservation and Natural Resources.
2. Construction or alteration of the Lake Tahoe shoreline below the high water elevation (6,229.1 feet) requires written permission from the State Department of Conservation and Natural Resources.
3. A permit must be denied when the source of domestic water or the place of disposal of sewage or other wastes would create a health hazard or the quality of Lake Tahoe waters would be impaired.
4. The State Department of Conservation and Natural Resources shall adopt regulations governing the issuance of permits under this section.

B. Clean Water Act

The Clean Water Act, CWA, applies to navigable "waters of the United States." Refer back to the discussion of the *Rapanos* case in Chapter 4 (Exhibit 4-2) to recall the controversy concerning the meaning of that term. The Act is primarily implemented and enforced by state agencies and/or the EPA and the U.S. Army Corps of Engineers. The CWA seeks to achieve its goals by:

- Authorizing **water quality standards** for surface waters,
- Requiring **permits** for point source discharges of pollutants into navigable waters,
- Assisting with funding for construction of municipal sewage treatment plants, and
- Planning for control of nonpoint source pollution.

Water Quality Standards
Standards for achieving designated uses

It's all about pollution, but where does the pollution come from? The distinction between **point sources** and **nonpoint sources (NPS)** of pollution is critical. The CWA defines "point source" as "any discernible, confined and discrete conveyance, including but not limited to any pipe, ditch, channel, tunnel, conduit, well, discrete fissure, container, rolling stock" from which pollutants are or may be discharged. Point sources include the discharge sites of municipal sewage treatment plants (described below as POTWs), industrial discharge sources, and confined animal feeding operations (**CAFOs**).

Point Sources
A discreet, identifiable source of discharge, such as a pipe

Nonpoint source pollution, unlike pollution from an identifiable point of release, comes from many diffuse sources. Imagine melting snow, running toward a stream, and picking up animal waste, leakage from vehicles, and pesticides. If the runoff is directed through a storm sewer system, that system may require a permit, as described later in this chapter. At first glance, the distinction between point and nonpoint sources may seem clear, but it has been the source of much litigation and clarification.

NPS
Nonpoint source; pollution is not discharged from an identifiable source, but comes from various sources (e.g., stormwater)

CAFOs
Confined/Concentrated Animal Feeding Operation

An **indirect discharger** is a nondomestic (commercial or industrial facility) source that discharges pollutants into a **publicly owned treatment works (POTW)**. A POTW is a system for the physical screening (primary treatment) and chemical and biological treatment (secondary treatment) of domestic and, in some municipalities, industrial wastes. Some industrial facilities do not use POTWs, but treat their own waste and discharge the end product as a point source.

Indirect Discharger
Source that discharges pollutants into POTW

POTW
Publicly Owned Treatment Works

In some municipalities POTWs also handle stormwater from, for example, drains along the curbs of roads. The disadvantage to such a **combined system** is that a heavy rain can overwhelm the system and cause the discharge of untreated waste.

Assignment 9-1

- ◆ Definitions are always open to interpretation. Search the Internet or use CALR to determine whether a permit for a point source would be required to conduct aerial pesticide spraying over a large area.
- ◆ Definitions may also change when states enact more stringent laws. For example, the Illinois Environmental Protection Act defines protected "waters" as "all accumulations of water, surface and underground,

natural and artificial, public and private, or parts thereof, which are wholly or partially within, flow through, or border upon this State." 415 ILCS 5/3.550. The definition is clearly intended to cover groundwater and wetlands as well as "navigable" water. Find the definition in your state's statute for the protection of water.

◆ Visit the CFR sections dealing with standards for issuance of permits, www.access.gpo.gov/nara/cfr/waisidx_02/40cfr125_02.html, find the definitions of POTW, industrial discharger, and pre-treatment.

1. Water Quality Standards and Permitting

How do we know whether water is polluted? States have authority to establish **water quality standards** (WQS) for their waters. The EPA must approve the standards; if the EPA does not reach an agreement with a state, it may promulgate water quality standards through the federal rulemaking process. State agencies may go further than required and apply standards to water not covered by the CWA. Water quality standards are scientifically measurable standards consisting of **designated uses, water quality criteria, and anti-degradation policies.**

a. Designated Uses

Designated Uses
The uses for which a body of water's quality standards are set

Designated uses are the uses of the water that society would like to achieve, such as drinking water, fishing, industrial water supply, or agricultural irrigation. Any body of water, or even part of a body of water, can have multiple uses. If a body of water has multiple designated uses, the designated uses requiring the highest water quality set the standard.

Designated uses must include any use that the water has achieved since November 28, 1975, even if not currently possible. Waste transport may never be a designated use. Because the goals of the CWA include fishing and swimming, every body of water must include those uses unless the water has been reclassified through the **downgrade process**, which requires proof that the water quality goals are unattainable because of natural background conditions, irreversible human-caused conditions, resulting substantial environmental harm, or excessive social and economic cost. An actual, existing use may never be removed from the designated uses for a body of water.

Downgrade Process
Reduction in the designated uses for a body of water

Assignment 9-2

◆ Choose a large, named body of water near your home. Start at www.epa.gov/waterscience/standards/wqslibrary/index.html. Find the relevant water quality standards and designated uses.

◆ **Acronym Roulette:** While in-depth discussion of the various pollutants that can be found in water is beyond the scope of this book, it is important that you be able to recognize the acronyms and be able to find more information when necessary. Using EPA websites, www.epa.gov/glossary/aarz.html#T, find the meanings of the acronyms DO, TDS, and PCB and using http://www.epa.gov/OCEPAterms/ find the definitions of pH, coliform organism, turbidity, and nutrients.

---

b.   Water Quality Criteria

Water Quality Criteria
Technical standards for achieving designated uses

Water quality criteria include specific technical conditions (see (e) on Exhibit 9-2) required for the designated uses, including:

- Concentrations of pollutants
- Temperature and pH
- "No toxic chemicals in toxic amounts"

The criteria can also include narrative descriptions that are difficult to scientifically quantify as shown by criteria (a) through (d) on Exhibit 9-2.

Anti-Degradation Standards
Standards for water of high quality

Anti-degradation policies apply to high water quality areas that currently exceed the standards for their designated uses. Anti-degradation generally has three tiers of protection: (1) protection and maintenance of existing uses of waters, (2) protection of high quality waters, and (3) outstanding national resource waters. The policies govern future uses that may have an adverse impact on the watershed, and therefore they protect these areas of water and prevent their degradation or loss of existing uses.

The EPA publishes recommended water quality criteria for a number of key designated uses (www.epa.gov/waterscience/standards/). States are not required to adopt the exact numbers that EPA has published, but if the EPA has issued a criterion, they must adopt a corresponding criterion that provides the same level of protection.

Mixing Zones
Area near a discharge point

The criteria may provide for **mixing zones**, areas or volumes of water adjacent to a wastewater discharge, where the water, because of the discharge, may not meet all applicable water quality criteria. These areas create a transition from a higher effluent concentration to a lower ambient concentration. Concentrations within a mixing zone may exceed criteria so long as the area is kept relatively small and the area does not overlap an important area, such as a swimming beach. A **design flow exemption** may provide for waiver of WQS during particular time periods (drought periods, wet weather periods).

Design Flow Exemption
Exemption from WQS during specified time periods

---

c.   Monitoring

§303(d) List
List of waters not meeting standards, submitted to EPA

Once a state has its standards, it must determine whether its waters are meeting those standards. The state first submits to the EPA a **§305(b) report**, including all it knows about all of its waters, then submits a **§303(d) list**, identifying waters that do not meet WQS.

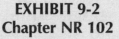

EXHIBIT 9-2
Chapter NR 102

WATER QUALITY STANDARDS FOR WISCONSIN SURFACE WATERS

1) GENERAL.

To preserve and enhance the quality of waters, standards are established to govern water management decisions. Practices attributable to municipal, industrial, commercial, domestic, agricultural, land development or other activities shall be controlled so that all waters including the mixing zone and the effluent channel meet the following conditions at all times and under all flow conditions:

(a) Substances that will cause objectionable deposits on the shore or in the bed of a body of water, shall not be present in such amounts as to interfere with public rights in waters of the state.

(b) Floating or submerged debris, oil, scum or other material shall not be present in such amounts as to interfere with public rights in waters of the state.

(c) Materials producing color, odor, taste or unsightliness shall not be present in such amounts as to interfere with public rights in waters of the state.

(d) Substances in concentrations or combinations which are toxic or harmful to humans shall not be present in amounts found to be of public health significance, nor shall substances be present in amounts which are acutely harmful to animal, plant or aquatic life. [material omitted]

(e) *Temperature and dissolved oxygen for cold waters.*

Streams classified as trout waters by the department of natural resources (Wisconsin Trout Streams, publication 6–3600 (80)) or as great lakes or cold water communities may not be altered from natural background temperature and dissolved oxygen levels to such an extent that trout populations are adversely affected.

1. There shall be no significant artificial increases in temperature where natural trout reproduction is to be protected.

2. Dissolved oxygen in classified trout streams shall not be artificially lowered to less than 6.0 mg/L at any time, nor shall the dissolved oxygen be lowered to less 7.0 mg/L during the spawning season.

3. The dissolved oxygen in great lakes tributaries used by stocked salmonids for spawning runs shall not be lowered below natural background during the period of habitation.

TMDL
Total Maximum Daily Load of pollutants allowable for a body of water, consisting of wasteload and load allocations

Wasteload Allocation
Component of TMDL attributable to point sources

Load Allocation
Component of TMDL attributable to nonpoint sources

If a body of water is not meeting the standards, the state must implement a strategy to achieve compliance. If the state does not submit a strategy that is approved by the EPA, the EPA can establish a strategy by federal rule. The most common strategy is the use of **total maximum daily load (TMDL)** limits. A TMDL limit is a calculation of the maximum amount of a pollutant that a body of water can receive and still meet water quality standards. That amount is then allocated among the sources of the pollutant. These allocations are called **wasteload allocations** for **point sources** and **load allocations** for **nonpoint sources**. The equation for determining wasteload allocations and load allocation includes a margin for safety and takes into account seasonal variations, to ensure that the allocations do not exceed the TMDL. The EPA does not dictate how the state should allocate TMDL among sources.

TMDLs are not self-executing. Permits are used to ensure that sources comply with the allocations and that pollutant levels decrease. The wasteload allocation for a point source is included in its permit for pollution discharge, as described in the next section.

After the initial listing, states must monitor their bodies of water and send reports to the EPA, generally on April 1 of even-numbered years. Monitoring is usually accomplished by random sampling because continuous monitoring is not possible.

The EPA makes some of the data it collects available to the public through its STORET system. Find out what is happening in your area by visiting http://cfpub.epa.gov/surf/locate/index.cfm.

EXHIBIT 9-3
Top 15 Causes of Impairment 1998 and 2000

From www.epa.gov.

Cause of Impairment	Count
Sediments	6,133
Metals	3,984
Dissolved Oxygen	3,772
Other Habitat Alterations	2,112
Temperature	1,884
pH	1,798
Impaired Biologic Community	1,440
Pathogens	5,281
Nutrients	4,773
Pesticides	1,432
Flow Alterations	1,099
Mercury	1,088
Organics	1,069
Noxious Aquatic Plants	831
Ammonia	752

**EXHIBIT 9-4
Map of CWA**

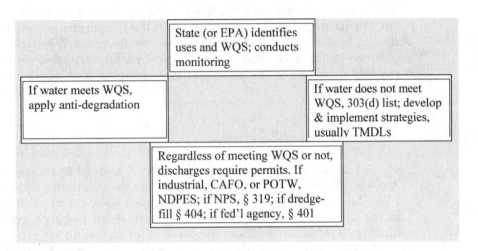

The term pollutant is broadly defined and includes, among other things, heat, waste, soil, rock, chemical materials (generally from industrial sources), and biological materials (generally bacteria, parasites, and viruses from human and animal wastes). For regulatory purposes, pollutants are categorized as: **conventional, toxic, and nonconventional**. There are five conventional pollutants: biochemical oxygen demand, total suspended solids, pH, fecal coliform, and oil and grease. Toxic, or priority pollutants include metals and manmade organic compounds. Nonconventional pollutants do not fit in either category and include substances such as ammonia, nitrogen, phosphorus, chemical oxygen demand, and whole effluent toxicity.

There are two types of permit: individual and general. A permit sets the allowable amount of each pollutant in a discharge; the wasteload allocation is included as part of the permit.

Industrial and commercial indirect dischargers are not required to obtain NPDES permits, but are required to pre-treat discharge before introducing it into a POTW. Wastewater discharged by industry is often contaminated by substances not common to domestic sources, such as lead, from the manufacture of batteries, or cyanide, used in electroplating. Such substances can harm municipal sewage systems, not designed to handle them. There are two uniform federal sets of standards for pre-treatment: "categorical pretreatment standards," which are technology-based limits on discharges that apply to specified industrial categories, and "prohibited discharge standards," which are general prohibitions applicable to businesses not covered by categorical standards. Specific prohibitions include wastes that create a fire or explosion hazard; are corrosive, unless the POTW is specifically designed to handle such waste; are solid or viscous pollutants in amounts that will obstruct flow in the system; are discharged in quantities sufficient to interfere with POTW operations regardless of what kind of pollutant; and discharges with temperatures above 104 degrees Fahrenheit (40 degrees Celsius) — or hot enough to interfere with biological processes — when they reach the treatment plant.

Information about TMDLs is available at www.epa.gov/owow/tmdl/. Find the map for your county.

2. National Pollutant Discharge Elimination System

NPDES
National Pollutant Discharge Elimination System; permit system for regulating point sources

How do we implement anti-degradation policies and TDMLs to prevent further pollution and, possibly, reduce existing pollution? The **National Pollutant Discharge Elimination System (NPDES)** requires a permit, issued by the state or by the EPA if the state does not have an approved program, before any pollutant can be discharged from a **point source** into navigable water. A permit is required regardless of the quality of the receiving water or whether the discharge causes pollution.

a. Individual Permits

Individual Permit
Not a general permit

An individual permit is a permit specifically tailored to an individual facility. A discharge source submits an application and the permitting authority (state or EPA) develops a permit for the particular facility based on information contained in the application (e.g., type of activity, nature of discharge, receiving water quality). The authority issues the permit for a specific time period (not to exceed five years) with a requirement that the facility reapply prior to the expiration date.

b. General Permits

General Permit
Covers multiple facilities in the same general category

A general permit covers multiple facilities within a category. General permits are cost-effective for permitting agencies because a large number of facilities within a geographic area (for example, a city, county, or state; a designated planning area; a sewage treatment district; a state highway system) can be covered under a single permit. Using a general permit ensures consistency of permit conditions for similar facilities. General permits may be written to cover categories of point sources having common elements, such as:

- Facilities that involve the same or substantially similar types of operations
- Facilities that discharge the same types of wastes or engage in the same types of sludge use or disposal practices
- Facilities that require the same effluent limits, operating conditions, or standards for sewage sludge use or disposal
- Facilities that require the same or similar monitoring

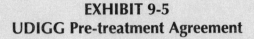

EXHIBIT 9-5
UDIGG Pre-treatment Agreement

An update on the folks at UDigg (Chapter 8): Because of the ethanol plant's proximity to a major POTW, UDigg will be able to discharge its wastewater to the city-owned plant. Based on the anticipated volume of wastewater, the city has asked for a pre-treatment agreement. Lisa found the following at http://66.113.195.234/IA/Iowa%20City/index.htm.

16-3E-4: PRETREATMENT STANDARDS:

A. General Standards:

1. Upon the promulgation of the federal categorical pretreatment standards for a particular industrial subcategory, if the federal standard is more stringent than limitations imposed under this article for sources in that subcategory, said federal categorical standards shall immediately supersede the limitations imposed under this article. This also applies to those federal categorical standards promulgated by EPA after the effective date hereof.
2. Where the city's wastewater treatment system achieves consistent removal of pollutants limited by federal pretreatment standards, the city may apply to the approval authority for modification of specific limits in the federal pretreatment standards. The city may then modify pollutant discharge limits in the federal pretreatment standards if the requirements contained in 40 CFR part 403, section 403.7, as amended, are fulfilled and prior approval from the approval authority is obtained.

B. Specific Standards:

1. An industrial user may not contribute to the POTW any substance which may cause pass through of any substance or any other product, such as residues, sludges or scums, which may cause the POTW effluent to be unsuitable for reclamation and reuse or to interfere with the reclamation process. In no case shall a substance discharged to the POTW cause the POTW to be in noncompliance with sludge use or disposal criteria, guidelines or regulations developed under section 405 of the act, as amended, with any criteria, guidelines or regulations affecting sludge use or disposal developed pursuant to the solid waste disposal act, the clean air act, the toxic substances control act, all as amended, or with state criteria applicable to the sludge management method being used. (1978 Code §33-30.13)
2. No industrial user shall discharge wastewater causing the following limitations to be exceeded at the north POTW treatment plant influent when measured in a twenty four (24) hour composite sample:

EXHIBIT 9-5
(continued)

Pollutant	Pounds Per Day
Ammonia	1,279.0
Cadmium	1.98
CBOD	10,000.0
Chromium	5.46
Copper	6.10
Cyanide	1.02
Lead	8.92
Mercury	0.02
Molybdenum	8.63
Nickel	5.18
pH	6.0 to 9.5
Phenols	55.15
Selenium	3.55
Silver	2.96
Toluene	55.15
TSS	9,893.0
Zinc	31.28

3. No industrial user shall discharge wastewater causing the following limitations to be exceeded at the south POTW treatment plant influent when measured in a twenty four (24) hour composite sample:

Pollutant	Pounds Per Day
Ammonia	1,900.00
Cadmium	5.17
CBOD	16,554.0
Chromium	16.93
Copper	21.02
Cyanide	2.08
Lead	12.22
Mercury	0.02
Molybdenum	6.72
Nickel	7.53
pH	6.0 to 9.5
Phenols	94.58
Selenium	5.29
Silver	6.29
Toluene	94.58
TSS	16,368.0
Zinc	63.05

EXHIBIT 9-5
(continued)

4. If the potable water supply exceeds the established pollutant limitations of subsection B2 or B3 of this section, industrial user discharge limitations shall be based on POTW performance and sludge disposal criteria. (1978 Code §33-30.13)

5. No individual user shall discharge wastewater having a pH lower than 5.0 or greater than 12.0 or having any other corrosive property capable of causing damage or hazard to POTW structures, equipment or personnel.

   a. Where a permittee continuously measures the pH of wastewater pursuant to a permit requirement, the permittee shall maintain the pH of such wastewater within the range set forth in the applicable permit, except excursions from the listed range are allowed subject to the following limitations: (1) The total time during which the pH values are outside the required range of pH values shall not exceed seven (7) hours and twenty six (26) minutes in any calendar month; and (2) No individual excursion from the range of pH values shall exceed sixty (60) minutes.

   b. The director may adjust the requirements set forth in subsection B5a of this section with respect to the length of individual excursions from the range of pH values if a different period of time is appropriate, based upon the treatment system, the plant configuration or other technical factors.

   c. For purposes of this subsection B5, an "excursion" is an unintentional and temporary incident in which the pH value of discharge wastewater exceeds the range set forth in the applicable effluent limitations guidelines.

6. No industrial user shall discharge any wastewater causing the POTW treatment plant influent wastewater temperature to exceed forty degrees centigrade (40°C) (104°F).

7. No industrial user shall discharge substances which create a fire or explosive hazard in the POTW, including, but not limited to, waste streams with a flashpoint of less than sixty degrees centigrade (60°C) (140°F) using the test methods specified in 40 CFR 261.21, as amended.

8. An industrial user shall notify, in writing, the POTW, the state and EPA of any discharge into the POTW of a substance which, if otherwise disposed of, would be considered hazardous waste. (1978 Code §33-30.13)

EXHIBIT 9-6
Discharges Prohibited and Permitted

From www.epa.gov/earth1r6/6en/w/cwa.htm.

A few examples of discharges that are prohibited without an NPDES permit:

- An industry discharging **process water** into a stream.
- A municipality's wastewater treatment facility discharging into a stream.
- Piping a sanitary drain directly into a lake.
- A city's **sanitary sewer line overflowing** into a street and then into a storm drain or creek bed.
- Dumping a drum of hazardous material into a wetland.
- Pouring used motor oil down a storm drain.
- A discharge from an **animal feedlot's** lagoon into a stream.
- **Power washer** that cleans such things as equipment, a restaurant's solid waste storage areas, or a parking lot and discharges the process water into a storm drain.
- Carpet cleaner that wet vacs carpet and discharges cleaning water into storm drain.
- **Car wash** that allows wash water to flow into a storm drain.
- **Storm water** runoff from **Industrial Activities**. . . . but . . .

From http://ecfr.gpoaccess.gov/cgi/t/text/text-idx?c=ecfr&tpl=/ecfrbrowse/Title40/ 40cfr122_main_02.tpl.

§122.3 Exclusions.

The following discharges do not require NPDES permits:

(a) Any discharge of sewage from vessels, effluent from properly functioning marine engines, laundry, shower, and galley sink wastes, or any other discharge incidental to the normal operation of a vessel. This exclusion does not apply to rubbish, trash, garbage, or other such materials discharged overboard; nor to other discharges when the vessel is operating in a capacity other than as a means of transportation such as when used as an energy or mining facility, a storage facility or a seafood processing facility, or when secured to a storage facility or a seafood processing facility, or when secured to the bed of the ocean, contiguous zone or waters of the United States for the purpose of mineral or oil exploration or development.

(b) Discharges of dredged or fill material into waters of the United States which are regulated under section 404 of CWA.

(c) The introduction of sewage, industrial wastes or other pollutants into publicly owned treatment works by indirect dischargers. Plans or agreements to switch to this method of disposal in the future do not relieve dischargers of the obligation to have and comply with permits until all discharges of pollutants

EXHIBIT 9-6
(continued)

to waters of the United States are eliminated. (See also §122.47(b)). This exclusion does not apply to the introduction of pollutants to privately owned treatment works or to other discharges through pipes, sewers, or other conveyances owned by a State, municipality, or other party not leading to treatment works.

(d) Any discharge in compliance with the instructions of an On-Scene Coordinator pursuant to 40 CFR part 300 (The National Oil and Hazardous Substances Pollution Contingency Plan) or 33 CFR 153.10(e) (Pollution by Oil and Hazardous Substances).

(e) Any introduction of pollutants from non point-source agricultural and silvicultural activities, including storm water runoff from orchards, cultivated crops, pastures, range lands, and forest lands, but not discharges from concentrated animal feeding operations as defined in §122.23, discharges from concentrated aquatic animal production facilities as defined in §122.24, discharges to aquaculture projects as defined in §122.25, and discharges from silvicultural point sources as defined in §122.27.

(f) Return flows from irrigated agriculture.

(g) Discharges into a privately owned treatment works, except as the Director may otherwise require under §122.44(m).

(h) The application of pesticides consistent with all relevant requirements under FIFRA (i.e., those relevant to protecting water quality), in the following two circumstances:

(1) The application of pesticides directly to waters of the United States in order to control pests. Examples of such applications include applications to control mosquito larvae, aquatic weeds, or other pests that are present in waters of the United States.

(2) The application of pesticides to control pests that are present over waters of the United States, including near such waters, where a portion of the pesticides will unavoidably be deposited to waters of the United States in order to target the pests effectively; for example, when insecticides are aerially applied to a forest canopy where waters of the United States may be present below the canopy or when pesticides are applied over or near water for control of adult mosquitoes or other pests.

c. Permit Conditions

A permit sets measurable limits on the amounts of pollutants allowed to be discharged. The limits may be based either on technology (technology limits) or water quality standards, and they are written so that they cannot be attained simply by dilution of the discharge. The permit may require continuous compliance or may include daily, weekly, monthly, or yearly requirements.

Example

From the EPA website.

Average Weekly Discharge Limitation
The highest allowable average of daily discharges over a calendar week, calculated as the sum of all daily discharges measured during a calendar week divided by the number of daily discharges measured during that week.

Effluent Limitations
Also called technology limits, limit the amount of pollutants discharged

Technology limits do not require precise equipment or operations, but limit the level of discharge (**effluent limitations**). These are sometimes called "TBELs" (technology-based effluent limitations). The level of discharge is determined by studying an industry and determining pollution levels that could be achieved if the most cost-effective pollution control techniques were used. These are "end of discharge pipe" limits and do not take into account the quality of the water into which the discharge is made. If the EPA has approved TMDLs for the water, the limits must be consistent with the wasteload allocation assigned to the source by the TMDL. If no standards have been established for a particular industry or discharge, **best professional judgment** is applied to set the permit limits. EPA effluent limit guidelines for categories of industry can be found at www.epa.gov/ebtpages/watewastewnationalpollutantdischargee.html.

Best Professional Judgment
How permit limits are set if EPA has not established technology standards for a particular industry or discharge

Technology-based limits for POTWs are, with some exceptions, the same everywhere. Permit requirements are expressed as levels of: (1) biochemical oxygen demand (BOD), (2) total suspended solids (TSS), and (3) pH acid/base balance. These levels can be achieved by well-operated sewage plants employing "secondary" treatment. Primary treatment involves screening and settling, while secondary treatment uses biological treatment in the form of "activated sludge."

WQBELs
Water Quality-Based Effluent Limitations

If end-of-pipe effluent limitations are not adequate to meet applicable water quality standard, the permit must impose limits beyond the technology-based limits. Remember those water quality standards are set by the state, based on designated uses and water quality criteria. **Water quality-based effluent limitations (WQBELs)** are related to the quality of water into which the discharge is made; these are considered "harm-based" limitations. WQBELs are also set by industry.

BAT/BCT
Standards for existing dischargers: Best Available Technology economically achievable or Best Conventional Technology

Permit limits also take into account whether the operator is a new discharger. For existing dischargers, depending on the type of pollutant, the **best available technology economically achievable (BAT)** or the best conventional pollutant control technology (BCT) is required. Under **anti-backsliding** rules a renewed or reissued permit cannot have less stringent conditions than those previously applied.

Example

An EPA Fact Sheet for proposed issuance of an NPDES permit, found at http://yosemite.epa.gov/r10/water.nsf/NPDES + Permits/Current + ID1319/$FILE/Sorrento_Fact_Sheet.pdf, indicates both TBELS:

Table C-1: Technology-Based Effluent Limits (40 CFR 405.65)				
Parameter	Maximum Daily Limit	Average Monthly Limit	Maximum Daily Limit	Average Monthly Limit
	lb/100 lb of BOD₅ input		based on 529,224 lb/day of BOD input (lb/day)	
BOD₅	0.016	0.008	85	42
pH	6.0 to 9.0		6.0 to 9.0	
Total Suspended Solids (TSS)	0.020	0.010	106	53

and WQBELS:

E. Coli Bacteria

The Lower Boise River is designated for primary contact recreation. The primary contact recreation criteria are a monthly geometric mean of 126 organisms/100 ml and a single sample maximum of 406 organisms/100ml. The draft permit contains water quality-based effluent limits requiring these criteria to be met before the effluent is discharged to the receiving water, in order to ensure consistency with the Lower Boise River TMDL.

As with the CAA, new dischargers are subject to **new source performance standards (NSPS)**, which are based on **best available demonstrated technology (BADT)** and are often more stringent than standards imposed on existing dischargers. As with the CAA, permit-holders try to avoid, and often challenge, classification as a "new source."

A variance from or a modification of the limits can be granted under limited circumstances described in the CWA. The most common type of variance is a **fundamentally different factor variance**; the EPA defines fundamentally different factors (**FDF**) as "those components of a petitioner's facility that are determined to be so unlike those components considered by EPA during the effluent limitation guideline and pretreatment standards rulemaking that the facility is worthy of a variance from the effluent limitations guidelines or categorical pretreatment standards." An FDF is not based on economic hardship. As the Supreme Court stated in *Chemical Mftrs. Assoc. v. Natural Resources Defense Council, Inc.*, 470 U.S. 116 (1985): "Some plants may find themselves classified within a category of sources from which they are, or claim to be, fundamentally different in terms of the statutory factors. As a result, EPA has developed its FDF variance as a mechanism for ensuring that its necessarily rough-hewn categories do not unfairly burden atypical plants."

EXHIBIT 9-7
Notice of Intent for NPDES Coverage Under General Permit

In addition to its discharge of waste into the municipal POTW, after pre-treatment, UDigg will discharge storm water from its property. Luckily, a general permit is available to cover the situation and Lisa found the application online.

**IOWA DEPARTMENT OF NATURAL RESOURCES
ENVIRONMENTAL PROTECTION DIVISION**

	IDNR CASHIER'S USE ONLY
	0253-542-SW08-0581

NOTICE OF INTENT FOR NPDES COVERAGE UNDER GENERAL PERMIT

No. 1 FOR "STORM WATER DISCHARGES ASSOCIATED WITH INDUSTRIAL ACTIVITY"

or

No. 2 FOR "STORM WATER DISCHARGES ASSOCIATED WITH INDUSTRIAL ACTIVITY FOR CONSTRUCTION ACTIVITIES"

or

No. 3 FOR "STORM WATER DISCHARGE ASSOCIATED WITH INDUSTRIAL ACTIVITY FOR ASPHALT PLANTS, CONCRETE BATCH PLANTS, ROCK CRUSHING PLANTS, AND CONSTRUCTION SAND AND GRAVEL FACILITIES."

PERMIT INFORMATION

Has this storm water discharge been previously permitted? ☐ Yes   ☐ No

If yes, please list authorization number _____
Under what General Permit are you applying for coverage?

General Permit No. 1 ☐   General Permit No. 2 ☐   General Permit No. 3 ☐

PERMIT FEE OPTIONS

For coverage under the NPDES General Permit the following fees apply:

☐ Annual Permit Fee $150 (per year) Maximum coverage is one year.
☐ 3-year Permit Fee $300 Maximum coverage is three years.
☐ 4-year Permit Fee $450 Maximum coverage is four years.
☐ 5-year Permit Fee $600 Maximum coverage is five years.

Checks should be made payable to: Iowa Department of Natural Resources.

FACILITY OR PROJECT INFORMATION
Enter the name and full address/location (not mailing address) of the facility or project for which permit coverage is requested.

NAME:	STREET ADDRESS OF SITE:		
CITY:	COUNTY:	STATE:	ZIP CODE:

CONTACT INFORMATION Give name, mailing address and telephone number of a contact person (Attach additional information on separate pages as needed). This will be the address to which all correspondence will be sent and to which all questions regarding your application and compliance with the permit will be directed.

NAME:		ADDRESS:		
CITY:	STATE:	ZIP CODE:	TELEPHONE ( )	

Check the appropriate box to indicate the legal status of the operator of the facility.
☐ Federal   ☐ State   ☐ Public   ☐ Private   ☐ Other (specify) _____

SIC CODE (General Permit No. 1 & 3 Applicants Only) [   ]

SIC code refers to Standard Industrial Classification code number used to classify establishments by type of economic activity.

Be sure to complete both sides of this form.

542-1415(Rev. 6/07)

EXHIBIT 9-7
(continued)

FACILITY LOCATION OR LOCATION OF CONSTRUCTION SITE
Give the location by ¼ section, section, township, range, (e.g., NW, 7, T78N, R3W).

1/4 SECTION	SECTION	TOWNSHIP	RANGE

MAIL TO:

STORM WATER COORDINATOR
IOWA DEPARTMENT OF
NATURAL RESOURCES
502 E. 9TH STREET
DES MOINES, IA 50319-0034

OWNER INFORMATION Enter the name and full address of the owner of the facility.

NAME:	ADDRESS:		
CITY:	STATE:	ZIP CODE:	TELEPHONE: ( )

OUTFALL INFORMATION

Discharge start date, i.e., when did/will the site begin operation or 10/1/92, whichever is later: _____

Is any storm water monitoring information available describing the concentration of pollutants in storm water discharges? ☐ Yes   ☐ No

NOTE: Do not attach any storm water monitoring information with the application.

Receiving water(s) to the first uniquely named waterway in Iowa, (e.g., road ditch to unnamed tributary to Mud Creek to South Skunk River):

Compliance With The Following Conditions:	Yes	No
Has the Storm Water Pollution Prevention Plan been developed prior to the submittal of this Notice of Intent and does the plan meet the requirements of the applicable General Permit? (do not submit the SWPPP with the application)		
Will the Storm Water Pollution Prevention Plan comply with approved State (Section 161A.64, Code of Iowa) or local sediment and erosion plans? (for General Permit 2 only)		
Have two public notices been published for at least one day, one each in the two newspapers with the largest circulation in the area where the discharge is located and are the proofs of notice attached? (new applications only)		

GENERAL PERMIT NO. 2 AND GENERAL PERMIT NO. 3 APPLICANTS COMPLETE THIS SECTION.

Description of Project (describe in one sentence what is being constructed):

For General Permit No. 3 - Is this facility to be moved this year?   Number of Acres of Disturbed Soil: _____
          ☐ Yes ☐ No   (Construction Activities Only)

Estimated Timetable For Activities / Projects, i.e., approximately when did/will the project begin and end:

CERTIFICATION – ALL APPLICATIONS MUST BE SIGNED

Only the following individuals may sign the certification: owner of site, principal executive officer of at least the level of vice-president of the company owning the site, a general partner of the company owning the site, principal executive officer or ranking elected official of the public entity owning the site, any of the above of the general contracting company for construction sites.

I certify under penalty of law that this document was prepared under my direction or supervision in accordance with a system designed to assure that qualified people properly gathered and evaluated the information submitted. Based on my inquiry of the person or persons who manage the system, or those persons directly responsible for gathering the information, this information is to the best of my knowledge and belief, true, accurate, and complete. I further certify that the terms and conditions of the general permit will be met. I am aware that there are significant penalties for submitting false information, including the possibility of fine and imprisonment for knowing violations.

NAME (please print)	TITLE:
SIGNATURE:	DATE:

d. Enforcement

Permits require the discharger to monitor compliance and submit information to the permitting agency at specified intervals. Many states now permit filing of compliance information over the Internet. A permit may be terminated or may be modified, among other reasons, if its conditions are violated, if there are changes to the facility or operation, if new information is disclosed, or there is a change in environmental conditions.

There are defenses for violations of permit conditions. A violation might have been caused by **upset**, factors beyond the operator's reasonable control. An operator may intentionally **bypass** treatment facilities for necessary maintenance, if the bypass does not cause violation of effluent limits. A bypass that causes violation of effluent limits may be excused if it was necessary to avoid personal injury or severe property damage. In cases involving any of these excuses, the operator must notify the permitting agency within 24 hours. In addition, an operator who believes that effluent limitations are not being met because of pollutants already present in water taken into its system may request **net limitations**, a credit for the pollutants already in the intake water.

A violation of NPDES permit requirements may result in enforcement actions by the state or the EPA. Enforcement may involve injunctions, fines, imprisonment, or supplemental environmental projects. Supplemental environmental projects require violators to spend more money on a project designed to benefit the environment than they would have spent paying a fine. Citizen suits are also authorized by the CWA, but 60-day notice must be provided to the EPA and the state so that the agency may take action.

e. Intake of Water

NPDES permits deal with what goes into the water, but what about what comes out? During the early years of the twenty-first century, the EPA attempted to regulate water intake facilities, which typically draw water for use in cooling a power plant or factory. In addition to the heat that is added if the water is returned to the river or lake (which would require an NPDES permit), large-scale withdrawal of water can have a devastating impact on aquatic life. As of this writing, the regulatory landscape is unclear. Major portions of EPA rules have been remanded by federal courts. Many of the challenges have been initiated by the "waterkeeper" family of environmental groups.

From *Riverkeeper, Inc. v. EPA*, 475 F.3d 83 (2d Cir. 2007):

> This is a case about fish and other aquatic organisms. Power plants and other industrial operations withdraw billions of gallons of water from the nation's waterways each day to cool their facilities. The flow of water into these plants traps (or 'impinges') large aquatic organisms against grills or screens, which cover the intake structures, and draws (or 'entrains') small aquatic organisms into the cooling mechanism; the resulting impingement and entrainment from these operations kill or injure billions of aquatic organisms every year. Petitioners here challenge a rule promulgated by the Environmental Protection Agency . . . pursuant to . . . the Clean Water Act . . . 33 U.S.C. §1326(b), that is intended to protect fish, shellfish, and other aquatic organisms from being harmed or killed by

---

Upset
Circumstances beyond reasonable control of operator cause violation of permit limits

Bypass
Discharge goes around treatment facilities, typically to allow maintenance to occur

Net Limitations
Taking into account pollution already in the water

EXHIBIT 9-8

The process for issuance of an individual NPDES permit, described in 40 C.F.R. 124, involves:

1. Permitting agency receives application from permittee.
2. Reviews application for completeness and accuracy.
3. Requests additional information as necessary.
4. Develops technology-based effluent limits using application data and other sources.
5. Develops water quality-based effluent limits using application data and other sources.
6. Compares water quality-based effluent limits with technology-based effluent limits and chooses the more stringent of the two as the effluent limits for the permit.
7. Develops monitoring requirements for each pollutant.
8. Develops special conditions.
9. Develops standard conditions.
10. Considers variances and other applicable regulations.
11. Prepares the fact sheet, summarizing the principal facts and the significant factual legal, methodological, and policy questions considered in preparing the draft permit including public notice of the draft permit and other supporting documentation.
12. Completes the review and issuance process.
13. Issues the final permit.
14. Issuance of a final permit may be appealed and is ultimately subject to judicial review.

All NPDES permits, at a minimum, have five general sections, although the contents of each section will vary:

- Cover Page — Typically contains the name and location of the permittee, a statement authorizing the discharge, and the specific locations for which a discharge is authorized.
- Effluent Limits — The primary mechanism for controlling discharges of pollutants to receiving waters. Permit writers spend a majority of their time deriving appropriate effluent limits based on applicable technology-based and water quality-based standards.
- Monitoring and Reporting Requirements — Used to characterize waste streams and receiving waters, evaluate wastewater treatment efficiency, and determine compliance with permit conditions.
- Special Conditions — Conditions developed to supplement effluent limit guidelines. Examples include best management practices (BMPs), additional monitoring activities, ambient stream surveys, and toxicity reduction evaluations (TREs).
- Standard Conditions — Preestablished conditions that apply to all NPDES permits and delineate the legal, administrative, and procedural requirements of the permit.

regulating 'cooling water intake structures' at large, existing power-producing facilities. [W]e grant in part and deny in part the petitions for review, concluding that certain aspects of the EPA's rule are based on a reasonable interpretation of the Act and supported by substantial evidence in the administrative record, but remanding several aspects of the rule because they are inadequately explained or inconsistent with the statute, or because the EPA failed to give adequate notice of its rulemaking.

Stay tuned! For recent developments, see http://www.waterkeeper.org/mainarticledetails.aspx?articleid=147.

f. Nonpoint Sources

NPS pollution includes runoff of fertilizers and pesticides, leakage from underground storage tanks, sediment, acid rain and other atmospheric deposits, and storm water and parking lot runoff containing oil and other vehicle fluids, trash, animal waste, road salt, and cleansers used in washing vehicles and building facades. Imagine the NPS pollution that followed Hurricane Katrina.[3]

Section 319
Permit for nonpoint source discharge through a system

Stormwater in a natural area is an NPS, but the discharge of stormwater or snow melt through a municipal storm sewer system, or an industrial facility is subject to **Section 319** permit requirements. The UDigg general permit will be a §319 permit. While states may have more stringent requirements, EPA NPDES stormwater permit regulations cover the following classes of stormwater discharges on a nationwide basis:

- Operators of Municipal Separate Storm Sewer Systems (sometimes called MS4s) located in "urbanized areas" as identified by the Bureau of the Census
- Industrial facilities that discharge to an MS4 or to waters of the United States; however, any industrial facility (except construction) may certify to a condition of "no exposure" if their industrial materials and operations are not exposed to stormwater, and eliminate the need to obtain stormwater permit coverage
- Operators of construction activity that disturbs one or more acres of land; construction sites less than one acre are covered if part of a larger plan of development

Although NPS is the largest contributor to water pollution, with the exception of Section 319 Permits, the CWA does not directly regulate NPS pollution. The Act does require states to establish area-wide plans to control both point and nonpoint sources. In addition, the law provides for grants to states to develop programs to manage NPS. State management plans, which require EPA approval, must identify waters impaired or threatened by NPS, establish goals for cleaning those waters, and list the BMP that will be used to achieve the goals.

---

[3]The devastation traveled to several states. For example, Mississippi's 2005 Report on its Nonpoint Source Management Program mentions the impact of the storm several times, http://www.deq.state.ms.us/mdeq.nsf/pdf/NPS_05AnnualReport/$File/2005%20Annual%20report%20FINAL_011006.pdf?OpenElement.

- ◆ Using a search engine, such as Google, enter "nonpoint source pollution [name of your state]." Write a short summary of what your state is doing about NPS pollution.
- ◆ Visit the website of the Environmental Appeals Board Practice Manual, www.epa.gov/eab/pman-appdx6.pdf, and find and print the form for a petition for review of a permitting decision.
- ◆ Permitting assignment:
  - ◆ Determine who has authority to issue NPDES permits for your state: www.epa.gov/npdes/images/State_NPDES_Prog_Auth.pdf.
  - ◆ If applicable, find your state contact information: http://cfpub.epa.gov/npdes/home.cfm?program_id=45.
  - ◆ If your state has a website concerning NPDES permits, use that site to answer the following questions. Otherwise, use the EPA site, NPDES Basics, http://cfpub.epa.gov/npdes/home.cfm?program_id=45.
    1. Find the form to apply for a permit for stormwater discharge from a construction site.
    2. For how long must a permit holder keep monitoring records?
    3. How long before discharge begins should an application be filed?
    4. What types of permitting actions require public notice?
    5. What should be contained in public notice?

3. Dredge and Fill Material Permits

Section 404 of the CWA regulates the deposit of dredged and fill material into waters of the United States. Dredged material is excavated from a body of water; fill material is material placed in the water, changing its character or elevation. The section includes exemptions for normal farming activities, such as plowing, and activities such as levee and bridge maintenance. Dredge and fill permits are generally issued by the **U.S. Army Corps of Engineers**, although individual states can assume responsibility for the program with EPA approval. The EPA can veto a decision by the Corps to issue a permit.

Section 404 serves as a wetland protection law even though wetlands are not specifically mentioned in the statute. Wetlands are areas that are sufficiently inundated with water to support the prevalent growth of vegetation adapted to growth in saturated soil. Wetlands serve a critical purpose in recharging the groundwater table. When a wetland must be damaged as part of a project, the permit often requires **mitigation** or payment of a fee **in lieu of mitigation**. A mitigation bank is a wetland, stream, or other aquatic resource area that has been restored, established, enhanced, or (in certain circumstances) preserved to compensate for unavoidable harm to aquatic resources permitted under Section 404 or a similar state or local wetland regulation. A mitigation bank may be created

Section 404 Permit
"Dredge and fill" permit

Army Corps of Engineers
Authorizes Section 404 dredge-and-fill permits

Mitigation
To compensate for unavoidable damage (typically to wetlands)

when a government agency, corporation, nonprofit organization, or other entity undertakes these activities under a formal agreement with a regulatory agency.

Assignment 9-4

Many administrative agencies provide regulatory guidance documents to assist the public in complying with regulations. Find an Army Corps of Engineers regulatory guidance letter concerning monitoring at mitigation projects, www.usace.army.mil/cw/cecwo/reg/rglsindx.htm.

C. Safe Drinking Water Act

SDWA
Safe Drinking Water Act

Public Water Systems
Governed by Safe Drinking Water Act

Primacy
State's authority to enforce federal law, granted by EPA

The **Safe Drinking Water Act (SDWA)** directs the EPA to set standards for drinking water and its sources: rivers, lakes, reservoirs, springs, and ground water wells. While SDWA applies to every **public water system** in the United States, with the exception of private wells that serve fewer than 25 people, different standards apply to systems, depending on the size and type of system. In setting the standards, the EPA considers both health risks and costs.

Most states have been granted **primacy** by the EPA and are authorized to implement SDWA because they were able to show that they have standards at least as stringent as EPA standards. Originally, SDWA focused primarily on treatment of drinking water, but 1996 amendments introduced source water protection, operator training, funding for water system improvements, and public information as components of safe drinking water. The states, or the EPA, make sure water systems test for contaminants, review plans for water system improvements, conduct on-site inspections and sanitary surveys, provide training and technical assistance, and take action against water systems not meeting standards.

Under SWDA, public water systems must ensure that contaminants in tap water do not exceed EPA standards by treating the water, testing it frequently, and reporting results to states. If a water system is not meeting standards, the system is responsible for notifying customers. Many water suppliers are also required to prepare annual reports for their customers. States and water suppliers must conduct assessments of water sources to see where they may be vulnerable to contamination. SDWA also mandates that states have programs to certify water system operators and make sure that new water systems have the technical, financial, and managerial capacity to provide safe drinking water.

Assignment 9-5

Your client is building a 50-unit senior citizens' residence in a rural area. The location is such that the cost of extending municipal water lines would be prohibitive. The client plans to use an on-site well to supply the tenants with water. Find your state's rules or publications to guide the client on his responsibilities for monitoring the quality of the water and providing notice to customers if the water violates standards. For example, in Illinois, water supply operators may have an obligation to give notice of violations in languages other than English.

EXHIBIT 9-9
Requirements for Languages Other than English

From   www.epa.state.il.us/water/compliance/drinking-water/collectors-handbook/ sample-collectors-handbook.pdf.

PN IN LANGUAGES OTHER THAN ENGLISH

If a large proportion of the population you serve does not speak English, you must provide multilingual notices. To assist in determining if you if have a large number of non-English speaking consumers visit http://www.factfinder.census.gov.

D.   Coastal Zone Management Act

The **Coastal Zone Management Act of 1972 (CZMA)** established a voluntary national program within the Department of Commerce to encourage coastal states to develop and implement coastal zone management plans to protect and, in some cases restore, coastal resources such as wetlands, floodplains, estuaries, beaches, dunes, barrier islands, and coral reefs, as well as the fish and wildlife using those habitats. To encourage participation, CZMA makes federal financial assistance available to any coastal state, tribe, or territory, including those on the Great Lakes, to develop and implement a program. Most eligible states and tribes are, or will be, participating in the program.

    The Act has been amended several times, to deal with new priorities and include additional grant funding. In reauthorizing the CZMA in 1990, Congress identified NPS pollution as a major factor in the degradation of coastal waters and requested that states with approved coastal zone management programs implement coastal NPS pollution control programs. The Section 6217 program includes grants to states for development of programs and for implementation and is administered at the federal level jointly by the EPA and the **National**

CZMA
Coastal Zone Management Act; voluntary program, states can obtain grants for protecting coastal areas

NOAA
National Oceanic and
Atmospheric Agency,
administers the CZMA

Oceanic and Atmospheric Agency (NOAA). EPA guidance on coastal NPS pollution addresses five major source categories: (1) urban runoff, (2) agriculture runoff, (3) forestry runoff, (4) marinas and recreational boating, and (5) hydromodification.

EXHIBIT 9-10
Coastal Zone Management Program

From www.coastalmanagement.noaa.gov/mystate/welcome.html.

Does your state have a coastal zone management program?

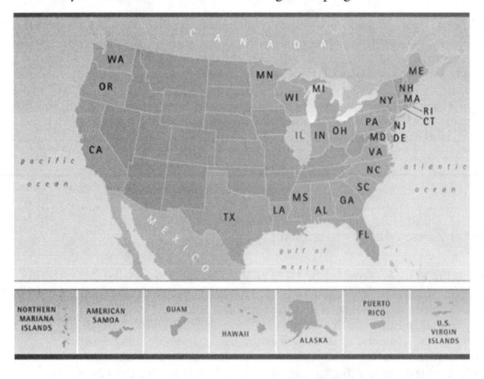

E. Oil Pollution Act and Ocean Dumping Ban Act

OPA
Oil Pollution Act

The **Oil Pollution Act (OPA)**, 33 U.S.C. §§2702 to 2761, increased the EPA's ability to prevent and respond to catastrophic oil spills. A trust fund financed by a tax on oil is available to clean up spills when the responsible party is incapable or unwilling to do so. The OPA requires oil storage facilities and vessels to submit plans detailing how they will respond to large discharges. The EPA has published regulations for aboveground storage facilities; the Coast Guard has done so for oil tankers. The OPA also requires development of Area Contingency Plans to prepare and plan for oil spill response on a regional scale.

An amendment to the **Marine Protection, Research, and Sanctuaries Act (MPRSA)**, 33 U.S.C. §1401 et seq., commonly called the **Ocean Dumping Act**, regulates, and in some cases bans, dumping of sewage sludge, medical waste, and industrial waste into ocean.

MPRSA
Marine Protection, Research, and Sanctuaries Act

Ocean Dumping Act
Amendment to Marine Protection, Research, and Sanctuaries Act

F. In the Field: Ethics and Disclosures

In Chapter 1, you were introduced to an important rule governing the conduct of legal professionals: Model Rule 1.6, Confidentiality. How do an attorney's obligations under the rule fit with the obligations of those who operate facilities with permits for air emissions, wastewater discharge, or waste disposal? As you have learned, those permits are generally subject to requirements concerning record retention and reporting. In addition to routine reporting, the permit holder is often required to report extraordinary events. These permit conditions often originate in statutes that provide for criminal sanctions in the event of intentional or

---

EXHIBIT 9-11
Client-Lawyer Relationship

Rule 1.6 Confidentiality of Information

(a) A lawyer shall not reveal information relating to the representation of a client unless the client gives informed consent, the disclosure is impliedly authorized in order to carry out the representation or the disclosure is permitted by paragraph (b).

(b) A lawyer may reveal information relating to the representation of a client to the extent the lawyer reasonably believes necessary:

(1) to prevent reasonably certain death or substantial bodily harm; (2) to prevent the client from committing a crime or fraud that is reasonably certain to result in substantial injury to the financial interests or property of another and in furtherance of which the client has used or is using the lawyer's services; (3) to prevent, mitigate or rectify substantial injury to the financial interests or property of another that is reasonably certain to result or has resulted from the client's commission of a crime or fraud in furtherance of which the client has used the lawyer's services; (4) [material omitted]; or (6) to comply with other law or a court order.

knowing failure to notify the appropriate agency in the event of a spill or accidental discharge. What is the obligation of a lawyer who becomes aware that a client/permit holder has not reported such an event?

The answer is not always clear, but the Rule provides guidance for some situations. Section (b)(1) requires disclosure if an attorney has information that a client is likely to commit a criminal or fraudulent act likely to result in death or substantial bodily harm to a person. Discharges of pollutants may endanger human health. The section refers to preventing a crime and the failure to report within a specified time period may have already occurred, but the continuing failure to report may constitute a continuing crime.

In other circumstances, sections (b)(2) or (3) may apply. The continuing or complete criminal failure to report may be reasonably certain to cause property damage or may have caused property damage and the client may have used the lawyer's services in connection with the incident. The issue is obviously very fact sensitive. In addition, each state adopts its own version of ethical rules for lawyers. Consult the rules in your state to determine whether a lawyer has the option, or even the duty, to disclose.

Key Terms

§303 List
§319 Permit
§404 Permit
Anti-backsliding
Anti-degradation Standards
Army Corps of Engineers
BADT
BAT/BCT
Best Professional Judgment
Bypass
CAFO
Combined System
CWA
CZMA
Design Flow Exemption
Designated Uses
Downgrade
Dredge and Fill
Effluent Limitations
FDF
General Permit
Ground Water
Indirect Source
Individual Permit
Littoral Rights
Load Allocation
Mitigation

Mixing Zone
MPRSA
Navigable
Net Limitations
NOAA
NPDES
NPS
NSPS
Ocean Dumping Act
OPA
Point Source
POTW
Primacy
Prior Appropriation
Public Trust Doctrine
Public Water Systems
WQBEL
Riparian Rights
SDWA
Stormwater
Surface Water
TMDL
Upset
Wasteload Allocation
Water Quality Criteria
Water Quality Standards
Wetlands

Review Questions

1. Explain the difference between a point source and a nonpoint source, giving an example of each.
2. What is an indirect source and what is required of indirect sources discharging into public treatment systems?
3. What is a Section 404 permit and which agency issues such a permit?
4. What is wetlands mitigation?
5. Are states on the coast required to have coastal zone management plans?
6. Explain some of the ways in which the Safe Drinking Water Act ensures safe drinking water.
7. How are designated uses determined and how does that relate to water quality standards?
8. How are TMDLs used to bring water into compliance with quality standards?
9. What is a general permit and when might it be used?
10. Who issues NPDES permits for your state?
11. Explain the difference between permit conditions imposing technology limits and those imposing water quality limitations.
12. How are new sources of water pollution treated differently than existing sources?
13. What are riparian rights and what is the relationship of riparian rights to the public trust doctrine?
14. The CWA does not directly regulate NPS discharge, so how does it attempt to deal with NPS?
15. What is an upset and what requirement is triggered by an upset?
16. If you live in a prior appropriation state, explain the doctrine.

KEY TERMS CROSSWORD

www.CrosswordWeaver.com

ACROSS

4. Army _____ of Engineers
5. SDWA governs _____ water sources
6. _____ limitations also called technology limitations
9. an effort to compensate for unavoidable harm to wetlands
10. _____ water, not surface water
13. total _____ daily load
14. areas very important to recharge of ground water
16. initials, an agricultural use that may require a permit
18. owners of property abutting a lake have these rights
19. _____ source, a discrete identifiable place of discharge
21. _____ uses dictate the quality standards for a body of water
22. violation due to circumstances beyond operator control
23. these limitations consider pollution already in the water
24. _____ permit covers multiple facilities
25. normally NPS, if this goes through a municipal or industrial system, a permit is required

DOWN

1. initials, system for issuance of permits under CWA
2. rights of owners adjoining water
3. a Section 404 permit covers dredge and _____
4. category of pollutants
7. initials, amount of pollution water can accept and remain within standards
8. authorization for states to enforce federal programs
11. CZMA is a _____ program
12. reduction in designated uses for water
15. load _____ allocation, component of TMDL attributable to NPS
17. to remove fill from wetlands
20. _____ sources must pre-treat

10

CERCLA, SARA, EPCRA, and TSCA

A.   Overview of CERCLA and SARA

You may remember the movie, "Erin Brockovich," in which a paralegal (played by Julia Roberts) discovers that Pacific Gas & Electric had stored the highly toxic chemical hexavalent chromium in unlined cooling ponds and the chromium had polluted the water table. The movie was based on a true story — one of many environmental catastrophes of the 1970s, including Love Canal, discussed in the Chapter 4 material on environmental justice, and Times Beach.[1] Years ago, people were less aware of how chemicals can affect health and the environment and disposed of dangerous chemicals carelessly, and dozens of similar stories made news. The **Comprehensive Environmental Response, Compensation, and Liability Act (CERCLA)**, commonly known as the **Superfund law**, was enacted in 1980 in response to such situations. The law's major functions are enabling cleanup of existing contaminated sites and allocating financial responsibility for the cleanups. This chapter is organized according to those functions.

CERCLA was amended by the **Superfund Amendments and Reauthorization Act (SARA)** in 1986 (42 U.S.C. §9601 et seq.). Several site-specific amendments, definitions clarifications, and technical requirements were added to the legislation, including additional enforcement authorities. Title III of SARA also authorized the **Emergency Planning and Community Right-to-Know Act (EPCRA)**. Because these laws are part of the same scheme, this chapter does not focus on whether various provisions originated with CERCLA or SARA.

You have already learned something very important about these laws in an earlier chapter, concerning due diligence. CERCLA is focused on liability and due diligence is necessary to avoid the liability created by CERCLA.

CERCLA is different than other environmental laws in that it is retroactive; it addresses events that have already occurred and imposes liability for actions taken before the law was enacted. Other environmental laws are generally concerned with permits to control what will happen in the future. While the CAA, the CWA, RCRA (next chapter), and NEPA deal with what parties are doing or intend to do, CERCLA deals with what they did — whether intentional or not. CERCLA also establishes unique rights of action and sanctions.

1.   Response Actions

The cleanup process begins with site discovery or notification of possible **release** of **hazardous substances** into the environment. Sites are discovered by various parties, including citizens, state agencies, and EPA regional offices.

CERCLA
Comprehensive Environmental Response, Compensation, and Liability Act (CERCLA), commonly known as the Superfund

SARA
1986 amendments to CERCLA

EPCRA
Establishes requirements for federal, state, and local governments and industry for emergency planning and reporting on hazardous and toxic chemicals

Hazardous Substances
More than 800 substances covered by CERCLA

---

[1]To read more about Times Beach and see pictures of what has become of the contaminated land, visit http://www.legendsofamerica.com/MO-TimesBeach.html.

EXHIBIT 10-1
Overview of CERCLA and the NCP

CERCLA

- Authorizes two kinds of response actions:
  - short-term removals, actions taken to address releases or threatened releases requiring prompt response.
  - long-term remedial response actions to permanently reduce dangers associated with releases or threats of releases of hazardous substances that are serious, but not immediately life threatening. These actions can be conducted (with federal funds) only at sites listed on the EPA's **National Priorities List (NPL)**.
- Provides for liability of persons responsible for releases of hazardous waste;
- Establishes prohibitions and requirements concerning closed and abandoned hazardous waste sites; and
- Establishes a trust fund to provide for cleanup when no responsible party can be identified.
- Enabled revision of the **National Contingency Plan (NCP)**. The NCP provided guidelines to respond to releases and threatened releases of hazardous substances, pollutants, or contaminants. The NCP also established the **NPL**.

NPL
List of sites eligible for Superfund cleanup

NCP
Includes guidelines for response to releases and threatened releases of hazardous substances, pollutants, or contaminants

THE NATIONAL CONTINGENCY PLAN (NCP)

The NCP is the federal government's blueprint for responding to both oil spills and hazardous substance releases; it sets forth the responsibilities of the National Response Teams, Regional Response Teams, On Scene Coordinators, Remedial Project Managers, and others that participate in responses to releases, describes how coordination among these groups is to occur, establishes methods for determining the appropriate extent of response, and outlines the procedures to be followed in performing cleanups. Compliance with the NCR is essential to eligibility for reimbursement of costs, discussed later in this chapter.

---

a. Release

Release is defined as "any spilling, leaking, pumping, pouring, emitting, emptying, discharging, injecting, escaping, leaching, dumping or disposing" **excluding** emissions:

- From exhaust engines
- Involving nuclear material (covered by Atomic Energy Act)

- From normal applications of fertilizer
- Occurring solely in a workplace (covered by OSHA, discussed in an earlier chapter)
- Covered by a federal permit.

This broad definition has been interpreted as covering "releases" from decomposition of storage tanks, migration of substances during rain and flooding, situations that create a threat of release, and even substances released from industrial workers who unknowingly carry particles home, as you will see when you read the cases at the end of this chapter. Under the theory of *res ipsa locquitur* (the thing speaks for itself), courts have even applied the term "release" to situations involving elevated levels of contamination from an unknown source.

Res Ipsa Locquitur
"The thing speaks for itself"; in negligence law, connection is obvious without evidence

b. Hazardous Substances

CERCLA includes references to four other laws, CWA, CAA, RCRA, and TSCA, to designate more than 800 substances as hazardous and identify many more as potentially hazardous based on their characteristics and the circumstances of their release. The definition, found in CERCLA §101(33), does not include petroleum, crude oil, or any fraction thereof that is not specifically listed as a hazardous substance, natural gas, liquefied natural gas, or synthetic gas of pipeline quality (or mixtures of natural gas and such synthetic gas). Petroleum releases are generally addressed under other laws such as the underground storage tank provisions of RCRA (discussed next chapter), or the CWA (discussed in a previous chapter). This so-called petroleum exemption is particularly important when you consider that the EPA estimates that approximately one-half of the estimated 450,000 contaminated sites in the United States are impacted by underground storage tanks or some type of petroleum contamination.

Because many sites contain petroleum contamination and petroleum frequently contains other listed hazardous substances, (e.g., BTX compounds such as benzene, toluene, and xylene), whether the exception applies to those substances within petroleum can be controversial. In general, indigenous, refinery-added hazardous substances are exempt, but substances added to petroleum as a result of contamination are not exempt. In other words, if petroleum is part of a hazardous mix, the mix may be covered by CERCLA.[2]

Note that a hazardous substance is not necessarily a waste product. While the RCRA, discussed in the next chapter, deals with "wastes," CERCLA also deals with substances that may be a valuable part of an industrial process.

CERCLA also authorizes the EPA to respond to "a release or substantial threat of release . . . of any **pollutant or contaminant** which may present an imminent and substantial danger to public health or welfare. . . ." The term "pollutants or contaminants" encompasses just about anything that, upon exposure "will or may reasonably be anticipated to cause" specified harmful health effects. While the

Pollutant or Contaminant
Anything that, upon exposure "will or may reasonably be anticipated to cause" specified harmful health effects

---

[2]Although a release may not be covered by CERCLA, for purposes of liability, it may require reporting under EPCRA. Petroleum releases fit in this category. To see a list of chemicals subject to EPCRA, visit http://www.epa.gov/ceppo/pubs/title3.pdf.

EPA can clean up a site polluted by a pollutant or contaminant, it is not authorized to recover its cleanup costs from private parties or to issue an order directing parties to perform a cleanup when the substance involved is only a pollutant or contaminant. In addition, many releases of pollutants or contaminants do not meet the requirement that there be an "imminent and substantial danger," a higher threshold than that for response to releases of hazardous substances. Therefore, while the definition of a pollutant or contaminant is broad, as a practical matter, CERCLA authority is rarely used to respond to such a release.

c. Reporting Releases

Under CERCLA the "person in charge" of a facility or vessel is required to report to the **National Response Center (NRC)** a release of a hazardous substance in a specified amount as soon as he or she has knowledge of the release. The NRC is the federal government's communications center, staffed 24 hours a day to receive reports. A report to the NRC triggers the NCP and the responses described in the next section.

NRC
Staffed 24 hours to receive reports of releases

The EPCRA contains a parallel requirement that the "owner or operator" of the facility report immediately to the state emergency response commission (EPCRA requires that states establish such commissions) and any local emergency planning commission (these are created by the state commission). Other laws contain similar requirements; the CWA and CAA, discussed in previous chapters, require reporting of unpermitted discharges.

CERCLA defines facility broadly to include any area where a hazardous substance is located, but the definition specifically excludes releases from consumer products in consumer use. A vessel is defined as any contrivance capable of being used for transportation on water. The EPA has broad authority to enter property to conduct inspections and take samples to enforce the law.

Assignment 10-1

◆ Use the EPA Superfund site, www.epa.gov/superfund/resources, to find the definition of "continuous" release and write a short report on how continuous releases are reported.
◆ Hazardous substances are listed at 40 C.F.R. §302.4, found at http://a257.g.akamaitech.net/7/257/2422/08aug20051500/edocket.access.gpo.gov/cfr_2005/julqtr/40cfr302.4.htm. Determine whether Acetone, a common ingredient in nail polish remover, is listed, and, if so, in what quantities is a release reportable?
◆ Identify your state's agency for reporting under EPCRA.
◆ Use the Cornell website to research CERCLA and determine
   a. What is the penalty for failure to notify the NRC of a release?
   b. Is spraying pesticide a reportable release?

EXHIBIT 10-2
Definition of a Hazardous Substance

From http://www.epa.gov/superfund/programs/er/hazsubs/lauths.htm.

Superfund's definition of a hazardous substance includes the following:

- Any element, compound, mixture, solution, or substance designated as hazardous under Section 102 of CERCLA.
- Any hazardous substance designated under Section 311(b)(2)(a) of the Clean Water Act, or any toxic pollutant listed under Section 307(a) of the Clean Water Act. There are over 400 substances designated as either hazardous or toxic under the CWA.
- Any hazardous waste having the characteristics identified or listed under Section 3001 of the Resource Conservation and Recovery Act.

Hazardous waste is defined under RCRA as a solid waste (or combination of solid wastes) which, because of its quantity, concentration, or physical, chemical, or infectious characteristics, may: (1) cause or contribute to an increase in mortality or an increase in serious irreversible, or incapacitating illness; or (2) pose a substantial present or potential hazard to human health or the environment when improperly treated, stored, transported, disposed of, or otherwise managed. In addition, under RCRA, EPA establishes four characteristics that will determine whether a substance is considered hazardous, including ignitability, corrosiveness, reactivity, and toxicity. Any solid waste that exhibits one or more of these characteristics is classified as a hazardous waste under RCRA and, in turn, as a hazardous substance under Superfund.

- Any hazardous air pollutant listed under Section 112 of the Clean Air Act, as amended. There are over 200 substances listed as hazardous air pollutants under the CAA.
- Any imminently hazardous chemical substance or mixture which the EPA Administrator has "taken action under" Section 7 of the Toxic Substances Control Act.

In all, more than 800 substances have been specifically identified as CERCLA hazardous substances under these laws.

CERCLIS
EPA computerized database of contaminated sites

After a release is reported, any site that is assessed as presenting a serious threat is entered into **Comprehensive Environmental Response, Compensation, and Liability Information System (CERCLIS)**, EPA's computerized inventory of potential release sites. The site may, or may not, be later identified as part of the NPL on that system. The next step is a response action. The EPA can enter into a voluntary cleanup agreement with potentially responsible parties; compel potentially responsible parties to respond, if the release may pose an "imminent and substantial danger"; or may initiate a response itself. The agency responsible for coordinating response efforts is called the **lead agency**. If the EPA itself handles the response, it will typically seek reimbursement from any **potentially responsible parties (PRPs)**.

d. Removal Actions

There are two types of response actions: "removals" and "remedial actions." A **removal action** is a response to an immediate danger to human health or the environment. **Remedial actions (RA)**, on the other hand, are long-term cleanups intended to permanently address the threat posed by contamination at a site. Removals may take weeks, but remedial actions may take years or even decades to complete. Because administrative requirements imposed on removal actions are less stringent than those for permanent response actions, removals are often conducted before and in conjunction with long-term remedial action for the site. There is, however, a limit on how much federal money may be used on a removal action before the site is listed on the NPL.

The decision to conduct a removal action, a remedial action, or some combination of the two is not often clear at the beginning of the process. The agency may begin the process for remedial action and, at any time, determine that a removal is required. There are three types of removal action: emergency, time critical, and non-time critical. **Emergency removals** are undertaken when the danger is so great that there is no time to undertake a planning process. **Time critical removals** are those actions for which there is a planning period of less than six months before site activities must be initiated. **Non-time critical removals** require at least six months but not more than twelve months of planning before the removal action will be performed.

Example

Typical removal actions might include providing alternate water supplies to residents whose groundwater has been polluted, immediate removal or cleanup of hazardous substances spilled from a container, or construction of a fence around a hazardous waste site.

As you read the following material, keep in mind that some removals are implemented by PRPs. Often removal is conducted by a governmental agency, which may then seek reimbursement from PRPs, as discussed in a later section.

Lead Agency
Agency charged with coordination of assessment and cleanup

PRPs
Current owners and operators; former owners and operators involved during time hazardous substance was disposed at facility; persons who arranged for disposal or treatment of hazardous substances; persons who accepted hazardous substances for transport to facilities they helped select

Removal Action
Short-term response to contamination that must be cleaned up immediately

RA
Actual cleanup of site

Emergency Removals
Removal without time for planning

Time Critical Removals
Actions for which there is a planning period of less than six months before site activities must be initiated

Non-time Critical Removals
Requires six to twelve months of planning before removal action

---

EXHIBIT 10-3
PRPs Under CERCLA

Remember: You have already learned about PRPs and possible defenses in an earlier chapter, dealing with Due Diligence.

PRPs under CERCLA §107(a) can be: (1) **current owners and operators** of the facility or vessel involved; (2) **former owners and operators** of a facility who were involved with the facility during the time any hazardous substance was disposed at the facility; (3) persons who **arranged for disposal or treatment** of hazardous substances that they owned or possessed at a facility; and (4) persons who **accepted hazardous substances for transport** to disposal or treatment facilities or sites that they helped select. These categories of liable parties are often referred to as: (1) owners and operators, (2) former owners and operators, (3) generators or arrangers, and (4) transporters.

---

i. Emergency Removals

Emergency removals are handled under the Superfund Emergency Response Program. When a release or spill occurs, the responsible party, its response contractors, local fire and police departments, and local emergency response personnel provide immediate response. State agencies are available to assist, if needed. If a local government or Indian tribe conducts temporary emergency measures in response to a hazardous substance release, but does not have emergency response funds, it can obtain reimbursement of up to $25,000 per incident from the EPA Local Governments Reimbursement Program.

If the release or oil spill exceeds the reporting trigger, as described in a previous section, the NRC is notified. When a report is made, the NRC notifies an **On-Scene Coordinator (OSC)**, based on the location of the spill.[3] The procedure for determining the lead agency is clearly defined so there is no confusion about who is in charge during a response. The OSC determines the status of local response to determine whether federal involvement is needed. The OSC must ensure that cleanup, whether implemented by industry, local, state, or federal officials is appropriate and timely. Depending on the duration of the removal effort, the OSC may be required to involve local officials and implement a community relations plan.

OSC
Responsible for coordinating removal efforts

---

[3] Statutorily defined as "Federal official predesignated by EPA, DOD, DOE, or SCG to *coordinate* and *direct* responses under Subpart D, or the government official designated by the lead agency to coordinate and direct removal actions under Subpart E of the NCP."

The OSC may determine that local action is sufficient and that no federal action is required. If the incident is large or complex, the OSC may remain on the scene to monitor the response and provide advice. However, the federal OSC will take over the response if:

- The party responsible for the chemical release or oil spill is unknown or not cooperative;
- The OSC determines that the spill or release is beyond the capacity of the company, local, or state responders to manage; or
- With respect to oil spills, the incident is determined to present a substantial threat to public health or welfare due to the size or character of the spill.

The OSC may request assistance from the EPA national Environmental Response Team, the National Oceanic and Atmospheric Administration, Regional Response Team, or other "special forces."

Factors in the decision to initiate a CERCLA removal action:

- Actual or potential exposure to nearby human populations, animals, or the food chain
- Actual or potential contamination of drinking water supplies or sensitive ecosystems
- Hazardous substances or pollutants or contaminants in drums, barrels, tanks, or other bulk storage containers that may pose a threat of release
- High levels of hazardous substances or pollutants or contaminants in soils largely at or near the surface that may migrate
- Weather conditions that may cause hazardous substances or pollutants or contaminants to migrate or be released
- Threat of fire or explosion
- Availability of other appropriate federal or state response mechanisms to respond to the release
- Other situations or factors that may pose threats to public health or welfare or the environment

ii.   *Time Critical and Non-Time Critical*

The planning process for nonemergency removals also begins with a **Preliminary Assessment**, which normally involves review of existing information and records to determine whether the release requires additional investigation or action; identification of the source and nature of a release; and identification of any other potentially responsible parties. The assessment can result in prompt removal action or further evaluation. Sites determined to pose no significant threat or potential threat to public health and the environment are excluded from further consideration by a site closeout report commonly referred to as a **no further remedial action planned (NFRAP) decision**.

Following the preliminary assessment, a **Site Investigation** may be conducted to determine whether there is a release or potential release and the nature of the associated threats and to augment data collected in the preliminary assessment. The investigation generates additional information to complete

Preliminary Assessment
Normally involves review of existing information and records

NFRAP Decision
Site closeout report — ends consideration for NPL

Site Investigation
Determines whether there is a release or potential release and nature of associated threats

HRS
Established by NCP, assigns
numerical values to health
and environmental risks

Hazard Ranking System (HRS) scoring; the HRS is a numerical ranking system contained in the NCP. The investigation can result in a NFRAP decision, removal action, or further remedial action. For non-time critical removals, an engineering evaluation/cost analysis is also prepared to analyze removal alternatives.

Removal actions must comply with "applicable or relevant and appropriate requirements" (ARARs) "to the extent practicable" considering the urgency of the situation and the scope of removal action to be taken. ARARs are requirements under other environmental laws that may apply to or be appropriate for the remedial action and are discussed further in the next section.

A removal may remediate the site so that remediation is not needed. If that is not the case, the process continues with a determination of whether the site should be listed on the NPL.

Assignment 10-2

Will I have to do that?

You might, but don't worry. There is lots of guidance available for preparation of a preliminary assessment or a site investigation or use of the HRS. Using the website, http://www.epa.gov/superfund/sites/npl/hrsres/, answer the following questions:

◆ What are the four "pathways" for purposes of organizing a preliminary assessment report?
◆ What are the four major activities that are part of a site investigation?

---

e. Remedial Actions

As described in the previous section, the level of threat presented by a release may have necessitated a removal. If a removal action involved a preliminary assessment and site investigation, those serve as the first steps for the remedial action process. If those steps were not taken in connection with a removal, they must be performed at the beginning of the remediation process. The site's HRS score, established during the preliminary assessment/site investigation phase, determines whether the site will be listed on the NPL and, therefore, eligible for remediation with Superfund trust money. A site does not have to be listed on the NPL for EPA in order for a removal, site investigation, or remedial design to be performed, or a remedial action enforced. NPL listing only limits EPA's performance of a remedial action using Superfund money.

EXHIBIT 10-4
National Priorities List

National Priorities List Sites in Pennsylvania

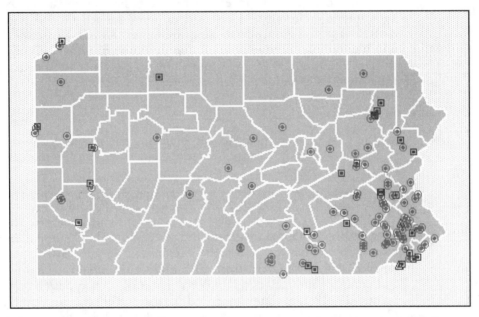

To find NPL sites in your state: www.epa.gov/superfund/sites/npl/npl.htm.

The NPL is included in the NCP and is updated annually. The HRS, developed by the EPA, determines priorities among releases and threatened releases throughout the nation. HRS criteria are based on risks to public health, welfare, or the environment, taking into account factors including the extent of population at risk, hazard potential of the facility's hazardous substances, potential for contamination of drinking water supplies, and threat to ambient air. Applying these criteria, EPA ranks sites for listing on the NPL. Once on the NPL, a facility becomes a priority for long-term remedial evaluation, funding, and response. For federal facilities, NPL status triggers numerous responsibilities and timelines for conducting remedial action.

i. Investigation

**Remedial Investigation/
Feasibility Study**
Done to determine nature
and extent of contamination
and explore alternatives for
remediation

ARARs
Level of cleanup is determined by standards set in
other relevant laws

The next step is a **remedial investigation/feasibility study** to determine the nature and extent of contamination and explore alternatives for remediation. Before conducting the remedial investigation, the lead agency prepares a plan, including a field sampling plan, describing the number, type, and location of samples, and type of analysis to be done. The agency also prepares a quality assurance project plan, describing policy, data quality objectives, and measures necessary to obtain adequate data to select the appropriate remedy. The lead agency then collects and analyzes data, identifies federal and state **Applicable or Relevant and Appropriate Requirements (ARARs)**, assesses the degree to which site releases of hazardous substances constitute a threat to human health and the environment, and identifies contaminant levels that are adequately protective for a site. The investigation can take years to complete.

> The EPA provides guidance for preparing the remedial investigation and feasibility study: http://www.epa.gov/superfund/resources/remedy/pdf/540g-89004-s.pdf.

The Feasibility Study evaluates options for remedial action. The lead agency must identify potential treatment and screening technologies, assemble technologies into alternatives, screen the alternatives, identify ARARs, and perform a detailed analysis of alternatives. The study must employ nine criteria to assess and compare alternatives: (1) protectiveness of human health and the environment; (2) ARARs compliance; (3) long-term effectiveness and permanence; (4) reduction of toxicity, volume, or mobility through treatment; (5) short-term effectiveness; (6) implementability; (7) cost; (8) state acceptance; and (9) community acceptance. The same criteria are used to select the remedial action.

ii. Level of Cleanup: ARARs

What degree of cleanup must be achieved before the site is considered clean? This is not always an easy decision. Every site is different with respect to contamination, risks, and the cost of cleanup. CERCLA favors remedies that are permanent, cost-effective, and involve the treatment of hazardous substances to reduce their volume, toxicity, or mobility, and disfavors transport and disposal of hazardous substances to another site without such treatment. If hazardous substances are left on-site at levels that will not allow unrestricted use and exposure, the EPA must review the adequacy of the remedy every five years.

The primary guidance for cleanup is a requirement that a remedy achieve all ARARs where hazardous substances are left on-site. Federal laws that provide ARARs include, but are not limited to, the Resource Conservation and Recovery Act (RCRA), and Toxic Substances Control Act (TSCA), discussed in later chapters, and the CAA, CWA, and SDWA, discussed in previous chapters; state laws that are more stringent than federal requirements may be ARARs.

Example

The SDWA governs allowable contaminant levels for drinking water provided to consumers; the law is not specifically applicable to cleanup of contaminated groundwater, but if that water is a potential source of drinking water, those standards may be ARARs. On the other hand, if the water has no potential for use as drinking water, SDWA standards might not be "relevant" or "appropriate." Similarly, if cleanup involves removing and treating contaminated groundwater and discharging the treated water into surface water, CWA water quality criteria and standards must be met.

You should remember that some of those laws require permits for discharges and emissions. CERCLA includes a permit exemption for removals and remedial actions conducted on-site or within the proximate area of contamination. A response that originates on the subject site or at another location to which the contamination has migrated may have off-site emissions, but it is exempt from permit requirements. This exemption prevents delay and costs that would be part of the permit process.

There are three types of ARARs: chemical-specific, which place a risk-based limit on the amount of a chemical that can be discharged into or present; action-specific, which restrict particular activities; and location-specific, which involve restrictions based on the location of the site. Essentially, application of ARARs generally means that remedies must achieve the highest cleanup levels established by other federal and state standards. There are, of course, exceptions, for situations in which achievement of ARARs is not feasible or in the best interests of the community.

For a more in-depth discussion of ARARs, visit http://www.epa.gov/superfund/contacts/sfhotlne/arar.pdf.

Before documenting its decision selecting a response action, the lead agency must publish notice of its selection and provide a reasonable opportunity for comments from the public, the state, and the EPA, if it is not the lead agency. Public input is essential and Community Relations Plans are required for certain response actions; the level of public involvement depends on the extent of the project. Comments become part of the administrative record, which is essential to subsequent judicial review of the agency's decision. Following the public comment period, the lead agency must prepare a written summary of comments, criticisms, and new relevant information submitted by the public. The lead agency then issues a **Record of Decision (ROD)**, which sets forth the selected remedy and the factors leading to its selection.

ROD
Lead agency sets forth its plan of action and justification

Remedial Action (RA) means the actual cleanup at the end of the long discovery, evaluation, and investigation process and **Remedial Design (RD)** refers to the engineering and construction plans and specifications prepared to implement the RA. The RD/RA phase is often called "turning dirt" because, unless there has been a removal action, this is the point at which the lead agency finally begins to clean the site. The RA/RD phase may include excavation, pumping, and

RD
Engineering plans and specifications to implement remedial action

treating contaminated groundwater, use of various containment mechanisms, use of institutional controls, and so on.

> The "best" remedial actions neutralize the contaminant; removing the contaminant to another site or encapsulating the contamination are not favored if a better alternative is possible. EPA guidance on RA/RD: http://www. epa.gov/superfund/whatissf/sfproces/rdra.htm.

Operation and Maintenance measures maintain the effectiveness of RAs and begin after the remedial action objectives in the ROD are achieved and may include institutional controls, five-year reviews, and deletion from the NPL.

Assignment 10-3

Using the Cornell website, used in a previous assignment, examine 42 U.S.C. §9604:

◆ Who is actually authorized to initiate removal or remediation?
◆ Examine §9615; to whom is authority delegated in situations relating to "illness, disease, or complaints thereof" under §9604(b)(1)?
◆ What does the section say about cost-sharing with the states?

2.   Enforcement Options

a.   *EPA: Enforcement First Strategy*

To further the goal of maximizing the number of privately funded cleanups, CERCLA authorizes the EPA to seek a court order requiring a PRP to abate an endangerment to public health, welfare, or the environment. The law also permits the EPA to take administrative actions to compel PRPs to respond as necessary to protect public health and welfare or the environment. To avoid delay, CERCLA limits the jurisdiction of courts to hearing challenges to response actions or administrative orders requiring PRPs to perform cleanups. The general rule is that there can be no judicial review prior to the completion of the response action. Failure to comply with an administrative order can result in the assessment of an administrative or judicial (civil) penalty or a criminal charge. The fines are high to motivate compliance.

> Courts do have jurisdiction to hear some types of claims, most of which are described in the next section: cost recovery actions or actions for

contribution; actions to enforce a CERCLA order or seek penalties for violation of such an order; actions for private party reimbursement from the Superfund; citizen suits alleging that a completed removal action violated CERCLA (except where a removal action is to be followed by a remedial action, in which case the action cannot be heard until the remedial action is concluded); or actions brought by the EPA seeking an order compelling a PRP to perform a cleanup.

The process of pursuing PRP-funded remediation or of obtaining reimbursement from PRPs starts by identifying PRPs. The EPA conducts site file searches, state agency and EPA file reviews, title searches, and constructs a history of operations that occurred at the site. The EPA may issue information-request letters to parties who may have information about the site, such as the names and addresses of owners or operators, the types of wastes found at the site, and/or possible generators and transporters associated with the site. Failure to respond adequately to an administrative subpoena or **Section 104(e) request** can result in civil penalties and even criminal prosecution.

§104(e) Request
EPA request for information about contaminated site

PRP Bounty Hunters: Any individual who provides information that leads to the arrest and conviction of violators subject to criminal penalties may be awarded up to $10,000.

Once the EPA has enough information to identify parties as potentially liable for contamination at a site, it begins communication by means of a notice of potential liability, also called a general notice letter, and/or a notice of opportunity to negotiate to conduct the response action, also called a special notice letter. A **general notice letter**, sent to all identified PRPs, notifies them of their potential liability and starts an informal information exchange concerning site conditions, PRP connections to the site, and identification of other PRPs.

General Notice Letter
Notifies PRPs of potential liability

For a sample of a general notice letter, visit http://www.epa.gov/region09/toxic/noa/eldorado/pdf/general-letter.pdf.

Based on information obtained during the PRP search and information exchange process, the EPA may choose to issue **Special Notice Letters (SNLs)** to PRPs to facilitate formal negotiations. The SNL includes the names and addresses of other PRPs, and, if available, the volume and nature of substances each PRP contributed and a ranking of the substances by volume. Other contents may include information about EPA discretionary authority to formally negotiate the terms of settlements; conditions of the enforcement moratorium described below; description of a good faith offer; description of future response actions, if

SNLs
Sent to PRPs, triggers moratorium to encourage negotiated settlement

known; statement of work to be performed; and a statement whether the site is eligible for orphan share compensation under the Orphan Share Policy.

Note the difference in tone in a special notice letter: http://yosemite.epa. gov/R10/CLEANUP.NSF/82751e55bf4ef18488256ecb00835666/ f0e551fb8a69dcd288256fac00064739/$FILE/UCRspecial%20notice% 20letter,%2010-10-03.pdf.

Moratorium
Activity is discontinued for a period of time

The SNL triggers a period of time called a **moratorium**, during which certain EPA response and abatement actions at the site may not be taken for 60 days. The goal of the moratorium is to reach a settlement in which the PRPs agree to conduct or finance response activities. If within 60 days the PRPs make a good faith offer to conduct the response action, the moratorium may be extended up to an additional 60 days to provide time for reaching a final settlement.

The EPA may, at its discretion, choose not to follow special notice procedures. It may instead send a letter to PRPs stating that it is not going to use special notice procedures because, for instance, negotiations are already underway, and outlining EPA's plans for the negotiations. Due to the urgency of emergency and time-critical removals, they do not follow special notice procedures.

Steering Committee
Committee of PRPs, formed to negotiate with the EPA or share costs of cleanup

Once they have received notice of their potential liability, PRPs may form a **steering committee** to work together to negotiate with the EPA or to minimize costs in implementing cleanup. During negotiations either the PRPs or the EPA may prepare a **nonbinding preliminary allocation of responsibility (NBAR)**, which is an allocation of total response costs among PRPs, based on various factors. An NBAR is not binding on the PRPs and cannot be used as evidence in court.

NBAR
Nonbinding Allocation of Responsibility prepared by the EPA or PRPs

Consent Decree
Judicial decree expressing a voluntary agreement between parties

If a settlement is reached before response is complete, the PRPs may conduct the response action under a **consent decree** or an **administrative order on consent** with EPA or EPA contractor oversight. If there is no good faith offer or if negotiations fail, EPA may conduct the response action and seek reimbursement.

De Minimis Settlements
Liability of small-volume contributors of hazardous substances is resolved by payment of a onetime "cashout"

Settlements and consent orders reduce litigation and speed the process of remediation. One of the most effective tools for expediting settlement is the use of **de minimis settlements**, by which the liability of small volume contributors of hazardous substances is resolved by payment of a onetime "cashout," based on contribution of hazardous substances. These settlements often include hundreds of parties, who are removed from potential litigation early in the process. PRPs who contributed the smallest quantities can enter into **de micromis settlements.** If a de micromis contributor is threatened with litigation by private parties, the EPA will settle with that party for $0, releasing the party from liability, to prevent other, large contributors from pulling them into expensive litigation. This works because of the rules pertaining to contribution, discussed below.

De Micromis Settlements
Settlements with the contributors of the smallest amounts of hazardous substances

EXHIBIT 10-5
Excerpt from Model Consent Decree

EPA makes efforts to make settlement less painful than litigation, including providing consent decree forms on the website. For a sample paragraph from a "cash out" consent decree, see http://www.epa.gov/compliance/resources/policies/cleanup/superfund/cashout-cd-mem.pdf.

IX. RESERVATION OF RIGHTS BY UNITED STATES

16. The United States reserves, and this Consent Decree is without prejudice to, all rights against Settling Defendants with respect to all matters not expressly included within the Covenant Not to Sue [if Settling Federal Agencies, delete "Not to Sue"] by United States in Paragraph 15 [if Settling Federal Agencies, insert, "and the Covenant by EPA in Paragraph 15.1."] Notwithstanding any other provision of this Consent Decree, the United States reserves all rights against Settling Defendants [if Settling Federal Agencies, insert, "and EPA and the federal natural resource trustees [and the State] reserve, and this Consent Decree is without prejudice to, all rights against Settling Federal Agencies,"] with respect to:

a. liability for failure of Settling Defendants [or Settling Federal Agencies] to meet a requirement of this Consent Decree;
b. criminal liability;
c. liability for damages for injury to, destruction of, or loss of natural resources, and for the costs of any natural resource damage assessments;

[NOTE: The precise terms of Subparagraph 16(d) may need to be changed for any Settlor who has a continuing relationship with the Site.] d. liability, based upon Settling Defendants' [or Settling Federal Agencies'] ownership or operation of the Site, or upon Settling Defendants' [or Settling Federal Agencies'] transportation, treatment, storage, or disposal, or the arrangement for the transportation, treatment, storage, or disposal, of a hazardous substance or a solid waste at or in connection with the Site, after signature of this Consent Decree by Settling Defendants [or Settling Federal Agencies];

e. liability arising from the past, present, or future disposal, release or threat of release of a hazardous substance, pollutant, or contaminant outside of the Site; [and] **[NOTE: Insert Subparagraph 16(f) if Settling Defendants (or Settling Federal Agencies) have not agreed in Section VI (Payment of Response Costs) to compensate EPA for the costs described in Subparagraph 16(f) through a premium payment or an Additional Response Costs billing provision.]** [f. liability for performance of response action or for reimbursement of response costs if total response costs incurred or to be incurred at or in connection with the Site by the United States or any other person exceed $____ [insert total response cost estimate upon which Settling Defendants' payment is based.] **[NOTE: If the State is a co-plaintiff, insert separate paragraphs for the State's covenant not to sue Settling Defendants (and Settling Federal Agencies, if any) and reservation of rights.]**

In cases where PRPs do not undertake cleanup and the EPA uses Superfund money to conduct remediation, CERCLA provides for recovery of response costs (as well as "overhead" and a variety of penalties and expenses, when applicable) from those PRPs. Unfortunately, it is estimated that about 30 percent of contaminated sites are "orphan" sites, for which no financially solvent PRP can be found. In such cases, the Superfund trust can fund the cleanup.

b. The Not-So-Super Fund

Initially the Superfund trust paid for cleanups by assessing a tax on the petroleum and chemical industries. The tax expired in 1995 and the trust was subsequently funded with general revenues. In the years that followed, the fund assisted in the cleanups of a number of national disasters: the destruction of the World Trade Center, flooding in the Midwest, and various hurricanes, including Katrina. According to the EPA, cleanups are now more complex. Many believe that the trust is under-funded and unable to fulfill its purpose. As a result, it is increasingly important to identify PRPs and require them to clean up sites or seek reimbursement for cleanups conducted with Superfund money under 42 U.S.C. §9607, which provides that a PRP is liable for: "(A) all costs of removal or remedial action incurred by the United States Government or a State or an Indian tribe not inconsistent with the national contingency plan."

c. Liability of PRPs and Contribution

While CERCLA's reporting requirements are triggered by the release of a specified minimum quantity, the law contains no requirement that a specified amount of a hazardous substance be present before a response action must be taken or a party found liable for a release or threat of release of such substance. The release of any quantity of a hazardous substance is sufficient to establish liability. In addition, CERCLA provides for **strict liability**. There is no need to prove fault or negligence on the part of a PRP; the fact that the PRP conducted activities consistent with standard industry practices is not a defense. In fact, there is no need to prove actual harm; the threat of a release is enough to trigger liability. **Indemnification clauses**, commonly used to shift risk between parties to a contract, are ineffective to protect a party from liability to the government as a PRP.

Strict Liability
Liability without regard to fault or negligence

Indemnification Clause
To agree to assume another party's liabilities, typically as part of a contract

The law does provide some defenses: A PRP may have a defense if it can establish that the release was caused by an "act of God," "act of war," or the acts of an unrelated third party. As described in Chapter 6, defenses are available for creditors, fiduciaries, contiguous owners, "innocent landowners," bona fide prospective purchasers, and those redeveloping brownfields. The 1991 Recycling Equity Act exempts "arrangers and transporters" of "recyclable material."

Residential property owners, operators, and lessees, as well as small businesses and not-for-profit organizations are exempt from liability as "generators" in sending waste to municipal solid waste facilities. Service stations have a limited exemption for oil recycling programs. The EPA has policies that it will not require residential owners to undertake response actions or pay response costs unless the residential homeowner's activities lead to a release or threatened release of hazardous substances and that it will not generally pursue a transporter of municipal waste. Other policies provide some protection for governmental entities that have acquired contaminated properties involuntarily and for PRPs not able to pay their total liability. For more information, see http://www.epa.gov/compliance/cleanup/superfund/liability.html.

A recent "hot topic" has been the liability of "interim owners" for passive migration. Can an owner who buys contaminated property and subsequently sells it later be held liable for having allowed the preexisting contamination to seep throughout the property? The majority of courts seem to be answering yes.

Liability is **joint and several**, meaning that all PRPs may be held liable or a plaintiff may sue any one of several PRPs for the entire cost of cleanup. A PRP may be able to defend against joint and several liability in a particular case if it can show that the harm for which it is responsible is divisible and reasonably capable of apportionment. Typically, however, hazardous substances are commingled following disposal at a site, and proof that a single PRP's contribution caused a distinct and segregable harm is not possible.

The law does, however, provide for **contribution actions**. Contribution actions are private suits among the PRPs to allocate responsibility and force all available, financially solvent PRPs to share the cost that may have already been borne by a single PRP. In allocating responsibility, courts look at a variety of factors, such as quantities of hazardous materials attributable to each defendant, the toxicity of the respective wastes, and the durability of the wastes. In a few contribution cases, courts have appeared willing to go beyond CERCLA's statutory defenses and consider defenses such as **laches**, **estoppel**, or **clean hands**. Whether a contribution action was available for a PRP who cleaned a site voluntarily, without EPA involvement, was debatable until recently, as discussed further in the next section.

d. Private Actions

While many environmental laws provide for citizens' suits in which private individuals sue to have the law enforced, CERCLA is unique in allowing private actions for compensation. Subsection (B) only addresses costs incurred consistent with the NCP. It does not address other personal damages, but the case summarized in Exhibit 10-6A demonstrates that state common law actions for damages from hazardous releases continue to be available, subject to CERCLA's limitations period.

Joint and Several Liability
Theory under which all defendants are liable for entire amount of damages and can be pursued individually or together

Contribution Actions
PRP asserts that other PRPs must contribute to judgment or cost of cleanup

Laches
Equitable concept — a claim will not be allowed if delayed so long as to disadvantage the other party

Estoppel
A party is barred from asserting a claim or defense based on own conduct — an equitable concept

Clean Hands
Refers to the theory that the party with "unclean hands" (acting in bad faith) is not entitled to equitable remedy

---

Under §9607 a PRP is liable for:

(A) all costs of removal or remedial action incurred by the United States Government or a State or an Indian tribe not inconsistent with the national contingency plan;

(B) any *other necessary costs of response incurred by any other person* consistent with the national contingency plan;

> (C) damages for injury to, destruction of, or loss of natural resources, including the reasonable costs of assessing such injury, destruction, or loss resulting from such a release; and
> (D) the costs of any health assessment or health effects study carried out under section 9604 (i) of this title.
> (Emphasis added.)

Subsection (C) refers to damages, rather than "costs" and, therefore, goes beyond the cost of cleanup. The provision allows federal, state, and Indian tribe natural resource trustees to sue for damages to natural resources. The definition of natural resources is broad and encompasses not only land, wildlife, and fish, but also air, water, groundwater, drinking water supplies, and other resources. It is limited, however, to resources owned, held in trust, or otherwise controlled by a federal or state government agency or an Indian tribe. Damages to private property are not recoverable. Natural resource damages are compensatory, rather than punitive, in nature. Any money recovered must be used for restoration or replacement of the resource or for acquisition of an equivalent resource. CERCLA also limits liability for natural resource damages to situations where the contamination that caused the damages occurred on or after December 11, 1980.

> While the Native American residents of tribal reservations do not share in the wealth of the industries that have polluted their lands, they do have to live with the consequences. A 1985 Environmental Protection Agency study of 25 reservations found 1,200 toxic waste sites, while another study showed 46 percent of all Native Americans live near abandoned toxic waste dumps. Poverty and political disenfranchisement have made reservations targets for exploitation. For more information about the situation on tribal lands and about legal theories being used to seek compensation, see www.law.duke. edu/shell/cite.pl?14 + Duke + Envtl. + L. + & + Pol'y + F. + 155 + pdf.[4]

These provisions obviously allow for recovery by non-PRPs; the language of 42 U.S.C. §9613 is equally clear in allowing PRPs to recover against each other when one of them has paid a disproportionate share as a result of a civil suit. Notice also the language of subsection (2), which provides strong motivation for PRPs to settle with the government — settling parties are exempt from contribution suits.

But what about a party who cleans up voluntarily, without any civil suit having been filed, and, therefore, does not fit the language of §9613(f)(1)? If the party undertaking cleanup was not a PRP, the answer is clearly that the suit would be for damages, not for contribution. But, if the party was a PRP, so that the suit would actually be for contribution, can the action proceed under §9607? Does it matter whether the party who undertook cleanup was "innocent" with respect to the contamination, despite being a PRP under the strict liability provisions of CERCLA? These questions were addressed in the case summarized in Exhibit 10-6B

---

[4]Kanner, Casey & Ristoph, New Opportunities for Native American Tribes to Pursue Environmental and Natural Resource Claims, 141 Duke Environmental Law and Policy Forum 155 (2004).

42 U.S.C. §9613
  (f) Contribution
    (1) Contribution
    Any person may seek contribution from any other person who is liable or potentially liable under section 9607 (a) of this title, *during or following any civil action* under section 9606 of this title or under section 9607 (a) of this title. Such claims shall be brought in accordance with this section and the Federal Rules of Civil Procedure, and shall be governed by Federal law. In resolving contribution claims, the court may *allocate response costs among liable parties using such equitable factors* as the court determines are appropriate. Nothing in this subsection shall diminish the right of any person to bring an action for contribution in the absence of a civil action under section 9606 of this title or section 9607 of this title.
    (2) Settlement
    A person who has resolved its liability to the United States or a State in an administrative or judicially approved settlement shall not be liable for claims for contribution regarding matters addressed in the settlement. Such settlement does not discharge any of the other potentially liable persons unless its terms so provide, but it reduces the potential liability of the others by the amount of the settlement.
    (3) Persons not party to settlement
        (A) If the United States or a State has obtained less than complete relief from a person who has resolved its liability to the United States or the State in an administrative or judicially approved settlement, the United States or the State may bring an action against any person who has not so resolved its liability.
        (B) A person who has resolved its liability to the United States or a State for some or all of a response action or for some or all of the costs of such action in an administrative or judicially approved settlement may seek contribution from any person who is not party to a settlement referred to in paragraph (2).
        (C) In any action under this paragraph, the rights of any person who has resolved its liability to the United States or a State shall be subordinate to the rights of the United States or the State. Any contribution action brought under this paragraph shall be governed by Federal law.
(Emphasis added.)

and in the Supreme Court decision, *United States v. Atlantic Research Corp.*, 127 S. Ct. 2331 (2007). The Court allowed Atlantic Research, a PRP that voluntarily cleaned up property, to recover costs from another PRP, the U.S. Department of Defense. Atlantic Research leased property at a naval ammunition depot to retrofit rocket motors. The work involved spraying the motors and burning rocket propellant pieces that dislodged. Propellant seeped into the soil and groundwater. Atlantic Research voluntarily cleaned up the site, then brought claims for contribution. Atlantic Research ultimately dropped its §113(f)(1) claim because the company had not been the subject of a §106 or §107 civil action and had not settled its liability with the government, but the Supreme Court held that the company was entitled to recover under §107(a)(4)(B). Are there questions remaining unanswered? Yes! Is a party who cleans up pursuant to a consent decree eligible to seek contribution? Stay tuned. . . .

Assignment 10-4
Case Questions

Read the cases summarized in Exhibit 10-6 and answer the following:

For Exhibit 10-6A:

◆ Are the plaintiffs attempting to enforce CERCLA (require that Goodyear clean up its plant) or using common law theories to claim damages?
◆ If this is not a case to enforce CERCLA, what is the importance of CERCLA to the case?
◆ What is the most important factor with respect to the negligence claim?
◆ What are the weaknesses of the strict liability claim?
◆ Do you agree with the court that this was a release into the environment?

For Exhibit 10-6B:

◆ Why was the property owner not entitled to contribution from the tenant under the specific contribution provisions of 42 U.S.C. §9613?
◆ Does this case resolve what would happen if the landlord had been at fault to some extent? For example, what if the landlord had stored a single barrel of chemicals on the property in 1943, which was long-forgotten, but leaked into the soil? What do you think would happen?
◆ Does the court's decision take away some of the EPA's leverage in obtaining settlements?

EXHIBIT 10-6A

DOROTHY J. KOWALSKI and LOUIS KOWALSKI, JR., v. GOODYEAR TIRE & RUBBER COMPANY

UNITED STATES DISTRICT COURT FOR THE WESTERN DISTRICT OF NEW YORK *841 F. Supp. 104* (1994)

Dorothy and Louis Kowalski bring this action in negligence and strict liability against Goodyear, alleging that Goodyear failed to prevent release of ortho-toluidine, an abnormally dangerous hazard, from its Niagara Falls plant, contaminating the plaintiffs and causing Mrs. Kowalski to contract bladder cancer. The release occurred when Mr. Kowalski, an employee of defendant, left the plant each day. Although he showered and changed his clothes, the configuration of the shower and locker facilities permitted the chemical to recontaminate his hair, skin, and street clothes.

Dorothy allegedly developed cancer as a result of 25 years of exposure to ortho-toluidine by handling her husband's clothing and spread of the chemical throughout their house. Plaintiffs assert that Goodyear knew the chemical could cause bladder cancer, yet failed to inform workers even after learning that several employees had contracted the disease. Plaintiffs seek recovery in strict liability, for personal injury and loss of consortium resulting from defendant's negligence, and for punitive damages.

Goodyear moves for summary judgment and contends that the statute of limitations bars this action. Secondly, Goodyear argues that plaintiffs have failed to define the abnormally dangerous activity. Finally, it asserts that plaintiffs have failed to state a claim of negligence because they have not alleged a duty which Goodyear owed Dorothy.

[Court rejects claim that suit was barred by state statute of limitations.] CERCLA provides a wide range of remedial action for problems of environmental waste. It is not limited to authorizing the federal government to file an action. The plain reading of §9658 suggests that preemption of a state statute of limitations was an additional remedy, not one confined to actual CERCLA actions.

Goodyear next argues that federal law only preempts the state accrual date if there is a "release," of a hazardous substance, into the "environment." The manner of alleged release is the carrying-out of the substance from the plant upon the clothes and person of the husband, and the environment is the home and auto, which Goodyear claims is not the "environment" contemplated by CERCLA. Plaintiffs cite *Staco, 684 F. Supp. 822 (D. Vt. 1988)*, which found that carrying home hazardous substances on clothing constitutes a "release into the environment" for purposes of CERCLA. This court agrees that the remedial purposes of the law and its language can include hazardous chemicals carried out of the workplace on employees' person and clothing which have the potential of causing injuries to those who come in contact with employees.

EXHIBIT 10-6A
(continued)

The commencement date under CERCLA §9658, is the date at which Dorothy knew or reasonably should have known that her cancer was caused by ortho-toluidine release. Plaintiffs allege that they had no knowledge that ortho-toluidine could cause cancer until Louis received a letter in 1990 from the National Institute for Occupational Safety and Health reporting results of a study done with men employed in Goodyear's plant, from which Louis retired in 1987. The suit was filed in 1992, within *N.Y.C.P.L.R §214-c* three-year limitation period and is not barred by the statute of limitations.

Engaging in an activity which is abnormally dangerous subjects the actor to strict liability for harm caused to his neighbors resulting from the abnormally dangerous character of the activity, even though the actor has exercised the utmost care and has acted without negligence. Restatement (Second) of Torts, §519. Plaintiffs claim that escape of the hazardous substance ortho-toluidine was the direct, proximate cause of Dorothy's cancer. Goodyear argues that these allegations, even if accepted as true, fail to establish a basis for imposing strict liability. The mere use of toxic chemicals in a plant with a risk of secondary exposure has never been held to constitute an abnormally dangerous activity.

New York courts use six factors to determine whether an activity is abnormally dangerous: (a) existence of a high degree of risk of harm to the person, land or chattels of others; (b) likelihood that harm that results from it will be great; (c) inability to eliminate risk by exercise of reasonable care; (d) extent to which the activity is not a matter of common usage; (e) inappropriateness of activity to the place where it is carried on; and (f) extent to which its value to the community is outweighed by its dangerous attributes.

Only (b) is clearly present. Ortho-toluidine is a known carcinogen that can cause injury through the skin. Bladder cancer is often a fatal disease, and there is a likelihood of great harm. The court is unable at this stage to determine the other factors. If Dorothy was able to contract the disease from her husband's clothing, it would imply some degree of risk to all people who habitually entered the plant. It is almost impossible to say that the company was unable to eliminate the risk by exercising reasonable care; plaintiffs allege that failure to provide in-house laundering, adequate showers, and lockers in an uncontaminated area caused ortho-toluidine to be released. Plaintiffs argue that Goodyear admitted releasing the chemical into the air, sewer system, and other sites as late as 1989, but that did not contribute to Dorothy's disease, and there is no evidence of risk associated with those releases. To find that use of the chemical was "common," "appropriate" to the setting, or of such value to the community that "its dangerous attributes" would be outweighed, the court must weigh more substantial evidence. Therefore, defendant's motion for judgment on this claim is denied at this stage.

To recover for negligence, plaintiffs must show that defendant owed them a duty of care. Goodyear argues that Dorothy has failed to show any legal duty.

EXHIBIT 10-6A
(continued)

Plaintiffs allege that Goodyear knew that exposure to ortho-toluidine through clothes, skin, and hair increased the risk of bladder cancer; knew or should have known that persons with secondary exposure, were within the zone of danger, and that, despite this knowledge, permitted the chemical to escape. Since Dorothy was a foreseeable plaintiff, the Kowalskis assert that a duty was owed to her to minimize the risk of harm, which Goodyear negligently failed to do. Whenever one person is placed in such a position with regard to another that every one of ordinary sense would recognize that if he did not use ordinary care and skill with regard to the circumstances he would cause danger of injury to the person or property of the other, a duty arises to use ordinary care and skill to avoid danger. The plaintiffs have alleged Goodyear's control over a known dangerous substance that carries with it a duty of ordinary care to protect persons and property within the scope of the danger. Goodyear owed a duty of care to all within the reach of the chemical's "known destructive power."

Goodyear argues that even if the court finds a duty to protect against known danger, it is not foreseeable that a wife who suffers secondary exposure through the handling of her husband's work clothes is at risk of cancer. Plaintiffs have provided evidence that by 1954 Goodyear perceived the danger of third-party exposure to ortho-toluidine from clothes, shoes, or gloves on which the chemical had spilled. They produced publications which warn against allowing employees to bring home work clothes or carry contamination from the change room to the showers. Plaintiffs have stated a claim and detailed Goodyear's duty based on foreseeability of harmful effects of secondary exposure sufficiently to survive a motion for summary judgment.

EXHIBIT 10-6B

METROPOLITAN WATER RECLAMATION DIST. OF GREATER CHICAGO v. NORTH AMERICAN GALVANIZING & COATINGS, INC.

UNITED STATES COURT OF APPEALS, 7th CIRCUIT *473 F.3d 824 (2007)*

Section *107(a)* of CERCLA imposes liability on certain private parties for cleanup costs associated with hazardous waste contamination. *Section 113(f)*, added by

---

EXHIBIT 10-6B
(continued)

SARA, allows those responsible for cleanup costs to bring actions for contribution against one another to apportion fault. Metropolitan brought this action under both provisions, seeking to recover cleanup costs that voluntarily incurred in remedying a parcel that it has leased for the past 50 years to Lake River. Lake River's parent, North American, moved to dismiss for failure to state a claim. The district court dismissed the *§113(f)* claim, but allowed a *§107(a)* claim to go forward. We affirm.

In the 1940s, Metropolitan leased about 50 acres to Lake River, which developed a facility to store, mix and package industrial chemicals, using above-ground storage tanks that were prone to leaks. During the tenancy, the tanks allegedly spilled close to 12,000 gallons of chemicals into the soil and groundwater. The toxins were hazardous substances and posed imminent danger. Metropolitan incurred substantial expenses investigating, monitoring and remedying the contaminated property.

Metropolitan sued Lake River to recoup costs. In ruling on the motion to dismiss, the district court distinguished the CERCLA claims. The court described *§107(a)*'s provisions as providing an implied cause of action for cost recovery in cases "where a party is seeking direct recovery of costs incurred in cleaning up a hazardous waste site." *Section 113(f)* claims for contribution are asserted by PRPs, seeking to apportion damages among themselves. The court recognized that Metropolitan, because it owned the property during the period of contamination, was a PRP under CERCLA. Normally PRPs are limited to claims under *§113(f)* and cannot recoup the full cost of remediation under the joint and several recovery of *§107(a)*. The Supreme Court had held recently in *Cooper Industries v. Aviall Services, Inc., 543 U.S. 157, (2004)*, that parties like Metropolitan who have commenced cleanup voluntarily, rather than being compelled to do so by civil suit, have no right to contribution under the wording of *§113(f)* (allowing contribution only "during or following any civil action"). The court held that, for PRPs who voluntarily undertake clean-up, an implied right to contribution under *§107(a)* is available, notwithstanding their status as liable parties. A contrary outcome would be contrary to the purposes of CERCLA to promote prompt and proper cleanup.

Enforcement of CERCLA rests primarily with the EPA, which has a range of enforcement options. To implement the statute, the EPA formulates the NCP, outlining steps that parties must take in choosing a remedial action and in cleanup. For sites that the EPA deems an imminent threat, it may issue an administrative compliance order or obtain a court injunction, directing a responsible party to respond. The EPA may commence cleanup on its own using the Superfund. After Superfund money has been spent, the EPA may recover costs from responsible parties:

(1) the owner and operator of a vessel or a facility,
(2) any person who at the time of disposal of any hazardous substance owned or operated any facility at which such hazardous substances were disposed of,

EXHIBIT 10-6B
(continued)

(3) any person who by contract, agreement, or otherwise arranged for disposal or treatment, or arranged with a transporter for transport for disposal or treatment, of hazardous substances . . . at any facility or incineration vessel owned or operated by another party or entity and containing such hazardous substances, and

(4) any person who accepts or accepted any hazardous substances for transport to disposal or treatment facilities, incineration vessels or sites selected by such person, from which there is a release, or a threatened release which causes the incurrence of response costs, of a hazardous substance. . . . *42 U.S.C. §9607.*

For these PRPs, liability under *§107(a)* is strict, joint and several; the EPA may recover costs in full from any responsible party, regardless of that party's relative fault. After CERCLA's passage, a question emerged: Whether a responsible party, who had been sued to commence cleanup or repay costs, may obtain contribution from other PRPs. In 1980, CERCLA did not provide expressly for a right of contribution. Courts recognized an implied right of contribution for PRPs who had been sued under *Section 107(a)* and, because of the joint-liability scheme, had been ordered to pay more than their pro rata share of cleanup costs.

Congress amended CERCLA by SARA to authorize a contribution action: "Any person may seek contribution from any other person who is liable or potentially liable under *section 9607(a)* of this title, during or following any civil action under *section 9606* of this title or under *section 9607(a)* of this title." *42 U.S.C. §9613(f)(1).* Under this provision, the court allocates costs using equitable principles. Liability is several, as opposed to *107(a)*'s joint and several scheme. SARA encourages parties to settle with the government by insulating any party that settles from a contribution action. SARA produced its own questions: Whether the new right of contribution was the only cause of action available to a PRP seeking to recover cleanup costs. PRPs who had expended costs understandably wished to seek joint and several cost recovery under *§107(a)*.

Every circuit to decide the issue held that, after SARA, PRPs were precluded generally from seeking joint and several recovery under *§107(a)*, and that any claim seeking to shift costs from one responsible party to another must be brought under *§113(f)*. The courts reasoned that a PRP, by definition, shares responsibility for contamination. Therefore, any action by one PRP against another to equitably apportion liability is a "quintessential claim for contribution" and it would be unfair to allow a PRP to recover 100 percent of response costs from others similarly situated. These courts reasoned that permitting a PRP to elect recovery under *§107(a)* would render *§113(f)* meaningless, as a PRP would readily abandon a *§113(f)(1)* suit in favor of more generous provisions of *§107(a)*.

CERCLA's strict liability yields a great number of potentially liable individuals, due to the reality that those truly responsible may not have the necessary

EXHIBIT 10-6B
(continued)

money for cleanup. An absentee landowner may be liable under *§107(a)* for the full cost of remedying a hazard caused by its tenant, even if the landowner had no reason to know that hazardous waste was being stored on its land. To blunt the force of a rule that limits the rights of these "innocent" parties under *§113(f)*, our cases developed the "innocent landowner" exception, under which a joint and several cost recovery action under *Section 107(a)* remains available to landowners who allege that they did not pollute the site in any way.

Recently, the Supreme Court discussed the interplay between *sections 107(a)* and *113(f)*, and decided a key issue concerning the timing of a *§113(f)* claim for contribution. In *Cooper Industries, 543 U.S. 157*, an owner and one time operator of airplane maintenance sites had sold the properties to another company in the early 1980s. After operating the sites for a number of years, the buyer, Aviall, discovered that both it and the seller, Cooper, had contaminated the facilities with hazardous substances that had leaked from storage containers. Aviall notified Texas authorities, who in turn directed Aviall to clean up the site. Aviall commenced cleanup and, after it incurred some $5 million in response costs, brought an action for contribution against Cooper under *CERCLA §113(f)*.

The Supreme Court held that *§113(f)* did not authorize Aviall's suit for contribution. The Court began by noting that the cost recovery remedy of §107(a) and the contribution remedy of §113(f)(1) are "clearly distinct." The Court then examined §113(f)(1), which provides that a claim for contribution may be brought "during or following any civil action under *section 9606* of this title or under *section 9607(a)* of this title." As the Court emphasized, Aviall had not been the subject of any civil action, and its claim based on *Section 113(f)* therefore was not "during or following any civil action." On this basis, the Court deemed Aviall's contribution action premature. Notably, the Court did not rule out a *§107(a)* action, observing that *§113(f)(1)* is not the "exclusive cause of action for contribution available to a PRP." The Court refused to speculate on the precise nature of the alternative remedy and decided only the question of Aviall's right to a *§113(f)* cause of action. The limited holding of *Cooper Industries* is that a party must have settled its liability with a government entity or been sued, for costs under *§107(a)* or for compliance under *§106*, before it may look to other responsible parties for contribution under *§113(f)(1)*. It is clear, at least, that Metropolitan cannot sue under *§113(f)* because it has not been subject to an action for damages or compliance.

Metropolitan urges that a right of action exists under *§107(a)* for private parties that, although potentially strictly liable, have voluntary undertaken remediation and have no right to contribution under *§113(f)(1)*. The text of *§107(a)*, they believe, authorizes such an action, providing that four categories of parties "shall be liable for" the government's remedial and removal costs, and for any other necessary costs of response incurred by any other person consistent with the national contingency plan. North American responds that *§107(a)(4)(B)* does

EXHIBIT 10-6B
(continued)

nothing more than spell out the potential liability of responsible parties and does not create authority to sue. Although *§107(a)(4)(B)* includes liability for the response costs of "any other person," North American maintains that it does not create a *cause of action* for "any other person," particularly for PRPs such as Metropolitan. The EPA agrees that Metropolitan has no claim under *§107(a)*, but interprets *§107(a)(4)(B)* to create a cause of action for some private parties. The agency disagrees with Metropolitan about who is authorized to sue, arguing that "any other person" distinguishes those who may sue for cleanup costs from the PRPs listed in *subsections (1)-(4) of Section 107(a)*. Thus, the EPA reasons, the phrase "any other person" refers to individuals who are not potentially responsible for cleanup costs. For parties like Metropolitan who are potentially liable for cleanup costs, the EPA submits, the only cause of action lies in the provisions of *§113(f)*, when available.

We reject the view that *§107(a)* does not create a cause of action. In *Key Tronic Corp. v. U.S., 511 U.S. 809 (1994)*, Key Tronic, one of several parties responsible for contaminating a landfill, settled a lawsuit with the EPA and then sued other responsible parties under *§113(f)* for recovery of part of its multi-million dollar commitment. Key Tronic also brought a claim under *§107(a)(4)(B)* for costs it incurred voluntarily before settling. The Court stated that "*§107* provides a cause of action for private parties to seek recovery of cleanup costs . . . this was implied rather than express. By imposing liability on responsible parties for costs "incurred by any other person," *§107(a)* "*implies* . . . that [PRPs] may have a claim for contribution against those treated as joint tortfeasors." The Court observed that, after SARA, "the statute now expressly authorizes a cause of action for contribution in *§113* and impliedly authorizes a . . . somewhat over-lapping remedy in *§107*."

These cases leave open the question of whether *§107(a)* authorizes a cause of action by PRPs in Metropolitan's situation. This question has been addressed by three federal courts of appeals in the aftermath of *Cooper Industries* . . . our colleagues on the Second Circuit held that parties such as Metropolitan may bring an action under *§107(a)* for response costs incurred voluntarily and the Eighth Circuit adopted the reasoning. However, most recently, the Third Circuit held that the Supreme Court's decision in *Cooper Industries* did not require it to revisit its prior holdings that "a PRP seeking to offset its cleanup costs must invoke contribution under *§113*."

After reviewing the decisions, we agree with the Second and Eighth Circuits. The Supreme Court's continued recognition of an implied cause of action in *§107(a)*, coupled with that subsection's plain language, convince us that Metropolitan may sue under *§107(a)* to recover necessary response costs. *Section 107(a)* states in relevant part that a responsible party

(4) . . . shall be liable for — (A) all costs of removal or remedial action incurred by the United States Government or a State or an Indian tribe not inconsistent with the

EXHIBIT 10-6B
(continued)

national contingency plan; (B) any other necessary costs of response incurred by any other person consistent with the national contingency plan;. . . .

Nothing in *(B)* indicates that a PRP, such as Metropolitan, should not be considered "any other person." The word "other" should be given meaning, but does not distinguish "any other person" from PRPs listed in *subsections (1)-(4)*. We read "other" as distinguishing "any other person" from "United States Government," "State" or "Indian tribe," listed in the immediately preceding subsection. These parties may recover costs "*not inconsistent* with the national contingency plan." By contrast, "any other person" is limited to recovery of costs "*consistent* with the national contingency plan." We read the subsections, and reference to "any other person," simply as a way of relaxing the burden of proof for governmental entities as opposed to private parties.

Recognizing in *§107(a)* a right of action for Metropolitan also appears in line with the savings clause found in §113(f)(1), which provides: "Nothing in this subsection shall diminish the right of any person to bring an action for contribution in the absence of a civil action under [*§106*] of this title or [*§107*] of this title." The sentence rebuts any presumption that the express right of contribution in *§113(f)* is the exclusive cause of action for contribution available to a PRP.

Prohibiting suit by a voluntary plaintiff like Metropolitan could undermine CERCLA's aims of encouraging expeditious, voluntary environmental cleanups while holding responsible parties accountable for the costs. To further CERCLA's policies, PRPs must be allowed to recover response costs even before they have been sued or have settled their CERCLA liability with a government entity. Were a cost recovery action unavailable in these circumstances, such parties would likely wait until they are sued to commence cleaning up a site for which they are not exclusively responsible because of their inability to be reimbursed for cleanup expenditures in the absence of a suit.

North American and the EPA respond that the government may lose settlement leverage if parties such as Metropolitan are allowed to bring suit under *§107(a)* in these circumstances. They point out that PRPs who settle with the United States enjoy protection from contribution suits by other parties and retain the ability to seek contribution themselves. By contrast, PRPs who choose not to settle are barred from seeking contribution under *§113(f)* from the settling parties and thus face potentially disproportionate liability. If the statute were to allow non-settling parties to sue under *§107(a)*, even when unable to do so under *§113(f)*, North American and the EPA contend that PRPs would be discouraged from settling with the United States. These concerns do not exist in the circumstances here; neither the EPA nor any other government entity has involved itself in the cleanup. Metropolitan's undertaking was completely voluntary and financed by Metropolitan alone. The EPA is not in the picture and has no reason to pursue a settlement.

The EPA also took steps to alleviate the PRPs' concerns about settlement, stating its position that an administrative order on consent qualifies as a settlement within the meaning of CERCLA §113(f)(3)(B). The agency amended its documentation for such orders accordingly, http://www.epa.gov/compliance/resources/policies/cleanup/superfund/interim-rev-aoc-mod-mem.pdf.

B.   Brownfields Programs

The term **brownfields** is used to describe contaminated property, typically in a developed urban area, that does not quality for Superfund remediation. Such property is typically stigmatized and unlikely to be put to productive use.

Brownfields Programs
Government provides incentives for redevelopment of contaminated site

Brownfields incentives programs serve two goals: alleviating the need to develop greenfields, land never previously developed, and, at the same time, increasing the likelihood that brownfields will be cleaned up and redeveloped. Without financial incentives, redevelopment of brownfields is considered too expensive and risky for most developers. The federal program in effect at the time of this writing provides that incentive by allowing environmental cleanup costs to be deducted in the year incurred, rather than capitalized over time. In addition, the EPA provides information, technical assistance, and grants and loans to promote brownfields projects. Developers are exempted from CERCLA liability. States have created their own programs to further promote **infill development** and redevelopment of brownfields.

Infill Development
Development of lots in an already urbanized area, rather than "sprawl" development outward from urban areas

C.   Emergency Planning and Community Right-to-Know Act

EPCRA, 42 U.S.C. §11001 et seq., was enacted in response to the 1984 disaster in Bhopal, India, in which more than 2,000 people suffered death or serious injury from the accidental release of methyl isocyanate. The following year, a release at a related facility in West Virginia sent hundreds to hospitals. The focus on the law is not actual regulation of the chemicals that might cause such a disaster, but on making communities aware of risks and able to prepare to deal with releases.

EPCRA requires establishment of State Emergency Response Commissions (SERCs). The SERC designates local emergency planning districts and appoints local committees, which must develop emergency response plans.

Local committees are to include broad representation by fire fighters, health officials, government and media representatives, community groups, industrial facilities, and emergency managers. While EPCRA does not place limits on which chemicals can be stored, used, released, disposed, or transferred at a facility, it does include requirements to ensure that communities are prepared to respond to chemical accidents.

Local Plans.   The plan developed by a local district must:

- Identify affected facilities and transportation routes;

- Describe emergency notification and response procedures;
- Designate community and facility emergency coordinators;
- Describe methods to determine the occurrence and extent of a release;
- Identify available response equipment and personnel;
- Outline evacuation plans;
- Describe training and practice programs and schedules; and
- Contain methods and schedules for exercising the plan.

Obligations of Facilities Subject to EPCRA. Any facility subject to EPCRA must notify both the SERC and local district within 60 days after it first receives a shipment or produces the substance on site. The facility must appoint an emergency response coordinator to work with the local district on developing and implementing the local plan at the facility. Any facility that has within its boundaries an amount of an EPA-listed "extremely hazardous substance" that is equal to or greater than the "threshold planning quantity" listed for the substance is subject to the EPCRA.

> An example of a facility that would be subject to EPCRA, depending on quantities present, is the vehicle and grounds maintenance shed at a college, because these facilities store or use paints, petroleum products, solvents, certain cleaning products, or batteries.

EPCRA exempts substances in the same packaging and concentration that is used in or purchased for home use. For example, materials in the form typically purchased in a hardware store are not usually subject to reporting requirements. Other exemptions apply to certain types of research laboratories, hospitals, and other research facilities.

Depending on local requirements, its size and the amounts and types of chemicals it has, a facility may be required to:

- Provide local officials with an MSDS for each above-threshold chemical on-site or a list of the chemicals grouped into categories (42 U.S.C. §11021)[5]
- Report to the SERC and local committee the amounts, location, and storage conditions of hazardous chemicals and mixtures containing hazardous chemicals present at the facility — the annual inventory of chemicals is sometimes called a "Tier II" report (42 U.S.C. §11022)
- Inform the public and officials about *routine* releases of toxic chemicals to the environment, using a Toxic Chemical Release Inventory Form (Form R) (42 U.S.C. §11023).

To see a detailed explanation of the reporting requirements, visit http://yosemite.epa.gov/oswer/ceppoweb.nsf/content/epcraOverview.htm.

---

[5]An MSDS, Material Data Safety Sheet, is required by OSHA for certain chemicals. See Exhibit 8-2 in this book.

The EPA uses Form R to maintain the Toxic Release Inventory (TRI), an inventory of routine toxic chemical emissions from certain facilities. While Form R, which consists of five pages, is too long to reproduce in this book, you can see the form and instructions for its use, along with other reporting forms at http:// www.epa.gov/tri/report/index.htm#forms.

A related law, the **Toxic Substances Control Act (TSCA)** of 1976, 15 U.S.C. §2601 et seq., enables the EPA the ability to track the 75,000 industrial chemicals currently produced or imported into the United States. The law is discussed in depth in the next chapter.

TSCA
Enables EPA to track, inventory, and, if necessary, ban, industrial chemicals

Emergency Notifications. Facilities must provide an emergency notification and a written follow-up notice to the local committee and the SERC for any area likely to be affected if there is a release into the environment of a hazardous substance that is equal to or exceeds the minimum reportable quantity set in the regulations. There are two types of chemicals that require reporting under this section: (1) Extremely Hazardous Substances (EHSs); and (2) Comprehensive Environmental Response, Compensation and Liability Act (CERCLA) hazardous substances.

Initial notification can be made by telephone, radio, or in person. In addition, CERCLA spills must also be reported to the National Response Center at (800) 424-8802. Emergency notification requirements involving transportation incidents can be met by dialing 911, or in the absence of a 911 emergency number, calling the local operator.

Emergency notification must include the chemical name; indication of whether the substance is extremely hazardous; estimate of the quantity released into the environment; time and duration of the release; whether the release occurred into air, water, and/or land; any known or anticipated acute or chronic health risks associated with the emergency and where necessary advice regarding medical attention for exposed individuals; proper precautions, such as evacuation or sheltering in place; and name and telephone number of contact person. A written follow-up notice must be submitted to the SERC and local committee as soon as practicable after the release. The follow-up notice must update information included in the initial notice and provide information on actual response actions taken and advice regarding medical attention necessary for citizens exposed.

While the law is entitled "Right to Know," few actually know the risks in their communities. The Sunshine Week project, which focuses on availability of public records, http://sunshineweek.blogs.com/my_weblog/2007/03/nationwide_info.html, found that a large percentage of officials in charge of community plans required by the Act did not know where the plan was located or were unwilling to provide access to the plan, http://www.sunshineweek.org/files/audit07.pdf. To find your local commission, do a zip code search at http://yosemite.epa.gov/oswer/lepcdb.nsf/SearchForm?OpenForm.

D. In the Field: Limited Liability Entities and CERCLA

As if trying to learn the environmental statutes weren't enough, you also have to know something about business structure and insurance to fully appreciate the reach of CERCLA.

Assignment 10-5
Where You Live

◆ Use CALR to search cases from the federal circuit courts of appeal to determine whether the circuit in which your state is located has ruled on the liability of interim owners for passive migration.

◆ Using http://www.epa.gov/triexplorer/, attempt to find information about toxic chemical emissions in your area.

◆ Using http://www.emich.edu/public/geo/557book/d374.brownfields. html, find and report on your state brownfields program.

Limited Liability Entities
Businesses structured so that owners risk only what they invest in the business

Businesses are often structured as **limited liability entities**, so that if the business is unable to pay its debts, then, absent a specific agreement to the contrary, creditors are out of luck and cannot go to the owners or officers demanding to be paid. A limited liability entity has a legal existence separate from its owners and directors. Limited liability entities include **corporations, limited liability companies**, and, to some extent, **limited partnerships**. The underlying owners of such businesses, called stockholders, members, or limited partners, are generally considered investors who risk only what they put into the business; their personal assets (house, car, other investors) are not at risk.

To take full advantage of the concept of limited liability, businesses sometimes set up complex arrangements, with entities owning other entities. For example, at the time of the 1978 Amoco Cadiz oil spill, the tanker that spilled its cargo was owned by Amoco Transport, which was a **subsidiary** of the **parent company** Standard Oil.

Subsidiary
Business entity owned by another business entity

Parent Company
Business entity that owns another business entity

Under environmental laws, especially CERCLA, the assumption that environmental liability is limited to the entity that owns or operates the contaminated property has not always proven true. Under a theory called **piercing the corporate veil** a court can disregard the structure of the entity and impose liability on others.

Piercing the Veil
Court can disregard structure of entity and impose liability on owners

A parent company can be liable for the acts of a subsidiary if the parent company actually "manage[s], direct[s], or conduct[s] operations specifically related to pollution, that is, operations having to do with the leakage or disposal of hazardous waste, or decisions about compliance with environmental regulations." Active participation in the general affairs of the subsidiary alone will not make a parent company liable, unless some other basis exists for piercing the corporate veil. *United States v. Bestfoods*, 524 U.S. 51 (1998).

The decision has implications beyond situations involving actual ownership and has been a particular concern for municipalities that have contracted with private waste disposal companies for disposal of waste and have retained significant control over the operation. A local government can subject itself to potential CERCLA liability if its regulation of a site exceeds the exercise of conventional police power and rises to the level of "macromanaging" a facility. In *United States v. Township of Brighton*, 153 F.3d 307 (6th Cir. 1998) the court refused to provide a "mechanical checklist" of factors for determining when regulation constitutes "macromanaging," but emphasized that the township had not operated at "arm's-length" with its contractor. The court stressed that (1) the disposal agreement made the dump subject to the township's specifications and supervision, (2) the town had made repeated and substantial ad hoc appropriations and arrangements for maintenance, and (3) the town "took responsibility for ameliorating the unacceptable conditions" at the dump before and after state authorities scrutinized the site.

If the PRP entity ceases to exist, any successor to its operation must be careful in structuring the transaction to avoid becoming a successor to its liability. A successor company might acquire a PRP by a stock buyout, so that it becomes the owner of every aspect of the PRP — including its liabilities. On the other hand, a successor might purchase only certain aspects of the business, such as its equipment.

Hot Topic: The interaction of CERCLA with the bankruptcy laws has been the subject of much discussion in the legal community. The goal of bankruptcy laws, to give a debtor a fresh start, free of crushing liabilities, is at odds with the goals of CERCLA, to make PRPs responsible for cleanups and remove that burden from taxpayers. This is discussed in further detail in the next chapter.

What about individual shareholders and officers of the company? CERCLA's "transporter liability" provision was at issue in *United States v. USX Corp.*, 68 F.3d 811 (3d Cir. 1995). The court stated that corporate officers or shareholders may be subject to liability only if they "actively participate in the process of accepting hazardous substances for transport and have a substantial role in the selection of the disposal facility," but that "[i]t is not necessary that the officer personally accept the waste for transport. Nor is it necessary that the officer participate in the selection of the disposal facility. Liability may be imposed where the officer is aware of the acceptance of materials for transport and of his company's substantial participation in the selection of the disposal facility. An officer who has authority to control the disposal decisions should not escape liability under §107(a)(4) when he or she has actual knowledge that a subordinate has selected a disposal site and, effectively, acquiesces in the subordinate's actions."

So, how can businesses protect themselves? As mentioned in a previous chapter, environmental insurance is available, usually to cover cost of remediation above a specified "cap" or to protect against tort claims by outside parties. If the parties rely on insurance, in addition to the stability of the insurer and policy limits, they should consider whether they are getting an **occurrence policy**, under which the date of the conduct giving rise to the claim determines whether the loss was within the policy period, or a **claims-made policy**, under which the date of injury or damage determines whether a claim is within the period covered by a policy.

Occurrence Policy
Date of conduct giving rise to claim determines whether loss was within policy period

Claims-made Policy
Date of injury or damage determines whether a claim is within the period covered by a policy

---

EXHIBIT 10-7
Environmental Insurance Policy Language

Timing Is Everything

The controversy had its beginnings in 1986, when a water well was constructed on the property of a Mrs. Neal, which was located opposite the store where the gasoline tanks had been located. After her well had been in use a short time, Mrs. Neal discovered her well contained oil. The South Carolina Department of Health and Environmental Control (DHEC) confirmed the presence of petroleum in the ground water in the area. Mrs. Neal proceeded to sue Meador [the supplier of gasoline stored in the tanks] for damage to her property. DHEC also notified Meador that it intended to seek recovery for all costs of conducting studies of the site as well as potential costs in any possible clean-up of the site. The present declaratory judgment action was then begun by Safeco [which argues] that there was no liability under its policy either to Mrs. Neal or DHEC because contaminants from the storage tank was not an "occurrence" as defined in its policy, and that "property damage" did not cover the discharge of the gasoline since the events did not qualify as an "accident" within the meaning of its policies, especially since its policy expressly requires that the leakage be "sudden." The word "occurrence" is defined in the policy to mean "an accident including continuous or repeated exposure, which results in bodily injury or property damage neither expected nor intended from the standpoint of the insured." Ruling in favor of Safeco, the court stated that "occurrence [in such a policy] is judged by the time at which the leakage and damage are first discovered" and the Safeco policy was not in effect at the time of discovery. *Safeco Ins. Co. v. Federated Mut. Ins. Co.*, 915 F.2d 1565 (4th Cir. 1990).

Key Terms

§104(e) Request	Contribution Claims
Applicable or Relevant and Appropriate Requirements (ARARs)	De Micromis Settlements
	De Minimis Settlements
Brownfields Programs	Emergency Planning and Community Right-to-Know Act (EPCRA)
Claims-made Policy	
Clean Hands	Emergency Removals
Comprehensive Environmental Response, Compensation, and Liability Information System (CERCLIS)	Estoppel
	General Notice Letter
	Hazard Ranking System (HRS)
	Hazardous Substances
Consent Decree	Indemnify

Infill Development
Joint and Several Liability
Laches
Lead Agency
Limited Liability Entities
Moratorium
National Contingency Plan (NCP)
National Priorities List (NPL)
National Response Center (NRC)
NBAR
No Further Remedial Action Planned
    (NFRAP) Decision
Non-Time Critical Removals
Occurrence Policy
On-Scene Coordinator (OSC)
Parent Company
Piercing the Veil
Pollutant or Contaminant
Potentially Responsible Parties (PRPs)

Preliminary Assessment
Record of Decision (ROD)
Remedial Action (RA)
Remedial Design (RD)
Remedial Investigation/Feasibility
    Study
Removal Action
Res Ipsa Locquitur
Site Investigation
Special Notice Letters (SNLs)
Strict Liability
Subsidiary
Superfund Amendments and
    Reauthorization Act (SARA)
Steering Committee
Superfund Law
Time Critical Removals
Toxic Substances Control Act
    (TSCA)

Review Questions

1. Identify potentially hazardous substances, the release of which would **not** be covered by CERCLA.
2. Under what circumstances might a parent company be responsible for environmental liabilities of a subsidiary? Could directors of a corporation ever be held personally liable?
3. What is meant by the "enforcement first" policy?
4. What are the three types of removal actions and how do they differ?
5. What steps must be followed prior to a long-term remedial activity?
6. Explain the use of ARARs.
7. How do EPA policies attempt to avoid delay in remedial actions and costly litigation?
8. How do brownfields programs work?
9. Explain the concepts of strict liability and joint and several liability.
10. Explain how a PRP may be taking a risk by voluntarily cleaning up a site for which other PRPs may also be responsible.
11. What are the basic requirements imposed by EPCRA on the state and on private facilities?

KEY TERMS CROSSWORD

www.CrosswordWeaver.com

ACROSS

3. removal with no time for planning
5. PRPs may seek from other PRPs
7. acronym, numerical ranking for describing risk at site
9. acronym, site close-out report
10. long-term response
11. _____ the corporate veil, a theory for liability of corp. stockholders
14. _____ law, aka CERCLA
16. sites must be on this list to be eligible for Superfund cleanup
19. a corporation is a limited _____ entity
22. short term response to release
23. _____ agency coordinates cleanup
24. EPA computerized inventory of sites
25. acronym, in charge of removal operation

DOWN

1. remedial process begins with preliminary _____
2. PRP = _____ responsible party
4. not quite a hazardous substance, but covered by CERCLA
6. initials, contains national priorities list and protocol for cleanup
8. a parent corp. may be liable for _____ corp.
12. acronym, requires reporting of releases to NRC
13. program to encourage re-use of contaminated land
14. liability without fault or negligence
15. _____ action, aka "turning dirt"
17. acronym, plural, determines level of cleanup
18. _____-critical removal must be performed in less than 6 mos
20. acronym, 1986 CERCLA amendment
21. CERCLA liability is _____ and several

11

Solid Waste, Hazardous Waste

◆ ◆ ◆

A. Overview of RCRA

The **Resource Conservation and Recovery Act (RCRA)** (lawyers and paralegals often say "rik-rah" or "rek-rah"), 42 U.S.C. §6901 et seq., like many of the environmental laws you have already studied, is actually a series of laws dealing with a particular problem. This chapter is intended to give you an overview and will not focus on which amendments established specific programs and requirements. The RCRA regulates hazardous waste (Subtitle C), nonhazardous solid waste (Subtitle D), and underground storage tanks (Subtitle I).

Cradle-to-Grave
RCRA objective of regulating hazardous waste from its creation to final disposal

The RCRA gives the EPA authority to control *hazardous waste* from **"cradle-to-grave."** Regulation follows hazardous waste from its generation, through transportation, treatment, storage, and disposal. The RCRA initially left regulation of nonhazardous waste largely to the states, with some assistance from the EPA. In the 1970s and 1980s, however, a number of events made clear the need for a greater federal role with respect to nonhazardous waste:

- A barge loaded with garbage from the northeast embarked on an international journey in search of a dump site. For more information on this strange event, which captured national attention in 1987, see http://www.newsoftheodd.com/content/view/216/29.
- A number of states publicized estimates that they had only a few years of landfill capacity remaining to accommodate municipal solid waste needs.
- As landfill capacity dwindled, the NIMBY (Not In My Back Yard) and NIMEY (Not In My Election Year) syndromes escalated. Every public notice for proposed landfill site drew significant protest.
- As public opposition to the siting of permitted landfills grew, instances of illegal "midnight dumping" increased because of the cost or lack of landfill facilities.
- The EPA proposed new operating standards for landfills which, it was estimated, would put 75 percent of landfills accepting municipal solid waste in the nation out of business.

As a result, the law was amended to establish a federal framework for management of nonhazardous wastes. Like many of the laws you have already studied, RCRA requires self-reporting and provides for criminal prosecution of "knowing" violations, civil penalties, and citizen suits after proper notice to the EPA.

RCRA focuses on active and future facilities, rather than abandoned or historical sites (such sites are covered by CERCLA, discussed in the previous chapter). This chapter will focus on the obligations of those who are currently involved in or plan to become involved in dealing with solid waste, hazardous waste, or underground storage tanks to determine which laws are relevant, establish the permitting process, and so on. Keep in mind, however, that the law does give the EPA authority over those whose past actions have resulted in an imminent and substantial endangerment to health or the environment.

Remember that CERCLA imposes strict liability on those involved with covered sites. Because RCRA is focused on present and future actions, most courts hold that its definitions do not create liability for parties who are totally passive, although there is disagreement. The issue was explored in *Carson Harbor Vill. Ltd. v. Unocal Corp.*, 270 F.3d 863 (9th Cir. 2001). The court stated that:

[W]hether the definition includes passive soil migration is an issue of first impression in this circuit. Other circuit courts have taken a variety of approaches . . . a careful reading of their holdings suggests a more nuanced range of views, depending in large part on the factual circumstances of the case. Compare *United States v. 150 Acres of Land*, 204 F.3d 698, 706 (6th Cir. 2000) (concluding that absent "any evidence that there was human activity involved in whatever movement of hazardous substances occurred on the property," there is no "disposal"), *ABB Indus. Sys., Inc. v. Prime Tech, Inc.*, 120 F.3d 351, 359 (2d Cir. 1997) (holding that prior owners are not liable for the gradual spread of contamination underground), and *United States v. CDMG Realty Co.*, 96 F.3d 706, 722 (3rd Cir. 1996) ("The passive spreading of contamination in a landfill does not constitute 'disposal' under CERCLA."), with *Nurad, Inc. v. William E. Hooper & Sons Co.*, 966 F.2d 837, 846 (4th Cir. 1992) (holding past owners liable for the "disposal" of hazardous wastes that leaked from an underground storage tank). . . .

We hold that the gradual passive migration of contamination through the soil that allegedly took place during the Partnership Defendants' ownership was not a "discharge, deposit, injection, dumping, spilling, leaking, or placing" and, therefore, was not a "disposal" within the meaning of §9607(a)(2). The contamination on the property included tar-like and slag materials. The tar-like material was highly viscous and uniform, without any breaks or stratification. The slag material had a vesicular structure and was more porous and rigid than the tar-like material. There was some evidence that the tar-like material moved through the soil and that lead and/or TPH may have moved from that material into the soil. If we try to characterize this passive soil migration in plain English, a number of words come to mind, including gradual "spreading," "migration," "seeping," "oozing," and possibly "leaching." But certainly none of those words fits within the plain and common meaning of "discharge, . . . injection, dumping, . . . or placing." 42 U.S.C. §6903(3). Although these words generally connote active conduct, even if we were to infuse passive meanings, these words simply do not describe the passive migration that occurred here. Nor can the gradual spread here be characterized as a "deposit," because there was neither a deposit by someone, nor does the term deposit encompass the gradual spread of contaminants. The term "spilling" is likewise inapposite. Nothing spilled out of or over anything. Unlike the spilling of a barrel or the spilling over of a holding pond, movement of the tar-like and slag materials was not a spill.

1. Definitions

How RCRA regulates waste depends on whether it is classified as simply "solid waste" or as "hazardous waste." The starting point is **"solid waste."** A material must be defined as a solid waste before it can be considered a hazardous waste. The statutory definition of a solid waste is not based on the physical form of the material (whether it is a solid as opposed to a liquid or gas), but on the fact that the material is waste. Some say that all waste that is not hazardous waste is solid waste, so the issue boils down to whether a substance is waste.

Solid Waste
Discarded material that is not classified as hazardous

a. Solid Waste

The term "solid waste" means any garbage, refuse, sludge from a waste treatment plant, water supply treatment plant, or air pollution control facility and other **discarded** material, including solid, liquid, semisolid, or contained gaseous material resulting from industrial, commercial, mining, and agricultural operations, and from community activities, but does not include solid or dissolved material in domestic sewage, or solid or dissolved materials in irrigation return flows or industrial discharges that are point sources subject to permits under section 1342 of title 33, or source, special nuclear, or byproduct material as defined by the Atomic Energy Act of 1954. 42 U.S.C. §6903 (27) (emphasis added).

This very broad statutory definition has been refined by regulations.

The word discarded has been defined by 40 C.F.R. §261.2(a) as including: (1) materials that are abandoned; (2) materials that are recycled; (3) materials that are inherently waste-like; and (4) waste military munitions.

Abandoned is defined in subsection (b) as material: disposed of; burned or incinerated; or accumulated, stored or treated in lieu of being disposed of, burned, or incinerated.

There is a common misconception that all recycling is exempt from RCRA; EPA does regulate some materials when recycled (e.g., spent materials). As you will see when you examine Exhibit 11-1, subsection (c) defines as recycled, but subject to regulation as solid waste, specific materials applied to or placed on the land in a manner that constitutes disposal, or burned for energy recovery, or reclaimed, or accumulated speculatively.

Inherently waste-like materials are defined in subsection (d).

Discarded material includes military munition identified in §266.202 as a solid waste when: disposed of, burned, or incinerated; removed from storage for disposal; leaking, deteriorated, or damaged; determined to be solid waste by a military official; or collected from a range and sent off site for treatment or disposal. Discharge of ammunition is normal and expected use, not hazardous waste disposal.

Are the definitions clear to you? They aren't entirely clear to the courts or to those regulated by the law. For example, whether a substance is exempt from the definition of regulated recycled material has generated much litigation. The analysis tends to be very fact specific.

Sham Recycling
EPA can deny a recycling exemption from solid waste regulation if there is no market for the resulting product

Accumulated Speculatively
Recycled material is not exempt from regulation as solid waste if accumulated speculatively

The EPA has established guidelines for what constitutes legitimate recycling and has described activities it considers to be **"sham recycling."** Considerations include whether the secondary material is effective for the claimed use, whether the secondary material is used in excess of the amount necessary, and whether the facility has maintained records of recycling transactions. In order to ensure that exempt materials are actually recycled, the regulations designate as solid wastes (not covered by the recycling exemption) certain materials that are **accumulated speculatively**. A material is accumulated speculatively if it has no viable market or if the person accumulating the material cannot demonstrate that 75 percent or more of the material is recycled in a calendar year.

Examine the text of the relevant CFR section, reproduced in Exhibit 11-1, and you will see that much recycled material is exempt from the definition; whether material fits within the exemption depends on the type of material and the manner of recycling. For example:

- A material is used or reused and therefore exempt if it is used as an ingredient in an industrial process to make a product (e.g., distillation bottoms[1] from one process used as feedstock in another process) or if it is used as an effective substitute for a commercial product (e.g., spent pickle liquor used as a sludge conditioner in wastewater treatment).

---

[1]Distillation "bottoms" are by-products of the distillation processes in re-refineries.

- A material is reclaimed and therefore exempt if it is processed to recover a usable product or if it is regenerated (e.g., regeneration of spent solvents).
- If a material is directly reused within an industrial process, despite being left over from another or the same part of the process, it usually is excluded from the definition as a solid waste.

EXHIBIT 11-1
Definition of Solid Waste

From 40 C.F.R. §261.2 (sections relating to recycled material are bold).

§261.2 Definition of solid waste.

(a)(1) A solid waste is any discarded material that is not excluded by §261.4(a) or that is not excluded by variance granted under §§260.30 and 260.31.

(2) A discarded material is any material which is:

(i) Abandoned, as explained in paragraph (b) of this section; or

(ii) Recycled, as explained in paragraph (c) of this section; or

(iii) Considered inherently waste-like, as explained in paragraph (d) of this section; or

(iv) A military munition identified as a solid waste in 40 CFR 266.202.

(b) Materials are solid waste if they are abandoned by being:

(1) Disposed of; or

(2) Burned or incinerated; or

(3) Accumulated, stored, or treated (but not recycled) before or in lieu of being abandoned by being disposed of, burned, or incinerated.

(c) Materials are solid wastes if they are recycled — or accumulated, stored, or treated before recycling — as specified in paragraphs (c)(1) through (4) of this section.

(1) Used in a manner constituting disposal.

(i) Materials noted with a "*" in Column 1 of Table 1 are solid wastes when they are:

(A) Applied to or placed on the land in a manner that constitutes disposal; or

(B) Used to produce products that are applied to or placed on the land or are otherwise contained in products that are applied to or placed on the land (in which cases the product itself remains a solid waste).

(ii) However, commercial chemical products listed in §261.33 are not solid wastes if they are applied to the land and that is their ordinary manner of use.

(2) Burning for energy recovery.

(i) Materials noted with a "*" in column 2 of Table 1 are solid wastes when they are:

(A) Burned to recover energy;

EXHIBIT 11-1
(continued)

(B) Used to produce a fuel or are otherwise contained in fuels (in which cases the fuel itself remains a solid waste).

(ii) However, commercial chemical products listed in §261.33 are not solid wastes if they are themselves fuels.

(3) Reclaimed. Materials noted with a "*" in column 3 of Table 1 are solid wastes when reclaimed (except as provided under §261.4(a)(17)). Materials noted with a " — " in column 3 of Table 1 are not solid wastes when reclaimed.

(4) Accumulated speculatively. Materials noted with a "*" in column 4 of Table 1 are solid wastes when accumulated speculatively.

Table 1

	Use constituting disposal (§261.2(c)(1))	*Energy recovery/ fuel (§261.2(c)(2))*	*Reclamation (§261.2(c)(3)) (except as provided in 261.4(a)(17) for mineral processing secondary materials)*	*Speculative accumulation (§261.2(c)(4))*
	1	2	3	4
Spent Materials	(*)	(*)	(*)	(*)
Sludges (listed in 40 CFR Part 261.31 or 261.32	(*)	(*)	(*)	(*)
Sludges exhibiting a characteristic of hazardous waste	(*)	(*)	—	(*)
By-products (listed in 40 CFR 261.31 or 261.32)	(*)	(*)	(*)	(*)

EXHIBIT 11-1
(continued)

	Use constituting disposal (§261.2(c)(1))	*Energy recovery/ fuel (§261.2(c)(2))*	*Reclamation (§261.2(c)(3)) (except as provided in 261.4(a)(17) for mineral processing secondary materials)*	*Speculative accumulation (§261.2(c)(4))*
By-products exhibiting a characteristic of hazardous waste	(*)	(*)	—	(*)
Commercial chemical products listed in 40 CFR 261.33	(*)	(*)	—	—
Scrap metal other than excluded scrap metal (see 261.1(c)(9))	(*)	(*)	(*)	(*)

Note: The terms "spent materials," "sludges," "by-products," and "scrap metal" and "processed scrap metal" are defined in §261.1.

(d) Inherently waste-like materials. The following materials are solid wastes when they are recycled in any manner:

(1) Hazardous Waste Nos. F020, F021 (unless used as an ingredient to make a product at the site of generation), F022, F023, F026, and F028.

(2) Secondary materials fed to a halogen acid furnace that exhibit a characteristic of a hazardous waste or are listed as a hazardous waste as defined in subparts C or D of this part, except for brominated material that meets the following criteria:

(i) The material must contain a bromine concentration of at least 45%; and

EXHIBIT 11-1
(continued)

(ii) The material must contain less than a total of 1% of toxic organic compounds listed in appendix VIII; and

(iii) The material is processed continually on-site in the halogen acid furnace via direct conveyance (hard piping).

(3) The Administrator will use the following criteria to add wastes to that list:

(i)(A) The materials are ordinarily disposed of, burned, or incinerated; or

(B) The materials contain toxic constituents listed in appendix VIII of part 261 and these constituents are not ordinarily found in raw materials or products for which the materials substitute (or are found in raw materials or products in smaller concentrations) and are not used or reused during the recycling process; and

(ii) The material may pose a substantial hazard to human health and the environment when recycled.

(e) Materials that are not solid waste when recycled.

(1) Materials are not solid wastes when they can be shown to be recycled by being:

(i) Used or reused as ingredients in an industrial process to make a product, provided the materials are not being reclaimed; or

(ii) Used or reused as effective substitutes for commercial products; or

(iii) Returned to the original process from which they are generated, without first being reclaimed or land disposed. The material must be returned as a substitute for feedstock materials. In cases where the original process to which the material is returned is a secondary process, the materials must be managed such that there is no placement on the land. In cases where the materials are generated and reclaimed within the primary mineral processing industry, the conditions of the exclusion found at §261.4(a)(17) apply rather than this paragraph.

(2) The following materials are solid wastes, even if the recycling involves use, reuse, or return to the original process (described in paragraphs (e)(1)(i) through (iii) of this section):

(i) Materials used in a manner constituting disposal, or used to produce products that are applied to the land; or

(ii) Materials burned for energy recovery, used to produce a fuel, or contained in fuels; or

(iii) Materials accumulated speculatively; or

EXHIBIT 11-1
(continued)

(iv) Materials listed in paragraphs (d)(1) and (d)(2) of this section.

(f) Documentation of claims that materials are not solid wastes or are conditionally exempt from regulation. Respondents in actions to enforce regulations implementing subtitle C of RCRA who raise a claim that a certain material is not a solid waste, or is conditionally exempt from regulation, must demonstrate that there is a known market or disposition for the material, and that they meet the terms of the exclusion or exemption. In doing so, they must provide appropriate documentation (such as contracts showing that a second person uses the material as an ingredient in a production process) to demonstrate that the material is not a waste, or is exempt from regulation. In addition, owners or operators of facilities claiming that they actually are recycling materials must show that they have the necessary equipment to do so.

b.   Hazardous Waste

If a material has been classified as a solid waste (not meeting any of the solid waste exclusions or exemptions), the next step in the hazardous waste identification process is to determine whether the solid waste meets the definition of a hazardous waste. **Hazardous waste** has properties that make it dangerous or potentially harmful to human health or the environment. The universe of hazardous wastes is large; hazardous wastes can be liquids, solids, contained gases, or sludges. They can be the by-products of manufacturing processes or simply discarded commercial products, such as cleaning fluids or pesticides. In regulatory terms, a RCRA hazardous waste is:

Hazardous Waste
Has properties that make it dangerous or potentially harmful to human health or the environment

1. A waste that appears on one of the four **hazardous wastes lists (F-list, K-list, P-list, or U-list):**
   - **F-list** (nonspecific source wastes) identifies wastes from common manufacturing and industrial processes, such as solvents that have been used in cleaning or degreasing operations. Because the processes producing these wastes can occur in different sectors of industry, the F-listed wastes are known as wastes from nonspecific sources.
   - **K-list** (source-specific wastes) includes certain wastes from specific industries, such as petroleum refining or pesticide manufacturing. Certain sludges and wastewaters from treatment and production processes in these industries are examples of source-specific wastes.

Hazardous Wastes Lists
CFR lists identifying hazardous wastes

- **P-list** and **U-list** (discarded commercial chemical products) lists include specific commercial chemical products in an unused form. Some pesticides and some pharmaceutical products become hazardous waste when discarded.

2. Or exhibits at least one of four characteristics — ignitability, corrosivity, reactivity, or toxicity:

Ignitable Waste
Capable of fire or explosion

- **Ignitable wastes** can create fires under certain conditions, are spontaneously combustible, or have a flashpoint less than 60 °C (140 °F). Examples include waste oils and used solvents.

Corrosive Wastes
Hazardous waste, acid or base, corrodes metal

- **Corrosive wastes** are acids or bases (pH less than or equal to 2, or greater than or equal to 12.5) that are capable of corroding metal containers, such as storage tanks, drums, and barrels. Battery acid is an example.

Reactive Waste
Unstable under normal circumstances

- **Reactive wastes** are unstable under "normal" conditions. They can cause explosions, toxic fumes, gases, or vapors when heated, compressed, or mixed with water. Nitroglycerin is an example.

Toxic wastes
Poses a risk to human health

- **Toxic wastes** are harmful or fatal when ingested or absorbed (e.g., containing mercury, lead, etc.). When toxic wastes are land disposed, contaminated liquid may leach from the waste and pollute ground water.

Mixtures of hazardous waste plus solid waste as well as substances derived from hazardous waste are generally assumed to be hazardous waste. The exemptions are beyond the scope of this chapter, but the dilution prohibition, discussed later in this chapter, will provide some insight. The EPA has a program for "de-listing" substances, see http://www.epa.gov/epaoswer/hazwaste/id/delist/index.htm.

Assignment 11-1

Using an online resource, such as http://www.findlaw.com/casecode/cfr.html:

◆ Examine 40 C.F.R. §261.4 and determine whether domestic sewage is excluded from the definition of solid waste. What about point source discharges subject to the CWA?

◆ Examine 40 C.F.R. §260.30 and §260.31; when might a variance from classification as a solid waste be available to a party that is accumulating material speculatively without sufficient amounts being recycled to fit within the exemption?

◆ Consider — if a waste is considered hazardous because of a characteristic, such as being corrosive, it might lose that characteristic and cease to be hazardous if combined with another substance or treated. However, if a waste is considered hazardous because it is listed, it still contains the listed chemical after it is treated or combined with another substance. It might no longer actually be hazardous, but would it be categorized as hazardous? Find the relevant C.F.R. provision.

◆ Examine 40 C.F.R. §261.1; find the definitions of "scrap metal" and "by product." Why are those definitions important to understanding the sections reproduced in Exhibit 11-1?

- Find the "F List" in the C.F.R. What is the first category listed?
- Where are the P and U lists located?
- Which part of C.F.R. Title 40 deals with determination of the adequacy of a state permit program? Which part sets forth criteria for MSWLs?
- Read the case summarized in Exhibit 11-2 and discuss the following:
  What is the difference between the "dry tomb" approach and a bioreactor?
  What is the "political agenda" behind this suit?
  Does the standing requirement serve any beneficial purpose or is it just a way of allowing agencies to act without being challenged?

EXHIBIT 11-2

GRASSROOTS RECYCLING NETWORK, INC. v. U.S. E.P.A.

429 F.3d 1109 (D.C. Cir. 2005)

In 2004, the EPA promulgated a rule that allows an approved state landfill program to issue research, development, and demonstration permits granting variances from certain criteria set by the EPA for sanitary landfills. GrassRoots challenges the rule as exceeding the agency's authority under the RCRA. We dismiss.

The RCRA establishes a federal program to regulate handling and disposal of solid waste; it requires the EPA to promulgate criteria for determining which facilities shall be classified as sanitary landfills and which shall be classified as [prohibited] open dumps. Under the regulations a municipal solid waste landfill (MSWLF) must maintain a level of run-on control and install a final cover system to minimize infiltration and erosion. Most MSWLFs are operated as "dry tombs," with the level of liquid in the landfill minimized to slow biodegradation and reduce production of gas. An MSWLF that uses liquid to increase biodegradation is known as a "bioreactor." The EPA prohibits bioreactors by banning, in most cases, addition of liquid waste to a MSWLF. *40 C.F.R. §258.28(a)-(b).*

States are responsible for enforcing the EPA's minimum criteria; the RCRA contemplates each State will develop a solid waste management plan, subject to approval of the EPA, which will not be forthcoming unless the plan provides for closing all "open dumps." The RCRA instructs the EPA to: "encourage . . . authorities . . . [to] promote . . . research . . . experiments . . . and studies relating to . . . new and improved methods of collecting and disposing of solid waste. *§6981(a)(6).* The EPA issued the RD&D Rule, hoping to stimulate development of new technologies and alternative processes for disposal of solid waste. The rule allows an approved state program to issue an RD&D permit for an MSWLF as to

EXHIBIT 11-2
(continued)

which the owner or operator proposes to utilize innovative methods of disposal. *40 C.F.R. §258.4(a)*. Such a permit may authorize use of a design that does not conform to usual criteria for run-on control systems, final cover, and the prohibition on adding liquids, but only if the permit includes conditions at least as protective as criteria for MSWLFs to assure protection of human health and the environment.

GrassRoots argues EPA violated RCRA by delegating to States authority to implement the [RD&D] permit process and to waive certain national criteria for sanitary landfills. An association, such as GrassRoots, has standing to sue on behalf of its members only if (1) at least one of its members would have standing to sue in his own right, (2) the interests the association seeks to protect are germane to its purpose, and (3) neither the claim asserted nor relief requested requires that an individual member of the association participate. Because we conclude no member of GrassRoots has standing to sue in his or her own right, GrassRoots lacks associational standing and its petition must be dismissed.

GrassRoots attached affidavits of two members, describing the injuries he or she claims to have suffered as a result of the RD&D Rule. Each member states that he or she lives approximately 1.5 miles from a landfill in a Wisconsin town. Wisconsin has proposed, but not adopted, a rule that would allow it to issue permits under the RD&D Rule. Petersen states: "If I had known that the Metro Landfill could be converted into a bioreactor . . . I would not have purchased my property, or I certainly would have paid considerably less." Fate states he "might not have" purchased his property had he known the landfill near his home might become a bioreactor. Neither affidavit is evidence of the "actual or imminent" injury required for standing to sue. Each affiant states that at the time of purchase his or her home would have been worth less to him or her, not that the home in fact is worth less, due to the RD&D Rule. GrassRoots fails to assert, much less to prove, that the value of any member's home is less than it would be but for the rule. [Grassroots] suggest the rule will cause the value of homes to decline in the future, the injury is conjectural and not imminent. Whether [either] landfill will be converted into a bioreactor depends upon whether third parties take several steps. First, the DNR must approve a rule for issuing RD&D permits. Next, the EPA must approve the proposal. The owner of the landfill must apply for a permit, and the DNR must, after a public hearing, grant the permit application. Even then, the value of homes might not decline; recall that each RD&D permit must be as protective of human health and the environment as would be a non-RD&D permit. This "multi-tiered speculation" instances events that, although by no means impossible, are at this time neither actual nor imminent. GrassRoots has no evidence of actual decline in market value of any member's home. Its petition is *Dismissed*.

2. Regulation

a. *Regulation of Landfills Accepting Solid Waste*

The RCRA bans open dumping of solid waste and authorizes the EPA to set standards for **municipal solid waste landfills (MSWLs).** An MSWL is a landfill that accepts household waste and may also accept nonhazardous sludge, industrial solid waste, and construction debris. MSWLs can also accept household appliances (**white goods**). Some appliances, such as refrigerators and window air conditioners, rely on ozone-depleting refrigerants and their substitutes; the landfill must follow special federally mandated disposal procedures for such appliances. Some materials may be banned from disposal in MSWLs, including common household items such as paints, cleaners, chemicals, motor oil, batteries, and pesticides. Leftover portions of these products are called **household hazardous waste** because they can cause harm if mishandled. Many municipal landfills have a household hazardous waste drop-off station for these materials.

The technical details of the requirements are too extensive for this book; they govern the location standards, facility design and operation, closure and post-closure care, financial assurance requirements, groundwater monitoring, and corrective action standards. Every MSWL must have:

- Siting plan — to prevent the siting of landfills in environmentally sensitive areas, such as wetlands, fault lines, and floodplains
- On-site environmental monitoring systems — which monitor for any sign of groundwater contamination and for landfill gas — providing additional safeguards
- Liners — a flexible membrane (geomembrane) overlaying two feet of compacted clay soil lining the bottom and sides of the landfill, to protect groundwater and the underlying soil from **leachate** releases
- Leachate collection and removal systems that sit on top of the composite liner and remove leachate from the landfill for treatment and disposal
- Corrective action provisions to control and clean up releases
- Operating practices that include compacting and cover waste frequently with several inches of soil to reduce odor and control litter, insects, and rodents
- Closure and post-closure care plan including covering the landfill and providing long-term care of closed landfills
- Financial assurances that provide funding for environmental protection during and after landfill closure (closure and post-closure care), which are often accomplished by the purchase of **surety bonds** from a third party, such as an insurance company

Some solid waste landfills are specialized:

Bioreactor landfills are MSWLs designed to quickly transform and degrade organic waste. The increase in waste degradation and stabilization is accomplished through the addition of liquid and, in some cases air, to enhance microbial processes. Bioreactors are a new approach to landfill design and operation that differ from the traditional "dry tomb" municipal landfill approach.

MSWL
Municipal Solid Waste Landfill

White Goods
Appliances, such as refrigerators, as waste

Household Hazardous Waste
Household chemical remnants

Leachate
Liquid formed when water (from rain) soaks through a landfill, picking up suspended and dissolved materials

Surety Bond
Method of providing financial assurances, involving a third party insuring obligations

Bioreactor Landfill
Designed to speed the breakdown of organic materials

Construction and Demolition Debris Landfill
Also called C&D landfill, handles debris from construction and demolition

Inert
Not active

Industrial Waste Landfill
Landfill specializing in disposal of industrial waste

Combustion or Incineration
Burning to reduce volume of waste

Construction and Demolition (C&D) Debris landfills accept only construction and demolition debris, such as concrete, asphalt, brick, wood, drywall, asphalt roofing shingles, metals, and some types of plastics. C&D landfills are subject to less stringent standards than municipal solid waste landfills due to the relatively **inert** nature of C&D debris materials.

Industrial Waste landfills are designed for nonhazardous industrial waste, which may consist of a wide variety of nonhazardous materials that result from the production of various products.

To reduce waste volume, landfill operators may implement a controlled burning process called **combustion or incineration**. In addition to reducing volume, combustors can fuel heating systems or generate electricity.

Hot Topics

Does incineration solve the problem or create new problems? Many people think that the U.S. Army's disposal of chemical weapons by incineration poses great risks to human health and that the burden is disproportionately borne by minorities and low-income people. See http://www.cwwg.org/Itswrong.html, the website for the Chemical Weapons Working Group or the Sierra Club site, http://www.sierraclub.org/pressroom/releases/pr2004-03-03.asp. Is chemical weapon incineration planned for your area?

Are landfills "dead" land? Not necessarily; there are businesses that specialize in redeveloping closed landfills as recreational facilities such as golf courses (see www.brownfieldsgolf.com), playing fields for team sports, and tennis courts. The redevelopment of the Meadowlands area of New Jersey is an example of making productive use of what was once useless and even dangerous property, http://www.reclaimingthemeadowlands.com/index.asp?AID=45.

RDF
Facilities that recover recyclables before incineration

Mass Burning
Burning waste without sorting out recyclables

Scrubbers
Devices that use a liquid spray to neutralize acid gases and filters to remove tiny ash particles

More than one-fifth of U.S. municipal solid waste incinerators use **refuse derived fuel (RDF)**; in contrast to **mass burning**—where the solid waste is introduced "as is" into the combustion chamber—RDF facilities recover recyclables (e.g., metals, cans, glass) first, then shred the combustible fraction into fluff for incineration. Pollution control technologies are used to reduce the gases emitted into the air, including **scrubbers,** which are devices that use a liquid spray to neutralize acid gases and filters to remove tiny ash particles. Burning waste at extremely high temperatures destroys chemical compounds and disease-causing bacteria. Regular testing ensures that residual ash is nonhazardous before it is placed in a landfill. About 10 percent of the total ash formed in the combustion process is used for beneficial use such as daily cover in landfills and road construction. In addition, many new landfills collect potentially harmful landfill **methane** gas emissions and convert the gas into energy.

The federal requirements have imposed high costs on the states. The states have only limited ability to control the volume of the waste stream for which they are responsible because, as discussed in a previous chapter, the United States Supreme Court has determined that garbage is "commerce." State regulatory authorities generally may not discriminate against waste received from out of state. Under the **market participant exception,** however, a governmental body that is a landfill owner or operator, rather than just a regulator, may do business with anyone it chooses, without regard to interstate commerce discrimination constraints.

Methane
A gas produced by landfills

Market Participant Exception
Government-owned landfills may refuse to accept out-of-state waste despite impact on interstate commerce

Assignment 11-2

1. Visit   bondhttp://www.westernsurety.com/news/surety_legislation_by_state.htm. Determine the bonding requirements, if any, for landfills in your state.
2. Examine the statute itself, http://www.law.cornell.edu/uscode/html/uscode42/usc_sup_01_42_10_82.html.
   ◆ Find the "whistleblower" provision
   ◆ Find the "citizen suit" provision
   ◆ Find the provision for closing or upgrading existing open dumps
3. Starting at http://www.epa.gov/epaoswer/osw/stateweb.htm, find answers to as many of the following questions as possible:
   ◆ Does your state have a form for a landfill surety bond?
   ◆ What are the siting requirements for an MSWL?
   ◆ Does the landfill permit process include a background check on the owner or operator?
   ◆ Does your state have a special program to deal with used computer component parts?
   ◆ Does your state have a special program to deal with used vehicle tires?
   ◆ Is there an online list of **solid waste transfer stations**?

Solid Waste Transfer Station
Location where waste is removed from collection trucks and loaded for longer trip to disposal

Waste transfer stations are facilities where solid waste is unloaded from collection vehicles and held while it is reloaded onto larger long-distance transport vehicles for shipment to landfills or other disposal facilities. By combining the loads of several individual collection trucks, communities can save money on labor and operating costs. Although transfer stations help reduce the number of trucks traveling to the disposal site, they can cause an increase in traffic in the area where they are located. If not properly sited, designed, and operated they can cause noise, odor, and trash problems for residents living near them.

b. *Regulation of Hazardous Waste*

Remember that material that might have been hazardous waste at one stage of its "life," can cease to be hazardous as the result of recycling described in the previous sections.

i. *Generators and Transporters*

As with solid waste, the EPA has delegated primary responsibility for implementation of hazardous waste regulation to the states. In regulating hazardous waste "cradle to grave," the RCRA regulates all who control hazardous wastes at some point in its cycle, including those who generate (create) and transport hazardous waste. A generator is any person, or site, whose processes and actions create hazardous waste. Transporters are individuals or entities that move hazardous waste from one site to another by highway, rail, water, or air. Generally any use of a public road constitutes a transport.

Generators are classified as large, small, or conditionally exempt small generators. All must comply with the RCRA, but each class of generator is obligated to comply with different requirements as shown on Exhibit 11-3. Whether a generator must obtain an EPA identification number or a permit and what procedures are mandated (e.g., having an emergency response plan) depend upon the quantity of waste produced per month and how long that waste is held (accumulated). It is, therefore, essential that generators and transporters not act outside the bounds of their definitions by, for example, holding hazardous waste for too long, http://www.epa.gov/epaoswer/osw/gen_trans/generate.htm.

As you can see from Exhibit 11-3, all large and small quantity generators must obtain an EPA identification number from their state environmental offices, comply with the manifest system, handle wastes properly before shipment (packaging, labeling, marking, placarding, accumulation time, etc.), and comply with record-keeping and reporting requirements. Note that large generators must file biennial reports that include a description of the efforts undertaken during the year to reduce the volume and toxicity of waste generated.

CoolClips.com

Have you ever wondered about signs and numbers on the placards on the side of trucks and rail cars? UN/NA numbers (the four digit number) found on bulk placards refer to specific chemicals or groups of chemicals and are assigned by the United Nations and/or the United States Department of Transportation. To see the various signs, visit http://environmentalchemistry.com/yogi/hazmat/placards/. The symbol on this page is used to indicate radioactive material.

Transporters must also obtain an EPA identification number, comply with the manifest system, and comply with regulations of the U.S. Department of Transportation and individual states. To see the Department of Transportation's (DOT)

EXHIBIT 11-3
Chart of Generators

From http://www.epa.gov/epaoswer/osw/gen_trans/summary.htm.

	CESQGs	SQGs	LQGs

Quantity Limits	≤ 100 kg/month
	  ≤ 1 kg/month of acute hazardous waste
	  ≤ 100 kg/month of acute spill residue or soil §§261.5(a) and (e)
		Between 100-1,000 kg/month §262.34(d)	≤ 1,000 kg/month
			  >1 kg/month of acute hazardous waste
			  >100 kg/month of acute spill residue or soil Part 262 and §261.5(e)

EPA ID Number	Not required §261.5	Required §262.12	Required §262.12

On-Site Accumulation Quantity	≤ 1,000 kg
	  ≤ 1 kg acute
	  ≤ 100 kg of acute spill residue or soil §§261.5(f)(2) and (g)(2)
		≤ 6,000 kg §262.34(d)(1)	No limit

Accumulation Time Limits	None §261.5	≤ 180 days or ≤ 270 days (if greater than 200 miles) §§262.34(d)(2) and (3)	≤ 90 days §262.34(a)
Storage Requirements	None §261.5	Basic requirements with technical standards for tanks or containers §§262.34(d)(2) and (3)	Full compliance for management of tanks, containers, drip pads, or containment buildings §262.34(a)
Sent To:	State approved or RCRA permitted/ interim status facility §§261.5(f)(3) and (g)(3)	RCRA permitted/ interim status facility §262.20(b)	RCRA permitted/ interim status facility §262.20(b)
Manifest	Not required §261.5	Required §262.20	Required §262.20
Biennial Report	Not required §261.5	Not required §262.44	Required §262.41
Personnel Training	Not required §261.5	Basic training required §262.34(d)(5)(iii)	Required §262.34(a)(4)
Contingency Plan	Not required §261.5	Basic plan §262.34(d)(5)(i)	Full plan required §262.34(a)(4)
Emergency Procedures	Not required §261.5	Required §262.34(d)(5)(iv)	Full plan required §262.34(a)(4)
DOT Transport Requirements	Yes (if required by DOT)	Yes §§262.30-262.33	Yes §§262.30-262.33

Post-9/11 Enhanced Security Requirements, visit http://hazmat.dot. gov/riskmgmt/hmt/Enhanced%20Security%20Requirements%20(General).pdf.

Manifest
Used for tracking hazardous waste, must be signed by generators, transporters, and disposal facilities

A **manifest**, which is used for tracking hazardous waste, contains information on the type and quantity of the waste being transported, instructions for handling the waste, and signature lines for all parties involved in the disposal process. Any party coming into custody of the waste receives a copy and can refuse to sign the manifest if the description does not match the physical reality of the waste — the waste must then be returned to the generator. The generator is also responsible for contacting the EPA if it does not receive confirmation that the waste has been received at the disposal site within the required time frame (an "exception report"). The manifest is required by both DOT and EPA. This "chain of custody" system is important to both environmental safety — ensuring safe handling and preventing illegal dumping — and national security. Examine the manifest form reproduced as Exhibit 11-4. Instructions for completing the form are available at http://www.epa.gov/epaoswer/hazwaste/gener/manifest/registry/man-inst.pdf.

LDR
Land Disposal Restrictions on hazardous waste include dilution, storage, and disposal prohibitions

Note the need for EPA identification numbers and codes to identify the wastes, as well as the space for reporting discrepancies. Your state may have its own requirements: http://www.epa.gov/epaoswer/hazwaste/gener/manifest/registry/states.htm.

As soon as a hazardous waste is generated, it is also subject to **Land Disposal Restrictions (LDR) Program** regulations, unless it is at concentrations already below LDR treatment standards. If a business generates hazardous wastes that are above the treatment standards, it must either treat the wastes on-site before having them disposed of or send them off-site for proper treatment and ultimate disposal. If the hazardous waste meets the LDR treatment standards, further treatment is not necessary prior to disposal. A generator must always inform the receiving treatment, storage, and disposal facility of the status of the hazardous waste and ensure that it is handled safely.

The EPA's LDR has three major components:

Disposal Prohibition
Prohibition on land disposal of untreated hazardous waste

- **Disposal Prohibition.** Before a hazardous waste can be land disposed, treatment standards specific to that waste material must be met. A facility may meet such standards by
  - Treating hazardous chemical constituents in the waste to meet required treatment levels. Any method of treatment can be used to bring concentrations to the appropriate level except dilution. OR
  - Treating hazardous waste using a treatment technology specified by EPA. Once the waste is treated with the technology required under LDR, it can be land disposed.

Dilution Prohibition
Prohibition on adding liquid or other nonhazardous material to hazardous waste to simply dilute its concentration without treating it

- **Dilution Prohibition.** Waste must be properly treated and not simply diluted in concentration by adding large amounts of water, soil, or nonhazardous waste. Dilution does not reduce the toxicity of the hazardous constituents.

Storage Prohibition
Waste must be treated and cannot be stored indefinitely

- **Storage Prohibition.** Waste must be treated and cannot be stored indefinitely. This prevents generators and treatment, storage, and disposal facilities from storing hazardous waste for long periods to avoid

EXHIBIT 11-4
Uniform Hazardous Waste Manifest

Please print or type. (Form designed for use on elite (12-pitch) typewriter.)   Form Approved. OMB No. 2050-0039

UNIFORM HAZARDOUS WASTE MANIFEST	1. Generator ID Number		2. Page 1 of	3. Emergency Response Phone	4. Manifest Tracking Number

5. Generator's Name and Mailing Address   Generator's Site Address (if different than mailing address)

Generator's Phone:

6. Transporter 1 Company Name	U.S. EPA ID Number

7. Transporter 2 Company Name	U.S. EPA ID Number

8. Designated Facility Name and Site Address	U.S. EPA ID Number

Facility's Phone:

9a. HM	9b. U.S. DOT Description (including Proper Shipping Name, Hazard Class, ID Number, and Packing Group (if any))	10. Containers No. / Type	11. Total Quantity	12. Unit Wt./Vol.	13. Waste Codes
	1.				
	2.				
	3.				
	4.				

14. Special Handling Instructions and Additional Information

15. GENERATOR'S/OFFEROR'S CERTIFICATION: I hereby declare that the contents of this consignment are fully and accurately described above by the proper shipping name, and are classified, packaged, marked and labeled/placarded, and are in all respects in proper condition for transport according to applicable international and national governmental regulations. If export shipment and I am the Primary Exporter, I certify that the contents of this consignment conform to the terms of the attached EPA Acknowledgment of Consent.
I certify that the waste minimization statement identified in 40 CFR 262.27(a) (if I am a large quantity generator) or (b) (if I am a small quantity generator) is true.

Generator's/Offeror's Printed/Typed Name	Signature	Month	Day	Year

16. International Shipments	☐ Import to U.S.	☐ Export from U.S.	Port of entry/exit:
Transporter signature (for exports only):			Date leaving U.S.:

17. Transporter Acknowledgment of Receipt of Materials

Transporter 1 Printed/Typed Name	Signature	Month	Day	Year

Transporter 2 Printed/Typed Name	Signature	Month	Day	Year

18. Discrepancy

18a. Discrepancy Indication Space	☐ Quantity	☐ Type	☐ Residue	☐ Partial Rejection	☐ Full Rejection

Manifest Reference Number:

18b. Alternate Facility (or Generator)	U.S. EPA ID Number

Facility's Phone:

18c. Signature of Alternate Facility (or Generator)	Month	Day	Year

19. Hazardous Waste Report Management Method Codes (i.e., codes for hazardous waste treatment, disposal, and recycling systems)

1.	2.	3.	4.

20. Designated Facility Owner or Operator: Certification of receipt of hazardous materials covered by the manifest except as noted in Item 18a

Printed/Typed Name	Signature	Month	Day	Year

EPA Form 8700-22 (Rev. 3-05) Previous editions are obsolete.   DESIGNATED FACILITY TO DESTINATION STATE (IF REQUIRED)

treatment. Waste may be stored, subject to the LDR, in tanks, containers, or containment buildings — but only for the purpose of accumulating quantities necessary to facilitate proper recovery, treatment, or disposal.

Standards for the treatment required to implement the LDR were developed in phases. Solvent and dioxin-containing wastes were the first group of wastes for which EPA established treatment standards. You may also hear of "California list" (the second phase), third list, second-thirds, and third-thirds. The EPA continues to develop treatments standards for newly identified hazardous wastes.

ii. Treatment, Storage, Disposal

TSDF Permits
Permit for transfer, storage, disposal facility handling hazardous waste

TSDF permits. Hazardous waste is generally stored before it is treated and must be treated before it can be disposed. Facilities that will treat, store, or dispose of hazardous waste must obtain **Treatment, Storage, Disposal Facility** (TSDF) **permits** prior to construction. **Interim status** was granted to TSDFs in existence when the RCRA was enacted in 1980 and can be retained until either the facility loses that status because of noncompliance with requirements or the facility is able to obtain permanent permitted status.

> No TSDF permit is needed for businesses that generate hazardous waste and transport it off-site without storing it for long periods of time, businesses that transport hazardous waste, or businesses that store hazardous waste for short periods of time without treating it.

The first step in the permit process is a properly advertised, informal public meeting. After considering input from the pre-application meeting, the applicant prepares a permit application, describing the proposed facility, how it will protect the environment, handle spills and emergencies, and provide for closure and cleanup. The permitting agency sends notice of the application to interested parties and makes the application available for public review. After reviewing the application, the agency may issue a **Notice of Deficiency (NOD)** identifying, and requesting that the applicant provide, missing information. Given the complex and technical nature of the required information, the review and revision process may take several years.

NOD
Notice of deficiency in permit application process

When revisions are complete, the agency makes a preliminary decision about whether to issue the permit. The agency may issue a "notice of intent to deny." If the agency decides that the application meets appropriate standards, it issues a draft permit containing the conditions under which the facility can operate if it receives final approval, and it publicizes the decision to start a public comment period. After considering public comments, the permitting agency reconsiders the draft permit or the notice of intent to deny and issues a "response to public comments," specifying any changes, before finally issuing or denying a permit. Facility owners and the public have a right to appeal the final decision; the appeal is usually decided by administrative law judges.

If a facility changes management procedures, mechanical operations, or the wastes it handles, it must obtain a permit modification. Modifications require public participation. If a facility violates the terms of its permit, the agency can terminate the permit.

The EPA is trying to make the process more efficient. Find out more about e-permitting for hazardous waste facilities at http://www.epa.gov/epaoswer/hazwaste/permit/epmt/epermit.htm#model.

Permit Conditions. TSDF permit holders are subject to requirements concerning recordkeeping and reporting, the manifest system, LDR, and obtaining an EPA identification number (described in previous sections). In addition TSDF facilities typically must:

- Control emissions of volatile organic compounds (VOCs) from certain hazardous waste treatment processes, equipment (e.g., valves, pumps, compressors), containers, tanks, and surface impoundments
- Train employees and provide adequate security
- Comply with general closure and post-closure care requirements applicable to all facilities, as well as unit specific requirements for facilities described below (landfill, tank, surface impoundment)
- Investigate and clean up hazardous waste releases
- Demonstrate financial resources adequate to properly close the facility when its operational life is over and provide the appropriate emergency response in case of an accidental release
- Monitor groundwater by installing groundwater monitoring wells and establishing a groundwater sampling plan
- Depending on the type of facility (landfill, storage tanks, incinerator), comply with relevant design and operating standards
- Submit biennial reports

Sample permits can be viewed at http://www.epa.gov/epaoswer/hazwaste/permit/sample.htm.

Do permit holders lose their Fourth Amendment rights? Not entirely. As noted in Chapter 2, administrative search warrants are easier to obtain than non-administrative warrants because of the lower expectation of privacy. In addition, facility operators rarely refuse entry and require the inspector to get a warrant for fear of arousing suspicion. The statute, 42 U.S.C. §6927(a), provides:

(a) Access entry

For purposes of developing or assisting in the development of any regulation or enforcing the provisions of this chapter, any person who generates, stores, treats, transports, disposes of, or otherwise handles or has handled hazardous wastes shall, upon request of any officer, employee or representative of the Environmental Protection Agency, duly designated by the Administrator, or upon request of any duly designated officer, employee or representative of a State having an authorized hazardous waste program, furnish information relating to such wastes and permit such person at all reasonable times to have access to, and to copy all records relating to such wastes. For the purposes of developing or assisting in the development of any regulation or enforcing the provisions of this chapter, such officers, employees or representatives are authorized—

(1) to enter at reasonable times any establishment or other place where hazardous wastes are or have been generated, stored, treated, disposed of, or transported from;

(2) to inspect and obtain samples from any person of any such wastes and samples of any containers or labeling for such wastes.

Each such inspection shall be commenced and completed with reasonable promptness. If the officer, employee or representative obtains any samples, prior to leaving the premises, he shall give to the owner, operator, or agent in charge a receipt describing the sample obtained and if requested a portion of each such sample equal in volume or weight to the portion retained. If any analysis is made of such samples, a copy of the results of such analysis shall be furnished promptly to the owner, operator, or agent in charge.

Note the reference to a facility that has handled hazardous waste. Inspections may be conducted after the waste has moved on. Permits typically mirror the law with respect to inspections. The following language was taken from the Martin Electronics permit, http://www.epa.gov/epaoswer/hazwaste/permit/martin.pdf.

> The permittee, by accepting this Permit, specifically agrees to allow authorized Department personnel, upon presentation of credentials or other documents as may be required by law, access to the premises, at reasonable times, where the permitted activity is located or conducted for the purpose of:
>
> a. Having access to and copying any records that must be kept under the conditions of the Permit;
>
> b. Inspecting the facility, equipment, practices, or operations regulated or required under this Permit; and
>
> c. Sampling or monitoring any substances or parameters at any location reasonably necessary to assure compliance with this Permit or Department rules.

Storage.   Regulations contained in the CFR (Title 40, Parts 264 and 265) describe the standards for storage units, including:

- **Containers**—portable devices in which a hazardous waste is stored, transported, treated, disposed, or otherwise handled. The most common hazardous waste container is the 55-gallon drum. Other examples of containers are tanker trucks, railroad cars, buckets, bags, and even test tubes.
- **Tanks**—stationary devices constructed of nonearthen materials used to store or treat hazardous waste. Tanks can be open-topped or completely enclosed and are constructed of a wide variety of materials including steel, plastic, fiberglass, and concrete.
- **Drip pads**—wood drying structures used by the pressure-treated wood industry to collect excess wood preservative drippage. Drip pads are constructed of nonearthen materials with a curbed, free-draining base that is

designed to convey wood preservative drippage to a collection system for proper management.

- **Containment buildings** — completely enclosed, self-supporting structures (four walls, a roof, and a floor) used to store or treat noncontainerized hazardous waste. A waste pile is an open, uncontained pile used for treating or storing waste.
- **Hazardous waste piles** — placed on top of a double liner system to ensure leachate from the waste does not contaminate surface or ground water supplies.
- **Surface impoundments** — natural topographical depressions, man-made excavations, or diked areas such as holding ponds, storage pits, or settling lagoons. Surface impoundments are formed primarily of earthen materials and are lined with synthetic plastic liners to prevent liquids from escaping.

Treatment. Treatment is any process that changes the physical, chemical, or biological character of the waste to make it less of an environmental threat. Treatment can neutralize the waste; recover energy or material resources from a waste; render the waste less hazardous; or make the waste safer to transport, store, or dispose. Treatment standards for each specific hazardous waste (by hazardous waste code) are outlined in the CFR.

Combustion or incineration is a common treatment method that destroys hazardous organic constituents and reduces the volume of waste. Depending upon the type of waste and its constituents, residual ash may be deposited in a landfill or may require further treatment.

Disposal. Final disposal of hazardous waste is subject to the LDR, discussed in the previous section. Disposal facilities must obtain a permit prior to construction. The most common methods of disposal are land disposal units, which include landfills, surface impoundments, and waste piles (described in previous sections), **land treatment units (LTUs),** which involve application of waste to the soil surface or the incorporation of waste into upper layers of the soil to degrade, transform, or immobilize hazardous constituents, and injection wells. **Underground injection wells** are the most commonly used disposal method for liquid hazardous waste. Because of their potential impact on drinking water resources, injection wells are also regulated under the Safe Drinking Water Act (discussed in an earlier chapter) and by the EPA's Underground Injection Control Program.

LTU
Land Treatment Unit; disposal of hazardous waste on or in land

Underground injection wells
Most commonly used disposal method for liquid hazardous waste.

c. Other Wastes

Some wastes are managed under special, tailored regulations:

Mixed waste is hazardous waste containing radionuclides and technologically enhanced, naturally occurring, and/or accelerator-produced radioactive material containing hazardous waste. Low-level mixed waste is exempt from some RCRA regulations if managed as radioactive waste in accordance with Nuclear Regulatory Commission or NRC-approved state regulations.

Mixed Waste
Hazardous waste containing radionuclides and technologically enhanced, naturally occurring and/or accelerator-produced radioactive material containing hazardous waste

Universal waste
Includes batteries, pesticides, fluorescent bulbs, and mercury-containing equipment (e.g., thermostats)

Universal waste includes batteries, pesticides, lamps (e.g., fluorescent bulbs), and mercury-containing equipment (e.g., thermostats). The federal rule, which has been modified in some states, makes it easier for businesses to handle covered products. For example, the rule extends the amount of time that businesses can accumulate these materials on-site. It also allows companies to transport the materials with a common carrier, instead of a hazardous waste transporter, and no longer requires companies to obtain a manifest. The rule makes it easier for companies to establish collection programs and participate in manufacturer take-back programs required by a number of states. As a result, many large manufacturers and trade associations plan national and regional collection programs for their products.

Used oil, tires, oil filters, and batteries from vehicles contain many toxic substances, so disposal is a particular problem. The EPA's **Used Oil Management Program** focuses on the recycling of petroleum-based or synthetic oil that has been used. To identify recycling or disposal centers for oil, as well as for tires, and other household wastes in your area visit the earth911 website, http://www.earth911.org/master.asp?s=ls&a=HHW&cat=9&serviceid=#13.

Are You Part of the Problem?

Do you have a new cell phone? The latest MP-3 player? What did you do with your old monitor when you got an LCD monitor for your computer? The EPA estimates that electronics comprise up to 4 percent of the municipal solid waste stream. This is not harmless, inert material. Electronic components typically include plastic, cadmium, lead, mercury, hexavalent chromium, and flame retardants. For a legal professional, environmental concerns are only half of the problem. Confidential information may have been stored on electronics used for work and, if disposal is not handled carefully, may land in the wrong hands.

Assignment 11-3

◆ In CFR Title 40, identify the part that describes standards for owners and operators of hazardous waste treatment facilities.
◆ In CFR Title 40, find the low-level mixed waste exemption.
◆ Find the EPA website that describes the Universal Waste Rule. Determine whether your state includes electronics in the category of universal waste.

◆ Examine the statute and find the section that requires those who generate, transport, or handle hazardous waste to allow the EPA access for inspection.

◆ Determine how/where used oil is recycled in your area.

◆ In preparation for the next two sections, find your state law dealing with medical waste, http://www.epa.gov/epaoswer/other/medical/programs.htm, and whether your state has an approved program for dealing with underground storage tanks, http://www.epa.gov/swerust1/fedlaws/spa_frs.htm.

---

d. Medical Waste

In the late 1980s, medical debris washed up on the shores of New York and New Jersey, closing beaches and raising public awareness of the disposal of medical waste. As a result of the public outrage, the **Medical Waste Tracking Act (MWTA)** 42 U.S.C. §6992 et seq., established a pilot program in several states with standards for tracking medical waste and penalties for violations. The MWTA resulted in model guidelines that have served as the basis for several state programs.

MWTA
Medical Waste Tracking Act

Some components of medical waste are directly federally regulated. Wastes containing mercury or other toxic metals are governed by the RCRA; medical wastes containing radioactive isotopes or materials are covered by NRC. The EPA also has regulations governing emissions from hospital, medical, or infectious waste incinerators. In addition, requirements under the Federal Insecticide, Fungicide, and Rodenticide Act (FIFRA—discussed in the next chapter) apply to medical waste treatment technologies that use chemicals for treating the waste.

Medical waste consists of infectious, hazardous, radioactive, and other general wastes from doctors' offices and hospitals. The MWTA defines medical waste as including:

- Cultures and stocks of infectious agents and associated biologicals, including cultures from medical and pathological laboratories, cultures and stocks of infectious agents from research and industrial laboratories, wastes from the production of biologicals, discarded live and attenuated vaccines, and culture dishes and devices used to transfer, inoculate, and mix cultures

- Pathological wastes, including tissues, organs, and body parts that are removed during surgery or autopsy

- Waste human blood and products of blood, including serum, plasma, and other blood components

- Sharps that have been used in patient care or in medical, research, or industrial laboratories, including hypodermic needles, syringes, pasteur pipettes, broken glass, and scalpel blades

- Contaminated animal carcasses, body parts, and bedding of animals that were exposed to infectious agents during research, production of biologicals, or testing of pharmaceuticals

- Wastes from surgery or autopsy that were in contact with infectious agents, including soiled dressings, sponges, drapes, lavage tubes, drainage sets, underpads, and surgical gloves
- Laboratory wastes from medical, pathological, pharmaceutical, or other research, commercial, or industrial laboratories that were in contact with infectious agents, including slides and cover slips, disposable gloves, laboratory coats, and aprons
- Dialysis wastes that were in contact with the blood of patients undergoing hemodialysis, including contaminated disposable equipment and supplies such as tubing, filters, disposable sheets, towels, gloves, aprons, and laboratory coats
- Discarded medical equipment and parts that were in contact with infectious agents
- Biological waste and discarded materials contaminated with blood, excretion, excudates, or secretion from human beings or animals who are isolated to protect others from communicable diseases
- Such other waste material that results from the administration of medical care to a patient by a health care provider and is found by the administrator to pose a threat to human health or the environment

The model guidelines require segregation of the waste at the generator site, placement of the waste in containers that should protect the handlers and the public from exposure, labeling of medical waste containers, and tracking of medical waste transportation from the generator site to the disposal facility with a uniform tracking form to be submitted to the administrator of the state environmental agency. The system should include confirmation that the waste was received by the disposal facility and whether the waste was incinerated.

3.   Underground Storage Tanks

UST
Underground storage tank

An **underground storage tank system (UST)** is defined as a tank and any underground piping connected to the tank that has at least 10 percent of its combined volume underground. Federal UST regulations apply only to underground tanks and piping storing either petroleum or specified hazardous substances. The EPA promulgates technical regulations to prevent, detect, and clean up releases and to ensure that UST owners demonstrate the financial ability to deal with releases and damages from releases. Installation of unprotected steel tanks and piping has been banned since 1985. As with much environmental law, the federal law allows state UST programs approved by EPA to operate in lieu of the federal program.

Common UST sites include service stations, convenience stores, fleet service operators, and local governments. Until the mid-1980s, most USTs were made of bare steel, which is likely to corrode over time and allow UST contents to leak into the environment. Faulty installation or inadequate operating and maintenance procedures also can cause USTs to release their contents into the environment.

LUST
Leaking underground storage tank

A leaking UST is often called a **LUST.** The greatest potential hazard from a leaking UST is that the petroleum or other hazardous substance can seep into the soil and contaminate groundwater, but a LUST can also result in a fire or explosion.

Some USTs are exempt from federal requirements, but may be regulated by states:

- Farm and residential tanks of 1,100 gallons or less capacity holding motor fuel used for noncommercial purposes
- Tanks storing heating oil used on the premises where it is stored
- Tanks on or above the floor of underground areas, such as basements or tunnels
- Septic tanks and systems for collecting stormwater and wastewater
- Flow-through process tanks
- Tanks of 110 gallons or less capacity
- Emergency spill and overfill tanks

The RCRA also establishes the LUST Trust Fund, which has two purposes: to provide money for overseeing and enforcing corrective action taken by the owner or operator of the LUST and to provide money for cleanups at sites where the owner or operator is unknown, unwilling, or unable to respond or that require emergency action. The fund is financed by a tax on gasoline.

B. Toxic Substances Control Act

The **Toxic Substances Control Act (TSCA),** 15 U.S.C. §2601, gives the EPA authority to evaluate and control risks that may be posed by chemical manufacture, processing, and use. Various sections may apply to any manufacturer, processor, or distributor of chemical substances. The Act covers all chemicals planned for production, manufactured, imported, or exported from the United States **except:**

TSCA
Toxic Substances Control Act

- Pesticides
- Tobacco (and tobacco products)
- Source material by-products or special nuclear material defined by the Atomic Energy Act
- Food, food additives, drugs, and cosmetics covered under the Federal Food, Drug, and Cosmetic Act

TSCA includes a **low-volume exemption**, an **exemption for naturally occurring substances,** and an exemption **for chemicals manufactured or processed solely for export** from the United States. Exporters are required to notify the EPA, which notifies the government of the country to which the chemical is exported. The TSCA supplements the CAA and the Toxic Release Inventory (discussed in previous chapters) in protecting against environmental harm caused by chemical releases.

1. TSCA Inventory

Under the Act, the EPA maintains the **TSCA Inventory** of every chemical substance that may be legally manufactured, processed, or imported in the United States. The TSCA Inventory consists of a public part and a confidential part. There are many ways to search the public portion. If the identity of an existing chemical is claimed as confidential business information, it will not be listed on the public portion. The EPA classifies chemical substances as either existing chemicals or new chemicals. Any substance that is not on the TSCA Inventory is considered a new chemical.

If a chemical is not already on the inventory, and has not been excluded by TSCA, a **pre-manufacture notice (PMN)** must be submitted to EPA before the chemical can be manufactured or imported. A PMN can also be required for **significant new use** of an existing chemical.

The PMN must identify the chemical and provide information on the chemical's use, by-products, health and environmental effects, and disposal practices. The PMN review process conducted by the EPA includes public notice and opportunity for comment; among other matters, the EPA reviews the economic benefits of the chemical proposed for listing and whether it might replace a more toxic listed substance.

To see an annotated version of the PMN form, visit http://www.epa.gov/opptintr/newchems/pubs/pmnforms.pdf.

---

2. Regulation of Chemicals

What does the EPA do with the PMN information? The TSCA provides the EPA with authority to:

- Require manufacturers, importers, and/or chemical processors to conduct specific toxicological tests on chemicals that EPA has identified as posing possible risks
- Limit use, require labeling, control exposure or releases, or even ban a substance before it enters commerce, if the substance may present an unreasonable risk
- Require manufacturers, chemical processors, importers, and some distributors to keep records and report information on chemical production and processing, allegations of significant adverse reactions to health or the environment, health and safety studies, and information concerning substantial risks

EXHIBIT 11-5
TSCA Section 5

TSCA Section 5 contains the basis of authority to restrict the manufacture of chemicals. Section 5 also authorizes the EPA to deal with quality control issues in the manufacture of chemicals. Note the boldface provisions.

(a) **Scope of regulation** If the Administrator finds that there is a reasonable basis to conclude that the manufacture, processing, distribution in commerce, use, or disposal of a chemical substance or mixture, or that any combination of such activities, presents or will present an unreasonable risk of injury to health or the environment, the Administrator shall by rule apply one or more of the following requirements to such substance or mixture to the extent necessary to protect adequately against such risk using the least burdensome requirements:

(1) A requirement

(A) **prohibiting the manufacturing**, processing, or distribution in commerce of such substance or mixture, or

(B) **limiting the amount** of such substance or mixture which may be manufactured, processed, or distributed in commerce.

(2) A requirement—

(A) **prohibiting** the manufacture, processing, or distribution in commerce of such substance or mixture for

(i) a **particular use** or

(ii) a particular use in a concentration in excess of a level specified by the Administrator in the rule imposing the requirement, or

(B) limiting the amount of such substance or mixture which may be manufactured, processed, or distributed in commerce for

(i) a particular use or

(ii) a particular use in a concentration in excess of a level specified by the Administrator in the rule imposing the requirement.

(3) A requirement that such substance or mixture or any article containing such substance or mixture be marked with or accompanied by clear and adequate **warnings and instructions** with respect to its use, distribution in commerce, or disposal or with respect to any combination of such activities. The form and content of such warnings and instructions shall be prescribed by the Administrator.

(4) A requirement that manufacturers and processors of such substance or mixture make and retain **records of the processes used to manufacture or process** such substance or mixture and monitor or **conduct tests which are reasonable and necessary to assure compliance** with the requirements of any rule applicable under this subsection.

(5) A requirement prohibiting or otherwise regulating any manner or method of commercial use of such substance or mixture.

(6) (A) A requirement prohibiting or otherwise **regulating any manner or method of disposal** of such substance or mixture, or of any article

---

EXHIBIT 11-5
(continued)

---

containing such substance or mixture, by its manufacturer or processor or by any other person who uses, or disposes of, it for commercial purposes.

(B) A requirement under subparagraph (A) may not require any person to take any action which would be in violation of any law or requirement of, or in effect for, a State or political subdivision, and shall require each person subject to it to notify each State and political subdivision in which a required disposal may occur of such disposal.

(7) A requirement directing manufacturers or processors of such substance or mixture

(A) to **give notice of such unreasonable risk of injury to distributors** in commerce of such substance or mixture and, to the extent reasonably ascertainable, to other persons in possession of such substance or mixture or exposed to such substance or mixture,

(B) to **give public notice of such risk of injury**, and

(C) to replace or repurchase such substance or mixture as elected by the person to which the requirement is directed.

---

3. Recordkeeping and Reporting

Recordkeeping and reporting requirements are major components of the TSCA. The law requires that chemical manufacturers periodically (four to five years, see http://www.epa.gov/oppt/iur/pubs/guidance/basic-information.htm) update their information in the TSCA Inventory because the chemicals may change and the quantity manufactured and industrial, commercial, and consumer uses of a chemical may also change.

Section 8(c) requires that manufacturers and processors keep records of significant adverse reactions to health or the environment alleged to have been caused by the substance. Records of employees reporting adverse reactions must be kept for 30 years.

In addition, Section 8(e) states that "any person who manufactures [including imports], processes, or distributes in commerce a chemical substance or mixture and who obtains information which reasonably supports the conclusion that such substance or mixture presents a *substantial risk* of injury to health or the environment shall immediately inform the [EPA] Administrator of such information unless such person has actual knowledge that the Administrator has been adequately informed of such information." (Emphasis added.) The reporting requirements under 8(e) are complicated. For more information see http://www.epa.gov/oppt/tsca8e/pubs/frequentlyaskedquestionsfaqs.htm.

4. Chemicals Posing Unreasonable Risk

Section 6 of the TSCA deals with the EPA's authority over chemicals that present an unreasonable risk of injury to health or the environment. The TSCA includes specific provisions dealing with specific high-risk chemicals: asbestos, chlorofluorocarbons (CFCs), lead, and polychlorinated biphenyls (PCBs).

Asbestos is the name for a group of naturally occurring minerals that separate into strong, very fine fibers. The fibers are heat-resistant and extremely durable. Asbestos tends to break down into a dust of microscopic fibers that remain suspended in the air for long periods of time and can easily penetrate body tissues after being inhaled or ingested. The fibers can remain in the body for many years and cause diseases. Symptoms of these diseases generally do not appear for 10 to 30 years after the exposure. There is no safe level of exposure known; therefore, exposure to **friable** asbestos should be avoided.

Friable
Easily crumbled or pulverized

Phase-out of asbestos in commercial products began in 1989, but a total ban has not occurred due to a federal court decision in 1991. Regulation of asbestos involves several federal agencies. For more information see http://www.epa.gov/asbestos/pubs/help.html. In 1978, the EPA banned manufacture and use of lead-based paint and lead-based paint products. Lead-based paint chips and dust, if ingested, can create severe, long-term health effects, especially for children. Lead is also a known **carcinogen.** To see regulations dealing with lead in soil and dust and with lead paint encountered during renovation, visit http://www.epa.gov/lead/pubs/regulation.htm.

Carcinogen
Cancer producing

Chlorofluorocarbons (CFCs) are chemical compounds originally developed for refrigeration systems. When released, CFCs break down and release chlorine, which damages the ozone layer. With limited exceptions, production of CFCs ended in 1995 in developed countries, including the United States. In addition to the phase-out, an excise tax was imposed on CFCs beginning in 1990.

PCBs are mixtures of synthetic organic chemicals with the same basic chemical structure and physical properties ranging from oily liquids to waxy solids. Due to their nonflammability, chemical stability, high boiling point, and electrical insulating properties, PCBs were used in hundreds of industrial and commercial applications including electrical, heat transfer, and hydraulic equipment, in paints, plastics, and rubber products, in pigments, dyes, and carbonless copy paper and many other applications. PCBs have significant ecological and human health effects, including carcinogenicity, neurotoxicity, reproductive and developmental toxicity, immune system suppression, liver damage, skin irritation, and endocrine disruption. PCBs do not break down readily in the environment, and are taken into the food chain by microorganisms. The manufacture and processing of PCBs is prohibited, except under specific conditions for certain types of equipment. The regulations for PCBs are found at 40 C.F.R. §761.

C. In the Field: Environmental Cleanups and Bankruptcy

1. Overview of Bankruptcy Law

Bankruptcy law allows a debtor, who is unable to pay **creditors**, to resolve his debts by dividing assets among his creditors. Bankruptcy law is contained in Title 11 of the U.S. Code and is litigated in and supervised by federal bankruptcy courts.

Creditors
Those to whom debts are owed

Bankruptcy law has two purposes. Court-supervised division of assets ensures equitable treatment of creditors. Imagine that the owner of a gasoline station knows that she will have to declare bankruptcy soon. She owes substantial debts to her suppliers and to her brother and may even have some potential liability to neighbors because of a spill. Might she favor one of those creditors over the others, by using her remaining funds to pay her brother? An additional purpose of bankruptcy is to allow some debtors to free themselves (to be **discharged**) of the financial obligations after their assets are distributed, even if their debts have not been paid in full. Other bankruptcy proceedings allow a debtor to stay in business and use earnings to resolve debts.

There are two basic types of bankruptcy proceedings. A filing under **Chapter 7** of the Bankruptcy Code, also called **liquidation**, is the most common type of bankruptcy and involves the appointment of a **trustee**. The trustee collects the nonexempt property of the debtor, sells it, and distributes the proceeds to creditors.

Bankruptcy under **Chapters 11, 12,** or **13** of the Code involves **rehabilitation** of the debtor to allow use of future earnings to pay off creditors. A trustee is appointed to supervise the rehabilitation.

Bankruptcy can be initiated voluntarily by a debtor or by creditors. After a bankruptcy petition is filed, creditors, for the most part, may not seek to collect debts outside of the proceeding. The debtor may not transfer property that has been declared part of the estate and certain pre-filing transfers of property, secured interests, and liens may be delayed or invalidated.

Various provisions of the Bankruptcy Code also establish the priority of creditors' interests. Expenses and claims that have priority include administrative expenses and certain charges against the bankruptcy estate; some debts incurred within 90 days; certain wages, commissions, and employee benefits; certain deposits made to purchase or rent property; some child support and alimony claims; some tax debts; and certain debts secured by lien. The expenses of environmental cleanups are not a priority in bankruptcy, which can leave innocent parties and the taxpayers "holding the bag."

Some believe that companies should be financially responsible for consequences of their decisions, whether the consequences were intended or not. But those consequences are sometimes caused by multiple factors or are the result of a lack of knowledge by society as a whole, not just the company. The interaction of the two areas of law is very complex and can involve issues beyond the scope of this book. For example, might expenses related to environmental cleanups ever be considered an administrative expense, necessary to keep the business in operation?

Chapter 7
Also called liquidation, bankruptcy in which assets are distributed and debtor discharged

Liquidation
To end business, gather assets, settle debts

Trustee
Oversees bankruptcy

Chapter 11
Also called rehabilitation, a bankruptcy in which business continues in operation

---

Assignment 11-4

Sometimes the government intervenes . . .

A century after it was established to consolidate the Rockefeller mining interests, with falling copper prices and a $54 million net loss for a six-month period, American Smelting & Refining Co. (Asarco) was sold for $817 million to Grupo Mexico S.A. de C.V. Grupo announced that it would sell Asarco assets to pay the debt it incurred in purchasing the company. The most valuable asset, a mining operation in Peru, would be sold to another Grupo subsidiary. The sale was blocked by the U.S. Department of Justice, which claimed the deal would be a fraudulent transfer of assets at below-market prices. The main concern was that Asarco would be unable to fund the cleanup of at least 27 polluted mining sites in 13 states if stripped of valuable, productive assets. It was estimated that the cost of cleaning up would be between $500 million and $1 billion.

. . . and sometimes it doesn't. Read the case summarized in Exhibit 11-6 and discuss:

◆ The court distinguishes between "damages" and an order to undertake cleanup, which will, of course, cost money. Explain the difference and why the plaintiffs thought they might be able to get the court to order cleanup, even though they acknowledged that they could not seek damages.
◆ Explain why, in the *Torwico* case, a bankrupt company was ordered to undertake cleanup.

EXHIBIT 11-6

KRAFCZEK v. EXIDE CORPORATION

U.S. District Court for the Eastern District of Pennsylvania
(2007 U.S. Dist. LEXIS 29248)

Plaintiffs filed this citizen suit under *RCRA §7002* against Exide to compel Exide to decontaminate their property to a level that is consistent with unrestricted residential use. Exide recycled used lead-acid batteries and battery parts, operated a secondary lead smelter, and manufactured lead batteries near the property. The process included storage of used batteries and battery parts, collection and treatment of spent battery acid, and generation of sludge from the emission control device for the secondary lead smelter. Plaintiffs allege that lead dust from Exide's facility contaminated plaintiffs' property.

Lead is a toxic metal linked with adverse effects including systemic and organ toxicity, blood disorders, learning disabilities, development delays, cardiovascular disease, kidney disease, hypertension, joint pain, chronic fatigue, and immune system damages. Humans can absorb lead by ingesting, inhaling, or touching sources of lead, including contact with industrially generated lead fumes or particulate, contact with wind borne lead, or contact with lead in soil. Lead also has a deleterious effect on plant and animal life.

EXHIBIT 11-6
(continued)

In a prior citizen suit *L.E.A.D. v. Exide*, EPA issued an Administrative Order on Consent requiring Exide to assure proper remediation for protection of health and environment. Plaintiffs' property was covered by the AOC. Remediation and cleanup was supposed to be complete by 2005. Exide has remediated only a small part of plaintiffs' property.

Exide filed a petition to reorganize under the Bankruptcy Code before the U.S. Bankruptcy Court. In 2004 the Bankruptcy Court entered a final Order approving a Plan of Reorganization submitted by Exide and creditors, which contains an injunction and discharge enjoining continuation or prosecution of claims submitted to or administered in the bankruptcy. Plaintiffs requested damages resulting from the contamination, but did not seek compensation for remediation because remediation was to be undertaken by Exide pursuant to the Consent Decree. The bankruptcy plan does not address the contamination on plaintiffs' property.

After Exide's bankruptcy this case returned to the docket in 2005. In a motion to dismiss defendant argues that plaintiffs' claim is barred and discharged by the injunction issued by the Bankruptcy Court. Pursuant to the Bankruptcy Code liabilities on claims are dischargeable. *11 U.S.C. §101(12) (2007)*. A claim is defined as a:

> (A) right to payment, whether or not such right is reduced to judgment, liquidated, unliquidated, fixed, contingent, matured, unmatured, disputed, undisputed, legal, equitable, secured, or unsecured; or
> (B) right to an equitable remedy for breach of performance if such breach gives rise to a right of payment, whether or not such right to an equitable remedy is reduced to judgment, fixed, contingent, matured, unmatured, disputed, undisputed, secured, or unsecured.

Exide argues that plaintiffs' request that Exide clean up plaintiffs' property is a claim and was discharged under the Reorganization. Plaintiffs recognize that under the Bankruptcy Code and defendant's plan they are enjoined from prosecuting "claims" against defendant, but argue that their action survives because it is not a "claim" under *In re Torwico Elecs., 8 F.3d 146 (3d Cir. 1993)*. In *Torwico*, the State demanded that a debtor ameliorate an ongoing hazard. The Court held that an injunction "may still present a 'claim'" if it is merely a repackaged claim for damages, but that a debtor cannot maintain an ongoing nuisance in violation of state law and the state can force compliance with its laws, even if a debtor must expend money to comply. *Torwico*, however, involved a state's right to force environmental cleanup and the present case concerns an individual's ability to do so. A state can exercise regulatory powers; individual plaintiffs may not. Plaintiffs' request for a mandatory injunction does not fall under the exclusion for state environmental law enforcement actions; their decontamination request is a "claim" barred by the Bankruptcy Court's injunction and the complaint is dismissed.

2. Professional Profile

"Environmental law is not a discrete field. To succeed you must be knowledgeable about a variety of subjects: in my case, knowledge of research, litigation process, medical terminology, jurisdictions, court rules, and bankruptcy have been key. Above all, you must keep learning and not stagnate."

Tracie Rose is a Principal with ENVIRON Corp., an international environmental consulting firm providing health, safety, and environmental services to address complex problems that challenge the business community. ENVIRON has offices in North America, Europe, Australia, and Asia and projects across 50 countries. Ms. Rose has more than 15 years of experience supporting all aspects of dispute resolution, including bankruptcies, arbitration, and real and threatened litigation. She is involved in a variety of business transactions including projecting future liabilities within due diligence projects. Ms. Rose has found and assisted in development of experts for court and consultation and has provided extensive support and development of definable and reproducible scientific opinions. She has assisted with development of demonstrative exhibits to present data understandable to an untrained or nontechnical audience.

With BA and MA degrees in Anthropology, Tracie studied cultural differences and similarities, societal norms and customs, and threats to populations. She participated in studies within the Physical Anthropology specialty, focusing on analysis of skeletal remains. After graduation, she earned an ABA-approved certificate in Paralegal Studies. Tracie began her paralegal career with a short stint in the medical malpractice arena, where she interviewed clients, responded to discovery, and gathered medical records. Building on her experience analyzing skeletal remains, she was able to quickly capture what was required and build on her knowledge.

The majority of Tracie's career has been spent in the toxic tort area of personal injury law. She first worked with in-house counsel for an insurer and then for its national trial counsel. She participated in management of cases throughout the country, coordinating and managing trial schedules and documents. She gained special expertise working with medical experts used by clients at trial, assisting with review materials, records, and trial preparation.

In her current position, Tracie assists clients by answering questions about risk management in their businesses. She manages all aspects of dispute resolution, research, and factual reconciliation, supervision of staff, project management, scheduling, and account management. She is involved in discovery, pre-trial, and trial preparation; legal and medical research; records management and file organization; contact with inside and outside counsel for national dockets; development, preparation, and identification of national experts; document review and analysis; compilation of exhibits; and preparation of trial presentations and demonstratives. Her firm stays current on rulings nationwide as well as on local, state, and federal rules of court.

Through her career, Tracie has found her paralegal education invaluable. She chose a program that provided experience in research, writing, and discovery topics. This gave her an ability to quickly learn and understand her role in the litigation team and how she might enhance and enlarge that role. Tracie has always strived to bring something new to the table — a new perspective or new process of managing cases or presenting data. Although Tracie has a limited background in science, that has never prevented her from moving forward. Tracie listens, asks, and educates herself in terminology and theories so she may better support her internal client, the trial or project team, and her external client. She is able to look at data as it is presented through the eyes of an audience not trained in science. She often finds it a challenge for science professionals to present data, results, or numbers to an audience such as a jury or judge in a way that is both understandable and relevant.

Key Terms

Accumulated Speculatively	Market Participant Exception
Asbestos	Mass Burning
Bioreactor Landfill	Methane
Carcinogen	Mixed Waste
Chapter 7	MSWL
Chapter 11	MWTA
Combustion and Incineration	NOD
Construction and Demolition Debris Landfill	PMN
	PCB
Corrosive Waste	R & D
Cradle-to-Grave	RDF
Creditors	Reactive Waste
Dilution Prohibition	Scrubbers
Dioxin	Sham Recycling
Disposal Prohibition	Surety Bond
Friable	Solid Waste
Hazardous Waste	Solid Waste Transfer Station
Hazardous Waste Lists	Storage Prohibition
Household Hazardous Waste	TSCA
Ignitable Waste	TSCA Inventory
Industrial Waste Landfill	TSDF Permit
LDR	Toxic Waste
Leachate	Trustee
Liquidation	Underground Injection Wells
LTU	Universal Waste
LUST	UST
Manifest	White Goods

Review Questions

1. How is solid waste defined by RCRA and how is it regulated? Can a liquid be a solid waste?
2. Is all recycling exempt from classification as waste? If not, how is exempt recycling distinguished from nonexempt recycling? What does the agency

look at to determine whether recycling is legitimate, for purposes of exemption?

3. How is hazardous waste distinguished from solid waste? What are the four characteristics that can identify a hazardous waste? What is the other means by which a waste can be identified as hazardous?

4. What is an MSWL and what must it have to comply with federal law? Identify some specialized types of MSWL.

5. Identify the types of businesses subject to hazardous waste restrictions. What are the common requirements for those businesses?

6. What are the LDRs? Identify matters covered by a hazardous waste disposal permit.

7. Identify common methods of storage and disposal of hazardous waste.

8. Define mixed waste and universal waste. How does your state regulate medical waste?

9. Identify parties exempt from UST regulations.

10. What powers does the EPA have under TSCA?

11. What is the relationship between liability for environmental harm and bankruptcy?

KEY TERMS CROSSWORD

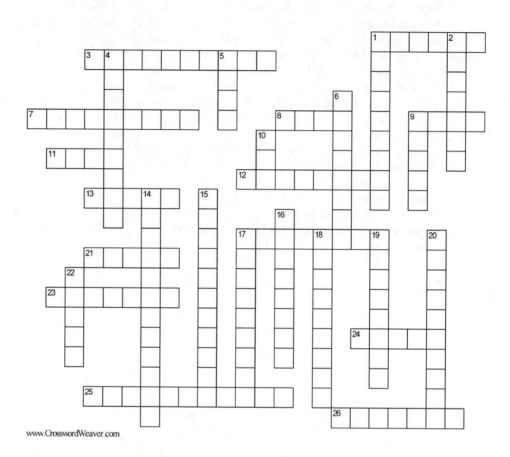

www.CrosswordWeaver.com

ACROSS

1. _____ bond, a means of financial assurance
3. landfill that promotes breakdown of substances by addition of liquid
7. _____ waste often includes batteries
8. initials, gives EPA authority to ban chemicals
9. initials, includes a model for state laws dealing with medical waste
11. initials, underground storage tank that is leaking
12. solid waste _____ station; waste is moved to bigger trucks
13. waste harmful or fatal if absorbed or digested
17. owed money
21. nonhazardous waste, even if liquid
23. _____ 11 refers to a section of the bankruptcy law
24. hazardous waste _____ in CFR identify substances so regulated
25. surface _____, method of storage or disposal
26. gas released from landfills

DOWN

1. used to neutralize gas during burning
2. appointed by bankruptcy court
4. underground _____ wells, a method of disposing of treated waste
5. initials, permit for disposal of hazardous waste
6. hazardous waste generators, transporters, disposal must use this
9. wastes contain radioactive material
10. initials, restrict land disposal of hazardous waste
14. burning
15. recycling exemption does not apply to material _____ speculatively
16. rain soaks landfill, forming this
17. _____ waste, acid or base
18. _____ waste can cause fire
19. wastes unstable under normal conditions
20. a method to reduce volume of waste
22. refrigerators, washing machines, _____ goods

12

◆ ◆ ◆

Wild Things, Wild Places: ESA, Federal Land, and FIFRA

◆ ◆ ◆

A. Overview of the Endangered Species Act

ESA
Endangered Species Act, 16 U.S.C. §1531 et seq.

The **Endangered Species Act (ESA)**, 16 U.S.C. §1531 et seq., was enacted by Congress in 1973 in response to an alarming decline in animal and plant species. It is one of many federal laws that protect plants and wild, farm, and domestic animals, birds, and fish. While some other similar laws are mentioned in this chapter, most are beyond the scope of this book. The University of New Mexico School of Law, Center for Wildlife Law, http://ipl.unm.edu/cwl/, has incredible links to summaries of state laws protecting wildlife and to federal laws, such as the Marine Mammal Protection Act, the Migratory Bird Conservation Act, and even the African Elephant Conservation Act. For more information on other laws and pending laws, visit the website of the Humane Society of the United States, http://www.hsus.org/legislation_laws/federal_legislation/.

NMFS
National Marine Fisheries Service, under Department of Commerce

FSW
U.S. Fish and Wildlife Service, within Department of Interior

Anadromous
Like salmon, return to rivers to breed

The ESA is not administered by the EPA. While all federal agencies must comply with the ESA, the **National Marine Fisheries Service (NMFS)** (under the U.S. Department of Commerce) and the **U.S. Fish and Wildlife Service (FWS)** (a unit of the U.S. Department of Interior) share responsibility for the administration of the ESA. Generally, the NMFS is responsible for species in marine environments and **anadromous** fish, while the FWS oversees terrestrial and freshwater species and migratory birds. Other agencies do have some responsibility for the fate of endangered species; for example, the EPA may prohibit the use of a pesticide that adversely affects the habitat of an endangered species.

The ESA includes incentives to encourage states to develop conservation plans for their listed species. The agencies may enter into agreements with individual states to authorize states to manage conservation areas. Financial assistance and incentives are provided to attract state participation. The ESA provides for citizens' suits and for civil penalties for substantive (not recordkeeping or reporting) violations committed "knowingly." Criminal fines and even imprisonment may also result from knowing violations.

Although most people agree with the goals of the law, its methods have been questioned and its continued existence is a political "hot potato." The ESA has been renewed on an annual basis since 1992, as debate drags on. Several environmental groups are strongly opposed to any significant revisions to one of the nation's toughest environmental laws, but those on the other side claim that the Act requires a few private landowners to bear the entire cost of public benefit — providing habitat for endangered species. To avoid costly land use regulations, property owners sometimes engage in preemptive destruction of currently unoccupied potential endangered species habitat, hinder collection of information about endangered species on their property, or even kill endangered species (commonly known as "shoot, shovel, and shut-up").

Why Bother?

There are a number of reasons for preserving a diversity of species, ranging from aesthetics to the value of plants and animals for medicine and medical research. **Biodiversity** is the variation of life forms within a given ecosystem and is often used as a measure of the health of biological systems. For an interesting analysis of the reasoning as applied to specific cases, visit http://www-phil.tamu.edu/~gary/ee2005a/russow.html.

Biodiversity
Variety and variability among living organisms and the ecological complexes in which they live

Does it work?

> Conservation actions carried out in the United States under the Endangered Species Act have been successful in preventing extinction for 99% of the species that are listed as endangered or threatened. — U.S. Fish and Wildlife Service

In 1941, the whooping crane population consisted of only 15 birds! With the help of the American and Canadian governments, captive breeding, a breeding-ground refuge in Texas, and a campaign by the National Audubon Society, the whooping crane population had increased to 48 birds by 1973. Since enactment of the ESA, the whooping crane population has climbed to 468 birds. In fact, very few species have become extinct while listed under the ESA, and 93 percent have had population increases or have remained stable.

The ESA protects only endangered and threatened species, so understanding the Act requires understanding how species are listed within those categories. Categorization depends on the degree of threat. An **endangered species** is one that is in danger of extinction throughout all or a significant portion of its range. A **threatened species** is one that is likely to become endangered in the foreseeable future. The ESA defines "species" broadly to include subspecies and (for vertebrates) distinct populations.

Endangered Species
In danger of extinction throughout all or a significant portion of its range

Threatened Species
Likely to become endangered in the foreseeable future

What is a species? There are lots of bears in the United States, but the polar bear may soon be listed, as described at the end of this chapter.

Taxonomic classification has seven levels. Here's how it works for a grizzly bear:

KINGDOM: Animalia
PHYLUM: Chordata
CLASS: Mammalia
ORDER: Carnivora
FAMILY: Ursidae
GENUS: Ursus
SPECIES: Ursus Arctos

Which is distinguishable from a polar bear:

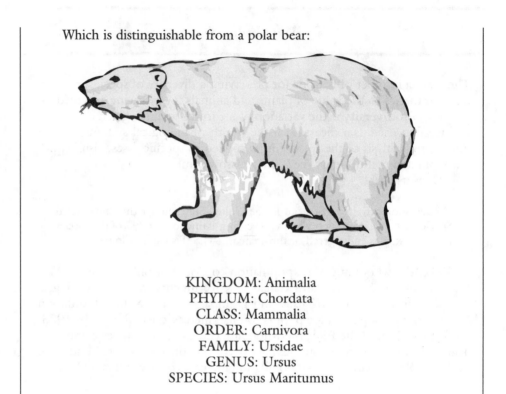

KINGDOM: Animalia
PHYLUM: Chordata
CLASS: Mammalia
ORDER: Carnivora
FAMILY: Ursidae
GENUS: Ursus
SPECIES: Ursus Maritumus

1. Listing Species

Species are brought to the attention of the agencies, and listing is initiated by the agency's staff, other government agencies, environmental groups, educators, and individuals. An individual can submit a formal petition for listing, supported by biological data. The agency conducts a review and must make a finding within 90 days of receiving a petition (if practicable) as to whether there is substantial information indicating that listing may be warranted. If the preliminary finding is positive, the agency will proceed as described below.

The agencies have developed a priority system in which the magnitude of threat is the highest criterion, followed by the immediacy of the threat and the **taxonomic** distinctiveness of the species; the system gives no preference to popular species or so-called higher life forms and does not take economic consequences into account.

The factors relevant to determining the level of threat include:

Taxonomic
Relating to science of classifying plants, animals, and microorganisms into increasingly broader categories based on shared features

- Present or threatened destruction, modification, or curtailment of the species' habitat or range
- Over-utilization for commercial, recreational, scientific, or educational purposes

- Disease or **predation**
- Inadequacy of existing regulatory mechanisms
- Other natural or manmade factors affecting the species' survival

Predation
Species being hunted, killed, or eaten by another

If the agency makes a positive "substantial information" finding, it begins a one-year period of review. At the end of the year, the agency will decide either that the information does not support a need for listing, that listing is **warranted but precluded** by a need to list species of higher priority, or that listing is warranted. A "warranted but precluded" finding requires subsequent findings on each succeeding anniversary of the petition until either a proposal is undertaken or a "not warranted" finding is made.

Warranted but Precluded
Listing of a species as endangered or threatened is warranted, but will not occur due to higher priorities

If the agency decides to pursue listing the species as endangered or threatened, it first publishes "notices of review" that identify "candidate" species to solicit biological information to complete the status reviews for the candidate species. Publication often covers multi-species proposals, in which several candidate species share a common ecosystem. Any interested person can comment and provide additional information on the proposal (generally during a 60-day comment period), and submit statements at any public hearings that may be held.

Information received during the comment period is analyzed and, within one year of a listing proposal, one of three actions is taken: (1) a final listing rule is published (as proposed or revised) because the best available biological data supports it; (2) the proposal is withdrawn because the biological information on hand does not support the listing; or (3) the proposal is extended (for six months) because, at the end of one year, there is substantial disagreement within the scientific community concerning the biological appropriateness of the listing. If approved, the final listing rule generally becomes effective 30 days after publication in the Federal Register.

If a "candidate" for listing (FWS term), also called a "species of concern" (NMFS term — more broadly defined), either does not qualify for listing or is not of high enough priority for listing, it is not protected by the ESA. In some cases, the agency may, nonetheless, initiate conservation activities, such as entering into agreements with other governmental or private agencies, or even with private individuals, to reduce the threat to the species. For example, the FWS can enter into a Candidate Conservation Agreements with Assurances for Non-Federal Landowners.

Once a species is listed, all protective measures authorized by the ESA apply to the species and its habitat, including protection from adverse effects of federal activities; restrictions on taking, transporting, or selling; recovery plans; acquisition of important habitat; and aid to state wildlife agencies. The agencies designate critical habitat and create a recovery plan outlining the goals, tasks required, likely costs, and estimated timeline to recover endangered species. Although the ESA does not specify a time limit, the FWS has a policy of recovering the endangered species within three years of being listed.

2. Critical Habitat

The ESA also requires designation of **critical habitat** either at the time of or within one year of a species being placed on the endangered list. Critical habitat consists of all areas essential to the conservation of the listed species. Listed species

Critical Habitat
Areas essential to conservation of listed species

are protected whether or not they are in an area designated as critical habitat. Designation of an area as critical habitat simply provides a means by which the habitat of an endangered or threatened species can be protected from adverse changes or destruction.

Although critical habitat can be designated on either public or private land, designation of private land in and of itself has no impact on private landowner activities that do not require federal funding or permits. The designation of critical habitat has its greatest impact on federal activities. Federal agencies are forbidden from authorizing, funding, or carrying out actions that jeopardize the continued existence of endangered or threatened species by altering critical habitat. For many projects, the key is "authorizing." State and local government agencies, corporations, and citizens need to obtain federal permits before any large-scale development, logging, or mining. Private owners are, however, subject to the protections of Section 9, discussed below.

Hot Topic

Invasive Species
Alien species whose introduction is likely to cause economic or environmental harm

Although most people are aware of the impact on biodiversity of what is taken from habitat by logging, mining, etc., many are not aware of the impact of what is added to habitat. In recent years, **invasive species** have reached a critical mass. Because of human travel, especially on public lands, agriculture, development, and other factors, the exponential growth of these species in many areas threatens endangered plants and animals. Many experts believe that native species — and the biological diversity that comes with them — could all but disappear, leaving the south blanketed in kudzu, western roadsides overrun with Scotch broom and southwestern waterways choked with tamarisk.

Conservation Easement
Voluntary, binding agreement between property owner and qualified conservation organization to restrict use of land

In order to protect critical habitat in private ownership, the agency (or an environmental group) sometimes purchases the land or obtains (by purchase or gift) a conservation easement over the land. A **conservation easement** is a voluntary, binding agreement between a property owner and a qualified conservation organization such as a land trust or government agency. The easement consists of restrictions on the use or development of land in order to protect its conservation values; easement restrictions vary greatly for each agency or organization. Because of limited funding to buy habitats, easements are a useful option; they are flexible and generally allow the owner to continue to use the land at some level and, in many areas, qualify the land for reduced taxes. The owner may also qualify for personal tax benefits if the easement is donated.

The agencies periodically award grants to state and local agencies, tribes, conservation groups, and individuals for preservation of critical habitat. On rare occasions, the agency will condemn land (take the land by power of eminent domain, paying just compensation) to create a reserve or refuge.

Assignment 12-1

◆ Using the FWS website, find information about Candidate Conservation Agreements with Assurances for Non-Federal Landowners. What is the major assurance the owners can obtain?

◆ Determine whether your county includes any critical habitat for listed species. http://criticalhabitat.fws.gov/.

◆ Listings are not generally nationwide. Determine whether the Karner blue butterfly is listed as endangered or threatened in your state.

◆ Regulations promulgated under the ESA are found in CFR Title 50; find a regulation that defines **ecosystem** in the context of fish habitat.

◆ That which is listed can be de-listed. Read the case summarized in Exhibit 12-1 and answer:

  • Leaving the Eagle Protection Act out of it, why is the presence of the eagle a problem for a private landowner?

  • In previous chapters, you've read that courts like to defer to agencies. In this case, the court rules in favor of an individual. Do you think the result would have been the same if the developer was challenging the listing of the eagle, rather than the agency's failure to follow through on de-listing?

Ecosystem
A localized group of interdependent organisms together with the environment that they inhabit and on which they depend

---

3. Protection of Listed Species Against Takings

a. Involvement by a Federal Agency

Section 7 of the Act directs all federal agencies to conserve threatened and endangered species and, in **consultation** with the FWS, to ensure that their actions do not jeopardize listed species or destroy or adversely modify critical habitat. Section 7 applies to management of federal lands and to other federal activities that may affect listed species, such as approval of private activities by issuance of permits or licenses.

In the FWS formal consultation process:

• The local FWS office is contacted to determine whether listed species are present within the action area.

• FWS responds by providing a list of species that are known to occur or may occur in the vicinity.

Consultation
Required of federal agencies prior to action that may affect listed species

---

EXHIBIT 12-1

CONTOSKI v. SCARLETT

**United States District Court for the
District of Minnesota, 2006 U.S. Dist. LEXIS 56345**

Contoski sued for failure to make a final determination on a proposed rule to delist the bald eagle. Defendants include the FWS and the Department of the Interior. The bald eagle has been protected under the ESA since 1978. The Act and regulations prohibit the "take" of any listed species. In addition, the Bald and Golden Eagle Protection Act also prohibits take of the bald eagle. The bald eagle population has increased since listing, and in 1999, the FWS published a proposed rule to delist the bald eagle. Defendants have not issued a final determination. In 2006, the FWS issued a new notice of the proposed rule to delist, and reopened the comment period. The FWS recently extended the comment period to June 19, 2006.

Contoski owns property on Sullivan Lake. In proposing a residential subdivision, Contoski learned of an active bald eagle's nest on his property. The Minnesota Department of Natural Resources issued a letter recommending that there be no development within a 330 feet radius of the nest to ensure compliance with the ESA and the Eagle Protection Act. Contoski argues that defendants have a non-discretionary duty to issue a final determination regarding the delisting, and that by failing to do so, have violated the ESA and the Administrative Procedures Act.

The ESA requires that final determination be made within one year of publication of a rule proposing to determine whether a species is endangered or threatened, or to designate or revise critical habitat. Defendants' failure to act violates *16 U.S.C. §1533(b)(6)(A)*. Defendants argue, however, that plaintiff does not have standing to bring this action, and that the action is prudentially moot because the FWS has now re-opened the comment period on the proposed rule.

To establish standing, a plaintiff must demonstrate that: 1) plaintiff has personally suffered an injury in fact; 2) the injury is fairly traceable to the challenged action of the defendant; and 3) it is likely that the injury will be redressed by a favorable decision. Here, plaintiff argues that he has suffered an injury in fact because the bald eagle is listed under the ESA, that the presence of a bald eagle nest on his property impairs his ability to develop his property, that his injury is traceable to defendants' failure to delist the bald eagle, and that a final determination delisting the bald eagle would remove one regulatory hurdle to development of his property.

Defendants argue that even if the bald eagle were removed from the ESA list, it would still receive protection under the Eagle Protection Act. Plaintiff responds that the Eagle Protection Act does not prohibit adverse habitat modification, and that development of his property could go forward if ESA protection were removed. There is no merit to the argument: Both the ESA and the Eagle Protection Act prohibit the take of bald eagles, and the respective definitions of "take" do not suggest that the ESA provides more protection than the Eagle Protection Act.

EXHIBIT 12-1
(continued)

Under ESA, the term "take" means to "harass, harm, pursue, hunt, shoot, wound, kill, trap, capture, or collect, or to attempt to engage in any such conduct." *16 U.S.C. §1532(19)*. The broadest verb is "harm," defined as "an act which actually kills or injures wildlife. Such act may include significant habitat modification or degradation where it actually kills or injures wildlife by significantly impairing essential behavioral patterns, including breeding, feeding or sheltering." *50 C.F.R. §17.3; see 515 U.S. 687 (1995)*. Under the Eagle Protection Act the term "take" means "pursue, shoot, shoot at, poison, wound, kill, capture, trap, collect, molest or disturb." *16 U.S.C. §668c*. Because the definition of "take" in the Eagle Protection Act does not include "harm," whether it prohibits adverse habitat modification depends on the interpretation of "disturb," which is the broadest verb used in the definition of "take" in the Eagle Protection Act. The USFWS has not yet defined "disturb" in a final rule.[n1]

The plain meaning of "disturb" is at least as broad as "harm," and both are broad enough to include adverse habitat modification. Protection against adverse habitat modification afforded under the Eagle Protection Act is at least as protective as provided by the ESA. Nevertheless, the Court holds that plaintiff's injury is redressible because the ESA is a barrier to development and a favorable decision would likely remove that barrier. It does not matter that other barriers continue to burden the property . . . plaintiff has standing to bring this lawsuit.

Although defendants concede that they have not complied with mandatory deadlines set forth in the ESA, they ask the Court to "exercise its discretion to withhold relief in this case." The FWS has reopened the comment period on its proposal to delist the bald eagle, and asserts that it would be inappropriate for the Court to compel a determination before it has an opportunity to examine comments generated during this comment period. Over five years have passed since defendants first issued the proposed rule, and they are no closer to issuing a final determination now than in 1999. There is no guarantee that defendants will not continue to delay a final determination. Nevertheless, the Court will consider the equities of the situation when determining the proper date. The information used in the proposed rule is approximately six years old, and the ESA mandates that the agency use the "best scientific and commercial data available." The Court will allow defendants a reasonable time to consider information received during the reopened comment period. Defendants shall issue a final determination no later than February 16, 2007, unless defendants present persuasive evidence of just cause for further limited delay. Plaintiff's request for an award of attorneys' fees, experts' fees, and costs is **DENIED**.

[n1]The USFWS published a proposed rule on the definition of the term "disturb" under the *Eagle Protection Act. Protection of Bald Eagles; Definition, 71 Fed. Reg. 8265, 8266*. The agency has proposed the following definition: "To agitate or bother a bald or golden eagle to the degree that interferes with or interrupts normal breeding, feeding, or sheltering habits, causing injury, death, or nest abandonment." *Id*.

- If FWS provides a negative response, no further consultation is required unless the project is altered or new information indicates that listed species may be affected.
- If listed species are present, the agency/applicant must determine whether the action may affect them.
  - A "may affect" determination includes actions not likely to adversely affect as well as likely to adversely affect listed species.
  - If the action is not likely to adversely affect listed species (e.g., the effects are beneficial, insignificant, or discountable), and the FWS agrees with that determination, no further consultation is required.
- If the agency/applicant determines that the action is likely to adversely affect listed species, then it must request initiation of formal consultation. This request is made in writing to the FWS, and includes a complete initiation package.
- When a request for formal consultation is received, the process becomes formal, and specific time frames come into play. Formal consultation is initiated on the date the package is received, unless the initiation package is incomplete. If the package is incomplete, the FWS notifies the agency/applicant of the deficiencies.
- From the date that formal consultation is initiated, the FWS has 90 days to consult with the agency/applicant and 45 days to prepare and submit a **biological opinion** (BiOp).

BiOp
Biological Opinion — document that states FWS opinion as to whether action is likely to jeopardize continued existence of listed species or result in destruction or adverse modification of critical habitat

If the BiOp indicates no jeopardy or adverse impact, the project may proceed. If the BiOp indicates some incidental impact, the project can proceed if the agency explores alternatives and imposes conditions. The agency can issue an incidental take statement, as described in the case summarized in Exhibit 12-2.

The conclusions of the BiOp may be challenged in court. Can a project ever proceed if the BiOp accurately concludes that it will jeopardize a species? The answer is: It's possible, but it almost never happens. You've undoubtedly heard of controversies that pit the economic "lives" of human beings against jeopardy to a listed species. An example is the notorious spotted owl controversy of the late 1980s: The listing of the spotted owl meant that timber companies would be required to leave at least 40 percent of the old-growth forests intact within a 1.3 mile radius of any spotted owl nest or activity site, costing many timber industry workers their jobs.

Endangered Species Committee
Can grant federal actions exemptions from "no jeopardy" rule

As originally enacted, the ESA was an absolute prohibition against activities that would jeopardize endangered species regardless of economic consequences, but the law was later amended to include a process by which economic and other impacts could be reviewed and projects exempted from restrictions that otherwise would apply. An **Endangered Species Committee** (sometimes referred to, by practitioners, as the "God Squad"), consisting of specified Cabinet officials and one individual from each affected state, reviews applications for exemptions. The application and requirements for exemption are so rigorous that few applications have ever been filed and the number granted remains in single digits as of this writing. Of particular importance in this century: An exemption must be granted for an agency action if the Secretary of Defense finds the exemption is necessary for reasons of national security and the President is authorized to make exemption determinations for a project for the repair or replacement of a public facility in a major disaster area. For more details about exemptions, see 50 C.F.R. §450.

Remember NEPA? Impact on listed species must also be considered by agencies implementing NEPA requirements. Any project qualifying as a major construction activity under NEPA requires a **biological assessment**. The contents of a biological assessment are determined by the action agency. The action agency should initiate informal consultation before the public scoping required for major construction activities as defined by NEPA. Formal consultation should be initiated prior to or at the time of release of the DEIS or EA (defined in Chapter 7). Section 7 consultation should be complete when the final EIS is issued. The Record of Decision for an EIS should address the results of the consultation.

Biological Assessment
Required by NEPA for major construction activities

b. Private Landowners

i. Prohibition on "Takes"

The key provisions of the ESA applicable to private landowners are found in Section 9. These provisions made it unlawful to **take** any endangered or threatened species on both public and private lands. "Take" is statutorily defined to mean "harass, harm, pursue, hunt, shoot, wound, kill, trap, capture, or collect." In 1975, the Secretary of the Interior clarified the broad definition of "take" by defining "harm" as: "An act or omission which actually injures or kills wildlife, including acts which annoy it to such an extent as to significantly disrupt essential behavioral patterns, which include, but are not limited to, breeding, feeding, or sheltering; significant environmental modification or degradation which has such effects is included within the meaning of 'harm.'"

Take
To harass, harm, pursue, hunt, shoot, wound, kill, trap, capture, or collect a listed species

ii. Other Violations

The Act also makes it unlawful to:

- Import, export, deliver, receive, carry, transport, or ship a listed species in interstate or foreign commerce in the course of a *commercial transaction*
- Offer for sale (without an indication of the need for a permit), or sell a listed species in interstate or foreign commerce
- Take a listed species on the high seas
- Possess, ship, deliver, carry, transport, sell, or receive unlawfully taken wildlife
- Remove and reduce to possession any listed plant from an area under federal jurisdiction
- Maliciously damage or destroy an endangered plant on areas under federal jurisdiction
- Remove, damage, or destroy an endangered plant in violations of state law

The prohibitions apply to live or dead animals, parts of those animals, and seeds. The ESA does include exemptions, although these situations may be covered by other laws:

- Species held in a controlled environment or in captivity at the time they were listed may continue to be held for noncommercial activities

- Transactions that take place entirely within a single state are not covered by the ESA, but may be covered by state law
- Antiques, such as scrimshaw, with proper documentation
- Noncommercial loans and gifts, such as breeding agreements between zoos
- **Hybrid** offspring of a listed parent and a non-listed parent, bred in captivity
- Seeds from artificially propagated specimens of threatened plants
- Situations covered by special rules — there are special rules for certain species, such as the American alligators and raptors and special rules for issuance of permits (discussed in the next section) for use of species for conservation education and captive breeding

Hybrid
Offspring of two different species

This list is not exhaustive. Other situations, such as killing in self-defense, for sustenance, or as part of religious observance, may be covered by limited exemptions depending on circumstances.

Several of the prohibitions relate to international trade. The **Convention on International Trade in Endangered Species of Wild Fauna and Flora (CITES)** is an international agreement that restricts the commerce of actually or potentially endangered plant and animal species. Like the ESA, it was signed by the United States in 1973. CITES includes all ESA-listed species as well as other plant and insect species. Compliance is voluntary; international trade in covered species is subject to controls. The Convention uses a licensing system to authorize import, export, and introduction of species. The system is administered by the parties to the Convention (individual nations). The FWS administers the program for the United States. For more information visit http://www.cites.org/.

CITES
Convention on International Trade in Endangered Species of Wild Fauna and Flora, an international agreement

There are circumstances under which an owner may be allowed to engage in otherwise prohibited activities pursuant to a permit. Most endangered species permits are issued by the agency's regional office for the area where the activity will take place. Interstate Commerce permits are issued by the office of the "lead region" for the affected species, not the region where the activity will take place. Permits for import and export are issued by International Affairs (Division of Management Authority). Fish and wildlife management is also handled by states, territories, and tribes, so an activity may require one or more permits from another regulatory agency.

Incidental Take Permit
Required when a nonfederal activity will result in "take" of a listed species — requires HCP

HCP
Habitat Conservation Plan — binding agreement between agency and private entity or state, specifies conservation measures to be implemented in exchange for permit

iii. *Permits*

To obtain an **Incidental Take Permit**, required when a nonfederal activity will result in "take" of a listed species, the applicant must develop a **Habitat Conservation Plan (HCP),** to offset any harmful effects the proposed activity might have on the species. To qualify for a permit, the taking must "not appreciably reduce the likelihood of the survival and recovery of the species in the wild."

HCPs are binding agreements between the agency and either a private entity or a state that specifies conservation measures that will be implemented in exchange for a permit. The HCP must minimize and mitigate impacts "to the maximum extent practicable," and must include adequate funding, and provisions to address "unforeseen circumstances." Examples of activities that may require an

Incidental Take Permit include construction and development activities. Issuance of an Incidental Take Permit involves a process that requires preparation of a BiOp compliance with NEPA, discussed earlier, and public comment.

To obtain an **Enhancement of Survival Permit**, for an activity that may benefit a listed species through the conservation of its habitat, the applicant must develop a **Safe Harbor Agreement** or a Candidate Conservation Agreement (discussed earlier in this chapter). An example of an activity that may require an Enhancement of Survival Permit is controlled burning.

Safe Harbor Agreements are voluntary agreements between the agency and cooperating nonfederal landowners that give owners assurances that the agency will not, in the future, impose restrictions on their land as a result of conservation actions on the owner's part. These agreements essentially relieve landowners of liability under the ESA in the event that conservation practices on their land attract or perpetuate listed species. To date, nearly three million acres of land have been enrolled in Safe Harbor Agreements.

A **Recovery and Interstate Commerce Permit** may be required to engage in scientific research on or conduct activities to enhance the propagation or survival of a listed species that will likely result in the species being harassed, captured, harmed, possessed, or killed. Examples of activities that may require such a permit include abundance surveys, genetic research, relocations, capture and marking, and telemetric monitoring. Under certain circumstances, a permit may also be required to possess tissues and/or body parts of listed species.

> **Enhancement of Survival Permit**
> May be required for an activity that may benefit a listed species through conservation of its habitat

> **Safe Harbor Agreement**
> Voluntary agreement between agency and nonfederal landowner to give owner assurances that agency will not later impose restrictions on land as a result of owner's conservation actions

> **Recovery and Interstate Commerce Permit**
> Required to engage in scientific research on or conduct activities to enhance the propagation or survival of a listed species, if those activities may result in "take"

Assignment 12-2

1. Use the Internet to find a BiOp and copy the table of contents.
2. Yikes! Bald eagles have been spotted on the UDigg property (being developed for an ethanol plant) along the Iowa River. Mr. Bushney is a great fan of eagles and the nesting area is on a part of the property furthest from construction. Still, the activity may disturb the eagles. Your mission:
   ◆ If the eagle is listed as endangered, what can UDigg do to avoid violating the ESA? Identify the regional FWS office with which the company will communicate if it should need a permit; find that office's online outline of the documents UDigg would need for that permit.
   ◆ Determine whether the eagle is still listed.
   ◆ Find the FWS voluntary Bald Eagle Management Guidelines and a regulatory definition of "disturb" under the Bald and Golden Eagle Protection Act.
3. Read the case summarized in Exhibit 12-2 and answer the following:
   ◆ Does this case stand for the proposition that once an activity has a permit it is safe from application of the ESA as long as it does not violate that permit?
   ◆ Given the facts that the salmon is now a listed species and is being harmed by the operation, will PG&E have to obtain an incidental take permit to continue its operation after the current permit expires?

◆ The Ninth Circuit issued a much-cited opinion concerning Incidental Take Statements in *Arizona Cattle Growers' Ass'n v. U.S. Fish and Wildlife Service*, 273 F.3d 1229 (9th Cir. 2001). Find the case and write a one-paragraph summary of the significant holding.

EXHIBIT 12-2

CALIFORNIA SPORTFISHING PROTECTION ALLIANCE; PACIFIC COAST FEDERATION OF FISHERMEN'S ASSOCIATIONS, INC. v. FEDERAL ENERGY REGULATORY COMM'N

United States Court of Appeals for the Ninth Circuit, 472 F.3d 593 (2006)

This is a petition to review a decision of the Federal Energy Regulatory Commission (FERC) not to initiate formal consultation with the NMFS about operation of the DeSabla-Centerville hydroelectric project, operated by Pacific Gas & Electric (PG&E) under a 30-year license that FERC issued in 1980. The project consists of dams, reservoirs, canals, and powerhouses that divert water from reservoirs and from Butte Creek into powerhouses for hydroelectric generation, then return water to Butte Creek downstream. The project affects the flow of water in the creek, which provides spawning grounds for Chinook Salmon. Nineteen years after FERC issued the license, the Chinook was declared a threatened species. After many fish died in Butte Creek in 2002 and 2003, NMFS requested FERC to initiate formal consultation pursuant to 50 C.F.R. §402.14(a). FERC did not do so. In 2004, California Sportfishing petitioned FERC to initiate formal consultation. FERC denied the petition.

ESA §7 provides for formal consultation with NMFS to insure that agency action does not jeopardize continued existence of an endangered species. The issue is whether there was any "action authorized, funded, or carried out" by a federal agency, that triggered the requirement in 1999. Petitioners want consultation to determine whether PG&E should change the way in which the project is operated pursuant to a license agreement issued by FERC in 1980. Statutory language, the regulations, and case law compel the conclusion that the **ESA** imposes no duty to consult about activities conducted by PG&E pursuant to a previously issued, license from FERC.

FERC could amend the license, which contains provisions authorizing FERC to modify the license to reflect changing environmental concerns. The **ESA** and applicable regulations, however, mandate consultation with NMFS only before an

EXHIBIT 12-2
(continued)

agency takes some affirmative action, such as issuing a license. Because FERC took no affirmative action concerning PG&E's existing license, we deny review.

A major component of consultation is production of a Biological Opinion (BiOp). In the BiOp, NMFS must determine whether the action under review is likely to jeopardize continued existence of a listed species or result in destruction or adverse modification of critical habitat. 50 C.F.R. §402.14(h)(3). If NMFS concludes that jeopardy is likely, it must issue reasonable and prudent alternatives to the action. Along with alternatives, NMFS issues an "incidental take" statement, which constitutes a **permit** for the agency or licensee to **take** endangered species, so long as they implement the reasonable and prudent alternatives and comply with conditions of the **incidental take** statement. The existing PG&E license expires in 2009, and consultation between FERC and NMFS has begun in renewal proceedings. In May 2005, California Sportfishing filed this petition for review of the FERC denials of consultation. PG&E intervened to defend the FERC denials.

PG&E argues that if there will be a preliminary BiOp in the renewal proceedings as to what may be done to protect the Chinook after 2009, no irreparable harm can result from failure to consult now. The consultation which petitioners seek, however, is aimed at measures to protect the Chinook under the existing license, not under the terms of a license that would go into effect in the future. That opinion will apply only to operations under the new license. Petitioners' concern is with ongoing operations affecting the Chinook now. There is a showing of irreparable harm and we have jurisdiction to consider whether the law requires consultation with NMFS in connection with ongoing operations under an existing license.

To support its position that the continuing operation of the project by PG&E is an agency "action," petitioners point to the Supreme Court's landmark decision in *Tenn. Valley Auth. v. Hill*, 437 U.S. 153, (1978). There, a project that had been approved repeatedly by Congress was required by the terms of the **ESA** to remain inoperative because, if the project became operational, it would result in the destruction of the habitat of a newly discovered, but endangered species of snail darter. The agency was ordered not to take action to operate the dam. In that case, the dam had not yet begun to operate and the contemplated government action was its start up. Here PG&E has been operating the project for more than 20 years. The question is whether ongoing operations are similarly subject to the **ESA**.

Congress could have provided that once a species is listed under the **ESA**, federal agencies must consult with expert agencies like NMFS about the impact of all operations, including those carried out pursuant to licenses. Congress did not do so. The statute requires agencies to consult with NMFS or another expert agency in connection with federal agency action in order to "insure that any action . . . is not likely to jeopardize the continued existence" of threatened species. The statute looks to the future effect of contemplated actions by the

---

EXHIBIT 12-2
(continued)

---

agency. The trigger is an agency action, not the listing of a species. Because the focus is on the future effect of the agency's action, the statute requires the government to insure that an action "is not likely to" jeopardize an endangered species. The phrase "likely to" does not refer to present effects but to the future. The regulations reinforce this purpose by requiring the agency to "review its actions at the earliest possible time."

The petitioners rely on *Turtle Island Restoration Network v. Nat'l Marine Fisheries Serv.*, 340 F.3d 969 (9th Cir. 2003). The case does not support petitioners. *Turtle Island* involved an ongoing program to issue fishing permits that could cause damage to sea turtles and other endangered species. We held that once a species was listed under the ESA, the agency was required to take into account the potential effect on the species before issuing future fishing permits. Permits issued in the past were not affected. Here the action of granting a permit is complete. The ongoing activity is that of operating pursuant to the permit. Plaintiffs are not challenging an ongoing program of issuing new permits that underlay our decision in *Turtle Island*.

In *W. Watersheds*, 456 F.3d at 930, plaintiffs challenged the agency's failure to consult on whether the agency should regulate rights-of-way used by private parties to divert water. In rejecting the claim, we explained that "consultation stems only from 'affirmative actions'" of an agency. Because private parties, not government, were diverting the water, there was no agency action triggering a duty to consult. This case is materially the same. PG&E, a private party, operates the project. FERC, the agency, has proposed no affirmative act that would trigger the consultation requirement for current operations. The regulations make clear that operation of a project pursuant to a permit is not a federal agency action. The regulations expressly define the term "action" to include the granting of licenses and permits.

Finally, Petitioners point to 50 C.F.R. §402.03, which provides that §7 requirements apply to all actions in which there is "discretionary Federal involvement or control." Petitioners contend that the reopener provisions, contained within the license, create such discretionary federal control within the meaning of the regulation. Article 37 gives FERC discretionary authority to require changes in the operation of the project, after notice and hearing. Article 15 requires the Licensee to make such modifications as may be ordered after FERC exercises such discretion. Thus, the provisions do no more than give the agency discretion to decide whether to exercise discretion. The provisions in and of themselves are not sufficient to constitute any discretionary agency "involvement or control" that might mandate consultation by FERC.

4. Native American Tribes and ESA

The interaction between the ESA and the rights of Native American tribes has raised interesting issues. The ESA is the "law of the land," but tribal governments are recognized as separate and sovereign nations. The tribes do not all acknowledge that the ESA applies to them. In addition, there is a unique "special trust" fiduciary relationship between the federal government and Indian tribes, created by treaties, statutes, executive orders, and judicial decisions — the U.S. government is required to protect tribal lands and resources, unless otherwise unencumbered through mutual agreement.

Examples of Conflict

- As you know, the bald eagle was listed as an endangered species, but the use of eagle feathers is central to many tribal religious customs. The result is the so-called eagle feather law, 50 C.F.R. §§22.1-22.32, which requires a permit for possession of eagle feathers for religious observance. While many feel that the permit requirement is an infringement on religious freedom because permits can be difficult to obtain, possession of feathers without a permit can result in a hefty fine.
- To extinguish the last conflicting claims to lands west of the Cascade Mountains and north of the Columbia River in what is now the State of Washington the United States entered into a series of treaties with Indian tribes in 1854 and 1855. The Indians relinquished their interest in most of the Territory in exchange for monetary payments. In addition, certain relatively small parcels of land were reserved for their exclusive use, and they were afforded other guarantees, including protection of their "right of taking fish, at all usual and accustomed grounds and stations . . . in common with all citizens of the Territory." But, several sub-species of Chinook salmon, native to that area, are now listed, as shown on Exhibit 12-3.

In an effort to resolve some of the issues, in 1997 the secretaries of Commerce and Interior issued a Joint Secretarial Order, directing NMFS and FWS to carry out their responsibilities in a manner that harmonizes the ESA with tribal rights.[1] The order directs the agencies to strive to ensure that tribes do not bear a disproportionate burden for conservation of species under the ESA; directs NMFS to notify and consult with Indian tribes on a government-to-government basis whenever a proposed action may affect fish, wildlife, or other resources that the federal government has a duty to protect in light of tribal interests (trust resources); provides that whenever NMFS enters formal consultation on a proposed action that may

---

[1] Secretarial Order #3206: American Indian Tribal Rights, Federal-Tribal Trust Responsibilities, and the Endangered Species Act (June 5, 1997).

EXHIBIT 12-3
Listing of Chinook Salmon

From http://ecos.fws.gov/tess_public/SpeciesReport.do?groups=E&listingType=L&mapstatus=1.

Salmon, chinook	*Oncorhynchus (=Salmo) tshawytscha*	Snake R. (U.S.A._ID, OR, WA) mainstem and the following sub-basins_Tucannon R., Grande Ronde R., Imnaha R., Salmon R, and Clearwater R.; fall run, natural population(s), wherever found	T
Salmon, chinook	*Oncorhynchus (=Salmo) tshawytscha*	Snake R. (U.S.A._ID, OR, WA) mainstem and the following subbasins_Tucannon R., Grande Ronde R., Imnaha R., and Salmon R.; spring/summer run, natural population(s), wherever found	T
Salmon, chinook	*Oncorhynchus (=Salmo) tshawytscha*	Sacramento R. (U.S.A._CA) winter run, wherever found	E
Salmon, chinook	*Oncorhynchus (=Salmo) tshawytscha*	U.S.A. (WA) all naturally spawned populations from rivers and streams flowing into Puget Sound, including the Straits of Juan De Fuca from the Elwha R. eastward, and Hood Canal, South Sound, North Sound and the Strait of Georgia	T
Salmon, chinook	*Oncorhynchus (=Salmo) tshawytscha*	U.S.A. (OR, WA) all naturally spawned populations from the Columbia R. and its tributaries upstream from its mouth to a point east of the Hood R. and White Salmon R. to Willamette Falls in Oregon, excluding the spring run in the Clackamas R.	T
Salmon, chinook	*Oncorhynchus (=Salmo) tshawytscha*	U.S.A. (OR) all naturally spawned populations in the Clackamas R. and the Willamette R. and its tributaries above Willamette Falls	T
Salmon, chinook	*Oncorhynchus (=Salmo) tshawytscha*	U.S.A. (WA) all naturally spawned populations in the Columbia R. tributaries upstream of Rock Island Dam and downstream of Chief Joseph Dam, excluding the Okanogan R., and the Columbia R. from a line between the west end of Clatsop jetty, OR, and the west end of Peacock jetty, WA, upstream to Chief Joseph Dam, including spring-run hatchery stocks (and their progeny) in Chiwawa R., Methow R., Twisp R., Chewuch R., White R., and Nason Creek	E
Salmon, chinook	*Oncorhynchus (=Salmo) tshawytscha*	U.S.A. (CA) all naturally spawned spring-run populations from the Sacramento San Joaquin R. mainstem and its tributaries	T
Salmon, chinook	*Oncorhynchus (=Salmo) tshawytscha*	U.S.A. (CA) from Redwood Creek south to Russian R., inclusive, all naturally spawned populations in mainstems and tributaries	T

affect tribal rights or trust resources that NMFS shall notify the affected tribe and give them an opportunity to participate in the consultation process; and directs NMFS to apply conservation standards upheld in the treaty fishing cases if NMFS determines that conservation measures affecting tribal rights or trust resources are necessary in order to protect listed species.

The order does not create new law or change existing law, but does clarify that:

- Critical habitat will not be designated on Indian lands unless it is determined essential to conserve a listed species.
- Proactive measures by the federal government to save endangered and threatened species on tribal lands are only considered at a tribe's request.
- Tribal conservation plans that address activities on Indian lands and address the conservation needs of the listed species are entitled to deference.
- Deference to tribal management plans for off-reservation tribal trust resources depends on the extent to which the plan addresses federal concerns.
- Upon request, the agencies may review and assess tribal conservation plans and other measures for conserving sensitive species.
- The development of reasonable and prudent alternatives (under Section 7) will continue to be scientifically based, but affected tribes may provide pertinent information and viewpoints that would enable the agencies to develop informed reasonable and prudent alternatives.
- The order does not override the prohibition against direct take. Whenever a situation arises that may raise the possible issue of direct take, a government-to-government consultation will occur.
- There is a five-prong test for application of incidental take restrictions to tribal treaty rights:
  - (i)   The restriction is reasonable and necessary for conservation of the species;
  - (ii) The conservation purpose of the restriction cannot be achieved by reasonable regulation of non-Indian activities;
  - (iii) The measure is the least restrictive alternative available to achieve the required conservation purpose;
  - (iv) The restriction does not discriminate against Indian activities, either as stated or applied; and
  - (v)   Voluntary tribal measures are not adequate to achieve the necessary conservation purpose.

It is important to recognize that while the federal government holds 95 million acres of land in a special trust for Indian tribes, tribal lands are separate by law from the federal land base and are recognized as being the "Indian land base." While tribal land is not part of the federal land base the federal government is still required to be responsible for the protection of these lands and tribal resources.

B.   Federal Lands

To understand federal administration of the Indian land base and the federal land base, which consists of general public land (managed by the Bureau of Land Management, BLM), national parks (managed by the National Park Service, NPS), national wildlife refuges (managed by FWS), and national forests (U.S. Forest Service — not on the chart, part of U.S. Department of Agriculture), examine the chart showing the structure of the Department of the Interior, Exhibit 12-4. The department is the largest federal conservation agency, with goals encompassing resource protection, resource use, and recreational activities.

Management of general public lands and national forests is guided by the Federal Land Policy and Management Act, 43 U.S.C. §1701, which provides for "multiple uses" of the lands. In other words, conservation, recreation, and environmental concerns are not always top priority; economic uses such as grazing, mineral extraction, and logging are possible and, in some cases, given priority. On the other hand, management of wildlife refuges, national parks, and national wilderness areas is focused on conservation.

The scope of this book is, unfortunately, limited. If you would like more information about protection of designated federal wilderness areas, visit http://www.blm.gov/nlcs/wilderness/faq.htm.

C.   Federal Insecticide, Fungicide, and Rodenticide Act

FIFRA
Federal Insecticide, Fungicide, and Rodenticide Act, 7 U.S.C. §136

The **Federal Insecticide, Fungicide, and Rodenticide Act (FIFRA)** authorizes the EPA to review and register pesticides for specified uses and to suspend or cancel the registration of a pesticide if subsequent information shows that continued use would pose unreasonable risks.

The term "pesticide" is defined as a substance intended for "preventing, destroying, repelling, or mitigating any pest" or for use as a "plant regulator, defoliant, or dessicant." The definition includes many kinds of ingredients in products, such as insect repellents, weed killers, disinfectants, and swimming pool chemicals that are designed to prevent, destroy, repel, or reduce pests of any sort, but it does *not* include substances that have the actual effect of a pesticide if those substances are not intended for that purpose.

Example: Application of pepper spray will, in fact, repel many pests, but pepper spray is not treated as a pesticide.

The term "pest" is defined as including "insects, rodents, worms, fungus, weeds, plants, virus, bacteria, micro-organisms, and other animal life."

EXHIBIT 12-4
U.S. Department of the Interior

U.S. Department of the Interior

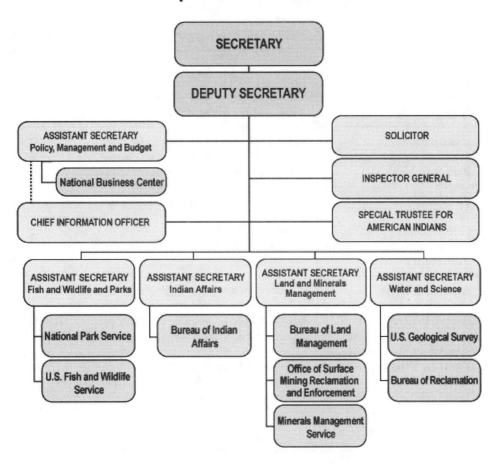

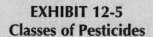

EXHIBIT 12-5
Classes of Pesticides

From www.epa.gov.

There are many classes of pesticides, each designed to destroy or repel certain species.	

Type	*Targets*
Insecticides	flying and crawling insects
Herbicides	undesirable plants/weeds
Rodenticides	mice, rats and other rodents
Fungicides	fungi that cause plant disease/wood rot, etc.
Nematicides	invertebrates (worms)
Fumigants	insects/fungi
Antimicrobials	microorganisms such as bacteria, molds, fungi
Biopesticides	natural materials such as animals, plants, bacteria, and certain minerals that target a variety of pests
Plant or insect growth regulators	plant (accelerate or retard, the rate of growth of a plant), insect (affect the growth of insects)

The EPA has a separate review processes for three categories of pesticides: Conventional Chemicals, **Antimicrobials**, and **Biopesticides**.

1. Registration

Pesticides must have an EPA registration before manufacture, transport, or sale. In the process of registering a pesticide, the EPA examines its ingredients, the particular site or crop on which it is to be used; the amount, frequency, and timing of its use; storage and disposal practices; and potential human health and

Antimicrobials
Capable of killing or inhibiting the growth of microorganisms, especially bacteria, fungi, or viruses

environmental effects. The producer of the pesticide must provide data from tests done according to EPA guidelines.

The registration program places high priority on registering pesticides that are safer than pesticides currently on the market, those pesticides with public health benefits, and pesticides that are of particular economic importance to producers. In addition to full federal registration, the EPA has authority to grant state-specific registrations, emergency exemptions, and experimental use permits. Experimental use permits may be "conditional," requiring monitoring or other measures.

The EPA also must approve the language that appears on each pesticide label. The label is a legal document; a pesticide can only be used legally according to the directions on the label accompanying it at the time of sale. Labels must conform to EPA requirements, even with respect to font size. Exhibit 12-6 shows some of the requirements for part of a label.

After a pesticide is registered by EPA, it may have to be registered in individual states, which may have more stringent requirements. Ultimately, states have primary responsibility (called primacy) for pesticides used within state borders. Does your state have a registration program: http://npic.orst.edu/state1.htm?

Preemption under FIFRA is a hot issue.

Biopesticides
Includes naturally occurring substances with pesticidal activities. Examples are attractants, repellents, plant growth regulators, bio-chemicals, microbial agents (e.g., Bacillus thuringiensis and its numerous strains, plant and/or insect viruses), products of modern bio-technology, and plant-incorporated protectants

---

> **7 U.S.C. §136v states:**
>   (a) In general
>   A state may regulate the sale or use of any federally registered pesticide or device in the State, but only if and to the extent the regulation does not permit any sale or use prohibited by this subchapter.
>   (b) Uniformity
>   Such state shall not impose or continue in effect any requirements for labeling or packaging in addition to or different from those required under this Act.

But, what are "requirements," and what falls within the scope of labeling? What kinds of requirements are "in addition to or different from" those required under FIFRA?

Many courts have held that state law claims alleging injury or damage from failure to warn of the toxic hazards of pesticides were preempted by FIFRA, but as of this writing, the Supreme Court has not addressed the issue.

Once a pesticide is registered, the registrant is required to submit information about adverse effects of its product to the EPA. Where do old pesticides go to die? Once a pesticide is disposed of, it is no longer subject to FIFRA, but is regulated by RCRA.

> Pesticide handling, storage, and disposal is a particular problem for farmers. The EPA publishes resources: http://www.epa.gov/pesticides/regulating/storage.htm#farmers.

EXHIBIT 12-6
Requirements for Pesticide Label

From http://www.epa.gov/oppfead1/labeling/lrm/chap-03.htm#labelformat.

A. **Front Panel**
   1. **Restricted Use Pesticide Statement** (Chapter 6) if applicable

      This section of the label, if applicable, includes the references to "restricted use," which under FIFRA Section 3 (d)(1)(C) describes those pesticides that require "additional regulatory restrictions" to avoid potential unreasonable adverse effects on the environment.
   2. **Product Name, Brand or Trademark** (Chapter 12)
   3. **Ingredient Statement** (Chapter 5)

      This section of the label identifies the name and the percentage by weight of each active ingredient and the percentage by weight of other/inert ingredients. If the size or form of the product package makes it impracticable to place the ingredient statement on the front panel of the label, permission may be granted for the ingredient statement to appear elsewhere. See 40 CFR 156.10(g)(2).
   4. **"Keep Out of Reach of Children" (KOOROC) Statement** (Chapter 7)

      This specific statement, which is commonly referred to as the KOOROC statement ("child hazard warning"), appears on almost all end use pesticide products except those pesticides that are intended for use on children or where it is demonstrated that children will not come in contact with the product. In these cases, a modified statement is allowed. See 40 CFR 156.66.
   5. **Signal Word** (Chapter 7)

      Signal words that correspond to the toxicity categories for product hazards (e.g., oral, dermal) appear on the front panel of the label. 40 CFR 56.60(a)(1).
   6. **First Aid** (Chapter 7)

      A first aid statement must appear on the front panel of all pesticides assigned to Toxicity Category I by any route of exposure, but the agency may allow reasonable variations in the placement of the statement. 40 CFR 156.68(d). The front panel must include a reference such as "See First Aid statement on back panel" near the word "poison" and the skull and crossbones if the Agency allows the first aid information to appear on the back panel. 40 CFR 156.68(d). First Aid statements for pesticides of other Toxicity Categories may appear on any panel of the label. 40 CFR 156.68(d).
   7. **"Skull & Crossbones" Symbol ☠ and the word "POISON"** (Chapter 7)

      FIFRA 2(q)(2)(D) requires labels of pesticides that contain substances in quantities highly toxic to man to include a skull and crossbones and the word "poison" prominently in red on a background of distinctly contrasting color. This requirement is further defined in 40 CFR 156.64(a)(1) as applying to pesticides in Toxicity Category I where such toxicity determination is based on oral, inhalation or dermal toxicity as opposed to skin or eye irritation.
   8. **Net Contents/Net Weight** (Chapter 17)

      This section identifies the weight or volume of pesticide in the container. See FIFRA 2(q)(2)(C)(iii); 40 CFR 156.10(a)(1)(iii).

The EPA is reviewing older pesticides (registered prior to November 1984) to ensure that they meet current scientific and regulatory standards and is reassessing tolerances (i.e., pesticide residue limits in food).

2. Federal Food, Drug, and Cosmetic Act

The **Federal Food, Drug, and Cosmetic Act (FFDCA)** requires the EPA to set pesticide tolerances for all pesticides used in or on food. A **tolerance** is the maximum permissible level for pesticide residues allowed in or on commodities for human food and animal feed. The EPA looks at:

FFDCA
Federal Food, Drug, and Cosmetic Act, 21 U.S.C. §301

Tolerance
Maximum permissible level of pesticide residue on food

- Aggregate exposures, including all dietary exposures, drinking water, and nonoccupational (e.g., residential) exposures;
- Cumulative effects and common mode of toxicity among related pesticides;
- Potential for endocrine disruption effects; and
- Protection of infants and children.

D. In the Field: Anatomy of a Listing — the Polar Bear

There are currently 19 polar bear populations in the Arctic, with an estimated total of 20,000-25,000 bears. Recent scientific studies of adult polar bears in Canada and in Alaska's Southern Beaufort Sea have shown weight loss and reduced cub survival. Current data indicates a rapid and unprecedented retreat of Arctic sea ice, including an earlier spring melt, a later fall freeze-up, and thinner ice, which could result in an ice-free Arctic Ocean in the future. Polar bears live on sea ice for a majority of the year and depend on sea ice habitats for their key life functions, so loss of sea ice would detrimentally affect all polar bears, worldwide.

In the case of the polar bear, the melting of sea ice is the potential threat to the species that appears to meet the five criteria for listing. The ESA does not discriminate between natural or manmade causes. "We have sufficient scientific evidence of a threat to the species to warrant proposing it for listing, but we still have a lot of work to do to enhance our scientific models and analyses before making a final decision," said U.S. Fish and Wildlife Service Director Dale Hall.

As a result, the polar bear was proposed for listing as a threatened species. The FWS published notices in the Federal Register. Not surprisingly, the oil and gas industry and others oppose the listing. Public comments can be seen at http://alaska.fws.gov/fisheries/mmm/polarbear/pdf/Summary%20of%20Comments%20from%20the%20Public_90_Day_Finding.pdf.

In January 2007, the FWS announced a 12-month finding on the petition, stating that:

> After review of all available scientific and commercial information, we find that listing the polar bear as a threatened species under the Act is warranted. Accordingly, we herein propose to list the polar bear as threatened throughout its range pursuant to the Act. This proposed rule, if made final, would extend the Act's protections to this species. Critical habitat for the polar bear is not determinable at this time. The Service

seeks data and comments from the public on this proposed listing rule. http://www.fws.gov/home/feature/2006/010907FRproposedrule.pdf.

The public was provided with information about making comments through April 9, 2007 on the FWS site, http://alaska.fws.gov/fisheries/mmm/polarbear/pdf/topics_card.pdf.

Subsistence Harvest
Required to obtain food for survival

The FWS has been monitoring the impact of **subsistence harvest** of polar bears by Alaska Natives since 1980. Harvest of polar bears by native peoples is allowed under the Marine Mammal Protection Act, but if the FWS finds that the harvesting negatively affects the polar bear population, it will not be allowed under the ESA. Other concerns that require further study include increased human habitation in polar bear areas and the impact of both onshore and offshore oil and gas development.

A final decision to list the polar bear as threatened would not have any direct effect on the predicted reduction in sea ice habitat. Listing would, however, require initiation of a recovery planning process, unless it is determined that this would not promote the conservation of the species. This process would involve cooperative efforts of international, federal, state, and local officials and agencies, Arctic Native groups, industry, and private entities to identify practical and feasible measures to provide for conservation of the species. It would also require federal agencies to consult with the FWS for any actions that would affect the polar bear. Experience indicates that these combined efforts will help increase public awareness about the status of polar bears and would assist in developing and implementing future polar bear management strategies.

Key Terms

Anadromous
Antimicrobials
Biological assessment
BiOp
Biopesticides
CITES
Conservation Easement
Consultation
Critical Habitat
Ecosystem
Endangered Species
Endangered Species Committee
Enhancement of Survival Permit
ESA
FFDCA
FIFRA

FSW
HCP
Hybrid
Incidental Take Permit
NMFS
Predation
Recovery and Interstate
    Commerce Permit
Safe Harbor Agreement
Subsistence Harvest
Take
Taxonomic
Threatened Species
Tolerance
Warranted but Precluded

Review Questions

1. Which agencies administer the ESA?
2. What is the process for listing a species as threatened or endangered, what criteria are relevant to the decision, and if a species meets the criteria for listing is it always listed?
3. How might a federal agency be involved in development of private property and, if an agency is involved in such development, what are its obligations under the ESA? Can an agency ever be exempted from those obligations?
4. What permits are available to allow a private party to take action that may have an impact on a protected species and what are the standards for those permits?
5. How are pesticides registered and what other obligations does the EPA have with respect to pesticides?
6. Do the ESA and FIFRA preempt state regulation? Is the ESA the only federal protection of animals?

KEY TERMS CROSSWORD

www.CrosswordWeaver.com

ACROSS

1. these are capable of killing or inhibiting growth of microorganisms
3. it is unlawful to _____ a listed species
10. enhancement of _____ permit
11. won't be listed because of higher priorities, warranted, but_____
14. habitat _____ plan, to obtain ITP
19. animals killing other animals
21. required of fed agencies considering issuing a permit that could impact listed species
23. initials, authorizes EPA to regulate pesticides
24. species likely to become endangered
25. ESA requires designation of critical _____

DOWN

2. FWS might take action to protect a _____ for listing
4. fish returns to river to breed
5. _____ take permit
6. initials, administers ESA with respect to marine environments
7. a consevation _____ is a voluntary agreement to restrict use of property
8. opinion needed for approval of ITP
9. natural products with pesticide properties
12. species in danger of extinction
13. kill plants
15. offspring of two species
16. kill worms
17. safe _____ agreement goes with a permit intended to enhance conservation of species
18. recovery and _____ commerce permit
20. relating to the science of classifying plants and animals
22. language on this must be approved before pesticide can be sold
23. initials, administers ESA with respect to birds

Glossary

§303 List: List of waters not meeting standards, submitted to EPA

§319 Permit: Permit for stormwater discharge from industrial facility

§404 Permit: "Dredge and fill" permit

§104(e) Request: EPA requests information about contaminated site

AAI: All Appropriate Inquiry for defense to CERCLA liability

Accessory Use: Use incidental to main use

Accumulated Speculatively: Recycled material is not exempt from regulation as solid waste if accumulated speculatively

Acid Deposition/Acid Rain: Mixture of wet and dry deposits from atmosphere, with higher-than-normal levels of nitric acids and sulfuric acids

Administrative Citation/Enforcement: Methods of enforcing pollution laws that do not necessitate resorting to the courts

Administrative Agencies: 1 of 5 sources of legal authority; administers a particular law or program

Administrative Law Judge (ALJ): Decision maker at agency hearing

Administrative Procedures Act (APA): Federal or state law governing procedures under which agencies operate

ADR: Alternative Dispute Resolution, resolving conflicts without court involvement

ADRA: Federal statute, Administrative Dispute Resolution Act of 1996

Adversarial: Argues a position

Affirm: Appellate or higher court's decision to support or uphold the decision of the lower court

Administrative Law Judge (ALJ): Decision maker at agency hearing

Allowance-Trading: Program under which sources are allocated "allowances" for emissions and may sell or trade those allowances

American Rule: In most litigation, each party pays own attorneys and costs

Analogize: To compare cases and find them similar

Annotated Statute: Statute with references to articles, cases, and other materials that explain and interpret the law

Anti-backsliding: New permit standards may not be lower than previous permit standards

Anti-degradation Standards: Standards for water of high quality

APA: Administrative Procedures Act — federal or state law governing procedures under which agencies operate

Appellant: Party bringing an appeal; lost in the lower court

Appellee: The party that won in the lower court

Applicable or Relevant and Appropriate Requirements (ARARs): Level of cleanup is determined by standards set in other relevant laws

AQCR: Air Quality Control Region

Arbitrary and Capricious: Decision not supported by the facts or law

Arbitration: Form of ADR — neutral party imposes a decision

Area Sources: Nonmajor sources that may be subject to NESHAPs

Army Corps of Engineers: Authorizes Section 404 dredge-and-fill permits

As-Applied Challenge: Challenge to constitutionality of a law as applied to particular situation

Asbestos: Chemical regulated by EPA as presenting unreasonable risk

ASTM: American Society for Testing and Materials

Attainment: Description of area in compliance with NAAQS

Attorneys' Fee Award: Also called fee reversal, losing party pays attorneys' fees of prevailing party

Audit: Procedure to determine environmental compliance

BACT: Best Available Control Technology; a standard for new sources

BADT: Best Available Demonstrated Technology, basis of NSPS

BAT/BCT: Standards for existing dischargers: Best Available Technology economically achievable or Best Conventional Technology

Bates Stamping: Numbering of documents, sequentially, chronologically, or by some other method

Best Professional Judgment: How permit limits are set if EPA has not established technology standards for a particular industry or discharge

Bioreactor Landfill: Designed to speed the breakdown of organic materials

Bona Fide Prospective Purchaser: Buyer who conducts AAI before purchasing may have CERCLA defense

Brief: Short case summary

Brownfields: Contaminated property

Brownfields Programs: Government provides incentives for redevelopment of contaminated site

Buffering: Shielding use from another, often by landscaping

Burden of Proof: Obligation to provide evidence of each element of a claim

Bypass: Discharge goes around treatment facilities, typically to allow maintenance to occur

CAAPP: Clean Air Act Permit Program or Program Permit — an operating permit

CAFO: Confined/Concentrated Animal Feeding Operation

CALR: Computer-Assisted Legal Research system

Caps: Limits on emissions

Carcinogen: Cancer producing

Case at Hand: The case under consideration

Case Law: Judicial decisions

Categorical Taking: Regulation takes away all economically viable use of property

Cause of Action: A recognized basis for a lawsuit

CEMS: Continuous Emissions Monitoring System — required to check compliance with emissions allowances

CERCLA: Comprehensive Environmental Response, Compensation and Liability Act — describes who is liable for contamination

CERCLIS: Comprehensive Environmental Response, Compensation, and Liability Information System — EPA computerized database of contaminated sites

CFCs: Chlorofluorocarbons — responsible for damage to stratospheric ozone

CFR: Code of Federal Regulations — compilation of rules, regulations of federal agencies

Chapter 11: Also called rehabilitation, a bankruptcy in which business continues in operation

Chapter 7: Also called liquidation, bankruptcy in which assets are distributed and debtor discharged

Citation: Address at which authority is found in law books or online

Cite: Verb form of citation (i.e., to cite)

Citizens' Suit: Private citizens sue to enforce environmental laws

Civil Law: Type of law pursued by an individual or group, business, or governmental body acting in a private capacity; result may be damages or court order

Claims-Made Policy: Insurance — looks at date of injury to determine coverage

Clean Hands: Refers to theory that party with "unclean hands" (acting in bad faith) is not entitled to equitable remedy

Cluster Development: Structures are grouped together so that open space is in large parcels

Code: Legislation; also called statute

Code of Federal Regulations: Compilation of rules, regulations of federal agencies

Codify: Statute entered into a topical system

Coding: Process of reviewing documents, summarizing key elements into a structured database format: e.g., date, doc type, Bates number, description, to whom, from whom, etc.

Combined System: A POTW that handles both sanitary waste and stormwater

Combustion and Incineration: Burning to reduce volume of waste

Comfort Letter: An advisory letter from the EPA, concerning the status of property

Comment: Right of public to have input in formal rule-making

Commerce Clause: Basis for most federal regulation of the environment

Commercial: Not residential, ASTM standards apply to commercial property

Common Law: Judicial decisions, also called precedent

Comprehensive Environmental Response, Compensation, and Liability Information System (CERCLIS): EPA computerized database of contaminated sites

Comprehensive Plan: Plan for community's future development

Computer Forensics: Science of discovering the history of electronic information, even if deleted

Concurring Opinion: Written by a judge who agrees with majority decision but for different reasons

Condemnation: See Eminent Domain

Conditional Use: A use that is permitted in a zone if it meets certain conditions

Connector: Symbol describing relationship between CALR search terms

Consent Decree: Judicial decree expressing a voluntary agreement between parties

Conservation Easements: Include agricultural and open space easements — give owners tax breaks for covenant not to develop

Constitution: 1 of 5 sources of legal authority

Construction and Demolition Debris Landfill: Also called C&D landfill, handles debris from construction and demolition

Contiguous Property Owner: Owner of property touching contaminated property, may have CERCLA defense

Contingency: Contract condition, may give a party an "out"

Continuing Trespass or Nuisance: Ongoing trespass or nuisance

Contribution Claims: PRP asserts that other PRPs must contribute to judgment or cost of cleanup

Contributory/Comparative Negligence: Defenses to negligence claim — plaintiff contributed to injury

Corrosive Waste: Hazardous waste, acid or base, corrodes metal

Costs: Expenses associated with litigation

Covenant: Promise or prohibition recorded against title to land

Cradle-to-Grave: RCRA objective of regulating hazardous waste from its creation to final disposal

Creditors: Those to whom debts are owed

Criminal Law: Category of law prosecuted by a governmental body involving a matter of concern to society as a whole

Criteria Pollutants: Lead, smog, carbon monoxide, nitrogen dioxide, sulfur oxides, particulate matter; regulated by NAAQS

CWA: Clean Water Act

CZMA: Coastal Zone Management Act; voluntary program, states can obtain grants for protecting coastal areas

Damages: Award of money

De Micromis Settlements: Settlements with the contributors of the smallest amounts of hazardous substances

De Minimis Settlements: Liability of small-volume contributors of hazardous substances resolved by single payment

De Novo Hearing: Review of evidence and testimony as finder of fact

Decision of the Court: Majority decision, governs outcome of the case

Design Flow Exemption: Exemption from WQS during specified time periods

Designated Uses: The uses for which a body of water's quality standards are set

Dilution Prohibition: Prohibition on adding liquid or other nonhazardous material to hazardous waste to simply dilute its concentration without treating it

Dioxin: An extremely toxic compound

Discovery: Pretrial process of gathering and sharing evidence

Discretion: Ability to exercise judgment in performing duties

Disposal Prohibition: Prohibition on land disposal of untreated hazardous waste

Dissenting Opinion: Opinion written by a judge who disagrees with the majority; not law but provides interesting facts and opinions about case

Distinguish: To compare cases and find them to be different

Document Unitization: Method of storing documents, can be by page or "as a whole"

Dormant Commerce Clause: State/local laws that discriminate to favor local interests or impact interstate commerce may be invalid even if Congress has not regulated

Downgrade: Reduction in the designated uses for a body of water

Dredge and Fill: Permits for dredge and fill of protected waters are covered by Section 404 of the CWA

Due Diligence: Careful inquiry

Duty: Element of negligence; obligation to act reasonably to avoid harm to others

Easement: A limited right to use property of another

E-discovery: Discovery of electronically stored information

Effluent Limitations: Also called technology limits, limit the amount of pollutants discharged

Elements, Cause of Action: Facts that must be proven to state claim

Elements, Comprehensive Plan: Parts of a comprehensive plan

Emergency Planning and Community Right-to-Know Act (EPCRA): Establishes requirements for federal, state, and local governments and industry for emergency planning and reporting on hazardous and toxic chemicals

Emergency Removals: Removal without time for planning

Eminent Domain: Also called condemnation, governmental power to take property for public purpose by paying just compensation

Enabling Act: Law creating administrative agency and defining its powers

Engineering Controls: Physical modification of property

Environmental Footprint: Measures impact of development on nature

EPCRA: Emergency Planning and Community Right-to-Know Act—establishes requirements for federal, state, and local governments and industry for emergency planning and reporting on hazardous and toxic chemicals

Equal Protection: Requirement that government justify unequal treatment of similarly situated parties

Equitable Remedy: A court order

Err: To make an error

ESI: Electronically stored information

Estoppel: A party is barred from asserting a claim or defense based on own conduct—an equitable concept

EU: European Union; responsible for some environmental treaties

Exaction: Requirement that developer make dedication as a condition to approval

Exclusionary: Zoning that excludes unpopular uses

Executive Action: 1 of 5 sources of legal authority; including orders signed by the president or governor

Executive Order: Order by president or governor, often implementing statute or governing operation of executive agencies

Exhaustion of Administrative Remedies: Requirement that a party pursue all levels of administrative review before seeking judicial review

Facial Challenge: Challenge to the constitutionality of a law as written

Factual Issues: Trial courts use testimony and evidence to decide facts, i.e., what happened

FDF: Fundamentally different factor variance from technology based permit standards

Federal Register: Daily publication for notice of federal agency rules

Fee Reversal: Court orders one party to pay other's legal fees

Fiduciary: One who acts on behalf of another, such as a trustee

Fields: Discrete pieces of information in document or database

Floating Zone: Zone that can be applied to land that meets criteria

FOIA: Freedom of Information Act — law requiring that agencies disclose non-exempt information upon request

Fraud: False statement of material fact, intended to induce reliance, on which a party does reasonably rely

Freedom of Information Act (FOIA): Law requiring that agencies disclose nonexempt information upon request

Friable: Easily crumbled or pulverized

FTCA: Federal Tort Claims Act — limits sovereign immunity

General Notice Letter: Notifies PRPs of potential liability

General Permit: Covers multiple facilities in same general category

GIS: Geographic Information System — mapping based on database

Global Warming: Climate change, assumed to result from destruction of stratospheric ozone layer

Grandfathered: Use that existed before zoning restrictions can continue

Ground water: Water beneath the surface

HAPs: Hazardous Air Pollutants — approximately 189 substances Congress has required the EPA to regulate

Hazard Ranking System (HRS): Established by NCP, assigns numerical values to health and environmental risks

Hazardous Substances: More than 800 substances covered by CERCLA

Hazardous Waste: Has properties that make it dangerous or potentially harmful to human health or the environment

Hazardous Waste Lists: CFR lists identifying hazardous wastes

Headnotes: Summaries of individual points made in the case

Hold Harmless: See Indemnification

Holding: Answer to the legal issue in a judicial decision

Household Hazardous Waste: Household chemical remnants

HRS: Hazard Ranking System — established by NCP, assigns numerical values to health, environmental risks

Ignitable Waste: Capable of fire or explosion

Imaged Format: Locked format such as PDF or TIFF

Immunity: Protection from prosecution

Incentive Zoning: Developer is offered breaks on zoning requirements in return for meeting municipal goals

Indemnification: Promise to reimburse for costs/losses

Indemnify: To agree to assume another party's liabilities, typically as part of a contract

Indirect Source: Discharges pollutants into POTW

Individual Permit: Not a general permit

Industrial Waste Landfill: Landfill specializing in disposal of industrial waste

Infill Development: Development of lots in already urbanized area, rather than "sprawl" development outward from urban areas

Innocent Landowner: Not involved in contamination, may have defense under CERCLA

Institutional Controls: Limits on use of property

Interpretive Rule: Agency's explanation of its actions or statement intended to provide guidance

Inverse Condemnation: Government "takes" property without instituting eminent domain or paying just compensation

Joint and Several Liability: Theory under which all defendants are liable for entire amount of damages and can be pursued individually or together

Judicial Decisions: 1 of 5 sources of legal authority; also called common law or precedent

Jump Cite: The exact page number on which a fact or quote appears in a case

Jurisdiction: Boundaries of decision makers' powers

Just Compensation: Must be paid in exercise of eminent domain

Kyoto Protocol: International treaty intended to deal with climate change (global warming)

Laches: Equitable concept—a claim will not be allowed if delayed so long as to disadvantage the other party

LAER: Lowest Available Emissions Rate—standard for new sources in non-attainment area

LDR: Land Disposal Restrictions on hazardous waste include dilution, storage, and disposal prohibitions

Leachate: Liquid formed when water (from rain) soaks through a landfill, picking up suspended and dissolved materials

Lead Agency: Agency charged with coordination of assessment and cleanup

Legal Issues: Determining appropriate consequences of the facts or whether a trial court handled a case properly

Legal Remedy: Damages, award of money

Legislation: 1 of 5 sources of legal authority; also called code or statute; enacted by an elected body (e.g., Congress)

Liable: To be found responsible

Limitations Period: Time limit for filing suit

Limited Liability Entities: Businesses structured so that owners risk only what they invest in the business

Liquidation: To end business, gather assets, settle debts

Littoral Rights: Rights of owners of lake frontage

Load Allocation: Component of TMDL attributable to nonpoint sources

LTU: Land Treatment Unit—disposal of hazardous waste on or in land

LUST: Leaking underground storage tank

MACT: Maximum Available Control Technology—basis of NESHAPs for major sources

Major Source: A source of emissions, so classified because of the volume of its emissions

Majority Decision: That which governs the outcome of cases; also called decision of the court

Manifest: Used for tracking hazardous waste, must be signed by generators, transporters, and disposal facilities

Market Participant Exception or Exemption: Government-owned landfills may refuse to accept out-of-state waste despite impact on interstate commerce

Market-Based Approach: EPA's preferred approach to regulation; includes incentives for earlier compliance, allowance trading programs

Mass Burning: Burning waste without sorting out recyclables

Mediation: Form of ADR—a neutral facilitates resolution crafted by parties

Methane: A gas produced by landfills

Ministerial Duties: Obligations that do not involve discretion

Mitigation: To compensate for unavoidable damage (typically to wetlands)

Mixed Use: Uses normally separated, such as commercial and residential, combined in a development

Mixed Waste: Hazardous waste containing radionuclides and technologically enhanced, naturally occurring and/or accelerator-produced radioactive material containing hazardous waste

Mixing Zone: Area near a discharge point

Mobile Sources: Vehicles and fuel

Modify: Appellate or higher court's decision to change the decision of the lower court

Moratorium: Activity is discontinued for a period of time

MPRSA: Marine Protection, Research, and Sanctuaries Act

MSDS: Material Data Safety Sheet—contains information about safe handling and disposal of potentially hazardous substances

MSWL: Municipal Solid Waste Landfill

Municipal Law: Local law (as opposed to federal or state law)

MWTA: Medical Waste Tracking Act

NAAQS: Primary and Secondary: National Ambient Air Quality Standards for levels of criteria pollutants: primary are concerned with health criteria; secondary with property damages and other concerns

NAFTA: North American Free Trade Agreement

National Contingency Plan (NCP): Includes guidelines for response to releases and threatened releases of hazardous substances, pollutants, or contaminants

National Priorities List (NPL): List of sites eligible for Superfund cleanup

National Response Center (NRC): Staffed 24 hours to receive reports of releases

Native Format: Format in which document was created

Navigable: Capable of navigation

NBAR: Nonbinding Allocation of Responsibility prepared by EPA or PRPs

Negligence: Failure to exercise reasonable care to avoid harm to others

Negligence Per Se: Breach of duty established by statutory standard

NESHAPs: National Emissions Standards for Hazardous Air Pollutants

Net Limitations: Taking into account pollution already in the water

NFRAP Decision: Site closeout report—ends consideration for NPL; See No Further Remedial Action Planned

NIMBY: Not In My Backyard; a person who opposes undesirable land uses in his community

NOAA: National Oceanic and Atmospheric Agency, administers the CZMA

NOD: Notice of deficiency in permit application process

No Further Remedial Action Planned Decision: Site closeout report—ends consideration for NPL

Nonconforming Use: Use that existed before zoning restrictions and does not comply with those restrictions

Non-time Critical Removals: Requires 6 to 12 months of planning before removal action

NPDES: National Pollutant Discharge Elimination System; permit system for regulating point sources

NPL: National Priorities List — list of sites eligible for Superfund cleanup

NPS: Nonpoint source; pollution is not discharged from an identifiable source, but comes from various sources (e.g., stormwater)

NRC: National Response Center staffed 24 hours to receive reports of releases

NSPS: New Source Performance Standards, based on BADT

NSR: New Source Review

Nuisance, Private: Interference with individual's use or enjoyment of property

Nuisance, Public: Interference with use and enjoyment of property common to the public

Objective Coding: Identifies commonly recognized fields, e.g., date and author

Occurrence Policy: Insurance looks at date of event causing liability to determine coverage

Ocean Dumping Act: Amendment to Marine Protection, Research, and Sanctuaries Act

OCR: Optical Character Recognition, method of scanning that makes document subject to search, alteration

Offsets: Part of market-based regulation; source increasing emission of one pollutant can offset by reduction of another

OIA: EPA Office of International Affairs

On-Scene Coordinator (OSC): Responsible for coordinating removal efforts

OPA: Oil Pollution Act

Open Meetings Act: See Sunshine Law

Operating Permit: Also called Title V Permit, issued to existing source

OSC: On-Scene Coordinator responsible for coordinating removal efforts

OSHA: Occupational Safety and Health Administration — concerned with indoor air pollution

Outsourcing: Sending work to an outside firm

Parent Company: Business entity that owns another business entity

PCB: Chemical regulated by EPA as presenting unreasonable risk

PDF/TIFF: Formats for saving documents as images, not subject to change by unauthorized parties

Per Se Taking: Physical occupation of or exclusion of owner from land

Permitted: Use identified as allowed in zoning district

Phase I: Environmental assessment without sampling, indicates what further testing may be needed

Phase II/III: Advanced environmental assessments, may include soil/water sampling

Piercing the Veil: Court can disregard structure of entity and impose liability on owners

Plaintiff: One who initiates lawsuit

Planner: Professional involved in zoning and planning land uses

PMN: Pre-manufacture notice for new chemical, filed under TSCA

Point Source: Discreet, identifiable source of discharge, e.g., pipe

Police Power: Inherent right of government to protect health, safety, and welfare

Pollutant or Contaminant: Anything that upon exposure "will or may reasonably be anticipated to cause" specified harmful health effects

Potentially Responsible Parties (PRPs): Current owners and operators; former owners and operators involved during time hazardous substance was disposed at facility; persons who arranged for disposal or treatment of hazardous substances; persons who accepted hazardous substances for transport to facilities they helped select

POTW: Publicly owned treatment works

Preemption: Federal law overrides state law; state law overrides local law

Preliminary Assessment: Normally involves review of existing information and records

Primacy: State's authority to enforce federal law, granted by EPA

Primary Authority: 1 of the 5 sources of law

Prior Appropriation: Doctrine for allocation of water rights in some states

Privacy Act: Law giving individual ability to prevent disclosure of information about the individual

Private Attorney General: Theory under which private citizens are allowed to prosecute "citizens' suits"

Privilege: A right to refuse to provide evidence/testimony, based on a relationship such as attorney-client

Procedural Due Process: Entitlement to notice and hearing before deprivation of constitutional right

Procedural History: The history of the court decisions that have moved the case to its current position

Procedural Rule: Governs agencies' own actions

Protocols: Sub-agreements to implement international treaties

Proximity Connector: Describes the distance between search terms in CALR

PRP: Potentially Responsible Party, possibly liable for contamination

PSD: Prevention of Significant Deterioration — emissions standard for sources in attainment areas

Public Trust Doctrine: Theory that resources are held in trust for public use

Public Water Systems: Governed by Safe Drinking Water Act

PUD: Planned Unit Development, zoning designation that can be applied to allow creative development of large tract

R&D: Research and development

RA: Remedial Action — actual cleanup of site

RACT: Reasonably Available Control Technology — standard for existing sources in nonattainment areas

RD: Remedial Design — engineering plans and specifications to implement remedial action

RDF: Facilities that recover recyclables before incineration

Reactive Waste: Unstable under normal circumstances

Reasoning: Summary of the court's explanation of its decision

Record of Decision (ROD): Lead agency sets forth its plan of action and justification

Redact: To remove information, typically due to privilege

Regulations: Established by administrative agencies

Regulatory Taking: Regulation of land goes "too far," takes property rights

Remand: Appellate or higher court's decision to send the case back to the lower court

Remedial Action (RA): Actual cleanup of site

Remedial Design (RD): Engineering plans and specifications to implement remedial action

Remedial Investigation/Feasibility Study: Done to determine nature and extent of contamination, explore alternatives for remediation

Remote-Sensing Technology: Used to monitor environment, e.g., satellite photography

Removal Action: Short-term response to contamination that must be cleaned up immediately

Reporters: Print volumes that contain judicial decisions

Res Ipsa Locquitur: "The thing speaks for itself"; in negligence law, connection is obvious without evidence

Reverse: Appellate or higher court's decision to invalidate the decision of the lower court

Riparian rights: Rights of adjoining landowners to use body of water

Ripeness: Requirement that plaintiff exhaust other possibilities before litigation

ROD: Record of Decision — lead agency sets forth its plan of action and justification

Root Expander: Symbol used to pick up word variations in a computer-based search

Savings Clause: Statutory provision preserving state or local law against preemption

Scanning: Conversion of paper documents to electronic images

Scrubbers: Devices that use a liquid spray to neutralize acid gases and filters to remove tiny ash particles

SDWA: Safe Drinking Water Act

Search Query: Terms and connectors or natural language used in CALR search

Search Warrant: A document issued by a judge or magistrate, authorizing a search

Secondary Authority: Material such as texts to help locate (finding tools) and understand primary law; form books, digests, handbooks, encyclopedias, etc.; not actual law

Self-Reporting: Requiring the regulated entity to keep and submit records of compliance

Setback: Distance between lot line and structure

Sham Recycling: EPA can deny recycling exemption from solid waste regulation if there is no market for resulting product

SIP: State Implementation Plan for achieving attainment with respect to NAAQS

Site Investigation: Determines whether there is a release or potential release and nature of associated threats

SLAPP: Strategic Lawsuit Against Public Participation

Smog: Also called ground-level ozone; one of the criteria pollutants

Solid Waste: Discarded material not classified as hazardous

Solid Waste Transfer Station: Location where waste is removed from collection trucks and loaded for longer trip to disposal

Sovereign Immunity: Government cannot be sued without its consent

Special Notice Letters (SNLs): Sent to PRPs, triggers moratorium to encourage negotiated settlement

Special Use: See Conditional Use

Spoliation: Destruction, alteration, or mutilation of evidence

Spot Zoning: Creates an island of use inconsistent with surrounding uses

Standing: Right to initiate a lawsuit, depends on whether and how plaintiff was injured by challenged action

Stationary Sources: Sources of pollution that are not mobile, such as factories

Statute: Legislation; also called code

Statute of Limitations: Law limiting time for filing suit

Statutory Construction: See Statutory Interpretation

Statutory Interpretation: Interpretation of statute's terms; also called statutory construction

Steering Committee: Committee of PRPs, formed to negotiate with EPA or share costs of cleanup

Storage Prohibition: Waste must be treated and cannot be stored indefinitely

Stormwater: Generally NPS pollution, but permit is required if discharged through municipal or industrial system

Stratospheric Ozone: Protective layer; the destruction of which is assumed responsible for global warming

Strict Liability: Liability without regard to fault or negligence

Subdivision: Creation of smaller lots from larger tract

Subjective Coding: Identification of fields requiring knowledge of case

Subpoena: An order to provide testimony or evidence

Subsidiary: Business entity owned by another business entity

Substantive Rule: Rule that implements statutory directive and has impact outside the agency

Sunshine Law: Requires agencies to hold meetings open to public

Superfund Amendments and Reauthorization Act (SARA): 1986 amendments to CERCLA

Superfund Law: Another name for CERCLA

Surety Bond: Method of providing financial assurances, involving a third party insuring obligations

Surface Water: Water above ground

Sustainable Development: Development that meets today's needs while preserving the ecosystems for future generations

Synopsis: Summary of case, often provided in publishers' enhancements

Takings Clause: Constitutional provision allowing taking of property with just compensation

TDR: Transfer development rights — ability to transfer right to develop a particular density to another owner

Tenth Amendment: Reserves powers to the states

Tier 1/Tier 2: Federal standards for vehicle emissions

Time Critical Removals: Actions with planning period of less than six months before site activities must be initiated

Timeline: Schedule of times at which certain events took place

Title: See Topic

Title V Permit: Also called an operating permit, issued to an existing source

TMDL: Total Maximum Daily Load of pollutants allowable for a body of water, consisting of wasteload and load allocations

Topic: Generally, statutes are organized by topic; breaking the code into Titles, Acts, Chapters, or Sections

Toxic Substances Control Act (TSCA): Enables EPA to track, inventory, and, if necessary, ban, industrial chemicals

Toxic Waste: Poses a risk to human health

Trade Secret Act (TSCA): Protects against agency disclosure of business secrets

Transaction Screen: Lowest level of environmental assessment, not always conducted by professionals

Transfer Development Rights: Ability to transfer right to develop a particular density to another owner

Treaties: International agreements

Trespass: To enter or cause entry on to property of another

Trial Courts: Court in which most cases start, generally concerned with deciding issues of fact

Trial Exhibits: Physical evidence prepared for trial

Tribal Courts: Courts established within and by Native American communities

Trustee: Oversees bankruptcy

TSCA: Toxic Substances Control Act

TSCA Inventory: Inventory of all chemicals produced in or imported to United States, maintained by EPA

TSDF Permit: Permit for transfer, storage, disposal facility handling hazardous waste

Ultra Vires: Beyond the authority granted in enabling act

UN: United Nations, responsible for much environmental use

Underground Injection Wells: Most commonly used disposal method for liquid hazardous waste

Universal waste: Includes batteries, pesticides, fluorescent bulbs, and mercury-containing equipment (e.g., thermostats)

Upset: Circumstances beyond reasonable control of operator cause violation of permit limits

UST: Underground storage tank

Variance: An exception to zoning laws

Vaughn Index: A list of documents withheld

Vested Rights: An absolute, legally recognized right

Wasteload Allocation: Component of TMDL attributable to point sources

Water Quality Criteria: Technical standards for achieving designated uses

Water Quality Standards: Standards for achieving designated uses

Wetlands: Areas sufficiently inundated with water to support prevalent growth of vegetation adapted to growth in saturated soil

White Goods: Appliances, such as refrigerators, as waste

Wildcard: Symbol used to pick up word variations in a computer-based search

WQBEL: Water Quality-Based Effluent Limitations

WTO: World Trade Organization

Zero Lot Line: Buildings are clustered without setbacks

Zoning: Division of land into districts according to use

Table of Acronyms

AAI: All appropriate inquiry—CERCLA liability defense

ADR: Alternative Dispute Resolution, resolving conflicts without court involvement

ADRA: Federal Administrative Dispute Resolution Act

ALJ: Administrative Law Judge—decision-maker at agency hearing

APA: Administrative Procedures Act—federal or state law governing procedures under which agencies operate

AQCR: Air quality control region

ARARs: Applicable or Relevant and Appropriate Requirements—level of cleanup determined by standards set in other relevant laws

ASTM: American Society for Testing and Materials

BACT: Best available control technology; a standard for new sources

BADT: Best available demonstrated technology, basis of NSPS

BAT/BCT: Standards for existing dischargers: best available technology economically achievable or best conventional technology

CAAPP: Clean Air Act Permit Program or Program Permit; an operating permit

CAFO: Confined/Concentrated Animal Feeding Operation

CALR: Computer-assisted legal research system

CEMS: Continuous Emissions Monitoring System—checks compliance with emissions allowances

CERCLA: Comprehensive Environmental Response, Compensation and Liability Act, establishes liability for contamination

CERCLIS: Comprehensive Environmental Response, Compensation, and Liability Information System—EPA computerized database of contaminated sites

CFCs: Chlorofluorocarbons—responsible for damage to stratospheric ozone

CFR: Code of Federal Regulations—compilation of rules, regulations of federal agencies

CWA: Clean Water Act

CZMA: Coastal Zone Management Act; voluntary program, states can obtain grants for protecting coastal areas

EPCRA: Emergency Planning and Community Right-to-Know Act—establishes requirements for emergency planning, reporting on hazardous chemicals

EU: European Union; responsible for some environmental treaties

FDF: Fundamentally different factor variance from technology based permit standards

FOIA: Freedom of Information Act—requires that agencies disclose non-exempt information upon request

FTCA: Federal Tort Claims Act—limits sovereign immunity

GIS: Geographic Information System—mapping database

HAPs: Hazardous Air Pollutants—approximately 189 substances Congress has required EPA to regulate

HRS: Hazard Ranking System—established by NCP, assigns numerical values to health and environmental risks

LAER: Lowest Available Emissions Rate—standard for new sources in non-attainment area

LDR: Land Disposal Restrictions on hazardous waste include dilution, storage, and disposal prohibitions

LTU: Land Treatment Unit; disposal of hazardous waste on or in land

LUST: Leaking underground storage tank

MACT: Maximum Available Control Technology—basis of NESHAPs for major sources

MPRSA: Marine Protection, Research, and Sanctuaries Act

MSDS: Material Data Safety Sheet, information about safe handling and disposal of hazardous substances

MSWL: Municipal Solid Waste Landfill

MWTA: Medical Waste Tracking Act

NAAQS: National Ambient Air Quality Standards for levels of criteria pollutants

NAFTA: North American Free Trade Agreement

NBAR: Nonbinding Allocation of Responsibility among PRPs

NCP: National Contingency Plan—includes guidelines for response to releases and threatened releases of hazardous substances, pollutants, or contaminants

NESHAPs: National Emissions Standards for Hazardous Air Pollutants

NFRAP decision: Site closeout report—ends consideration for NPL; No further remedial action planned

NIMBY: Not in My Backyard; a person who opposes undesirable land uses in his community

NOAA: National Oceanic and Atmospheric Agency, administers the CZMA

NOD: Notice of deficiency in permit application process

NPDES: National Pollutant Discharge Elimination System; permit system for regulating point sources

NPL: National Priorities List—sites eligible for Superfund cleanup

NPS: Non-point source; pollution is not discharged from an identifiable source, but comes from various sources (e.g., stormwater)

NRC: National Response Center—staffed 24 hours to receive reports of releases

NSPS: New source performance standards based on BADT

NSR/NSPS: New source review/new source performance standards

OCR: Optical Character Recognition, method of scanning that makes document subject to search, alteration

OIA: EPA Office of International Affairs

OPA: Oil Pollution Act

OSC: On-Scene Coordinator for removal efforts

OSHA: Occupational Safety and Health Administration — concerned with indoor air pollution

PCB: Chemical regulated by EPA

PMN: Pre-manufacture notice for new chemical, filed under TSCA

POWT: Publicly-owned water treatment facility

PRP: Potentially Responsible Party, possibly liable for contamination

PSD: Prevention of Significant Deterioration — emissions standard for sources in attainment areas

PUD: Planned Unit Development, zoning designation applied to allow creative development of large tract

R & D: Research and development

RA: Remedial Action — actual cleanup of site

RACT: Reasonably Available Control Technology — for existing sources in non-attainment areas

RD: Remedial Design — engineering plans and specifications to implement remedial action

RDF: Recovers recyclables before incineration

ROD: Record of Decision — plan of action and justification set forth by lead agency

SARA: 1986 amendments to CERCLA — Superfund Amendments and Reauthorization Act

SDWA: Safe Drinking Water Act

SIP: State Implementation Plan for achieving NAAQS

SLAPP: Strategic Lawsuit Against Public Participation

SNLs: Special Notice Letters — sent to PRPs, triggers moratorium to encourage negotiated settlement

TSCA: Toxic Substances Control Act — enables EPA to track, inventory, and ban industrial chemicals

TSDF permit: Permit for transfer, storage, disposal facility handling hazardous waste

UN: United Nations

UST: Underground storage tank

WQBEL: Water quality-based effluent limitations

WTO: World Trade Organization

Index